AF831980

Letter forwarded to George Soros
by the New York City Post Office

The Paradoxes of Unintended Consequences

The Paradoxes of Unintended Consequences

Edited by

LORD DAHRENDORF
YEHUDA ELKANA
ARYEH NEIER
WILLIAM NEWTON-SMITH
ISTVÁN RÉV

CEU PRESS

Central European University Press

Published by
Central European University Press

Nádor utca 15
H-1051 Budapest
Hungary

400 West 59th Street
New York, NY 10019
USA

Photo of George Soros by Vesna Pavlovic

Distributed in the United Kingdom and Western Europe by
Plymbridge Distributors Ltd., Estover Road , Plymouth PL6 7PZ,
United Kingdom

ISBN 963 9241 09 1

Library of Congress Cataloging in Publication Data
A CIP catalog record for this book is available upon request

Printed in Hungary by Akaprint

To George Soros
on his seventieth birthday by his friends:
admirers, critics and critical admirers

Table of Contents

List of Tables

Preface

When we first planned a volume of essays to be collected in a Festschrift to honor George Soros' seventieth birthday, we thought of the title "The Paradoxes of Unintended Consequences: the Past, Present and Future of Open Society". For reasons not quite clear to us, the first part of the title caught the fancy of the prospective authors more than the second, and since the essays have actually very little to do with the subtitle, we decided to drop it.

The authors we approached had either contributed directly to the development and growth of the huge philanthropic empire built by Soros, or could reasonably be expected, bearing in mind their own work, to produce an essay relevant to that world. It was, of course, impossible to approach even a small fraction of those who would have fitted the above description, so we tried, to the best of our ability, to strike an acceptable balance.

Having made the selection and sent out the letters of invitation, we refrained from acting as a critical, interfering and nagging editorial committee: we did not even try to exercise a judgment on the essays as to their degree of suitability to the chosen topic, nor did we entertain the idea of returning papers for rewriting or correction. This was not so much due to the time constraint as to the somewhat ceremonial character of the book—even though, by the very choice of the theme and its handling, we were attempting to be as informal as we could.

The original letter to the contributors contained the following remarks: "The very title suggests that we have in mind a critical, dialogical approach and on no account a hagiography. The participants invited to write would come from the different but intersecting worlds of academe, politics, and business…Adding an interesting twist to the process, we commissioned for the CEU atrium a sculpture of Giordano Bruno, burnt at the stake four hundred years ago, the anniversary of whose death will fall on 17 February 2000. His case beautifully exemplifies paradox: he is a symbol of martyrdom for holding views considered to be heretical by a society which was anything but open and tolerant. Yet the views of the man whom it was decided to eliminate were probably much more illiberal, undemocratic, and far from representing an open society than the views of those who condemned him. Yet our ideal is to live in open societies where even such views can be held without punishment. This example shows how seriously we take the title of the book."

The idea behind this approach was that any complex social process, any intervention in people's lives, any political attempt to change (for the better) the lives of the many, must involve unintended consequences, usually of a paradoxical nature, as well as their mirror image: self-fulfilling prophecies. The awareness of such possibilities, while not weakening the eros of doing, must perforce push the actor towards self-critical modesty and openness, and it is this aspect that we were hoping to bring out in the diverse essays.

We are not indulging in self-congratulatory satisfaction at our success. Many of the essays only hint at the above point of view, and a different process of editing probably would have done much to strengthen the focus of the book. Yet, after reading it through in its entirety, we do have the feeling that we are offering George Soros and the, hopefully, many readers, a good read.

The contributions, due to their variety, could appropriately be divided into six sections, although, naturally, many of the essays could have been placed differently, fitting at least one, if not several, other categories.

In the first section we collected statements by some exemplary thinkers and politicians who have influenced the emergence of open society in their own countries. The other five sections, which we called "dimensions", are intended to cover the various dimensions of the problem of "unintended consequences" and their paradoxes. These sections could also have been called "vectors", indicating that these are the directions in which interventions in societies can radiate their impact.

A close look at the titles of the books, essays, and op-eds written by George Soros, and the list of his philanthropic initiatives (to be found at the end of the volume, following his short biography), will reveal to the reader that each section relates to a cluster of these initiatives, and each and every essay relates to some of these activities.

It would be inconceivable, in a book dedicated to George Soros, not to mention the work and impact of his great, self-appointed teacher, Sir Karl Popper. We have no reason to question the testimony of Soros that Popper had a deep and lasting influence on his thinking. However, we have every reason to consider this, in itself, to be an example of unintended consequence, rich in paradoxes. Popper himself was a very demanding, often dogmatic thinker, who tolerated no opposition and had very little patience for genuine critical dialogue. He was a past master at guiding every discussion into his own intellectual court, thus actually preventing the dialogue that would have characterized an open society. While Popper had several disciples, he did not in fact have students with whom he might have conducted friendly, critical dialogue—dialogue between equals working on shared problems. Popper was an anti-positivist compared with the logical positivists, but very much a non-contextual thinker, whose readiness to relativize was minimal, and who, though reintroducing metaphysics to science, was the sharpest opponent of Thomas Kuhn (and thus of Kuhn's much more important precursor, Ludwik Fleck). The flexible, pragmatic, philosophically nimble, not always systematic mind of George Soros, to which he can attribute much of his success, is much closer to Kuhn and to the Fleckian *Denkkollektive*, than to Popper. And yet Popper did write the influential *Open Society and its Enemies* which, without doubt, influenced George Soros and his whole philanthropic enterprise. For Popper, the open society was what he thought he had learned from science and its success, yet one of the paradoxes of open society is that it cannot be modeled on science, or, for that matter, on any coherent corpus of knowledge. By its very nature it has to respect differences and thrive on contextual changes, nor can it afford time- and place-independent universal generalizations. The metaphor that suits it best is a permanent "trading zone" between partially explicated theories. The term "trading zone" is taken from anthropology and has been brilliantly used by historians of science with respect to intellectual discourse.

As several of the essays clearly show (even if not formulating the point in such terms), "unintended consequences" are not just consequences that had not been thought of, but rather consequences that could not have been thought of. Rather, these are consequences that should actually force us to reconsider our original theory. They did not occur to those who entertained a theory, because they could not have followed from that theory; unintended consequences show the weak points, or even the deep fissures, in a theory.

Some essays touch on a fundamental feature of all attempts to cope with social phenomena, whether in legal, political, economic, or cultural terms: the ever more poignant realization that there is a shifting boundary between the private and the public, as much as between the local and the universal. In none of our established scholarly disciplines can we approach the world with our coherently developed universal theories as they have matured through the last three hundred years; we are up against new social phenomena, new cultural traits, and possibly (and this is an open, fascinating debate) against different sets of quasi-universal values. The forces of globalization are dialectically intertwined with strong local counter-forces that have to be accounted for when wishing to deal with the different "others" in economic, political, cultural, or even military terms. As to "universals", we probably have to begin to think in terms of "negotiated universals", which presuppose a process totally different from that of announcing to all mankind in the name of Enlightenment what is to be held universally. Non-negotiated universals all suffer from the fact that they stem from what the late Ernest Gellner called "Enlightenment Fundamentalism".

The papers on matters economic, and not less those on philosophical/moral issues touching on economic matters, amply illustrate the lack of a comprehensive, successful theory of market and morals. Every analysis, every economic consideration, opens up a host of moral issues which must all be dealt with if we wish to live in a prosperous, just, decent, and democratic open society. George Soros' own example emphasizes this: from being a successful speculator, which allowed him to lay the foundations of his huge fortune, he turned into a deeply reflective moral thinker. The thoughts which are at the base of his philanthropic activities, and which probably could never have permitted him to build up such a fortune, are glaring examples of "unintended consequences", also showing that market-oriented thinking cannot have theoretical elements that could have predicted those consequences. Indeed, the theoretical base from which the unintended consequences do not follow is in itself the case for the "self-not-fulfilling prophecy". A genuinely self-fulfilling prophecy is rooted in a coherent theory.

A prominent feature of the collection of essays is that they all point to the interrelatedness of culture and education. Much as one could wish to concentrate on the direct political-economic-legal aspects of democracy and open society, while regarding the esoteric, "orchid-like" cultural luxuries as less important and for the time being irrelevant, one is forced to acknowledge that the seemingly least relevant cultural aspects are as necessary for an open society as the obvious ones. Be it music through the ages, the visual arts, the history of ideas, or literary products, as integral parts of the human mind they are all indispensable in the effort to bring about open societies. And this is a striking message: we would all like to concentrate our efforts on first bringing people social and political benefits, and we would like to believe that the cultural luxuries can be postponed until later—yet this is not so. Open society, freedom, and democracy are all that constitute the human being. At the same time, we are warned that the cultural is not above the political, nor can it or should it be so regarded. What is the right measure? Where is the balance? Another trading zone.

A final word about Giordano Bruno. He is emblematic of paradoxes and of unintended consequences. He was a dark, dogmatic, hermetic thinker whose thoughts and life represent the opposite of an open, democratic, "scientific" spirit. Many of his anti-Copernican, "anti-scientific" ideas became the opening chapters of some of our later, glorious intellectual achievements; without Bruno there is no Vico, without Vico there is no Canetti, and without Vico and Canetti it is difficult to imagine a new social science that would finally rid us of the bane of methodological individualism that stands in the way of a renewed attempt to solve the paradoxes of the individual against society, abandoned by Durkheim in the middle of his efforts. We live in a world which once again forces upon us the need to rethink it from the foundation. Living as we do in a globalized world, the small group who will do the rethinking must consist of intellectuals from all over the world.

Y. E.

I The Political Dimension

1 *Man of the Year**

BRONISŁAW GEREMEK

The granting of this award to George Soros offers a special opportunity to examine the personal achievements of the laureate and the milestones of his life.

It is an uncommon biography. It has been a long road from being a fourteen-year-old boy who, in 1944, risked his life to accompany a Hungarian official as his pretended son, to becoming one of the world's premier financiers, capable of risk taking and of exposing even powerful countries to the risk of financial disaster. In 1947, he left Hungary and studied in England, and in 1956 he settled in the USA. After many years of discreet silence surrounding his private life, as was the custom with the financial elite of the City and of Wall Street, George Soros decided to come into direct contact with public opinion. And it is thanks to this that we now know a lot about the various fields in which he is active. *The Alchemy of Finance: Reading the Mind of the Market*—in which, in 1987, he divulged his philosophy and some of the secrets behind his operations on the money markets—became a bestseller. *Opening the Soviet System*, published in 1990, and *Underwriting Democracy*, from 1991, expound the motives and plans of his actions in support of the transformation process in Central and Eastern Europe. In 1998, his *Crisis of Global Capitalism* provided the fullest explanation of Soros's philosophical and economic concepts, and presented a critical vision of contemporary capitalism and the new prospects for "open society". Soros has announced that the second—thoroughly revised—edition of the book is to be published in the near future. In his 1995 book/interview, *Soros on Soros*, he combined the story of his life with a presentation of his

* Laudatio in honor of Mr George Soros, Laureate of *Gazeta Wyborcza* "Man of the Year" Prize, Warsaw, 8 May 2000

views and his programs. If we add to this the dozens of articles by Soros and the hundreds of articles about Soros we can say that the *Gazeta Wyborcza* award honors a person already very much in the limelight.

Let me leave aside the main sphere of Soros's activity, the building of a personal fortune. I will not examine his financial successes and setbacks, since I know little about making money. My admiration for George Soros is connected with the way he spends money, and also with his intellectual concern for the fate of the world. In the dissident circles of Central and Eastern Europe we used to speak of "anti-political politics", or "antipolitics". And that is the kind of politics that Soros is involved in; he does not participate in opportunist political games, he does not stand in elections, he has little use for political parties. But he has a penchant for backing future-oriented projects—occasionally he initiates them himself, and he promotes dialog and actions to facilitate the fulfillment of such projects.

He once said that it was excess of money—and not altruism—that induced him to take up philanthropy. He had come to the conclusion that he had earned more money than he needed. And the formula for amassing a fortune is simple: it is enough to have an annual profit of 30 to 40 percent over twenty-five years, and even if you are starting with very little—as he did—you cannot help ending up with a fabulous fortune. Since he had no desire or need to spend his accumulated wealth he decided to use it to further his ideas. He became one of the greatest philanthropists of our times, though he is ambivalent about philanthropy itself. He believes that philanthropy corrupts both the donor and the recipient. The donor becomes an object of charity. One could recall here David Griffith's rapacious and cruel 1916 movie *Intolerance*, which showed how philanthropy foments hatred and contempt between the donor and the recipient. Accordingly, Soros practiced philanthropy in a way calculated to minimize that paradox of charity. He subordinated the technique of philanthropy to the idea of a self-organizing system, treating foundations as institutions of civil society. The Soros foundations became a worldwide network of social initiatives.

Enormous financial success has been attained by a man who had no sympathy for money, who was not infatuated by wealth, but who treated money and wealth as means for promoting and implementing a certain idea of public order. During the years of study at the London School of Economics he became fascinated with the idea of the "open society". He learned about it from the writings of Henri Bergson, but most of all from the lectures and philosophical writings of Karl Popper. When George Soros takes up philosophy—and he does so with gusto—he always follows in the footsteps of his London professor: he continues the direction of his thinking about the philosophy of science, he ascribes fundamental significance to Popper's method of falsification, he accepts the deductive model of the scientific method. But he also recognizes the significance of the principle of human fallibility, he accepts the theory of chaos, and he seeks to transcend the opposition between truth and falsehood—in relation to social facts—by introducing the category of indeterminate statement that enters into interaction with social reality. Soros uses the term "reflexivity" to describe the influence of people's thinking or expectations on reality. Sometimes he refers to himself as a failed philosopher ("A Failed Philosopher Tries Again" is the title of his 1995 Vienna lecture), though he reinforces the power of his philosophical theories with a practical argument: he derived the strategy for his financial operations from the thesis of human fallibility and from the thesis about the interaction of indeterminate statements with reality. So, the empirical corroborated the philosophical.

I have decided to follow Soros into philosophy—an area that offers uncertain footing for a historian—only to emphasize the significance he imparts to ideas. This applies most of all to George Soros's commitment to the idea of open society. Karl Popper's book, written during the last war and first published in 1945, after a prolonged conspiracy of silence, gained a well-deserved academic fame. It was banned to the east of the Elbe; in Poland it did not manage to break the resistance of the censors, either during the post-October thaw in 1957, or during the post-August renewal in 1981. It was not until 1987 that it was published clandestinely by Krytyka. However, despite its academic fame, it was only Soros who turned this powerful refutation of Plato, Hegel, and Marx—which, at the same time, was a vision of a social order—into a program of action. In the idea of open society he not only saw an instrument for struggle against the totalitarian ideology and system, but also a vision of a society as a self-organizing system, built on the foundation of freedom and individual responsibility. For one can perceive in the universal model of open society—as opposed to the closed society in which "the individual is nothing, and the party everything", in which passive obedience is the highest virtue and ties of blood the basic binder—a fusion of the freedom of man and the fundamental supremacy of human rights, the laws of the market and property, the democratic state and rule of law, and of the democratic political culture and civil society. No one possesses the ultimate truth. In such a comprehension of the social world Soros discovered an attitude of fundamental criticism, conviction about human fallibility, or even an expression of human uncertainty expressed in the principle of the indeterminacy of quantum mechanics. Foundations—themselves perceived as miniature open societies—were to be the instruments of implementing open society. But let us not forget: in the beginning were those two words, in the beginning was the idea, in the beginning was philosophy. And then there was money.

In 1979, he embraced the idea of promoting open society. Soros gained his first philanthropic experience in 1980 in South Africa—a classical closed society. However, apartheid wrecked his plans. It was in Central Europe—with the mounting resistance to communism after the period of Polish Solidarity—that Soros found conditions for the implementation of his program. So he started off by setting up an Open Society Fund to enable Czechoslovak, Polish, and Hungarian intellectual dissidents to travel to the United States to pursue their studies. In Bohemia this benefited the Charter 77 community, while in Poland Soros established contacts not only with intellectuals but also with the Polish Committee for Science and Education, a clandestine Solidarity structure better known under its Polish acronym OKNO. In Hungary he succeeded in creating the first foundation. The authorities at first refused him permission to add the "open society" qualifier to its name, but in 1984, he was allowed to register it under the designation "Soros Foundation". In Poland Soros was then in close contact with Klemens Szaniawski, and in Hungary with Miklós Vásárhelyi, the 1956 Imre Nagy government spokesman who was subsequently held in prison for years by the Kádár regime. In 1988, the Stefan Batory Foundation was established in Poland and became the flagship of the Soros network. Taking advantage of "glasnost" and "perestroika", George Soros started operations in the Soviet Union in 1987, and subsequently institutionalized them, undeterred by Andrei Sakharov's warnings.

So the path was plotted well before the onset of the revolutionary changes that swept across Central Europe in 1989, and before the implosion of the Soviet Union. His institutions first came into being in Hungary, then in Poland, and then in Russia. After the breakthrough Soros foundations began to mushroom in all countries of the region, and today they make up a vast network, consisting of thirty foundations, which covers nearly all of the "Other Europe" and the post-Soviet part of Asia. The list of countries benefiting from its operations makes an interesting read. It includes Albania, Armenia, Azerbaijan, Bosnia and Herzegovina, Bulgaria, Croatia, the Czech Republic, Estonia, Georgia, Hungary, Yugoslavia, Kazakhstan, Kyrgyzstan, Lithuania, Latvia, Macedonia, Moldova, Mongolia, Poland, Russia, Slovakia, Slovenia, Tajikistan, Ukraine, and Uzbekistan. Soros has launched a number of similar projects in other continents as well, but the post-communist area that witnessed the most dramatic pre- and post-1989 confrontation between "open society" and its foes, between freedom and subjugation, remains his number one stamping ground. In 1998 alone, the aggregate expenditure of the foundation network and the cost of Soros's special programs amounted to $575 million. Thus, in his capacity as a philanthropist, George Soros dispenses billions, which places him next to America's greatest—John D. Rockefeller and Andrew Carnegie. What is no less remarkable, however, is that Soros is consistent in his strivings, and that his pragmatic, politically realistic initiatives stem from his unswervingly coherent view of the world, from *Weltanschauung* perhaps, or—more simply—from a certain dream. In the beginning must be a dream for a worthy political project to materialize, as Martin Luther King would have put it.

When asked by Oxford University—when it was about to bestow an honorary doctorate on him—what he would like to be called, George Soros replied: "I would like to be called a financial, philanthropic, and philosophical speculator."

I like that answer. Firstly, because it is evocative of the original meaning of the word "speculation", which stood for "observation" both in Latin and in other languages of Europe, then shifted to "indulging in theories" in the late Middle Ages, assuming a financial connotation only in the late eighteenth century. Secondly, because it points to a commonality of Soros's approach to money, philanthropy, and philosophy. In all these three fields of endeavor his political actions are preceded by analysis and theory.

George Soros's programs highlight science and education as areas of paramount importance for the implementation of the idea of "open society". These areas figure most prominently on the priority lists of individual Soros foundations and claim a third of their financial resources. In addition to launching several specialist educational programs, Soros also decided to set up a Central European University. This was his response to the idea of cooperation between Czechoslovakia, Poland, and Hungary that we discussed back in 1989 and 1990: the university was to be located in Budapest, Warsaw, and Prague. Ultimately, it was set up only in Budapest, and Soros's idea to establish a university in Warsaw has, unfortunately, not been brought to life so far, for which the Polish side is to blame. Supporting universities and other academic schools was an important elite-forming instrument and an integral part of the transformation process.

In making her case for the recognition of the philosophical dimension of the world of action, Hannah Arendt set out to prove that the human condition was political. This is precisely how I see George Soros's activities. He is out to influence politics because he believes that in the 1990s the basic elements of the international situation changed, and that all major world institutions, namely, the United Nations system, the United States, the European Union, and the North Atlantic Alliance should adapt themselves to the new situation. He subjects the capitalist system to a critical analysis (just like Fernand Braudel he enjoys the market but has no sympathy for capitalism) while supporting post-communist states' economic progress towards capitalism. His direct involvement in politics has been at its deepest in Russia, but I am not sure it is a source of full satisfaction for him.

However, he can derive satisfaction from his commitment to the dissemination of open-society ideas in Central and Eastern Europe, as well as in Central Asia. He can derive satisfaction from shoring up the ideas of tolerance, freedom of the media, and economic cooperation in a war-engulfed and hate-infected Balkan Peninsula. He must feel satisfaction at being the one who, in the morning after the collapse of communism in Europe, was capable of outlining a plan for supporting the rebirth of free societies—very much in the spirit of George Marshall's post-World War II plan for the effective defense of the free world against communism. According to Karl Popper, it is necessary constantly to look for optimistic hypotheses. In projecting a vision of a global alliance for open society, George Soros spells out an optimistic prospect for the process of globalization. In so doing, he seems to be invoking the "eternal peace project" of Immanuel Kant, the Krolewiec philosopher, who is remembered as the advocate of a global *polis*. It is this cosmopolitan vision of a world built upon freedom that can provide accommodation for the idea of open society.

George Soros fully deserves the *Gazeta Wyborcza* award, conferred upon him in recognition of his understanding of the global challenge of post-communism, and in appreciation of his work in support of the magnificent idea of open society. For the Soros case resembles that of *Gazeta Wyborcza*, in that in the beginning there was the idea—and the adventure.

2 *Hungary and the Open Society*

ÁRPÁD GÖNCZ

Let us suppose—and trust—that the open society is the society of the future. Even so, all societies—whether warped or open — are rooted in the past, and logically grow through it into their own future.

This is true of Hungarian society as well. I myself have lived through several steps of our society's development. My years of coming to consciousness fell under the years of authoritarian dictatorship, the years of the shock of Trianon, when Hungarian society writhed under the almost unbearable pains of its recent past, and—understandably—tried to restore its own **past**. True, at a level lower than at its peak. This is because society was in a state of narcosis, a state fed by the illusion of the unchanging. Not only individuals—even societies are unable to step away from their own shadows. I could go so far as to say that Hungarian society was vulnerable between the two World Wars, that it was prey to the consequences of its own immediate past. Desires compensated for society's loss with dreams of fulfillment. Its isolation arose unavoidably from its obligatory belief in its superiority, from the fact that it believed those who had 'caused' its problems were of a lower caste. And there is nothing more poisoning to a society than when its members measure each other and their 'lebensraum' based on the yardstick of origin and national identity.

It is understandable, then, that given the historical circumstances Hungarian society was unable to break beyond the framework that enclosed it, that there came to be a gaping hole in its perception of reality, and that it suffered the greatest failure of its history. For in the Second World War Hungarian society can be placed not only among the military losers, but among the moral losers as well: nearly half the nation's property was lost, and society was mercilessly forced to face the bankruptcy of its shabby belief system.

Hungarian society would have had—and did have—the ability and will to face itself, and only the circumstances of the new occupation were able to prevent this. It prevented this reassessment by forcing Hungarian society into new ideological irrealities, which were comprised of a strange combinations of imported ideologies, the patriotic melancholy compensating for two lost World Wars, and social prejudices which had been turned inside out, but were similarly pigheaded.

1956 was a spontaneous attempt towards the self-purification which had been twice denied. It was not directed against anybody, the elements which comprised it lacked any desire to repress others, and it was entirely infused with the desire for liberation. This desire—this demand—was wholly realistic: it reflected the common will and was lacking only in an understanding and comprehension of the development of the international political situation. This could not have been otherwise, for this situation took a sharp turn barely two weeks into the revolution.

The promise of an open society, which was embedded within the spontaneous popular movements of 1956, turned again upon itself, and in the end retaliation and continuous repression gave birth to another form of exclusion. The desire for an open society again hid under the surface of society, and was only barely detectable under the blanket of denial and 'lies'. But even so, covered in a mist, it carried with itself the unspoken desire and demand for independence.

I am convinced that this desire, this demand, was the invisible force behind the slow, hesitant, and belated "consolidation" under the repressive powers, which established a bridge toward the institutional system of a democratic society.

It is completely understandable, then, that as a result of the change of systems, the institutional system created in the end reflected social consensus—the common interests of the three social strata who carried out the 'undefeated' revolution. It reflected the interests of reform communists who changed from believing Marxists into believers in democratic socialism; it reflected the interests of the "democratic opposition" who gave expression to the self-will of society; and it reflected the strata of "national conservatives" who had a grasp of social realities.

It reasonably included all of the internal safeguards and balances which could insure institutional stability in case any of these forces came to power, and it even provided for the ability to fill the vacuum which would be created if any of these forces attempted to empty it.

On this basis democratic society—or, more accurately, the political elite which brought about the changes—was able to carry out such daunting tasks as privatization, which went on to a greater extent than had ever been carried out anywhere in the world. We should add that it was done slaphazardly, on an ocean of legal loopholes, for the system of economic regulation was still in its infancy and there were no older legal precedents to fall back upon. And what is more, it was pushed through the braking power of the still developing, half-state, half-market temporary economy. Still, this was what enabled Hungary to become the first sustainable market economy amongst the formerly socialist countries.

It became a market economy, but was still far from being an open society. Partly because society, which had once enjoyed full employment but which was by now very unstable, had not prepared itself to be open. It measured its experiences from the preceding forty years of life, and the market economy deprived it precisely of what it believed was a self-evident right—the social security of one-third of the populace. This social strata naturally could not recognize the possibilities inherent in freedom, for in the lack of material resources it was unable, and still is unable today to take advantage of this potential. The willful demand for an open society is, therefore, primarily held by those with the material ability to take advantage of it.

We might point out here that in the thousand-year history of the Hungarian State never have so many come to a realization of the desire for an open society as today. Nonetheless it is also true that an open society is only truly open if the channels leading toward freedom are—at least in theory—open to everyone.

Today, however, we cannot say that our entire legal system has come to this realization. Our best social legislation (for instance, regarding the right to equality) only promises the realization of the desired norms over the decades to come, and society is rather more conscious of disadvantages, and at times rather holds the unconscious and violent demand for discrimination, than an instinctive attempt to recognize the rights of poorer, less educated, or otherwise disadvantaged people—even at its own disadvantage.

I believe that much time and a great deal of experience is necessary to make such an inclination general.

I am convinced that the Hungarian judicial system—in its entirety—serves this goal even at times when the day-to-day realities of Hungarian politics are much more likely to reflect the desire to brutally satisfy selfish individualistic demands, which can only be blocked through the collective social checks provided by an eventual social solidarity.

We must also deal with the fact that our society, just as every society, is simultaneously filled with the fast changing remains of past ideologies—including bestial ideologies. Every ideology has its own half-life. An ideology does not disappear because of the coming of a new system, a new age, or of economic changes. Ideologies are passed on within families, from father to son, and only the strength of conviction of uncompromising reality can erase an ideology from human minds.

From this we can conclude that the demand for an open society—for equality and freedom—is alive and developing, but hardly without hindrances. It must struggle with all the restraints of the past, even in its daily life.

I believe that this is the right place to recall the achievements of the Soros Foundation. George Soros is one of the vital personalities who has shaped our age. He was one of the first to recognize, and take practical steps toward the realization of this demand, the demand for an open society, in Hungary and throughout the world. The Foundation continuously changed its goals in an attempt to meet the demands and needs which were most pressing at any given moment. In the beginning this was the freedom of expression and its dissemination, then the provision of medical equipment, and then the spread of acquaintance with the world at large, and the widening of intellectual horizons. Today support for the masses of the disadvantaged, and the nurturing of intellectuals are the Foundation's primary goals. It has accurately recognized the weaker points of social coexistence and awareness, and as always focuses its fire where it can most fully strike its target.

I believe that this is true not only of the Hungarian Foundation, but of Soros Foundations worldwide, proving that their founder's, George Soros' wide vision is one of a clear understanding of society. I can surely also say that in Hungary alone tens and tens of thousands of people directly—and hundreds of thousands indirectly—have experienced the power of this support.

There is no doubt: The Soros Foundation and The Open Society Foundation are unable to establish an open society on their own. Only society can do this. But they can create the demand for an open society, and they can create the solidarity with which society will free itself.

3 *Travel Notes of an Eastern European in America*

ANDREI PLEŞU

To the ubiquitous presence of George Soros

Berkeley, 10 October 1994

I've been in Berkeley for a week and I feel no compulsion to make "European" comments on America. By "European comments" I mean the blasé jeer that joins elderly wisdom and narrow-mindedness. As a rule, we tend to visit America with the ironic mien of higher officers on inspection. No doubt we know that we are to encounter wondrous things, a "different world", but we also know that the Americans are rather "naïve", unsophisticated, that they "stole our best brains", that you must not walk at night in certain neighborhoods, etc. Europe fears Americanization as a new form of barbarity, as a species of mental regression. Consequently, it misses two targets at once: it utterly fails to grasp the *symbolic* stature of America in contemporary history; and it loses sight of its own barbarisms and regressions. The evil lies always across the Ocean. Everything is just fine here on the old continent...In other words, we've managed to make the United States the supply for a European superiority complex, at once inelegant and unprofitable. We would gain more if we strove to see in the *actual* America the shape of things still *virtual* in our world. America is as yet the most consistent *project* of humanity. It is the setting for a formidable "unseen war", whose unforeseeable outcome concerns all of us to the highest degree. To ignore this war with a kind of tourist self-sufficiency is to be blind to the signs of the times; it is to experience history like a game with nothing at stake. What are the stakes in this case? A new metaphysical grounding for human *liberty* and a correlated reformulation of the problem of *evil*. These are, undoubtedly, the grand themes of European civilization as well. However, what now amounts, for the Europeans, to no more than a *theme*, a speculation, a debate, a mere cultural virtuosity, the Americans have turned into their immediate reality. They *wage* a war we can only *comment* upon. And this is precisely because their lifestyle is "naïve", because they "have no history". The Americans have regained for us the *innocence of fighting*. Even the "adversary" is innocent. It may be that *this* is a new strategy. You can see it in America better than anywhere else: the new mythology of the age is no longer the geometric confrontation of angelic good and perfidious evil, but a struggle where good and evil both use the same weapon—innocence.

As innocence is the practice of both good and evil, *the same things* may appear as concurrently good and bad in the American environment. The risk of innocence is that it may give up its discriminating power too easily. Aware of this risk, the Americans occasionally submit themselves to compensating fits of rigor: prohibition, the ban on smoking, the drama of sexual harassment, the exigency of political correctness, etc. What transpire in all these cases are strict *rules*, rather than actual *criteria*. When innocence resorts to criticism too heavily, the result is a form of fanaticism. What is typical of the fanaticism in the intellectual debates of the American academe is not the draconian separation of good from evil, but rather the relativization of this separation. It is no longer a contention over what is good and what is evil: instead, it has to do with what is *legitimate* and what is not. Whatever traditionally passed for evil can now be deemed legitimate, just as whatever was recorded as good by tradition may now lack legitimacy. For instance, being gay (an instance of "evil" from a "conservative" viewpoint) is now a "legitimate option". To be courteous to women (a "good" thing for the accepted "etiquette") is now unacceptable behavior, which may hurt the "victim's" dignity. No doubt behind these efforts to chart another map of social and moral guilt lies an *egalitarian* passion: homosexuals deserve the same treatment as heterosexuals, women deserve the same treatment as men. On the other hand, the new ethics exalts to the brink of demagogy the pride in *difference*: difference has to be *respected*, not merely tolerated, it has to be acknowledged for its uniqueness. To speak of racial or ethnic *uniformity* in this context, or not to promote the autonomy of any minorities, their right to unmistakable uniqueness—these are attitudes to be unconditionally castigated. Consequently, equality is good and difference is good, too. To be more precise, equality may be both good (as the non-discriminating "effacing of differences") and bad (as the effacing of "legitimate" differences). Similarly, difference may be both good (as the right to be different) and bad (as the source of various forms of exclusivism). Theoretically, such nuances are plausible and harmless. In practice, however, they end by causing perplexity and chaos. While the egalitarian principle forbids you to be courteous to women, the principle of legitimate difference allows for, even recommends, the courteous homage paid to that same difference. And how are you supposed to respect homosexuals both because they are like you and because they are not like you? Treat them as if they were not gay and you will be reproached with being uncivil to their option. Treat them naturally, for what they are, and they will charge you with implied discrimination.

In the ambiance of universal innocence and readiness for "political correctness", human relationships risk being blocked or becoming hypocritical. And we have the Americans to thank for this *new beginning* of wisdom...

Berkeley, 17 October 1994

The egalitarian passion that supports the intense cult of *difference* causes a lot of confusion and countless dilemmas, not only on the turf of sexual minorities but on that of ethnic minorities as well. For the prophets of "multiculturalism" the most significant component of an individual is the "subgroup" to which he/she belongs: a *certain* nation, a *certain* race or class, a *certain* gender, if not a *certain* sexual practice. To be black or "Latino" (that is, Hispanic) or Jewish are all *decisive* determinations to be considered with utmost solicitude. John Searle, a philosophy professor at Berkeley, talks of an explosive depreciation of the "universal" in American universities: the "liberal" culture of the older generations prompted the intellectual solidarity of the *entire* human community. Now, everyone is encouraged to valorize his/her difference, to define his/her self through membership in a "subgroup". However, it is particularly difficult to find the right proportion between the legitimate right to be *different* and the pride of sui generis identity. If your ethnic "subgroup" is so important, and if your "national particularity" is the keynote of your discourse and your destiny, how do you avoid nationalism, the denial of any "integration", the pride in being "untranslatable"? Cultivating one's particularity will not give way to nationalist excess, they will reply, as long as it makes provisions for the particularity of others. I agree, but these are only a few happy exceptions. Generally, though, being enamored of one's tribe is not the most direct step toward a cosmopolitan openness. Exalting one's *differentia* rather abates the authority of the *genus proximus*. A dilemma, then! It is required of the

Mexican in California to be *very* Mexican, but not *too* Mexican. He is also asked to believe that it is the most extraordinary thing in the world to be Mexican (Searle quotes the confession of a woman academic from another university in California, according to whom the most significant event of her life was that she was born a woman), but also that, when speaking to a Japanese, the most terrific thing in the world is being Japanese. It all amounts to one merry Babel where the authenticity of what one feels is demolished in the name of what you *ought to* correctly feel. Except that in fields where there are no mathematical or grammatical rules, correctness cannot be measured. This is the greatest problem faced by "political correctness": it attempts to find quantitative criteria for the diaphanous. As a result, it turns into a "bureaucracy of the good", as Richard Bernstein calls it in his recent polemical book *The Dictatorship of Virtue and the Battle for the Future of America*. Bernstein is mistaken, though: it is the future of the entire planet that is at stake.

Come to think about it, the question of "being *unique together* with others" (themselves unique) is quite ancient: it is the question of religious life. Christianity, for instance, simultaneously asserts the *uniqueness of the person* and the *efficacy of the communal spirit*. I hesitate, though, to continue the discussion in these terms. My shabby "political correctness" would no doubt be taxed as even shabbier than it really is. For there lies yet another dilemma! Although life in America envelops you in a confusing diversity of religious "solutions" (each more exotic and heterodox than the other), in academic circles (at Berkeley, in particular) being religious has a bad ring to it. I am immediately informed that there is no "department for the history of religions" at Berkeley. This seems to be the object of some local pride, directly connected with the very charter of the university (founded in the second half of the nineteenth century). Berkeley was born in a secular, liberal atmosphere („Athens-like" one of the professors explains). In that case, it looks like Socrates was the first victim of "political correctness" in an age when its "ghost" was haunting "Greek democracy". He must have talked too freely of the gods...

At Berkeley, more than in other American universities, they don't particularly appreciate stilted outfits. Apart from rather exceptional occasions (a public conference, a pretentious dinner party), the academics work under a sporting, "informal" cover, so they may become indistinguishable from the students. In other words, the *counter-uniform* is mandatory. The same for one's behavior: casual, devoid of protocol, making the most of first names. Politeness calls for extensive apologies, at least each time your presence becomes noticeable from the rest (as when you want to shift position, make your way to a bookshelf, ask a question, etc.). On the other hand, any gesture that might betray an excessive sense of hierarchy or a courteous maneuver toward "the other sex" will deliver you to accusations of being retrograde or "sexist". You are reminded that "you are at Berkeley". This implies that you are in a place where the bourgeois style simply won't do: you do not stand up when a lady enters the room or when she stands up herself, you do not ask permission to take off your jacket, and you may not compliment fellow workers. You're at Berkeley. Recently, Professor L. was reprimanded for calling a woman colleague in his department "charming". The characterization struck many as intolerably erotic (especially the women...).

In a way, we are once more confronted with contradictory exigencies: the gesticulation of traditional propriety is dismissed as reactionary, discriminating, and "macho" (when you are too polite to a woman it means you are approaching her from a position of condescending "power"); but you are at the same time invaded by a secondary set of interdictions meant to induce perpetual prudence and to inhibit any imaginative impulse. You have to be concomitantly at ease and tense, always ready to relax but also always on the lookout for the rigors of an unpredictable code.

Cornered by all these "environmental" niceties I sometimes think I feel a Balkan grimace in the corner of my mouth...

Chicago, 24 October 1994

It would be just as wrong to think America is dominated by the "dictatorship" of political correctness as it is to think that the strict rules imposed on American smokers have universally suspended smoking. Smokers go on smoking in America. They do it less comfortably, more acrobatically, more tensely, but they also do it with the additional obstinacy that comes from the feeling of being persecuted. Similarly, the *ethics of extreme susceptibility*, hailed by the supporters of "political correctness", though a quite lively "intellectual fashion", is far from having gained unanimous support. The example set by America lies in its *palpable* diversity of opinions, in the liveliness of the debate. What has gained a certain aura of authority at Berkeley may very well be immaterial in Chicago. Nor have they reached any "consensus" inside Berkeley. John Searle is of a different persuasion than Tom Laqueur; Bernard Williams does not necessarily see eye to eye with David Cohen. Beside Bernstein's already cited work, two other books have managed to "destabilize" the utopian party of the "experts in equity": Russell Jacoby's *Dogmatic Wisdom* and Robert Hughes's *Culture of Complaint*. They both challenge the "pious stupidities" of the new cultural commissars and demonstrate that, most of the time, the remedies proposed by the therapists of political correctness are worse than the very disease they claim to be curing.

At times, it feels like the excesses of the fashionable ideologies are not even domestic inventions, although nowhere else in the world do they rise to such intensity: one journalist from the *San Francisco Examiner* (Gary Kamiya)—nor is he the only one—is of the opinion that the themes of "political correctness" were engendered by politicizing the philosophy of deconstruction imported from across the Ocean. Michel Foucault and Derrida are enjoying an uncanny success, at least at Berkeley. They are the ones who, seconded by local stars (such as Rorty, for instance), have provoked the crisis of the notion of "objectivity" (exposed as always "interested") and opened the path to a "multiculturalism" where nothing is really "better" than the rest, nothing can function as a valid criterion for definitive moral and intellectual hierarchies.

...There lies another proof that the United States appropriates for itself the wars in Europe and in the world at large with a pathos that should put our nonchalance to shame. The Americans have the candid courage to *live* and *experience* what is no more than mental juggling for the European metaphysicians. And if, when put into practice, "our" ideas generate confusion rather than anything else, well then so much the worse for them.

In a bookshop I thumb through an album of photographs taken between the two world wars. They relate to the artistic milieu of Paris and to a famous model, Alice Ernestine Prin, alias Kiki, loved and drawn by most of the geniuses of the time. In countless pictures at cafes or in studios, Kiki exhibits her charms uneconomically and without prejudice. No doubt she was an "emancipated" woman, ready to practice "sexual harassment" both as the "victim" and as the "aggressor". Is there any room left for characters such as her in our world today?

Is there a Kiki today? Certainly. And she behaves in the exact same way, even though she may invoke different reasons, even though she is a feminist and she "deconstructs" everything she touches. Kiki is smart. She is not apocalyptic, she does not take the intellectual battles seriously. And if she occasionally adopts a doctrinaire stance, it is merely for the sake of amusement: she knows that a touch of ideological dressing adds a lethal *je ne sais quoi* to her native grace and renders all theorists helpless...

Los Angeles, 31 October 1994

"When there is *quality*, the only problem we are left with is *quantity*", Constantin Noica used to say to the occasional unpersevering disciple. But when there is both quality and quantity, as in America, the problem is their *ratio*, their measure. Quantity may stifle quality, make it too rich, unpalatable. An orchid's splendor may become terrifying through amplification. Quantity generates an "off-scale" deviation of quality, a monstrous *dilatatio* that inhibits, rather than stimulates, consumption.

American quality is corroded by the inflation of quantity. You ask for a glass of milk and you are given half a pint. You ask for a sandwich and you are given a compact block of food that bears no relation to a normal bite. A "medium" pizza is gigantic, a small one is medium, and a large one is the size of Sylvester Stallone's back. Any one serving is an orgy in itself. It is also drowned in mandatory annexes filled with unprejudiced combinations of spices and sauces that don't necessarily go together. *Softness* reigns tacitly: the bread is mollified to the limit of insubstantiality, the sandwich verges on the suspect homogeneity of a prechewed substance. They drink lots of milk, non-alcoholic beer, weak coffee. There's an excess of ground ice, which turns all liquids into a sort of cold lava, paralyzing the deglutition tract. Castrated foods are the fashion: eggs without cholesterol, non-alcoholic alcohol, sugar-free sugar, decaffeinated coffee, fat-free dairy products. Here quality shines in the negative: it is a value of insufficiency. To render it harmless, they turn food into the mere appearance of food, into illusion. Thus, they entertain a new subversion of quantity: if what you eat is "cleansed" of all harmful components, then you are free to eat *as much as you like*, with no ensuing risks. I noticed a new type of obesity, especially in women: an obesity resulting from diet, abundant and flaccid, massive and atonic—the culmination of no-calorie inflatability. The body looks like two cones joined at the base: a whirligig afflicted with steatopygia, a resurrection of the prehistoric Venuses from Lespugne and Willendorf. Morphologically speaking, I can't help evoking the silhouettes of the Hindu *preta* spirits: posthumous images of greed, gigantic bodies with tiny mouths that keep nutrition always below the level of their appetites and their abdominal capacity.

...But all these nasty things one says about America are really unfair. I go again over the lines above and realize how unfair I have been to the seafood restaurant in San Francisco or to the Californian wines, to the fresh peach, grape, or pineapple juice, to the pink steaks, the lamb chops, and the omelets with Dutch cheese.

To say nothing of the "multicultural" grace of American femininity, which has survived untainted in spite of all diets.

You cannot really contemplate the downtown area of the great American metropolises (New York, Chicago, Los Angeles, or San Francisco) without an eschatological *tremor*. The agglomeration of translucent skyscrapers, the bold play of volumes, the crystal structure of the ensembles are all awe inspiring. You are tempted to think that you are looking at the first installment of the heavenly Jerusalem, a terrestrial anticipation of the final city: mineral splendor, uprightness, and brilliance. On the other hand, you sense precisely in this tempting analogy the risk of diversion, a possible trap for the spirit: *no one* lives in the admirable prismatic diamonds downtown. The city is reserved for labor, mechanical existence, and routine. It is as beautiful and frightening as the Apocalypse...

II The Social–Intellectual Dimension

4 *The Strange (Re)Discovery of Corruption**

IVAN KRASTEV

In Italy it all began with a woman scorned. Mario Chiesa and the Italian political establishment were surprised to learn that the failure to pay a few million lire maintenance payment to an estranged wife could destroy a political system. It was bad enough for the wife, Lara Sala, that her husband had taken up with another woman twenty years younger. But what broke her was her husband's stinginess. She complained to the authorities that he had not been making the payments she considered appropriate for a man of his standing. His salary, as head of an old people's home in Milan, was modest. But she told the authorities that she knew that her husband, a functionary of the Italian Socialist Party, had other sources of income. Lara Sala asked the authorities for justice. She was right to ask that income from corruption should be considered in deciding on proper maintenance payments.

The story continued when a businessman decided to speak out. This businessman, Luca Magni, had gone to the authorities to complain that he had been asked to pay Mario Chiesa in order to win a cleaning contract for the old people's home.

The arrest of Chiesa following a bribe of 7 million lire (around $5000) was the opening act of what would become known as "Operation Clean Hands". The final act is well known—the collapse of the old republic, more than 3,500 investigations of political and business leaders, court cases, suicides, the total reshaping of the party system. In the days of "Operation Clean Hands" the prison in Milan looked like La Scala on a first night—every eminent citizen was there.

"Operation Clean Hands" was not about the discovery that Italy was corrupted. For decades Italy had been the paradigmatic case of "corrupt democracy". What the public discovered in 1992 was the scale and the institutional form of this corruption. Money paid in bribes in the late 1980s and early 1990s was estimated at more than ten billion dollars per year. It appeared that it was almost impossible to obtain a public contract without paying "party tax". Corruption was not a distortion of the system but itself a system with rules and rule enforcement.

What shocked the public most was the discovery that it was politics that corrupts business. Rather than big businesses willingly giving money to big politicians, it was politicians extracting money from business. The scale of corruption was so impressive and communism appeared so dead that the public silence was violently broken. The anti-corruption revolution in Italy was not only about judges making their verdicts, it was about people publicly telling their stories.

For years corruption was one discourse that always demanded stories. Numbers alone did not excite the imagination. Most people sensed that there was no such thing as an objective social science about corruption. Corruption was one science where every victim felt expert. This was why corruption demanded narratives. It required the presence of a storyteller, who was ironically juxtaposed to the policy makers breathing reform. Corruption discourse was about juicy details, names, places, conspiratorial fantasies. Corruption was seen as sleazy, ambiguous, and impossible to put into meaningful mathematical models. Corruption, like cooking and gardening, was recognized as a subject in the kingdom of local knowledge. People were usually skeptical about the chances of fighting corruption. Anti-corruption campaigns have always been viewed with enthusiasm in the beginning and cynicism in the end.

All that is no longer true. Corruption, now, is a discourse that does not demand anecdotes. Corruption—a realm of anthropologists, sociologists, and political scientists—has been conquered by economists. A global anti-corruption campaign, led by the World Bank, is under way, and almost nobody dares to be skeptical about it.

How did all this become possible? This is the question that I attempt to answer in this paper. The subject of the paper is what Shalini Randeria once called the "Washington consensus on corruption".

The paper focuses on the interrelations between the leading global discourses on corruption—the economists' discourse, the discourse of the IMF and the World Bank, the discourse of leading multinational companies, and the discourse of Transparency International as the leading global NGO involved in the anti-corruption business. In telling the story of how corruption was constructed as a global policy issue and how the global policy response to corruption was designed, my paper will take the form of three small stories that will meet in the end.

The first story is the story of why corruption became a global concern; the second story is the story of why corruption became the concern of the institutions of the Washington consensus; the third story is the story of how a new science of corruption was discovered. The conclusion desperately tries to bring these stories together.

Why Corruption Became a Global Concern

The last decade of the twentieth century was remarkable for the global explosion of interest in corruption. Between 1982 and 1987 the word "corruption" appeared on average 229 times a year on the pages of *The Economist* and the *Financial Times*. In the period between 1989 and 1992 "corruption" appeared on average 502 times a year. In 1993 the word was mentioned 1,076 times in the two most respected European publications on politics and finance. In 1994 corruption was mentioned 1,099 times, and in 1995 a total of 1,246 times.

A search in Amazon.com for the word "corruption" yields 1,529 titles, while the word "globalization" leads to only 581. In the last five years the name of Russia's Grand Duke of Corruption, Boris Beržovsky, has been mentioned twice as often on the pages of *The Economist* than the name of the president of the World Bank, James Wolfensohn.

However, the popularity of corruption is not limited to publications. The IMF and the World Bank have included transparency clauses in their loan-giving practices. The OECD has adopted an anti-bribery act. In 1997 the IMF suspended a 227 million dollar loan to Kenya because of bad governance concerns. In 1997 the annual meetings of the World Bank and the IMF took corruption as their special focus. Billions of dollars have been spent in the last five years on anti-corruption projects. Corruption hit the top of the political agenda in countries as different as Russia, China, the US, Germany, Mexico, and Nigeria.

What has happened? Do we have more corruption today? Do we have more damaging corruption? Why has the world became less tolerant of it than in the days before globalization?

The answer has something to do with the end of the Cold War, which simply put an end to a period of political hypocrisy. There was no longer any reason for Western democracies to support corrupt dictators. When the Soviet threat was removed, corruption began to be a security issue.

The end of the Cold War was also the end of the great ideological confrontation within developed and developing countries. Explaining the success of "Operation Clean Hands" in Italy, Romano Prodi used only one word—"Yalta". The end of Yalta convinced Italian businesses that paying the "party tax" was no longer legitimate.

The end of communism challenged the very legitimacy of democracy. Deprived of the great ideological narratives, and after mourning at the funeral of the best enemy they ever had, citizens in the Western democracies focused their attention on the integrity and personality of people in politics. As a result of the "Americanization" of European politics, the old economy of "selling policies" was replaced by the new economy of "selling leaders". The moral values and personal integrity of the politicians captured the imagination of the public.

In Eastern Europe, the end of the Cold War made corruption the new game in town. The old system of exchanges of favors, which was massively spread in the communist period, was replaced by less sophisticated bribery. Eastern Europe made the transition from a "do me a favor" society into a "give me a bribe" society.

The eruption of social inequality that took place in post-communist countries was difficult to explain in terms of entrepreneurship and hard work. The emergence of new rich and new poor, and the unexplained reasons for success and failure, led people to believe that corruption was the only credible explanation. Large-scale privatization was the other critical factor increasing the incentives for corrupt behavior. One only has to imagine the scale of the redistribution of wealth taking place in the former Soviet bloc in order to understand Eastern Europe's fixation with corruption.

Just one footnote should be added to the unwritten history of post-communist corruption. The spread of corrupt activities led to the invention of new measurement units in the sphere of post-communist finance. When your Russian partner offers you a diplomatic bag as the price for your expert advice, do not hesitate to accept it and do not blame him for being vague. A diplomatic bag is not a metaphor, it is a measurement unit. One bag contains exactly 500,000 dollars, in 100-dollar banknotes.

The new global information environment and the popularity of investigative journalism is the other factor contributing to the new visibility of corruption. Today, just by the click of a mouse, people can learn about the Kohl Affair in Germany, the Kremlin credit-card scandal, or the Bank of New York scandal. They can even find out information about a former Bulgarian minister of the interior who has accused his own government of corruption. Corruption sells well. Bribery is "as intimate as seduction and as coercive as rape". Publishing corruption stories pays as nicely as investing in Internet stock—and the risk is lower.

The spread of democracy is also part of the explanation as to why corruption has become the subject of such debate. Democracies are not by definition any more transparent than non-democratic regimes, but in democratic countries governments have to face the ballot box and even risk not being re-elected. Electoral competition increases the probability that acts of corruption will come to the surface. The fact that more countries are going to the polls has made corruption more visible and important on a global scale.

Growing mobility and the new global market have also contributed to the visibility of corruption. In the words of Vito Tanzi, "globalization has brought individuals from countries with little corruption into frequent contact with those from countries where corruption is endemic. These contacts have increased the international attention paid to corruption, especially when some companies believed that they were cut out of certain contracts because the winning company had paid a bribe" (Tanzi 1998).

The rise of civil society and the public awareness campaigns arranged by NGOs have mobilized significant anti-corruption sentiments. Civic lobbying is partially responsible for making corruption not simply the problem of the corrupted countries, but also a problem for the countries and foreign companies corrupting them. It was civil activists who focused attention on the fact that money acquired through corruption in the East is kept in the banks of the West.

When Interpol reported that the estimated profits from organized crime for the year 1999 alone were between 400 billion dollars and 650 billion dollars, governments and societies began to believe that corruption mattered. In the language of political science, corruption and organized crime are structurally connected. Corruption weakens the state, preventing it from being an effective third party. The failure of the state to enforce rules creates a vacuum that is then filled by organized crime. When the government and the judicial system are so corrupted that they are unable to help you have a contract enforced, the only available enforcer is the mafia. And in many countries it is no longer possible to tell where the government leaves the scene and where the mafia enters.

All these factors, and many others, explain the new visibility of corruption. In many parts of the world everyday experiences explain why both ministers and the unemployed are obsessed with corruption. Such experiences illustrate the urgency with which corruption has become a global concern. But all these factors are still unable to explain how corruption was turned into a global policy issue and why it was addressed by the World Bank and the IMF as a primarily economic issue.

The dozens of corruption scandals that erupted in the last decade do not differ greatly from the waves of scandals in the past. It is enough to recall the corrupt 1970s, with Watergate and the famous Lockheed scandal—when it was proved that Lockheed had paid 25 million dollars in bribes to different members of the Japanese establishment, including the former prime minister. It is enough to recall the Flick affair in Germany and the series of scandals that have come to light in Latin America. Throughout the Cold War, corruption was a major issue with respect to developing countries and there was constant media investigation into the holy triangle of diamonds and oil, African dictators, and Western elites.

In spite of the fact that corruption was a major concern it remained a non-issue in the field of international politics. Why has it become an issue now? Has the amount of corruption increased, or has the world changed? Maybe both—but what mainly interests me is to see corruption's rise to importance as one of the ways to reflect on globalization and the problem of global governance, skipping the usual descriptive approach expressed in numerous references to the new communication technologies and the free flow of capital

In *Great Transformation* Karl Polany argues that the discovery of unemployment by governments was an introduction to the failure of the "first globalization". Can the present corruption debate give us a hint about the survival chances of the new globalization?

Why Corruption Was Discovered as a Global Issue

The official story of how the World Bank, the IMF, and the OECD discovered corruption reads like a civil society manifesto. In the official version, the new global response to corruption came as a result of the OECD governments' estimation of the new risk associated with corruption, but also as a response to the pressure coming from the democratic public. It was the newly emerging global civil society pushing for global anti-corruption policy.

This story tells how in the beginning was Transparency International (TI). It was founded in 1993 by a group of former World Bank executives. Loosely modeled on the concept of Amnesty International, TI dedicated itself to fighting corruption and promoting transparency around the world. After a few years TI made a difference. It was pressure coming from TI that urged international organizations to realize that corruption is a global problem that cannot be located in the Third World and Eastern Europe. The manner in which OECD countries treated corruption outside their borders was made responsible for the present "corruption epidemic". It was this dissident message coming from TI that provoked the applause of civic activists around the world. For many leftists, anti-corruption rhetoric was perceived as an opportunity to attack both their governments and the West. In the writings of human rights activists in Eastern Europe the significance of the contemporary fight against corruption was declared comparable with the significance of the fight for human rights in the 1970s.

Civil society's version of the present outburst of honesty is a persuasive one, but reading the archives of the current anti-corruption revolution suggests other answers to the question of how corruption became a global issue.

In this alternative story, in the beginning was not Transparency International but the US State Department. In the words of Patrick Glynn, Stephen Korbin, and Moises Naim, "a major shift in American policy on the bribery question came after the trade-minded Clinton administration assumed office in 1993. Departing from their predecessors' back-burner approach, Secretary of State Warren Christopher and Daniel Tarullo, assistant secretary of state for economic and business affairs, decided to make the OECD bribery negotiation a State Department priority. Both reflected the long-dominant wish in the American business community for a level playing field" (Elliot 1997). The American business community's obsession with corruption goes back to the 1970s. The post-Watergate spirit of "soul searching" and the shock of the Lockheed scandal pushed American legislators to introduce the Foreign Corruption Practices Act in 1977 (amended in 1988) that made the bribery of foreign officials by American citizens and companies a criminal offense. In the 1970s the American business community began to complain that the US's tougher position on corruption was significantly affecting the trade opportunities of American companies working in Third World environments where bribes were expected. A 1996 Commerce Department report estimated (with the assistance of the US intelligence agencies) that in the years 1994 and 1995 American firms had lost 11 billion dollars' worth of business to competitors who paid bribes. *The Economist* quotes another government study claiming that in 1994 and 1995 American firms lost some 100 deals worth 45 billion dollars to less principled rivals. The underlying analyses remained classified so it is difficult to know how the loss was estimated, but on the basis of such figures the US started its campaign to press the other OECD countries to criminalize the payment of bribes to foreign officials and to change the rules making bribes tax deductible in countries like Germany and France. A major factor in the US's policy in the area of bribe negotiations was the public pressure on European governments. "The embarrassment factor in these negotiations was very high"—confessed one of the European negotiators.

The trade version of the discovery of corruption shows that the discovery of corruption as a global policy issue cannot be reduced to the fashionable "pressure from below": it was much more a combination of pressure from below and pressure from above, in which both sides use and misuse each other in the global anti-corruption dance.

There were at least two other global players that had good and very specific reasons to change their attitude with respect to corruption—multinational companies and Bretton Woods institutions.

In the traditional perception of corruption, the "conversion" of multinational companies from sources of corruption into fighters against corruption is a dramatic change. To illustrate the extent to which foreign capital was once seen as a source of corruption we have only to point out that in the Bulgarian language, all French, German, and English words for doing business—*Geschäft*, for example—have the connotation of performing a corrupt act.

In the 1960s and 1970s, foreign investors considered corruption to be a useful vehicle for opening up and modernizing the economies of developing countries. Corruption was seen as an instrument to break the official protectionist barriers that were imposed by the governments of the post-colonial states.

In the new world of global finance and free trade, protectionism is an unaffordable luxury for most governments. In the transition economies of Central and Eastern Europe, protectionism is simply unthinkable. Their dependency on IMF loans and their competition for foreign direct investments has forced them to open their economies and to adopt non-protectionist legislation. This new, open environment is the major reason for the multinationals' change of mind with respect to corruption. What companies like Shell and Lockheed have discovered is that corruption has turned into a hidden form of protectionism.

Compared with the normal markets for goods and services, corrupted markets are characterized by the very high value of local knowledge. In order to corrupt public officials and to win contracts one cannot rely simply on offering the biggest bribe in the biggest brown paper bag. The market in corruption services is a clandestine, closed market. In order to be competitive on this market one has to know whether to offer a bribe, to whom to offer the bribe, and how to offer it. Local businesses are much better positioned in the corruption market because they are plugged into the existing networks and because they possess local knowledge. In other words, a corrupted business environment is much more favorable to local businesses than to foreign investors. The great corruption scandals in Eastern Europe in recent years are not scandals of multinationals winning contracts, they are scandals of multinationals losing contracts or seeing their property rights undermined. The bitter story of the BP/Amoco venture in Russia is an illustration of the fact that only insiders can survive in the oil fields of Siberia.

In a private conversation, a senior British diplomat complained to me that Western investors are simply not allowed to enter the corrupt market. "They simply do not want us" said the diplomat, "they do not want our investments, they do not even want our bribes".

It was this discovery that corruption is a hidden form of protectionism that is mainly responsible for multinationals joining anti-corruption movements and pressing for the effective curbing of corruption. It does not mean that multinationals are no longer corrupting, it simply means that they now prefer the normal markets.

But it was not only the US and the multinationals that discovered that corruption is bad. The World Bank and (by association) the IMF discovered that corruption is a problem that they can solve.

It tends to be forgotten that both the World Bank and the IMF were Cold War institutions and that their missions were shaped in the context of the global confrontation between the free world and communism. The World Bank played an important role in preventing the invasion of communism in poor Third World countries. In playing its role of assisting, but also containing, the World Bank was particularly cautious with the sensitivities of its Third World clients. Throughout the Cold War period the word "corruption" was simply absent from the vocabulary of the IMF and the World Bank. "When I came to the World Bank", wrote James Wolfensohn, "I was told that there was one word I could not use, which was the 'C' word, the 'C' word being 'corruption'. Corruption, you see, was identified with politics, and if I got into that I would have a terrible time with my Board." (Remarks at the Global Forum on Fighting Corruption.)

However, from 1996 the World Bank and the IMF were not in a position to keep corruption outside their sphere of concern. There are four main reasons for the World Bank and the IMF turning to face corruption. The first reason was pressure for greater transparency and accountability with respect to World Bank and IMF programs. The second reason was that the US government wanted the word to be mentioned. The third was the tension and competition that existed between the IMF and the World Bank; and the final reason was the escalating criticism of the Washington consensus, especially with respect to IMF and World Bank policies in Russia, and pressure from influential conservative circles in the US to close the World Bank or at least to minimize its role (Naim 2000).

When it was created at the end of the Second World War, the International Bank for Reconstruction and Development (the World Bank) had a clear purpose: to help finance the rebuilding of war-ravaged Europe. In the 1950s, that job accomplished, it became the main vehicle through which governments in Europe and North America dispersed capital to poorer nations. In the 1980s, as the free market came into fashion, the bank became a fount of economic advice. But today things have changed. "If the World Bank did not exist", wrote *The Economist* in 1997, "the 180 governments which own it would not bother to create it."

But the Bank did exist, with 10,100 employees, more than 183 billion in loans outstanding in 1997, and an imposing new office complex in Washington, DC. The fight against corruption became part of the new strategy of the World Bank, and to a lesser extent of the IMF, in order to prove their usefulness in the post-Cold War world.

For the Bank, an agenda of good governance and transparency led to three distinctive gains. It put into one package the management restructuring of the institution undertaken by the new president James Wolfensohn and the new stress on institution building and knowledge. Secondly, it improved the image of the Bank; and thirdly, it allowed the Bank to distinguish itself from the orthodox policies of the IMF.

In its 1997 report the Bank rediscovered the state and reformulated its position on relations between the state and the market. The conclusion of the Bank was that a functioning market is impossible in the absence of a functioning state, and that institution building should be the priority in the process of transition. It was not wrong policies but wrong priorities that were blamed for policy failures. In the vocabulary of the Washington consensus, the weak institutional environment was responsible for the failure of the initial reform package in places like Russia. Corruption served the role of a general explanation for a variety of policy failures in different environments. What emerged as a commonplace between the different cases of failure was the existence of endemic corruption. Prior to becoming a buzzword in Bank proposals, "corruption" was already a buzzword in its reports. However, in order to address corruption the World Bank needed to depoliticize it. "I visited a number of countries", recalled Wolfensohn, "and I decided that I would redefine the 'C' word not as a political issue but as something social and economic." The redefinition took place in 1996. Corruption was not about politics any more.

The success of the second generation reforms was declared conditional on the successful elimination of hyper-corruption. There was a need for a comprehensive global anti-corruption initiative. But was it possible to shape successful anti-corruption policies while divorcing corruption from its context? Was an objective social science of corruption possible?

How the New Science of Corruption Was Born

This, the most intriguing story in this paper, is not about American pressure on OECD negotiations on bribery, nor does it concern World Bank survival strategies and its institutional interest in turning corruption into an economic issue. It is not a story about the role of the global NGOs. It is a story about the social sciences.

The invention of corruption as a global policy issue that can be solved with the "one size fits all" policy would have been unimaginable without the radical discovery that corruption is measurable. It was the radical transformation of the discourse of the social sciences on corruption that made the current global anti-corruption campaign possible.

Corruption was traditionally an issue foreign to the social sciences. It is almost absent from theoretical discourse at the end of the nineteenth and the beginning of the twentieth century. "Corruption" is absent in the indexes of the collected volumes of Marx and Mill. In the nineteenth century corruption was something to live with, something to gossip about, and something to rail against, but not something to reflect upon. "Corruption" could be found in newspapers and pamphlets but not in the works of scholars.

It was the perception of corruption mainly as a moral issue that kept it out of the interest of social researchers. In his book *Corruption. Ethics and Power in Florence in 1600–1770*, Jean-Claude Waquet shows that in the period in question discourse on corruption was not a discourse on government but a discourse on human nature. This is why corruption was reported but not reflected on in the political literature. The modern conviction that corrupted individuals corrupt institutions has made corruption marginal to the debate on institutions.

In recent times the uneasiness of the social sciences with respect to corruption is related to the problem of definition. A definition is needed that is universal enough to include all acts of corruption in different cultures and at different historical times; this definition must also turn the debate on corruption into something more than a series of case studies.

Three basic approaches are competing in the attempt to define political corruption. According to the first, corruption is defined as an abuse of public office for private gain. In the second, corruption is defined with respect to the public interest and public opinion. In the third, the definition is market centered: corruption is defined as market-type behavior outside the realm of the market. All these definitions have their strong and weak points. They all define, in different ways, what it is we study when we study corruption (Heywood 1997). The definition debate was constantly confronted with questions such as: "Can we confine our research on corruption to acts of the misuse of public office that are criminalized by the law, or should we also include acts of corruption that are still not criminalized?" "How should we treat the situation when certain acts are perceived as corrupt by the existing colonial legislation but public opinion does not perceive them as corrupt?" "If we adopt definitions of corruption centered on public interest or public opinion, how do we define the public interest and whose opinion is public opinion?" "Should we confine corruption to its monetary forms, or should we include also non-monetary forms of bribery?" "How should private gain be defined in the context of corruption research?" All these questions are well known to scholars of corruption.

But the major problem with regard to corruption was never really how to agree on a working definition. The problem was not definition, but data. Corruption is a crime, but it is a crime that nobody is interested in reporting. The number of cases of corruption that end up in court is insignificant in comparison with the number of corrupt transactions taking place. And the number of cases of corruption that are proved is ridiculously small. Reliance on public opinion can also be misleading. Anti-corruption rhetoric is often used for political purposes, and people's belief that their own or their neighbors' society is corrupt is more often indicative of the prevalence of anti-corruption rhetoric than of the actual state of affairs.

The data problem is also a problem of legitimacy in measuring corruption. What are we claiming when we say that corruption has increased in a certain country? Are we claiming that there are more corrupt transactions per person? Are we saying that more people are involved in acts of corruption? Are we claiming that in the public perception a particular country is more corrupt? Are we claiming that corruption has reached the highest levels of power?

Another difficulty with corruption is defining its functions in society. The present consensus that corruption harms development is a new phenomenon. In the 1960s and 1970s corruption was an issue of extensive debate with respect to the Third World, but there was no consensus on its effects on development. The economic miracle in Asia did not support a hard stand on corruption. Southeast Asian tigers did well, despite the fact that they were perceived as corrupt. The other reason for scholars and policy makers to be cautious in condemning corruption was political. In the Cold War period corruption was viewed by many as a democratic disease, and many military coups and communist takeovers in different parts of the world were legitimized using anti-corruption rhetoric. "Graft is a factor in the Cold War", wrote *The Economist* in 1957.

In the 1960s and 1970s there were two principal schools in assessing the role of corruption in developing countries. In the view of people like Huntington, corruption could have positive effects. It reduced violence and was a form of adjustment to modernization, and it was anti-revolutionary. "He who corrupts a system's police officer", claimed Huntington, "is more likely to identify with the system than he who storms the system's police station" (Huntington 1968).

Corruption apologists adopted Robert Merton's functionalist analysis of the political machines in the US in showing that corruption cannot be analyzed outside the concrete context in which it appears and that in many cases corruption is functional for the development of society.

In his book *Comparative Political Corruption* James Scott demonstrates several hidden functions of corruption in the context of post-colonial modernization. Corruption, for example, was the only channel by which the Chinese minority in Malaysia could have access to political decision making. In the case of Soviet Union, "blat" (non-monetary exchange of favors) was perceived as a form of adaptation on the part of the population to the shortage economy. In late 1964, Nathaniel Leff of Columbia University argued that "corruption may introduce an element of competition into what is otherwise a comfortably monopolistic industry...and a tendency towards efficiency can be introduced into the system". Bribery was also rationalized as a time saving mechanism for transactions taking place in a highly bureaucratic environment.

The moralizing school in the corruption debate was not ready to accept the progressive role of bribery in the developing countries, pointing to the lasting effect of corruption on the functioning of the national administration and its negative effect on civic culture. But what was commonplace between apologists and moralizers was the understanding that corruption is a context-sensitive issue and that any analysis of corruption should be contextual in its nature. It was a heresy in the 1960s and 1970s to believe that a global anti-corruption policy package could be designed and that it could be offered to Nigeria, Russia, Mexico, and China at the same time.

In the context of this old debate the current anti-corruption paradigm is distinctively new. The decontextualization of anti-corruption knowledge started with the turning of corruption from a political into an economic problem. Three major "discoveries" followed: the discovery that corruption is an institutional problem; the discovery that "old corruption knowledge" is policy irrelevant; and finally the great discovery that corruption can be quantified.

The story of these three great discoveries is the story of how economic discourse marginalized all other discourses in the debate about corruption. The understanding of corruption was based mainly on the assumption that a corrupt act is an example of rational behavior that takes place under certain incentives. Putting incentives right was declared sufficient to reduce the endemic corrupt behavior. If, in the seventeenth century, people tended to believe that corrupt people corrupt institutions, recent years have demonstrated not simply that institutions corrupt people, but that the problem of corruption is the problem of policy choices. People are corrupted because they implement policies that sustain corruption. "The growth of corruption", wrote Vito Tanzi, "is the long-term effect of the growth of the role of the government in the economy." And he continues "I would hypothesize that the impact that high taxes, a high level of spending, and new regulations have on acts of corruption is not immediate, but rather a function of time" (Tanzi 1998). Tanzi's hypothesis is at the heart of the new understanding of corruption. Corruption was constructed as a long-term effect of the function of the interventionist state. Lord Acton's famous saying that power corrupts and absolute power corrupts absolutely was replaced by the vision that governments corrupt and big governments corrupt absolutely, but in the long term. Corruption was translated into the language of the Washington consensus. Big government was singled out as the major source of corruption, and the foundations for new global anti-corruption policies were laid down. In its economic formulation corruption is decontextualized and normative. Economists started with the assumption that it is big government that corrupts, so the next logical step was to suggest that the only successful anti-corruption campaign is the withdrawal of government from economy.

This decontextualization of the understanding of corruption became possible because non-economists failed to argue the risks of global anti-corruption policy. The failure of anthropologists, sociologists, and political scientists to challenge the economists' monopoly over the corruption debate has to do with the discovery of the political incorrectness of the cultural arguments with respect to corruption. In the development debate in the 1960s many anthropologists and political scientists focused their attention on case studies of corruption, illustrating the fact that different political and cultural regimes are characterized by different forms of corruption. Differentiation was the basic methodology in studying corruption. The old discourse on corruption argued that different political regimes create conditions for different types of corruption, and that there is no direct connection between the spread of petty corruption and the rise of political corruption. The old discourse was looking for explanations. It was a corruption and not an anti-corruption discourse.

In arguing that Western norms for corrupt behavior were not applicable to non-Western societies, most anthropologists and political scientists perceived their position as a defense of non-Western societies against the accusation of over-corruption. In the 1980s the same arguments for cultural distinctiveness started to be read as a pretext for treating these societies as inferior with respect to development and economic growth. Anthropologist found their position severely attacked by their beloved natives.

The Washington consensus that was the flavor of the 1980 arked the end of the split between development economics and mainstream economic theory. It was accepted that the way in which nations become prosperous is not different in different parts of the world. Furthermore, it was discovered that prosperity could be achieved simply by adopting the right policies and sticking to them.

In 1755 Adam Smith famously remarked that "Little else is a requisite to carry a state to the highest degree of opulence from the lowest barbarism, but peace, easy taxes, and tolerable administration of justice." Jeffrey Sachs referred to Smith in his 1996 article on the prospects of economic growth in Africa. Sachs was an optimist with respect to African growth. There was not much peace or tolerable administration of justice in Africa, but there was a readiness to go for easy taxes.

This radical turn in the understanding of development reformulated the major findings of the old corruption studies. It was a commonplace in the 1960s that poorer countries tend to be more corrupted. In the 1990s the commonsense opinion was that it is not that poor countries are more corrupted, but that corrupted countries are poor.

The claim of the new anti-corruption science was that corruption has nothing to do with culture. Corruption is characteristic of institutional environments and characteristic of certain policies. However, all this new knowledge on corruption was normative in its nature. It was very difficult to verify it because corruption was not measurable. Once corruption was turned into a depoliticized economic issue new tools were required for studying it.

The new moment in constructing corruption as a global issue was the discovery that corruption can be measured. Like all great discoveries this was a child of luck, interest, and accident. In their eagerness to influence the public and to mobilize support for global anti-corruption actions, TI decided to produce a ranking of countries according to the way their level of corruption was perceived by the senior executives of multinational companies. In 1994 TI produced its first corruption perception index. Interviewing senior and experienced executives of multinational companies and balancing their answers with information coming from other sources, TI came up with a table ranking fifty-three countries in the world. The impact of the corruption index was shattering. All major newspapers around the world published it and commented on it. Opposition parties started to refer to it. Governments began attacking it. But the most important effect was the public conviction that it was possible to compare levels of corruption in certain countries and to monitor the rise of corruption in any one individual country.

The estimation of corruption on a national level was not the invention of TI: Political Risk Services had already been making estimates of the corruptness of the environment in different countries. It had offered these estimates to business clients, but these estimates were never presented as "measurements of corruption". Political Risk Services kept its estimates confidential and never made a scientific claim with respect to its ranking tables. The company knew that its corruption estimates were based on impressionistic evidence.

When publicizing its corruption perception index TI did not claim to have succeeded in measuring actual corruption. TI's experts underlined that this was a perception index, and over the years they worked constantly on their methodology. But the first step had been taken. The ranking table was in the newspapers. The next stage was easy. When the ranking table was produced econometrists started to work on this ranking, or on the ranking compiled by Political Risk Services, producing cross-country regress analyses. Among the findings it was shown that corruption hurts economic growth and reduces the level of foreign investments—that is, if two countries have otherwise equal conditions FDI will go to the less corrupted one. Corruption hurts mostly poor people, it distorts the logic of public investment (governments favor projects with higher corruption potential), and so on.

Corruption was no longer about anecdotes and context-sensitive analysis: the study of corruption was portrayed as similar to the study of inflation. The causes of corruption were reduced to the effect of a government's role in politics. The TI index that was designed as a PR instrument was manipulatively turned into hard data, on the basis of which the new anti-corruption policies started to be designed. Economists managed to solve the basic problem with respect to corruption—that is, the lack of data—and, on the basis of the legitimacy enjoyed by any quantitative type of analysis, radically marginalized non-economic discourses on corruption. Recently several researchers, including World Bank in-house researchers (Daniel Kaufman, www.worldbank.org/wbi/gac), have criticized the methodology of Transparency International and have tried to limit the speculations coming from the quantitative analysis of corruption. However, this clarification cannot change the fact that the discovery of the measurement of corruption radically changed the discourse on it. The latest publications on the subject are full of statistical correlations.

It was this major change in the study of corruption that legitimized and made possible the new global anti-corruption package.

Conclusions

Reflection on the construction of corruption as a global issue and on the formulation of the global response to corruption provides an opportunity to look at the work of the new global governance. The rhetoric of anti-corruption, or more precisely the rhetoric of transparency, became the meeting point between the aspirations of the public for more democracy and political accountability, and the aspirations of the market for more openness and less government in economy. This global anti-corruption coalition came into being as a result of a major transformation in the international political and economic environment that took place after the end of the Cold War. The new visibility of corruption made it a global concern. But it was the pressure exerted by the US government in protecting its trade interests, the search by the World Bank for a new mission and legitimacy, and the pressure exerted by NGOs for more voice and greater visibility that made corruption a global policy issue. The global anti-corruption coalition was shaped as a discourse coalition, a coalition of actors sharing a definite social construct of what corruption is about and how to challenge it. This discourse coalition came into being as a result of a radical change in the theoretical discourse on corruption. It was "discovered" that corruption is measurable and that corruption was constructed as a result of the long-term effect of the interventionist state. The old "science" of corruption was replaced by the new anti-corruption science. Non-economic discourses on corruption were found irrelevant in terms of policy. They simply explained corruption at a time when there was a need to defeat it. Corruption was constituted as an economic and not a political problem, a problem that could be studied in the same way as economists study inflation.

The global anti-corruption response prepared by the World Bank contains three major elements—a package of economic policies; a package of policies directed at the reform of civil administration and institution building in general; and, as a third component, a collection of "spiritual practices" in the fashion of early Calvinism, for example the request that before entering a bid firms should make anti-bribery pledges.

Is this package going to be successful? Probably not. The economic policies are just recycled versions of the Washington consensus—privatization, deregulation, competitiveness, openness...The institution-building package is difficult to implement in a policy environment dominated by a growing number of weak states. The Protestant flavor is simply a matter of bad taste. In addition, the stress on auditing as the major form of accountability risks disturbing the work of inefficient national administrations. (Last year, for example, Tanzania was obliged to produce around 1,200 reports for its Western donors.)

The basic problem with the new, global anti-corruption campaign is that it is based on policy irrelevant knowledge. The hundreds of pages of statistical correlations between corruption and all other measurable entities ignore the basic fact that the effect of corruption cannot be calculated outside its local context, and that corruption cannot be measured.

Corruption is basically a political issue. It has to do with the very definition of the "political". National anti-corruption campaigns and the debate that they provoke are forms of redefining and renegotiating the borders between public and private. The success of "Operation Clean Hands" in Italy cannot be understood outside this constituting role played by the anti-corruption discourse in redefining politics and the public interest in general: the changes in Italy started with a woman being scorned but ended with the redefinition of the role of politics and political parties in public life. In the current global anti-corruption debate this societal dimension of the old anti-corruption reforms is missing. World Bank economists and civil society activists commit themselves to the current war against corruption, failing to recognize that they are hunting after different animals. But maybe this is the way global governance works?

References

Anechiarico, Frank and James B. Jacobs (1996). *The Pursuit of Absolute Integrity: How Corruption Control Makes Government Ineffective.* Chicago: University of Chicago Press.

Coulloudon, Virginie (1997). "The Criminalization of the Russian Political Elite". *East European Constitutional Review* 6: 73–78.

De Sardan, Olivier J. P. (1999). "A Moral Economy of Corruption in Africa?" *Journal of Modern African Studies*, 37, 1: 25–52.

Elliot, Kimberly Ann (ed.) (1997). *Corruption and the Global Economy.* Washington, D.C.: Institute for International Economics.

Heidenheimer, Arnold, J. (1970). *Political Corruption. Readings in Comparative Analysis.* New York: Holt, Rinehart and Winston, Inc.

Heywood, Paul (ed.) (1997). *Political Corruption.* Oxford: Blackwell Publishers.

Huntington, Samuel (1968). *Political Order in Changing Societies.* New Haven, Connecticut: Yale University Press.

Naim, Moises (2000). "Washington Consensus or Washington Confusion". *Foreign Policy*, Spring: 87–101.

Rose-Ackerman, Susan (1999). *Corruption and Government.* Cambridge: Cambridge University Press.

Tanzi, Vito (1998). "Corruption Around the World. Causes, Consequences, Scope, and Cures". IMF Staff Paper.

Transparency International and the Economic Development Institute of the World Bank joint publication (1998). *New Perspectives in Combating Corruption.*

Visvanatan, S. and Sethi H. (eds.) (1998). *Foul Play*. New Delhi: Banyan Books.

Wedel, Janine (1998). *Collision and Collusion: The Strange Case of Western Aid to Eastern Europe*. St Martin's Press.

Williamson, John (1990). "What Washington Means by Policy Reform". In John Williamson (ed.), *Latin American Adjustment: How Much Has Happened?* Washington Institute for International Economics.

5 *Music and Freedom: A Polemical History**

LEON BOTSTEIN

I.

It has become increasingly difficult to locate or to justify the purpose, much less the actual function, of so-called high art traditions, particularly with respect to music, in contemporary post-communist political and social life. This is as true for the former Eastern bloc countries, including the Soviet Union, as it is in the rest of Europe and North America. What follows is a provocation with a purpose. It contains the suggestion of a response to the marginal status of so-called classical or serious concert music, based on a reading of the historical career of music. The core of the issue is whether the traditions of high art music can be crucial to the creation and maintenance of a free, democratic or "open" society in this new century.

Before the late 1980s the communist regimes in the East followed a distinct line in Marxist theory that led the state to support the dissemination of the traditions of classical music to the masses. The popular music of the West was identified as decadent and bourgeois; monopoly capitalism, it was alleged, had created a highly successful and alluring mass cultural production that served only to affirm its unwarranted legitimacy. High art traditions in music were also supported by the state in Soviet Russia, as they were in the Eastern bloc countries, as means to elevate the tastes of the masses. Music, partly because of its character as a performance art that possessed neither language nor imagery, was seen as a benign public tool of culture capable of communicating an aesthetic of solidarity and universality. An eighteenth-century conceit regarding music as a universal language of human sentiment was appropriated by communist regimes. Furthermore, during the Cold War classical music became a potentially neutral arena of export beyond the Iron Curtain. Like sports (consider the investment in participation in the Olympic Games), music assumed a prestige status. Communist countries exported their leading composers, performers, and ensembles in highly regulated tours of the Western world as vehicles of propaganda.

The collaboration between the regimes and the high art musical establishment in each nation had its share of remarkable results. The post-World War II levels of musical education and training, performance standards, and scholarly and editorial ambitions in the East became extraordinarily high. But most significantly, classical music, particularly in its historical incarnation as presenting the repertory from the past, permitted communist regimes the possibility of allowing nationalism to flourish through music. The traditional concert music and folk music of each ethnicity and nationality were celebrated and manipulated as bastions against foreign influences, particularly from the West. Furthermore, cultural nationalism through music offered an innocent and compatible outlet from, and alternative to, the transnational claims of communist ideology that had been superimposed on older nationalist political traditions.

The collapse of communism in the late 1980s and early 1990s released the forces of reaction to this system. Popular music from the West had long been an underground medium of rebellion and resistance among the young against the repressive state. When market forces took over from the state monopoly in the arena of culture, audiences began to desert the classical traditions. Throughout the 1990s state funding gradually collapsed. There was a flight of talent to the more affluent West. Conservatories, opera houses, symphonic ensembles, and music publishing were left, so to speak, in the dust and experienced significant deterioration, even in the former GDR. In the West, the traditions of classical music had become, by the 1970s, largely superfluous and marginal with respect to politics and culture. By comparison, in the former communist countries the trajectory of change in the 1990s was more striking on account of the lingering memory of state support and collusion. The East caught up quickly with the West.

Reactionary skeptics in the East, who feared the onslaught of mass culture from the West after the fall of communism, have been largely vindicated in terms of music. Market forces and globalization are regularly held responsible for the lowering of cultural standards worldwide; they are accused of bringing an unwanted Americanization of native cultural traditions and languages. This tragedy, in terms of music, seems to be somewhat different. The former communist countries, with remarkable rapidity, have encountered the paradoxes of an open society long familiar to North American and European countries that have little to do with recent history. These paradoxes have their own longer history.

One can trace from Alexis de Tocqueville onwards a profound unease with respect to the cultural consequences of democratization and the extension of liberty and political rights. Insofar as political oligarchy and enlightened despotism were linked historically, through patronage, to the flourishing of high culture and taste, already in the early nineteenth century the prospect of an open society was understood as a tragic necessity, whose price would be the lowering of standards in terms of taste and civilization. Jakob Burckhardt and Friedrich Nietzsche (not to speak of Matthew Arnold), and, several decades earlier, Balzac, deemed modern economic progress, the growth of the city, the spread of literacy, and the extension of political rights responsible for cultural corruption and aesthetic, if not ethical, degradation. No amount of education could possibly avert the triumph of vulgarity and the trivial in music, art, and literature in a mass democratic society—in an open society driven exclusively by a free market that defined all cultural production in terms of its profitability. A link between the defenders of a pre-capitalist feudal aristocracy and advocates of communism can be found in their shared contempt for the cultural consequences of uncontrolled capitalism. Beyond the havoc capitalism would wreak on the material condition of the overwhelming mass of humanity, there was the prospect that their spiritual and cultural well-being was at risk as well.

Whether this tradition of cultural pessimism is legitimate or warranted is not, for the purposes of the argument that follows, germane. Rather, a challenge inherent in the various kinds of logic defending notions of an open society is how to construct and sustain, in a condition of freedom and open skepticism, effective avenues of human expression that challenge the dominance, if not monopoly, of market and economic criteria of judgment. Is there a role for forms of cultural production that have no mass audience and are not commercially viable? How can critique and dissent flourish in art forms if concessions to mass taste and conventions hold exclusively the keys to artistic survival?

By what criteria does one defend and support the unpopular, the difficult, and the so-called elite forms of aesthetic expression and communication? American social reformers from the late nineteenth century through to the era of the Great Depression retained the naïve conceit that one should improve the uneducated masses by introducing them to the traditions of classical music. This thinly veiled fear of what the mass of humanity might prefer was the flip side of a thoughtless upper-middle-class embrace of musical culture at the end of the nineteenth century and throughout the twentieth century. The haute bourgeoisie celebrated classical musical culture as the signifier of superior taste and social status. They dragged their reluctant children to concerts and piano lessons. They, in fact, imitated the habits of an older, landed aristocracy who had been legendary as patrons and participants in the extraordinary musical culture of Viennese classicism. Bourgeois confidence in its own cultural capacities was indeed weak; the *ancien régime* in culture thrived long after its political defeat.

Within a morass of conflicting and contradicting social appropriations of the classical musical tradition in modern history a key question remains unanswered. Is there a reason, in nations both East and West, for anyone to be concerned about the future of Western classical music in its historical and contemporary incarnations, both as a museum or as a forum for new generations to express themselves in music? In other words, are the traditions of classical and concert music relevant today to an open society? Can they contribute to sustaining and improving freedom and the quality of life in those societies? Since, by the standards of modern commerce, these traditions are not viable in terms of the economic marketplace, their survival is dependent on direct and indirect forms of state patronage. There are two categories of support—direct state tax-based revenue allocations and subventions by individuals and corporations sanctioned by the state and encouraged by tax codes. These both involve a political judgment regarding the priorities of an open society.

If the classical musical tradition is little more than a luxury item with no larger purpose or meaning, one might well leave it to suffer its fate alongside expensive vacations, jewelry, racing cars, and yachts. If the rich do not wish to buy tickets and underwrite a symphony orchestra, then there is no legitimate reason for the state to train musicians and maintain symphony orchestras. Now that all classical music recording has been abandoned as commercially non-competitive by the massive multinational entertainment, publishing, and communications conglomerates, without indirect or direct public patronage, the future of classical music in open societies is at risk. Apart from nostalgia, is there a reason to be concerned? Does this matter? What do the traditions of classical music, old and new, have to offer that cannot be supplied by other cultural formations, particularly those that appeal on a mass basis through mediums of entertainment and communication enhanced by modern computer technology?

The argument that follows does not offer an answer. Rather, it outlines a history of the political significance of the classical concert music tradition and its attendant philosophical justifications. From the late eighteenth century on, history reveals that the forms of music subsequently appropriated by the communist regimes, manipulated by fascism, and long supported by the monarchical state have been, as Thucydides might have expressed it, "a human thing". They represent a unique reflection of the human imagination and potential; a "form of life" as the philosopher Ludwig Wittgenstein put it. Insofar as the theory of an open society owes its origin to Karl Popper, Popper's own deep personal engagement with music and his lifelong advocacy of it as essential suggest that the connections between the Western tradition of classical music and a successful open society demand further exploration. If, as George Soros has argued, there is a danger in reducing the ideal of the open society to the sum of that which the free market generates, then the question of what cultural formations and institutions need protection from the monopoly of the market in an open society becomes pertinent. In that negotiation, regarding what, in civil society, demands protection from the will of the majority and the market, it is important that the connection between music and politics, and, more precisely, the connections between certain forms of musical expression and dissent, innovation, and freedom, be well understood.

II.

In theory and practice, the role of the aesthetic in democracy has had an uneasy history. The eighteenth century offered a privileged account of how certain of the high arts, particularly music, might influence the sensibilities. Friedrich von Schiller's *On the Aesthetic Education of Man* (1795) offers perhaps the most eloquent argument that the capacity for judgment, cultivated intuition, and awe for the imagination in terms of the aesthetic are necessary for nurturing the values of freedom, tolerance, and respect for individuality. The task of cultivating the human spirit so that it can thrive in freedom is placed in the hands (or rather at the feet) of an encounter with art.

In the decades before the French and American Revolutions, music assumed a central role in eighteenth-century constructs of art and culture on account of its presumed unique and seemingly contradictory nature as distinct from the visual and linguistic. The aristocracy and the urban elite of civil servants, professionals, and merchants that were the patrons of Gluck, Haydn, Mozart, and Beethoven in Vienna and London were amateurs and listeners attached to long forms of instrumental discourse. They supported and used the vast output, between 1770 and 1815, of solo keyboard essays in sonata form, free keyboard fantasias, music for chamber ensembles—trios and quartets—and lastly large instrumental assemblages organized to deliver multi-movement symphonies. Instrumental music was understood as having no evident illustrative elements. It was not overtly grammatical, and its rules and elements could not be easily construed as offering any sort of explicit argument. It seemed entirely divorced from external reality except in some emotional sense; music could, however, mirror and trigger emotions.

Although music inhabited the aesthetic realm and appeared entirely abstract, at the same time it was logical in terms of its structure and organization. It possessed some sort of narrative. For Beethoven and his Bonn teacher Christian Gottlob Neefe, instrumental music (as it had been for J.S. Bach's most gifted son C.P.E. Bach) was actually a medium for the expression of sentiments, states of mind, moral claims, and above all the emotional response to external events. Yet all this occurred beneath a surface entirely opaque. When repressive censorship enveloped the Habsburg monarchy after 1815, the Austrian playwright and acquaintance of Beethoven, Franz Grillparzer (himself an accomplished amateur musician), lamented his fate as a writer, since composers were much more likely to escape the censor's pen. Implied in this observation was the tacit admission that musicians could actually say something censors would be interested in cutting out and suppressing. Tragic theater was at risk, particularly of the sort cast in the image of Shakespeare and Schiller's historical dramas. The fairy tale and farcical domestic satire flourished in post-1815 Vienna, since the causes of laughter and the subject matter seemed to the witless censor perfectly innocent. The intelligence of censors is never to be overestimated.

Eighteenth-century traditions of instrumental music and their counterparts in the early nineteenth century therefore offered listeners some sort of argument. The power of that argument was twofold. First, even in the era of enlightened despotism there was nothing like the expectation of free expression and rights in the face of political and police authority characteristic of the late twentieth century. Not only did music artificially create an extended and entirely constructed unit of time possessed of aesthetic content, but it was susceptible to subsequent linguistic description and analysis. Yet it remained impervious to facile external control and interpretation. At the same time it also sustained a seemingly innocent occasion for public assembly. Throughout the era of Viennese classicism and well into the age of early romanticism, between 1770 and 1848, all public events, including concerts, required police permits and were scrutinized by the state authorities. In the 1820s, even the semi-public gatherings of private associations were subject to espionage. The Gesellschaft der Musikfreunde, founded in Vienna in 1812, was an association requiring political authorization. It came as no surprise to skeptical reactionaries that many leaders on the barricades in the March 1848 revolution included members of the recently formed Wiener Männergesangverein (1843), the Gesellschaft, and other music societies. After all, music had provided the basis for the few institutions of society in the era of post-Napoleonic reaction that could sponsor organized regular public events and semi-public gatherings of an elite.

The second advantage possessed by music in its long instrumental forms, and also later, after 1820, in its incarnation in shorter instrumental pieces and within the art song (*Lieder*), was music's inherent capacity, apart from language, to communicate meanings without suggesting any uniformity in those meanings. Balzac, in his short novel *Gambara* (1837), describes the strikingly divergent visual images and imaginary scenes triggered in the minds of the fashionable audience by the same piece of music. In silence, without any necessity for disclosure, music could generate an intimate space and offer each individual a structured and socially acceptable occasion for the free and personal exercise of extended thought, rumination, fantasy, the visual imagination, and daydreaming. In sum, for the late eighteenth and early nineteenth centuries, the materials of instrumental music in the classical tradition were an essential and unique dimension of freedom in two respects: as a rare opportunity for freedom of expression and for freedom of assembly.

The key to the success of music was a shared understanding with respect to the logic of musical form. Meaning and expression were dependent on listener expectations regarding the formal procedures in the manipulation of musical materials. An extended argument required duration. Significant duration permitted contrast, variation, and the transformation of materials, and it demanded repetition. These qualities were sufficient to complete and bring home a weighty argument. The late eighteenth century bequeathed to the nineteenth century the essential elements of a sort of musical prose, despite the fact that the romantic poets, particularly Novalis, understood music as essentially poetic. They in fact sought to endow poetry with a musical character. Music was considered the idealized language of nature and was defined as inherently poetic. However, in terms of the transaction between composer and listener, the poetic character of music—that is, its elusive nature and its resemblance to symbolism, allegory, and metaphor—was explicitly tempered by the necessity for music to communicate differentially but with a high degree of subjective clarity. Beethoven, after all, wrote one of the best battle symphonies, celebrating Wellington's victory in Spain.

Despite its non-denotative character, eighteenth-century music assumed a linguistic and pseudo-grammatical character in terms of the expectations of its listeners. In the tempered scale, for example, each key represented a mood or a sentiment. For Christian Friedrich Daniel Schubart, whose writings exerted a profound influence on Beethoven's generation, A major was the key of emotional satisfaction and hope, D major that of triumph, and G major that of the idyllic and the rural, the key of eclogues. Furthermore, music was written with an ear for rhetorical gesture that followed the traditional rules of rhetorical conventions in speech. Formal rhetoric, in terms of oratory and argument, were transposed into musical form. And most importantly, instrumental music developed its own musical logic by which cells, or rather musical ideas, underwent transformations within larger structures governed by harmonic conventions involving the notion of root key relationships. A system of tonality evolved which created a sense of spatial orientation, involving a notion of home, travel, and return.

It should come as no surprise, therefore, that musical communication and the participation in musical culture seemed essential to eighteenth-century thinkers, particularly those interested in democratic theory. One need only cite Jefferson and Franklin on the American side. For the English, when Haydn appeared in London, in the 1790s, it was an occasion for celebration. Eighteenth-century theorists from Hume to Burke, including in particular Adam Smith, went to great lengths to endow music with philosophical significance. Listening to instrumental music required a sort of philosophical listening. The arena in which music could excel was in the area of moral and ethical philosophy. The later symphonies of Haydn can be understood as presenting moral arguments and laying ethical claims that were grasped at first hearing by audiences.

This entire, constructed private aesthetic but public edifice was understood as explicitly artificial. When Goethe remarked to his friend, the composer Zelter (the teacher of Mendelssohn), that a string quartet was a conversation, he directly identified the magic of that conversation in the fact that it was not literally so. The artificiality of musical elements placed music at a distance from words and images. The direct illusion of realism and the conventions of portraiture, landscape painting, and narration associated with the eighteenth-century visual arts and the novel, particularly in England, were not available to music. It was obvious that pitch and harmony, as well as rhythmic patterns, were in no immediate sense natural. There was no music, in the sense of the conventions of composition, in nature itself.

This paradox did not, however, diminish music's utility as an instrument of realism. As Mendelssohn argued in the 1840s, music in fact possessed its own clarity, greater than that possessed by any words. In aesthetic philosophy there were certainly those who placed music below poetry and painting on account of its apparent artificiality. They followed in the footsteps of Plato. But the Greeks, particularly Plato, understood that music, like myth, despite its apparent artificiality, exerted a deleterious, if not narcotic, effect. It could be dangerous and misleading. Although artificial in terms of external reality, it was, in terms of human nature, somehow decidedly real and natural. Music's role in the history of aesthetic realism from the eighteenth century on was to assume a place as a metaphorical mirror of the uniqueness of the human soul. Insofar as music—in terms of its realization as late-eighteenth-century instrumental music—was the expression or reflection of the human soul, or—for those with an eighteenth-century materialist associationist view of the mind—a mirror and forum of the psychological workings of the mind, music assumed a particular prestige. It was the realistic medium of the human interior. The expansion and protection of musical culture in the decades preceding and succeeding the French Revolution and its Napoleonic aftermath, seemed essential to defenders of liberty, freedom, and the rights of man. Music was the aesthetic reflection of man's inalienable right to think, to will, and to feel. It reflected a private realm that demanded protection against the state. Its defenders knew that even music commissioned by the state and designed to serve political power would not necessarily be heard as communicating the intent of its patrons. Music had become a powerful, covert medium of ideas, out of the reach of control on account of its very nature.

Therefore, when music was combined with words, in sacred forms such as the Mass and the oratorio, or in secular forms, particularly opera and song, music was not understood as providing merely a background or supplemental illustration. The key difference between the way music functions in opera where there are words and visual tableaux, and the way it works in film and television, is that in the former music is never, from the perspective of composer and listener, relegated to mere illustration. The instrumental musical conventions, so elaborately and brilliantly articulated by Mozart and Haydn, at one and the same time augmented and influenced the role of music in the massive operatic output of both composers. In the operas of Mozart, particularly *Figaro* (1786), *Don Giovanni* (1787), and *The Magic Flute* (1791), as well as in the oratorios of Haydn, *Il ritorno di Tobia* (1774–75), *The Creation* (1796–98), and *The Seasons* (1799–1801), music provided a level of meaning beyond that which words and plot-lines were able to communicate. The reference to Haydn's oratorios is made because of their relative fame as opposed to Haydn's massive operatic output, which is unfortunately largely unknown to modern audiences. This point was not lost on the church hierarchy in the late eighteenth century. The debate over the proper use of music in the setting of the Catholic Mass centered on an effort to control theological interpretation. The Masses of Haydn and Mozart—the appropriation of operatic and instrumental conventions into the arena of sacred music—were regarded with extreme suspicion by church authorities and after 1790 fell into disfavor. How, after all, could the musical conventions made popular among the aristocratic and non-aristocratic urban elite by Freemasons be consistent with religious orthodoxy? Could the type of music employed by Mozart in the *Magic Flute*, designed to communicate the power of secular humanistic conceits characteristic of the Enlightenment, be acceptable as a medium for the communication of a Catholic faith defined strictly in the terms set by the counter-reformation? Could it be adequate as a means to help distinguish the faithful, true Catholicism from nascent heresies and divergent types of Protestantism?

III.

The romantic reaction to the Enlightenment, in particular to the reign of terror and the career of Napoleon, altered the trajectory of music's role in politics and culture. However, one must distinguish between shifts in the way philosophers understood music, and the actual career of musical culture in nineteenth-century Europe. This, perhaps, is another way of saying that one ought not to read Hegel too closely. The French Revolution accelerated the expansion of forms of popular music that derived from the aristocratic traditions of instrumental music and opera. Music became an instrument of politics as it sought to reach an ever-growing audience using simplified adaptations of classical models. The French operas of the 1790s; the new, romantic German opera, best exemplified by Carl Maria von Weber; and the meteoric success of Rossini, all point at an underlying pressure to reach a larger audience, whose freedom of movement and assembly had been enhanced by the political and economic transformations.

The decades from the mid-1790s to 1848 reveal a striking increase in the popularity of music as mass entertainment through opera and the emergence of international star virtuosos such as Liszt and Paganini. Amateur instrumental, choral, and concert societies sprang up all over Europe. It was in this period that the piano underwent rapid technological change. It was to become the nearly universal dominant instrument of music throughout Europe and America. By the 1890s, the triumph of the piano had been secured. It was a user-friendly mechanical instrument of musical reproduction. It permitted a fundamental democratization of musical literacy. Like the personal computer in the later twentieth century, the piano became a leading consumer product, whose unit price declined precipitously owing to the transformation of piano manufacture. A product of artisan craftsmanship became the product of the factory system. The wealthy could purchase parlor grands, and workers could afford miniaturized uprights. To use it one did not need to be musical in the sense of pitch discrimination. Playing by numbers, using numerical fingerings became popular, since a piano remained in tune without the user needing to tune it. Furthermore, the piano could suggest a complete ensemble and reproduce the sounds of opera and orchestral music.

The shift in Europe and America from rural to urban life created a demand which Offenbach, von Suppé, Sullivan, and Johann Strauss successfully met—for light opera and operetta. A new class of urban popular music, that of dance and song, as closely linked to classical concert music as operetta was to opera, flourished. Popular, salon, and high art music developed in an interrelated and symbiotic manner. In terms of high art classical music, during the first half of the nineteenth century music took on a new role as the language of an endangered nature and a lost past. From the early nineteenth century onwards, instrumental and vocal music in the classical tradition provided a forum through which discontent and skepticism regarding the progress of urban modernity and new technologies such as the steam engine could be articulated.

Beethoven's "Pastoral" Symphony (1808) marks the beginning point of this aspect of music's career in the nineteenth century. It was, as Beethoven himself claimed, the articulation and expression of an individual's reaction to nature. It illustrated the ambivalence of the city dweller. In it, rural life was subject to idealization, as were its inhabitants. The terrifying power of nature, represented by storms and lightning, was understood as a warning against the arrogance of man, who sought to use modern technology and science to harness nature for human use. The spiritual corruption of urban life was placed, through music, in contrast to the ethical clarity and moral decency of simple rural folk. Through the medium of instrumental music the listener could escape the artificiality and cramped density of urban life. In the romantic era, music created a dream world, a medium of escape from the terrifyingly rapid industrialization, mechanization, and rationalization of economic and social life. Music became the vehicle of private subjectivity.

The period of political reaction and repression that took hold of Europe after 1815 enhanced the already established power of music as an instrument of psychological realism. Even in Franz Schubert's music, however, the psychological intersected with the political. Although those who gathered in the Schubertiads cherished the intimacy of the musical communication, there remained a thinly veiled political meaning. Schubert himself had been arrested and his friend and beloved text writer, the poet Mayrhofer, had turned into a government informer.

Much to the horror of mid-century proponents of aesthetic formalism, such as Eduard Hanslick, adherents of musical culture, as participants and listeners, embraced the traditions of classical music in part because they offered a forum of interior inward expressiveness protected from political control. But the content of that interior life had changed. The philosophical aspirations of the eighteenth century were replaced with the desire to expand the inner life of the individual away from the public sphere and the marketplace. Music was privileged because it helped created a private world of dreams and an intimate forum for visual fantasy. But the transposition of the private to the public did not lag far behind. By the 1850s, larger orchestral forms, in the hands of the New German School of Liszt and Wagner and through the innovations of Berlioz, had assumed a new illustrative and narrative function. Ever increasing numbers of city dwellers went to concert halls to listen to instrumental narratives that evoked for them an Ossianic Celtic past (Mendelssohn), the epic adventures of medieval and classical heroes (Liszt), and unreachable landscapes otherwise inaccessible. For example, in the late nineteenth century, audiences went to listen again and again to the depictions of the seven seas in Anton Rubinstein's "Ocean" Symphony (1851–80). Tchaikovsky's "Winter Dreams" Symphony (1874) is another example of this use of the symphonic form.

Insofar as nationalism had emerged as a novel political sentiment at odds with the remnants of dynastic absolutism, music took on a special role in the nineteenth century, particularly in Eastern Europe. Through the music of Smetana and Dvorák, the aspirations of a new Czech nationalism could be most freely expressed during the second half of the nineteenth century. It is for this reason that the triumph of the fall of communism found one of its most searing public expressions in a Prague performance (immediately distributed in CD form), attended by Václav Havel, of Smetana's *Má vlast* (c.1872–79). It was conducted by the late Rafael Kubelik. He and Rudolf Firkusný, the great pianist and pupil of Janacek, were among the first to be honored by the Charles University. They were most visible bearers of a nationalist musical tradition, dating back to the mid-nineteenth century, who returned from self-imposed exile to celebrate the liberation of their homeland.

The composer who most effectively exploited music as a popular instrument of nationalist politics and as a medium for the interior resistance to modernity and its attendant economic rationality was Richard Wagner. In his music dramas, the eighteenth-century conventions of music making—those that had survived as protected and insulated from state censorship—were transformed. He relied on a wide palette of color, easily identified musical elements, and a seamless fabric of repetition. Wagner had been a participant in the 1848 revolution. He understood music's allure and therefore perfected and extended the power of music to illustrate and to narrate. He realized the power of music to transform and subordinate, for the listener, the clock of daily time.

One of the consequences of the factory system, urban life, and modern commerce was the triumph of standardized time measurement. The clock, as Nietzsche's Zarathustra understood all too well, was a symbol of how man sought to orient himself within nature. The analog clock face was a circle that divided time into equal segments in defiance of the natural distinctions of dawn and dusk, day and night. Combined with the advances in artificial illumination, people began to work and live in cities in defiance of the natural course of the day. Seconds, minutes, and hours became the universal instruments of measuring work. Time, money, and value intersected and trampled claims for the primacy of nature in the definition of time; they created a powerful nexus of standardization that defied facile claims to individuality.

The tyranny of the clock, however, could be relinquished as an individual stepped into a concert hall or an opera house. Music could redefine time. It could expand its meaning so that a single minute could assume the aspect of extended duration (without, of course, a sense of boredom). In Wagner, however, the lengthening of time within the framework of opera became an essential attribute. The nearly six hours it takes to perform *Tristan* (1857–59) permitted the individual the chance, psychologically, to gradually lose all contact with the ordinary measurement of time in daily life. The prelude to Act I served to detach the listener immediately from reliance on conventional measurements of time and space. The listener entered an entirely new magical and fantastic context. Bruckner, Wagner's self-appointed disciple, translated that experience into symphonic form. Mahler, likewise, wrote single symphonic works lasting well over an hour, designed by their very length to transport the listener away from the experience of time dictated by the rituals of work, movement, school, and family.

Owing once again to music's paradoxical nature—the abstract and unreal character of its surface and materials and its unique connection to the emotions and the imagination—romantic music, through Wagner, created its own expectations and clichés, and a new vocabulary with which to spin its own special realist illusions. But this realism was explicitly defiant of external reality. It was a realism of myth as well as of private space; it generated a musical equivalent of prose fiction. Like the reader of the nineteenth-century novel, the listener was transported beyond the constraints of reality by the aesthetic devices of realism. The listener entered, like Ludwig II of Bavaria, Wagner's patron, into a realm of myth and aspiration that seemed more real and important than all externalities. Music challenged the present by disconnecting the listener from it. Music created a new form of dissent cloaked in symbols and images of the mythic past and visions of a utopian future. Wagner's popularity was immense. Many, including Harvard's first professor of music, John Knowles Paine, considered his influence on the young potentially dangerous. Max Bruch sought, in the 1870s, to counter Wagner's influence by reviving the secular oratorio and placing it in the service of a less illusion-filled and subversive engagement with music. His popular *Odysseus* (1872) was written to celebrate the unification of Germany; it employed an amalgam of Wagnerism and pre-romantic classical models to serve more concrete political ends. The irony was that the subversive element in Wagner was itself illusory. The fantasy world it induced inspired most of its listeners to affirm their drab realities.

IV.

The fact that until the twentieth century the political structures of Europe did not offer even its most privileged inhabitants the advantages of an open society bears repeating. The ever-growing public for instrumental and operatic music before 1918 in Europe found in that art form a surrogate for genuine political participation, freedom of expression, and freedom of movement. At the same time, however, by the end of the century the narcotic aspect of a widespread musical culture came to be understood as too affirmative of un-freedom. Aestheticism—art for art's sake—seemed to thrive at the expense of political engagement. Musical culture and cultivation, the very success of the escape from reality through music, were challenged by the generation of composers and musicians born in the 1860s and 1870s, who came of age at the turn of the century. The distance between fantasy and reality was attacked through post-Wagnerian musical innovations. This became most apparent in the work of Richard Strauss and Gustav Mahler. The audiences of the 1890s and the first decade of the twentieth century were jolted out of the comfortable reveries so powerfully generated by Wagner and his immediate followers, such as Humperdinck (in, for example, his 1893 *Hansel und Gretel*).

The generation following Strauss and Mahler went even further. Schoenberg and Stravinsky, in separate and distinct ways, both explicitly broke with the conventions of romanticism. They put forward a radical neoclassicism that sought to reconcile the aspirations of eighteenth-century instrumental music—its philosophical idealism and formal integrity in terms of musical logic—with sounds and musical techniques derived directly from, and adequate to, the contradictions of modernity. Neoclassicism in the early twentieth century was communicated through a musical texture that was explicitly harsh, non-illustrative, dense, angular, asymmetrical. The illusion of narrative continuity was shattered. The illusion of realism was undermined by the use of technical advances in musical sound. These, in turn, challenged the complacency of judgment on the part of listeners wedded to the romantic musical phantasmagoria.

As Walter Benjamin described it, writing in the mid-1930s, the nineteenth-century, middle-class, cultured individual had allowed the inherent critical and political potential within aesthetic culture—in the novel, the photograph, architecture, opera, and concert music—to be (with few exceptions) overwhelmed. What remained was the appropriation of high culture in the service of economic oppression, social inequality, and political un-freedom.

In the early twentieth century the movement known as modernism in music, like its counterparts in art and literature, sought to render new music an instrument of progressive politics. Art emerged in the substantially freer Europe of the 1920s, before the onset of fascism and Stalinism, as a medium of utopianism and an agent of radical reform. It sought to awaken its audience out of its self-imposed dream world. Bartók, in Hungary, would seek the sources of modernism in the forgotten rural folk traditions that had survived the onslaught of urbanization and industrialization.

However, music in the twentieth century did not directly follow in the path of painting, architecture, and literature. New forms of technological innovations transformed its trajectory and career. With the advent of the piano roll and the player piano, the gramophone, and the radio, the mechanical reproduction of music triumphed. It did so by enshrining history as a bulwark against new composition. The piano industry collapsed. Each home had a new means of making music that required no skill. The nineteenth-century audience of active amateurs was replaced by passive listeners. Even the simplified forms of musical literacy popularized by the piano were no longer necessary. Democratization of access was so effective that the modernist innovations never took hold. Instead, live performance and recorded music concentrated on the repertoire of the past.

Unlike modernism in literature and painting, modernism in music, through its attack on the conventions of romanticism, lost its audience. In the post-World War II world, when freedom of expression and political participation became widespread in Europe and America, and particularly in the context of the allure of the moving image with sound—film and television—the traditions of eighteenth- and nineteenth-century music making were overwhelmed. The concert hall was no longer a unique forum for assembly. Escapism and assent through fantasy, guided by a manipulation of time, did not require the coded and sometimes opaque medium of complex musical forms. The film offered an easier route. Modernism in music became unnecessary. Popular music, and even political music, for example in the cases of Hanns Eisler and Kurt Weill, used traditional simplified means of music making derived from the eighteenth and nineteenth century and adapted them. Nationalism, in its musical modernist incarnations, as in the case of Szymanowski, Enescu, and Janácek, used folk traditions within an essentially conservative tonal framework. Jazz and popular music from America, beginning in the 1920s, offered new avenues of expression and entertainment that rendered the radical innovations of musical modernism marginal, particularly for the musical theater. Musical modernism encountered strong opposition, as in the case of Hans Pfitzner, whose explicitly conservative *Palestrina* (1915) was hailed by Thomas Mann as offering the proper alternative in the necessary effort to preserve cultural values against modernist radicalism.

The prestige of musical modernism survived its lack of audience. The reason for this was the extraordinary lengths to which Nazi Germany and Stalinist Russia went in their attempts to suppress it. Modernism remained a symbol of resistance to fascism well into the 1960s. Yet in the repressive context of Russia, until the 1980s traditional classical music continued to play a role reminiscent of the 1815 to 1848 period. Assembling in concert halls and listening to music on the radio continued to be important rituals of covert and protected personal and political expression. Music's capacity to conceal attributed meaning and therefore to place the expression of emotion in public beyond suspicion, made it possible for ordinary people to cry and express collective enthusiasm at concerts of the standard repertory. For them, the "Pathétique" Symphony (1893) by Tchaikovsky sustained its meaning in political terms. It helped individuals to display in public pent-up emotion and, for a moment, to escape unharmed from tyranny and elude the absence of real freedom of expression.

Whether or not one wishes to accept the claim that for most of his life Shostakovich sought to express, beneath the affirmative surface of his music, dissent, there is no doubt that the claim itself is plausible. The wide public for music used the official sanction of the classical and operatic repertoire for its own purposes. It could hear, despite the stringent requirements placed on modern composition, echoes and suggestions of dissent and free expression. For a brief moment it could experience, through music in public, that which was dangerous to express in language, even in private. Modernism functioned for Soviet composers as an overt language of resistance, which is why in 1948, as in the mid-1930s, Stalin waged an intense public campaign against it.

In contrast, the Nazi endorsement of late romanticism as its official aesthetic permitted the regime to appropriate successfully the entire legacy of German music, including Mozart and Beethoven, for its political ends. Modernism went entirely underground. Karl Amadeus Hartmann represents a perhaps unique example of a non-Jewish German who remained in Germany and declined to participate in public musical life. In this self-imposed exile he wrote new music, that he kept secret, in the expressionist language of modernism. The connection between modernism and progressive politics was not always neat. Although his music was banned and his opportunity to function as a musician was curtailed, Anton von Webern, the visionary Austrian modernist, became a fanatical adherent of the Nazi cause. It is poignant to recall that the Jewish victims of the Nazis, in their segregated enclaves during the 1930s in Germany and in the ghettos and concentration camps of the 1940s, utilized the very repertoire appropriated by the Nazis as a medium of protected personal expression and hope. The traditions of eighteenth- and nineteenth-century music defied the powerful attempt on the part of repressive dictatorships to define and control the meaning of music.

V.

The factors that have lent the classical music tradition, dating from the late eighteenth century, this power as an expressive medium of personal aspiration, hope, and dissent are in the end its formal qualities and dimensions. These include the capacity of instrumental music without words or images to be sustained over a long period. Within this range of duration the materials of music can follow an extended logic of development and variation. The function of jazz in the African–American community in the long history of its un-freedom is analogous to the European tradition. Length of duration is crucial to the transformation of ordinary time and the creation of a framework for contemplation and the reassessment of experience. Music communicates precisely to the individual without requiring the denotative attributes of the visual and linguistic. Despite the potential and recent history of popular music as an aspect of protest politics, it can be argued that both for the private realm and in public discourse new complex and longer forms of musical expression are needed. In a society where mass communication and the centralization of the economic forces controlling entertainment promise increased standardization, an alternative is imperative.

For Balzac and Benjamin, writing a century apart, the nineteenth century was the era of arcades, journalists, and parvenus. The bourgeoisie affirmed a corrupt political and economic environment by immersing itself in the fantastic riches of its own culture and material goods, retaining only a faint recognition of the criticism and satire communicated by poets, writers, and composers. Nonetheless, under the cloak of the aesthetic, a tradition of critique and assent was sustained.

The twentieth century witnessed the expansion of the consumer economy, symbolized best by the mall. A dissenting high culture had become marginal. The pseudo-utopian cyberspace of the twenty-first century may promise little more than a technologically advanced equivalent of the stalls and shops of the nineteenth-century city and the malls of the twentieth. The dissenter through high art must find a way to function even indirectly. Artists themselves, particularly composers, may be driven overtly by an autopoetic discourse concerned only with originality and aesthetic innovation. They may indeed be elitists and severely critical of mass taste and the power of commerce in art and culture. Yet despite a purely aesthetic intention, in music a lineage of covert protest and dissent has been a part of its history of reception. Music has spurred the critique of accepted norms that define the self-conscious role of the artist, particularly the musician. No matter how small the audience, it is from the high art aesthetic enterprise that the charge of fallibility can be directed against reigning conventions and mass tastes. Music can develop new structures and paradigms of meaning and expression.

Music has functioned as a refuge and exit from the limits and constraints of un-freedom. In an open society, it can function as a challenge to the tyranny of public opinion, routine, and standardization. If an open society can be sustained only by the existence of innovation in the form of protest and dissent (which an open society is designed to protect, if for no other reason than to remind its beneficiaries of the limits of their own conceits), then the traditions of concert music that emerged in the late eighteenth century in a closed society will still be relevant. This relevance will come from the constant reinterpretation of works from the musical past and the creation of new music. Open societies, East and

West, must sustain this tradition for their own sakes, if only to protect the future from succumbing to patterns of spiritual uniformity and intellectual standardization. These are so deeply internalized that sameness is often mistaken for difference, and genuine innovation suppressed as bad art in both the public and private spheres. The ambitions of the aesthetic dimension become useful, not when they are explicitly utilitarian but when they, by design or appearance, seem to have little to do with politics. That is the lesson (if there is one at all) of the history of music since the late eighteenth century.

6 *Democracy in a Non-Democratic Society*

EDMUND MOKRZYCKI

The most popular, if not stereotypical, view of Eastern Europe is that this is a region in "transition" (some would say under "transformation") from a planned ("command") economy to a market economy, and from an authoritarian (totalitarian) one-party state to democracy. This paper deals, in a somewhat critical manner, with the second aspect of East European "transition", that is to say, with the process of democratization.

The Political Setting

Democracy has many shades. If democratization simply means more freedom and the manifested plurality of opinion, then there are good reasons to claim that the whole region, including Lukashenko's Belarus, is a more democratic place now than it was in the 1980s. If democracy is characterized in terms of its intrinsic institutions—such as universal suffrage, rival political parties, regular free elections, and an independent judiciary—then Eastern Europe looks more like a complicated mosaic with many unclear or discouraging spots, particularly in the southern and eastern parts of the region. And finally, if democracy is defined by its goal, that is, as the rule of the demos, then I am afraid that the very idea of "transition to democracy" in the post-communist countries calls for qualification. This paper suggests such a qualification by way of examining how the rule of the demos is exercised in Polish democracy.

There are three salient elements in Polish politics today: political elites, jointly called the "political class"; the democratic mechanism embedded in democratic institutions; and the demos, or "the people", who, according to any theory of democracy, use the democratic mechanism in order to exercise popular sovereignty.

As comparative studies show, the Polish political class is relatively well educated, experienced, politically and ideologically differentiated, and accustomed to seeking legitimacy in free competitive elections.[1] Polish post-communists, unlike their counterparts in several post-Soviet countries, embraced democracy and are masters in using democratic procedures in the power game. They are also enthusiastically pro-Western and pro-NATO. The democratic mechanism is firmly established in the Polish political system. Theorists of "transitology" do not seem to realize that, by their standards, several Central European countries have long passed the two winning-posts on the track of "transition". If standard transitology criteria are applied, then it is difficult to deny that, at least with respect to Hungary, Poland, and the Czech Republic, transition is "complete" and democracy has been "consolidated".[2] The explanation is simple: the non-democratic regimes in Central Europe ceased to exist virtually overnight as a result of the implosion of the whole communist system. Democracy in their region became "the only game in town" by virtue of the political vacuum around it and not by contest, as has been the case in Latin America.

As for "the people", the situation is much more complex. On the one hand, democracy has traditionally been among cherished national ideas due to political (rather than ideological) reasons. Poland was denied independence by three authoritarian monarchies. The articulation of democracy became a part of national ideology. The communist experience reinforced this trend. The "Solidarity" movement of 1980 to 1981 was indicative of the unity of the nation formed around the values of democracy qua liberty.

On the other hand, those were values of democracy as articulated in abstract democratic doctrine. In the West, democracy had been practiced before it was articulated. In Poland it was the other way around. Except for the turbulent "partocracy" of 1918 to 1926 and the semi-authoritarian regime of 1926 to 1939, Polish society has never, until 1989, experienced democratic political order.

The smooth change of regime in 1989, and the ease with which new democratic institutions started to operate, should be credited not so much to "resurrected civil society" as to intellectual and political elites and their ability to apply Western patterns in a new sociopolitical environment. The masses, including millions of former "Solidarity" members, supported democracy mostly in the form of a political *carte blanche* for the "democratic opposition". The famous individual "picture with Wałęsa" during the 1989 parliamentary election made redundant or irrelevant, as the case may have been, any ideological proclamation or political program on the part of the MP candidate.

Illusory Civil Society

Few people remember that it was mostly because of the Solidarity movement and its supporters that the forgotten concept of civil society reemerged and briskly made a career in academic and political debates. Scholars and politicians, fascinated with the spontaneous and yet orderly and efficient opposition movement that at one moment involved the great majority of the population, attached universal meaning to Polish events. The concept of civil society, and of an independent citizenry curtailing the power of the party-state and creating an alternative polity, seemed to provide a self-evident explanation of the phenomenon of Solidarity. For many liberal intellectuals it constituted a case proving that civility, civic culture, and social self-organization can accomplish a lot, even in the most adverse circumstances. Some scholars suggested that the Polish experience could be instructive with respect to other East European countries, or, indeed, Western democracies. Michael H. Bernhard believed that in the case of Poland "the reconstruction of civil society preceded similar development in other countries in the region by ten years".[3] Jean L. Cohen and Andrew Arato in turn asserted that "it is quite possible that some of the emerging Eastern constitutions will embody new sensitivity to an active civil society, a sensitivity that should in turn influence Western constitutional developments".[4]

Not much is left of this optimistic diagnosis. The Solidarity movement appealed to liberal intellectuals for what it was and for what it was not. On the one hand, it was an authentic and spontaneous movement of concerned citizens, people of all strata of society united by a noble cause. On the other, the program was not predicated upon economy. As Jerzy Szacki has observed, "the civil society paradigm that had been hammered out much earlier by Western political thought disintegrated in Eastern Europe. The citizen of Eastern Europe is not a bourgeois".[5]

A *burgerliche Gesellschaft* without the *burgerlich*? Indeed, many liberal intellectuals were hoping that Poland after communism would move towards freedom and democracy without market and inequality. It proved to be another intellectual utopia. The "civil society", constructed as if class interests and economy did not matter, proved to be a historical ephemera.

The Solidarity movement, with its idea of the "Self-Governed Republic", has not outlasted the very system it opposed. There were specific local circumstances in the crumbling Polish communism of the late 1970s that brought Solidarity into being and endowed it with the most salient features of civil society. The collapse of communism was followed not only by "the war at the top" (Wałęsa's slogan during his attempt to regain full power after several successful months of Mazowiecki's premiership), but also by the irresistible disintegration of the "civil society".

The first clear signal that there was something wrong with Polish "civil society" came during the first presidential election when Stan Tyminski, a mediocre man from nowhere, posing as a Canadian businessman, was able to excite savage populism and came a strong second with 21.1 percent of the vote, humiliating Mazowiecki (with 18%) and forcing all "concerned citizens" to support Wałęsa in the second round, whether they liked him or not.

In the few years since the collapse of communism, the fascinating "civil society" has given way to what, under communism, was named a "social vacuum". True, there are close to 20,000 NGOs in Poland, but they form a reality *sui generis*, regarded by both the political class and the "people" as a blend of hobby and philanthropy.

Everyday life is characterized by indifference, dishonesty, brutality, and respect for ruthless swindling and unmitigated force. People tend to perceive the social world as the field of a zero-sum game: some have to lose if some are to gain.

Paradoxically, this type of social philosophy, destructive as it is to interpersonal relations, coexists with solidarity of a kind, that is, with traditional Polish thinking in terms of "us" versus "them": us—the people; them—the government, the political class, the state.[6] Here we touch upon one of the main historical impediments on the way to democracy. As long as the popular view of the state suggests that rather than being a form of political self-organization of society—good or bad—it is a force over society, alien by definition and hostile de facto, democracy cannot mean much more than a new form of selecting "them".

Who Are the People?

In some countries, democracy ends at the polling station, which is not to say that it is meaningless. As Adam Przeworski has demonstrated, even in its minimalist, Schumpaterian version democracy is worth defending because voting constitutes the "flexing of muscles" and thus "provides a reading of chances in a violent conflict"[7]. In other words, ballots generate information indicative of the distribution of force, which by itself is an important factor in preventing and regulating conflicts.

Polish democracy seems to be a more sophisticated instrument. It seems that the democratic mechanism works beyond periodical voting, in the realm of everyday parliamentary and governmental decisions, particularly those related to the redistribution of wealth. All the democratically elected Polish governments, whether from the Left or from the Right, have been more than attentive to the "voice of the people". The question is, who are the people?

On the one hand, Poland is a typical case of a "new democracy", which means that the masses have inadequate understanding of democratic politics and that their political behavior is regulated by their pre-democratic experience. The masses in Poland look upon the government as an intrinsically authoritarian actor, and so they expect the government to be a good *gospodarz*. "*Gospodarz*" has a multitude of connotations, including landlord, landholder, farmer, master of the house, head of the family, manager, caretaker. In the most abstract sense *gospodarz* is a paternal figure, willful but mostly positive. The idea of social service is only beginning to take root among elites. The call for political participation is perceived as a meaningless slogan. All the major public opinion polls show that a political career is at the bottom of the occupational prestige scale.

On the other hand, there are very strong interest groups supported by, and representing the interests of, selected parts of the population. These groups exercise real control of the government. They are efficient, well organized, and led by experienced politicians qua labor union activists. The line between labor union and state politics is blurred—both on the Right, dominated by former and present Solidarity activists; and on the Left, where OPZZ, the reformed communist labor union, is influential. As for today, about 60 percent of parliamentary members have their roots in labor union politics. Pressuring the government on behalf of a strong occupational group is the best starting point for a political career. This is one aspect of a general pattern: a continuation of the type of politics that developed during the last two decades of communist Poland when strikes and negotiations substituted the incapacitated communist system of central distribution. Direct negotiations between striking workers and communist officials bypassed all the constitutional channels of articulation of interest, even though they resulted in substantial changes of state economic policy, particularly in the area of the allocation of resources and the redistribution of national wealth.

Today, of course, strike-negotiation politics play a less important role in the system, and the constitutional agencies are real and no longer operate on behalf of a single political party. Nevertheless, it is the most effective method of articulating particular group interests and, as such, it has become an unconstitutional yet extremely powerful corrective mechanism in the state machinery. Needless to say, it works to the benefit of strong social groups targeted by activist-politicians, and at the expense of weak social groups, particularly those that need the assistance of the state most. It is characteristic that even the procedural aspects of the "negotiations" have been preserved, including the role of the Roman Catholic Church which "mediates" between disputing parties, one of which is still called "the social" as opposed to "the governmental".

Most importantly, the results of "negotiations" take precedence over official state policy. Under "social" pressure, or in the anticipation of such pressure, the government makes decisions that impair the general public interest, manipulates economic figures to cover undue adjustments, alters budgetary provisions, ceases to collect taxes from the biggest factories, and provides illicit loans, etc. Sometimes, when the pressuring group is really strong and turns violent, the government refrains from prosecuting even serious law-breaking. During Andrzej Lepper's revolt (1999) the "Right-Center" government, humiliated by open and manifested violation of the law and yet afraid to act, issued an equivocal interpretation of the events that Andrzej Lepper, as well as his followers and sympathizers, could—and did—read as a post facto legalization of the revolt. The question of whether post facto legalization by the government is possible at all was not considered. This by itself is indicative of a legal and political culture stemming from past experience. Under communism the government could "legalize" anything whether, post or ante facto.

Seen from a sociological perspective the Polish political scene is composed of three elements:

(1) a competent but arrogant and corrupted political class;
(2) weak and resourceless masses (would-be civil society);
(3) strong, aggressive, and ruthless pressure groups.

The political game is in fact being played by two partners only: (1) and (3). Partner (2) joins the game incidentally, in times of voting. As a result, Polish politics is characterized by two systems, partly parallel, partly overlapping. The first pertains to the whole society and is driven by the democratic mechanism. The second links the political class with a relatively stable number of "social partners", that is, the most aggressive and most powerful pressure groups. This system is driven by the strike-negotiation mechanism developed and institutionalized (in the sociological sense of the term) during the last decades of communism.

Economic, and indeed social, policy is controlled mostly by the second system. The role of the masses is quite illusory. "Flexing muscles" is a factor, ballots do work like "paper stones", but the fact is that the masses are used to the dual structure of the world: "us" versus "them". The government is, by its very nature, "them", and the pressure groups, like in the old days, are of "us". In other words, the political mood of the masses is modulated by the actions of the pressure groups. Not perhaps as much as it was under communism, when the opposition groups were seen as a moral representation of the nation, but strongly enough make the political class believe that "muscles" are being flexed in fact by the most powerful pressure groups. That is why Polish politicians, whether on the Left or the Right, always get extremely nervous at any sign of possible unrest among coal miners, who by Polish standards are probably the most privileged workers (this dates back to the times of a "planned" economy with its extreme over-consumption of energy), and are most indifferent to the misery of hundreds of thousands of former state farm workers, even though in terms of sheer numbers they represent, together with their families, a formidable political force.

Between Democracy and Oligarchy

This double-system politics has good and bad consequences. It can be best appreciated if Poland is compared to Russia. Strong pressure groups that claim, with social consent, the mandate of the demos, prevented Poland from taking the course of Russian "democratic" oligarchy. This course was not unlikely in Poland, given our political traditions, the weakness of civil society, and the strength of bureaucratic elites of all kinds. The strong pressure groups counterbalanced those elites and introduced a measure of political equilibrium in the country.

On the other hand, these opposing major actors play a game of particular interests in which the general interest of the society is losing dramatically. The public sector consumes over 45 percent of GDP, which is a lot in a country that wants to radically improve its economic status in Europe in a decade or two. And yet all the major state functions are neglected in a most blatant manner. Education, the administration of justice, the police, science and scholarship, the fine arts, public transport, roads, crime prevention, health care, social security—all these areas (and more), which in the post-communist situation depend heavily or entirely on state subsidies, are in a miserable condition. While, during the first few years of "transformation", this fact could be explained in terms of budgetary difficulties, it is clear by now that the real source of the problem is structural. The state, with all its resources (about 40 percent of

GDP comes from the "public", i.e. the state sector), has become a contested domain exploited by various segments of the political class on the one side, and by several powerful pressure groups on the other. Appealing to the "silent majority", as Polish academics did last year, brings no results whatsoever. The "silent majority" as a rule supports in words all noble causes, irrespective of the fact that they often exclude each other. When it comes to real politics, however, the "silent majority" considers advocates of the particular group interest as representatives of "the people", and thus, paradoxically, as advocates of the general interest.

A political system thus constructed is intrinsically unresponsive to real social problems. The politicians are accountable for their actions to partners in the political game rather than to "the people". This explains their arrogance and unconcealed greed, as well as the disrespect for social norms that bewildered intellectuals read as "suicidal irresponsibility". In fact, it is rational behavior on their part, because in Polish politics "anything goes" that does not become a weapon in the political power game played by selected political actors. As soon as the new, more "democratic" (self-government ideal) system of local government was passed, local politicians, almost all of them from Left to Right, granted themselves absurd salaries. A little provincial bureaucrat would earn more than the president of the country. All of that from the budget of the local community populated by people "flexing muscles".

Young Democracy?

There is no reason to believe that with the passing of time, the aconstitutional, if not unconstitutional, distribution of real political power will wither away. Poland is certainly a new democracy, but whether it is—as transitology would have it—a young democracy is an open question. A young democracy, by its very nature, will mature and in due course will become a full-fledged democracy. I have tried to show some of the structural characteristics of the Polish political system that make it a specific, rather than young, democracy, the specificity being caused by the characteristics of Polish society.

Giuseppe di Palma believes that "democracy can grow in many soils".[8] This is certainly true. But it seems to be equally true that the variety of soils is matched by the variety of democracies, only some of which resemble Western democracy, even if all meet procedural criteria.

Western democracy was born not of political crafting and the recomposition of the political scene, but of the changing structure of group interest. The idea that democracy is good for everybody or, in any case, for all segments of the population, is a convenient ideological statement but it cannot be taken seriously as a sociological proposition. In the modern complex society with conflicting group interests, no political system can be equally good or equally bad for all the groups concerned. Western democracy developed at the end of the long struggle over the distribution of power between those who owned their wealth and social position mostly to their own effort and abilities, and those who, having privileged access to state power (because of birth or for other reasons), enjoyed political rent. In other words, democracy developed as a response to the demand for equal access to state power and was in the interest of those strata that later formed what is now known as the middle class. If the middle class guarantee democratic development, as it is often pointed out, it is not because it is located "in the middle", but because democracy is its political habitat.

The question that follows from looking at Polish politics concerns the relevance of the procedural conception of democracy. Political science has developed an impressive theory of democracy as an elaborate system of procedures. This theory is often used as if procedures as such constituted democracy and so were its essential, rather than instrumental, elements. Such an approach has one great advantage: it provides universal criteria for democratization. However, as the Polish case shows, it can be misleading, if only because it misrepresents the real political relations. If democracy is about equal access to state power (which prevents capitalizing on political privileges), then Polish procedural democracy, good as it is, has a long way to go before it becomes the rule of the demos in a meaningful sense.

Notes

1 Cf., for example, Jacek Wasilewski (ed.) (1999). *Elita Polityczna 1998.* ISP PAN.

2 For a systematic elaboration of these criteria see Juan J. Linz, and Alfred Stepan (1996). *Problems of Democratic Transformation and Consolidation: Southern Europe, South America, and the Post-Communist Europe.* Baltimore and London: The Johns Hopkins University Press.

3 Michael H. Bernhard (1993). *The Origins of Democratizations in Poland.* New York: Columbia University Press, p. 10.

4 Jean L. Cohen, and Andrew Arato (1992). *Civil Society and Political Theory.* Cambridge, Mass.: The MIT Press, p.17.

5 Jerzy Szacki (1995). *Liberalism after Communism*. Budapest: Central European University Press, p.101.

6 Actually, the concept used is "*władza*", which, very much like Russian "*vlast*" has a substantial connotation. It is usually translated as "power" but in fact it denotes those who possess or represent the power of the state.

7 Adam Przeworski (1999). "Minimalist Conception of Democracy: A Defence". In Ian Shapiro, and Casiano Hacker-Cordon (eds.), *Democracy's Value*, Cambridge: Cambridge University Press, pp. 48 and 49.

8 Giuseppe di Palma (1990). *To Craft Democracies*. Berkeley: University of California Press.

7 *Boors and Angels*

ADAM MICHNIK

Half a century ago I was a small child who did not understand anything about anything. But when I watched the behaviour of the "March" (March 1968) journalists thirty years ago, I understood a few things. I understood the power of unbridled boorishness. Therefore I can understand writers who feel alarmed at yet another onslaught of boorishness in Polish public life. However, I think it is wrong to associate this exclusively with the coming to power of the communists. It is not true that "uneducated louts, ignoramuses and boors" got into power then. The laments we are hearing have a long history.

I.

Edmund Burke, without a doubt one of the most distinguished political writers of his day, wrote in his memorable *Reflections on the French Revolution*:

> ...the time of chivalry is over. Today is a time of sophists, economists and schemers, and Europe's glory is fading for good. Never again shall we see that magnanimous loyalty toward one's birthright or sex, never again shall we see that proud submission, dignified obedience and sincere devotion which stirred people's souls with freedom even during slavery. The God-given charm of life, a readiness to defend the fatherland, a desire for manliness and heroism belong to the past! An attachment to principles and an integrity which, when wounded, aroused courage but did not spread as far as cruelty, an integrity which ennobled everything it touched and even made an offence lose half its evil, shedding vulgarity, have gone. (...) Life is brutally shed of all its decency. All the noble

> ideas, stemming from the treasury of moral feelings, residing in the heart but acknowledged by the mind as essential in order to cover the faults of our naked, defective souls and give it honour in our own eyes, are henceforth to be rejected as ridiculous, absurd and outdated relics. (...) When a king's subjects adopt rebellion as their principle, the king adopts tyranny as his strategy.
> When we are deprived of certain convictions and principles of life, we lose something exceedingly precious. From that moment on we have no compass by which to guide ourselves, neither do we know exactly to which port we are heading.

II.

Twenty years ago, a well-known right-wing political essayist wrote his "Treatise on Lice", a sharp feuilleton attacking the opportunism and hypocrisy of the Polish cultural élites. The guiding thought of the essay itself was that the élites had assumed the form of lice—cowardly scribblers who justified their servitude to totalitarian rule in devious ways. I was alarmed by the biased and boorish picture of the world painted in that essay. I myself felt I was a "louse" and I penned a response, to which I gave the title "Lice and Angels". Years later I read a feuilleton that was equally well written, but equally biased in its construction: a feuilleton about "Boors", praising the "illustrious" and the "highborn". Therefore, I would like to declare: I am a "Boor". Or, to put it differently, I think that all of us from KOR (the Workers' Defence Committee) and from underground Solidarity are "Boors". And not just from today. We have been Boors for a long time.

III.

Chateaubriand, an aristocrat in mind and body, a master of penetrating analysis and of the pen, noted in his *Memoirs from beyond the Grave*:

> 14 July, the storming of the Bastille. I witnessed this attack on several invalids and a scared warder. If the gates had been kept locked the crowd would never have gained entry to the fortress. Two or three cannon shots were fired, but not by the invalids. They were fired by French guardsmen in the towers. De Launay, having been dragged from his hiding place and subjected to thousands of insults, was massacred on the steps of the City Hall. Flesselles, the mayor of Paris, had his head smashed by a bullet from a pistol. That was a scene which heartless hypocrites consider to be so wonderful. While the murdering was taking place,

> orgies occurred as in the Rome riots during the rule of Otto and Vitelius. The takers of the Bastille paraded about in coaches; happy drunks, declared victors, paraded in the taverns. Their escorts were prostitutes and sans-culottes, who were now begging to rule. Paying honour out of fear, passers-by raised their hats to these heroes, many of whom did not survive their triumph through over-exhaustion. Keys to the Bastille were duplicated. They were sent to every important idiot in all four corners of the world. (...) The most famous speakers met, the most illustrious writers and painters, the most popular actors and actresses, dancers, famous foreigners, courtiers and European ambassadors: the old France came to this place in order to expire, and the new France came in order to be born.
> The storming of the Bastille—"a bloody indulgence"—opened a new era.
> In the eyes of the people, the Bastille was a symbol of vanquished servility. They saw it as a kind of executioner of their liberties at the entry to Paris.

The Boor entered the city centre before the Red Army conquered Poland. The Boor entered the city centre over the body of the Bastille.

IV.

The last 100 years of Polish history have been a discourse between Kordian and the Boor. Kordian was a patriot, and the Boor a primitive fool, a manipulated simpleton, a politician who did not know how to tie his tie, who had only just abandoned his pitchfork and was now forcing his way into salons.

But Kordian needed the Boor. Hence, the Boor was idealised by insurrectionists and revolutionaries because without him, no insurrection or revolution could succeed. Hence, the Boor found his way to the national Pantheon without difficulty: as the brave Bartosz Glowacki, scythe-wielder at the battle of Raclawice; or as the brave Jan Kilinski, the patriotic shoemaker of Warsaw; or as Wojciech Drzymala, who fooled the German administration with his famous wagon.

The Boor was reviled and insulted by the conservatives because he had his own memory, his own aspirations, his own scent. The spectre of the Boor, making his way into the salons, fascinated the progressives and dismayed the traditionalists. But the Boor remained a boor, a symbol of the Galician "massacre" when they "wielded the saw", a symbol of the calamity of 1863 when the peasants betrayed insurrectionists to the Russians, although it was said at the time that "kings fight the most bravely, but peasants die in the biggest numbers".

The ideas of freedom, independence and the Revolution were élitist, each in its own way. Each of them had its own specific First Brigade, which was fed by a conviction regarding the nobility of a small group of martyrs among a multitude of cowards and boors. Aleksander Fredro, author of *Zemsta* (Revenge) and *Sluby Panienskie* (The Weddings) and every inch a conservative, wrote: "Squires deserve to have patriarchal authority, no one can replace it effectively."

Kordian conspired with the Boor, but the lord, his close cousin, was able to show the Boor his place.

V.

Writing about the twenty years between the world wars, Witold Gombrowicz wrote several times about his fear of the Boor. This fear has great eyes and a long history. It survives to this day. This fear is not absurd.

Ortega y Gasset, author of the famous treatise on the "Revolt of the Masses", claimed that a regression towards barbarity, in other words a "return to a naiveté and primitivism of people who either have no past or have forgotten they have one" began already in the nineteenth century. In Ortega's opinion, "Bolshevism and Fascism are typical mass movements led by inferior people living beyond the limits of time, people devoid of memory and historical consciousness."

However, Bolshevism and Fascism were not invented by boors, but by intellectuals who were less (Gobineau) or more (Marx) cunning. For the Boor, there was room only in militant groups or in the lower echelons of authority. The top echelons and the salons were reserved for people from the new élites, obsessed by a narcotic fascination with power and the charms of their own ideology. It is not Fascism or Bolshevism that paved the Boor's way into the salons, but the principle of universal, democratic parliamentary elections. The Boor's voice became important; his opinion had to be respected. The election results could very well depend on the Boor. The Boor could stage a factory strike, or he could work obediently. The Boor organised rallies. The Boor demanded an eight-hour working day. The Boor started to run for parliament.

Until, eventually, the Boor spoke in his own voice. When Conservative deputies summoned the spectre of a "new Szela" in the Galician Sejm in 1912, Wincenty Witos, leader of the people's faction, said in the Sejm in Lwow:

> I must firmly oppose a summoning of the spectres of 1848, [I am] against a rekindling of old wounds, against bringing this deed to the minds of people who had no part in it and who were not to be blamed for it. Although the great poet

> K. Ujejski has granted a general absolution to the powers that were ignorant of this great massacre, putting the blame on other satans who had been active there, I do not think it will harm anyone if I say that this terrible deed was done by people under the influence of frenzy and passion, bitter because of the harm which they had suffered for centuries. On your part, however, this was caused by your centuries of neglect in bringing up the people under your authority, by the terrible harm and exploitation which you inflicted upon them. After all, you were lords over life and death. You taught the lessons, and the peasant passed the examination.

Such was the response of the Boor who demanded dignity on the threshold of the twentieth century.

VI.

Then came the long war and the wonderful moment when independence was restored. Kordian's virtues were rewarded. But the euphoria was short-lived. Already in 1920, the fate of the young Republic hung in the balance—the Bolshevik army entered Poland, proclaiming the slogan: "All power is in the hands of the Boors."

But the Boor did not listen to the Bolsheviks. He joined the Polish army and defended the Republic against Red Army liberators. This was written about by the deeply shocked Stefan Zeromski, who asked:

> How can it be that, like Tsarist commissars in the past, now Soviet commissars have found their way to our towns and villages, to our churches, houses and works of art? How is it that both the former, and those of today, have found acknowledgement among the Polish people? It must be said openly that the slovenliness of the spirit of Poland, resurrected as if by a miracle, has brought the whip of Bolshevism. Poland lived with a slovenly spirit, haunted by all kinds of roguery, profiteering, corruption, careerism at the expense of others, rampant bureaucracy and a desire to obtain absolute power. All the noble sentiments conceived under bondage died in this first day of freedom. The struggle for power, no doubt in existence throughout the world as an expression of the strength of social groups, parties and camps, assumed monstrous proportions in Poland. It is not wise, distinguished, intelligent and educated people, of whom we have many in Poland, who have come to power, but the most capable or the most cunning leaders of parties. It is as if the waters in a pond have receded, and at the bottom we see a huge breeding-ground of reptiles and amphibians. When this became visible to everyone, everything underneath remained as if it were in bondage. In the Kingdom itself there is a huge army of landless and homeless people. (…) A new generation of dispossessed persons has been formed in the space of nineteen years. Seasonal migration is halted by the post-war status quo, and industry does

not exist. (...) He who, when the Muscovites came to Poland, stood in defence of his palace, manor, townhouse, property or apartment full of furniture and works of art, his hovel on a plot of land, his lands and possessions, knew what he was defending when he defended his country. But he who had absolutely nothing and stood in defence of his country did not know what he was fighting for. He was fighting for his country's future prosperity. He was defending other people's property, the inviolability of a palace, the prosperity of a manor, the right to rent from a townhouse, apartments which he had never seen and never would see, and, finally, he was defending the power which had often trodden on him remorselessly. A landowner is like a bush at the side of the road. The enemy can tread upon it, kick it and pull it apart, but the bush will soon spread new roots, grow again and appear in spring in brand-new greenery. A homeless man is like a heap of manure which nourishes grain, fruit, vegetables, grass and most beautiful flowers. It should make no difference to him who plants him, treads upon him or drinks his juices. If this social manure, upon which we have trodden just like our overlords—the Russians and Germans—did before us, seizes a rifle and opposes the enemy together with the gentry, bourgeoisie, intelligentsia, farmers and factory workers, experiences bloodshed in battle and wins victory alongside the rest, his deed is an obligation upon all of us. He should not expect grace or a reward for the blood he spilled, but the surrender of everything that lies in his country. It is necessary to heave oneself up from the slovenliness of spirit. The same blood, sacrificial and holy for us forever, that flowed on the battlefield of Warsaw from the heart of Father Skorupko, the nation's hero, also flowed in streams from the wounds of nameless Polish soldiers and landless peasants. (...)

With our deeds, we must now convince the world and tell it the truth that the ideas for which our soldiers died in the battle against the Red Army stood far above the rights, defined by a narrow body of Moscow oligarchs, which they tried to impose on us. If we have not yet implemented these rights, then we carry images of them in our souls. We must shed opinions whereby we are a nation of gentry and noblemen, a country of obscurantism, a kind of army of white knights of Pilsudski. The working world in the East and in the West, in England, France, Italy, America and Germany itself, and in Russia, must realise that it is not true that Poland was the gendarme of bourgeois Europe, carrying the disaster of world progress on its banners. We must not let our defeat of the Red Army in defence of our fatherland; in defence of our monoglot, indivisible and self-governing people; and in defence of our language and self-determination, be perceived as a victory of a stratum of rich men, gentry and landowners, and the defeat of the poor people, as well as the speed of world progress. Having defeated Bolshevism on the battlefield, we must now defeat its mentality. Bolshevism must give way to higher, more just, more intelligent and more perfect principles. It is necessary to stir into action the old, dirt-encrusted Poland, imbued with the poison of invaders. The August storm (...) must cleanse our air from the fumes of meanness.

That is what Kordian wrote about the Boor after the victorious war against the Bolsheviks in 1920.

VII.

"The fumes of meanness." That phrase of Stefan Zeromski is as broad as it is far from synonymity. What were the countenances of meanness in that time?

It was certainly scorn for the Boor, displayed by the "high born" and "Enlightened Ones". However, it was also a brutal display of greed by the Boors, who had forced their way into the salons. Corruption, opportunism—all this marked the presence of the common people on the parliamentary benches. However, the corruption and egoism of the "high born" provided a pattern for the egoism and corruption of the Boors.

I feel genetically linked to the Boors, I feel snobbism and jealousy at the sight of the lightning careers of the high born. But when I see a Boor making room for himself using elbow tactics, I feel anger and shame. Nevertheless, I share a feeling of solidarity with the Boor; we possess the same brutality, the same ambitions, the same complexes.

That is why I am immune to anti-Boor rhetoric. I remember that Wincenty Witos himself was a Boor, as well as Roman Dmowski. I also remember that Jozef Pilsudski, the great architect of the struggle for Poland's independence, used language that was far from parliamentary when he wrote about a "toilet" or when he insulted parliamentarians. This nobleman, opposed to the servility of his own social class, also acted like a Boor.

Dabrowska wrote that it is a paradox of Polish history that

> …the May coup, carried out by forces that were inclined towards democracy and supported by radical social groups, quickly developed into an openly anti-democratic system of government. Perhaps the oddness and paradox of this phenomenon is only apparent. We Poles need not even point at Sorel, or the socialist background of Mussolini, Hitler, or Stalin, in order to perceive the evident link between extremist and doctrinaire social revolutionary thinking on the one hand, and anti-democratic moods, arising from this thinking, on the other. We need only read Ludwik Mieroslawski's *Poznan Uprising*. There, we will find a nucleus of dictatorship, state totalitarianism, the seeds of today's idea of "leadership", the mystic thoughts of rationalism and the military responsibility of the whole of society, raised to the highest principle of social life. (…) The new government line was recognised as the principle of the "strong arm", capable of

counteracting "irresponsible social experiments", among which the landowners included the land reform in particular.

While on the subject of the "fumes of meanness", one must remember the outburst of demagogy served to public opinion in the Second Republic by virtually every single political camp. Wincenty Witos warned the peasants: "Be careful that no empty-minded, loud-mouthed people climb their way up on your backs. These people honour you as long as they need you, but later they are as little concerned about you as they are about broken tools. (...) If you (...) are incapable of using your strength, if the shout of an agitator throws you off balance, if the slightest breath of demagogy makes you sway, then you will pay very dearly for what you have experienced."

And they did pay, and not just the peasants. Polish semi-dictatorship squeezed between the Nazi Reich and the Stalinist Soviet Union, was incapable of forming a government of "national conciliation" even in the face of the Nazi threat. The government of the Republic was incapable of performing even a magnanimous act of reconciliation vis-à-vis its opponents, distinguished citizens like Witos or Korfanty, who had returned from abroad.

Scorn for the Boor was related to scorn for the political culture and democratic order.

VIII.

Maria Dabrowska commented on Polish history with bitterness: "The venomous seeds of severance, sown for centuries, have received strong nourishment, and the nobility, in their zeal, have merely broadened the gulf." In her moving *Crossroads*, Dabrowska quotes the author of *Warsaw Memoirs*, who believed that the "self-liberation of the dim peasants will be like a sword in the hand of a madman". Indeed, noted the author of *Nights and Days*: "A Pole was able to bear with dignity the loss of his privileges and lands, taken away by the enemy. For a thousand good or bad reasons, he was also able to dispose of his property carelessly. He lost the sacred and beloved land of his fathers at games of cards and other diversions. He used it to pay his debts to Jews and Germans. But there was one person to whom he never wanted to give either land or money—the peasant, the heart and soul of the nation."

For the high born, it was obvious where the land reform was leading. "It was the same in Russia. The campaign against the land reform, just like many other depressing events of our lives, is just a 'digression' in the great and spontaneous movement of the socio-political reaction. We cannot perceive here a connection with the most important and most difficult cause of our century. Reaction might be very much in fashion today, just like progressivism used to be in fashion. (...) Most of the slogans now being used, and even the methods of government now being propagated (a longing for the whip), are merely a return to the reaction and coercion which were disgraced a long time ago. No one should be fooled by the new names. Just like every evil, reaction often wears a mask." "The ghost of the past often forges his passport", she quotes Victor Hugo.

IX.

However, the real "forging of passports" commenced after 1945. That was when, at the same time as the social revolution imposed by Soviet bayonets against the will of the people, a specific Polish knot was tied: beneath the banner of social justice, the "high born" were disenfranchised and deprived of their property, buildings and positions in the state and society. Maria Dabrowska's dire warning, expressed on the threshold of the Second Republic, was fulfilled: "If today's conservatives, using the danger of communism as an excuse, choose social reaction, and if that is the second reason behind the strong campaign against the land reform, then that is a bad sign. For he who chooses pressure and reaction, whether he governs or is governed, chooses the chief danger—unrest and revolution."

The point is that the Great Change was accompanied by a Great Destruction: the Boor reached for other people's property and positions, destroying what was left of the national traditions, democracy and customs of a law-governed country. However, the Polish paradox is something else altogether: a coalition between the Boor and Bolshevism was justified by other "high born" people, the children of bourgeois homes fascinated by the Social Revolution. One of them wrote:

> The lone anger of a man of the intelligentsia,
> He who remembers the tomb of Agamemnon
> As he remembers the tomb in the Wawel,
> Is worthy of a song, yet the song
> Deserted him a long time ago:
> Now it rides on a russet tank, bearing a soldier's hat

with a youthful zeal and independent,
and under its rough tunic
the heart is pounding.
He is not to be judged by a mob now.
He sees the bright redness,
Pale with anger he listens to the street,
He was a revolutionary at heart,
"And now, look, the Boors are ruling,
they are sealing their appeals to the crowd with red wax.
That was not what we wanted.
The Marshal would not have abandoned the cause thus."

Is this not an appropriate, though grotesquely malevolent, description of today's awareness by Andrzej Szczypiorski?

After all, one must remember that the coalition between the Boor and Soviet Bolshevism, unfortunately a genuine coalition, was opposed not by the high born, but by the Boors themselves: Stanislaw Mikolajczyk, leader of the Polish peasants; Cardinal Stefan Wyszynski, leader of the Polish church; Wladyslaw Gomulka, leader of "right-wing nationalistic deviation" among the Polish communists. It is they who became the symbols of opposition to Stalinist oppression. That is also the path—opposition, exile and the prison cell—by which the masses entered the city centre.

The "high born" and the "enlightened" were just as divided as the Boors. One need only mention the Skamandrites on the one hand—Lechon, Wierzynski, and Witlin living abroad; and on the other hand Iwaszkiewicz, Slonimski and Tuwim. It is enough to remember Boleslaw Piasecki's friends from the National-Radical Camp who found themselves in PAX, and Wojciech Wasiutynski in the National Party abroad. It is enough to recall the two Bochenski brothers: Innocenty Maria, a Dominican, professor in Fribourg and the author of revealing works on Soviet Marxism; and Aleksander, a deputy in the Stalinist Sejm and the author of *The History of Polish Stupidity*, in which he denounced romantic notions and extolled the need to co-operate with the communist regime.

One must not confuse communist rule with Boorish rule. We Boors were everywhere, among the officers of the Secret Police and among its prisoners. Just as the "high born" and "enlightened" person was not a synonym for a Soviet agent, so too the Boor was not a synonym for opportunist and traitor. They were everywhere.

X.

As a result of the Nazi and Soviet occupation, emigrations and executions, Poland became boorish. The whole of Poland became boorish—the communist, collaborating part, and the anti-communist, anti-Soviet part. It is the Boor who collectivised Poland, made it atheist and Soviet. And it was a different Boor who opposed this. A Boor reviled Poland, and a Boor defended it.

I am not accusing the "high born" and "Enlightened Ones". They, too, were on both sides of the barricade. However, they were in a somewhat different position. They understood the complexity of the world, the secrets of dialectics, the secret of geopolitics, and the need to protect the nation's substance.

The Boor served communism without a thought, and also without a thought he kindled unrest—in Poznan in 1956, in March 1968, in December 1970. Not until 1976 did the rebellious Boor meet with the rebellious "Enlightened One". The rebellious "Enlightened One" formulated a thesis about a civic society or civil defence. The Boor spoke with his guts rather than with his brain. That is why he kept saying: "yes, yes", or "no, no". He said "yes" more often. Nevertheless, he was able to say "no" vehemently enough to move the foundations of the Soviet Empire.

This Boor was an odd fellow. There was no shortage of PZPR members among the leaders of the strikes in 1970 and 1980. Let us try to understand that. The People's Republic of Poland appreciated the Boor, gave him land, and let him advance from the village to the city. Ultimately, the People's Republic gave him a sense of dignity, albeit an illusory one.

The Boor was glorified at every single opportunity—worker, farmer, work leader or secret agent. The Boor listened with pleasure when people said "You have become an officer not thanks to study, but thanks to your strong will." He was overjoyed when he was appointed managing director as a reward for his background. In other words, the Boor, now flaunting about in the salons, was an inseparable part of the communist lie about social justice. But a different Boor discovered the lies of the communists and the deceit of the salons of power—in the name of a less illusory dignity. Lech Walesa, Zbigniew Bujak, Wladyslaw Frasyniuk—these were they, these Boors from Solidarity, who overthrew communism. That is why I was, remain, and always will be on the side of the Boors. That is why I find it easy to cite the communist poet:

A man covered in dust walks along the road,
Carrying on his back logs cut in the forest.
Ask him and he will tell you:
More than one century has dealt him wounds.
He is the blood and salt of this earth.
Old history exerts pain through him.
He carried the burden of other sins.
But "WHO IS OTHER THAN A COMMON MAN?"

XI.

But I know it is not quite so simple. From the very beginning, the alliance between the left-wing intelligentsia and the common man, in other words between the "Boor" and the "Enlightened One", has been based on lies and aimed at creating successive lies.

Let us recall that the "Boor" approved communist rule because communist rule did not make him take off his hat and kiss the landlord's hand, and it brought an end to the daily indignities. The left-wing "Enlightened One" rebelled against the conventions of the ancien régime, of which the above indignity formed part, and did not wish to take part in it.

The remainder of this history has been described in a masterly way by Slawomir Mrozek in his *Tango*, and subsequently interpreted by Jan Blonski in his *Collected Plays of Slawomir Mrozek*.

An exceptionally astute analyst and raconteur of the secrets of Polish fortunes, Mrozek described the family homes of left-wing "Enlightened Ones": "It was said there that 'happiness is the right and duty of people who have been liberated in our new age. (…) There is only one rule. One must not be afraid to do whatever one feels. (…) A man reaches for himself, discards his old gods, and mounts the pedestal.'" Recalling this period of rebellion against tradition and customs, Mrozek's hero says: "Do you think we were nothing but blind anarchists? We also marched towards the future, in a historic movement. (…) Rebellion is the rock on which progress builds its church. The greater the rebellion, the more extensive this church."

Blonski says that the result of this religion of rebellion and progress was "first of all a belief that evil can be removed from the world together with a king's privileges, the church's power, and even inbred injustice." Then there will be "social equilibrium, where values hitherto suppressed by institutional restrictions will bloom. These values shall be freedom and chastity, as the Jacobins wanted, and enterprise and prosperity, as the utilitarians wanted."

However, the result of this permanent dialogue between dreamers in the salons was not freedom, chastity, or prosperity, but the era of Edek—a rustic who considers vim and a lack of principles to be the New Rules governing interpersonal relationships. "It seemed to me, most Enlightened One, that we are governed by what is interpersonal and tormented by what is personal. But then I saw it was only Edek." "Edek" is a "downright Boor", freedom changed to free choice. The rebellion of the "Enlightened Ones" against religion, convention and tradition was a "farewell to an era" which "they considered to be the start of a new era", whilst the new era, Edek's victory, was a "revolution of nihilism". The "rebellion against convention ended in a caveman's hole", Blonski wrote.

XII.

Mrozek, and via him Blonski, give an accurate description of the singular evolution of fascination with "Boors" among circles of rebellious "Enlightened Ones". From Mrozek's drama, one gets the impression that, after all the daydreaming, ambitions and manipulations of the "Enlightened Ones", at a moment of calamity, war or revolution only the "Boor" is left standing, and a "Boor" is someone who knows what he wants, just like Edek in *Tango*, "someone who is sure of his interests and his body, who feels at home like a cow or shark. In a word, someone for whom existence is not a problem."

There is no communication with a Boor. (…) The Boor is unfathomable."

What feelings does a Boor arouse? "A fear of crowds, which cause nothing but noise." A Boor has no social standing. "Of course, he or his father used to be in service, hence his fear that he will insist upon being served, that he will wreak vengeance, that he will touch everything with a heavy, punitive hand. But now he appears as a simple man, someone who is establishing wealth, in other words a petty bourgeois, or even a monarch—in other words, a dignitary."

The Boor's habits are crude, but "thanks to his excellent nonproblematic nature, the Boor is a metaphysical phenomenon rather than a social one."

The key to Blonski's pronouncement is that "in every man, a stereotype and an animal exist side by side…deep inside there is a dormant Boor and a swaggering intellectual puppet."

XIII.

However, this "swaggering intellectual puppet" can become a bold and clever intellectual, capable of heroic deeds; however, this "Boor" knows how to transform himself into a bold leader—first of the Great Strike, and then of the entire nation. This Boor has transfixed the entire world in wonder. He has moved the world.

Poland's latest history is fickle. People have changed their masks, faces, attitudes and characters. Just like in Stevenson's novel, the good, mild Dr. Jekyll becomes the evil, criminal Mr. Hyde.

Jan Blonski is right. A metamorphosis like that is programmed inside each of us. A lout can behave like a statesman, and a ruffian can summon up enough heroism to defend freedom and independence. Unfortunately, the opposite also occurs—heroes become bogged down in senseless intrigues, and proverbial "incorruptible people" become embedded in corruption. Modesty and tolerance turn into vanity and fanaticism.

This applies both to "Boors" and to the "high born" or "Enlightened Ones".

Why, then, do I feel I am a "Boor" rather than an "Enlightened One"? Because we Boors do not know how to lie properly—we are betrayed by our primitive manners, simple language and involuntary honesty, which is the result of the absence of an exquisite imagination.

We "Boors" know that, just like revolution, our simplicity and brutality in public life stem from poverty and indignity, or from participation in despotic rule which causes the indignity of others. We are brutal and boorish, but at least we do not tell old wives' tales about historic tradition, national substance and the historic missions revealed to monarchs. And, of course, when we watch our brothers demonstrating in the mines, steelworks and shipyards, when we see their despairing faces and listen to their meaningless slogans, we know what is going on. It is they who "were striking" for freedom, and it is they who fell victims to it. They believed that with their strikes they would achieve calm and prosperity. Yet, after the victory of freedom, all they got was unemployment. It is they who feel they have lost through no fault of their own. They are the ones who have had a rough time.

We Boors realise that a market economy has its own laws, but we also know that fear and pain have their own laws, too.

We Boors know that a triumphant ignoramus with a doctor's degree, who pretends he is Kordian, is no different at all from the "Boor" inside the party apparatus. He is merely more hypocritical.

XIV.

I do not think this has anything to do with my education or occupation. It is more a question of identity: to be in a boorish condition is the same as approving the aspirations of those who have been harmed and degraded, and feeling a part of their world. One can be at odds with one's own world, as long as one retains one's sensitivity to the misfortunes of those who have suffered and lost.

A Great Lament resounds over Poland's beautiful countryside. The angels are lamenting the sins of Poles. Ten years ago there was a lament that Polish intellectuals were "lice"—cowards, hypocritical opportunists, collaborators. During martial law we heard a lament that Poland was in the throes of the evil spirit of anti-state radicalism. Now, we hear everywhere that Poland is disintegrating through the fault of covert communists disguised as liberals, once again via the all-pervading rule of the "Boors".

Each of these laments is as false as it is useful—false like every generalisation, and useful like every sign that says "Malfunction".

"From the small seed of truth, they cultivate the plant of lies." That is how Czeslaw Milosz described the doings of the worshippers of the Spirit of History fifty years ago. Although the lamenting angels are behaving in a similar way, I do not wish to ascribe to them any perfidious intentions. One can understand their cries of despair that "the bottle is half empty". But in a country where the bottles were completely empty for centuries, there is reason to rejoice in the fact that they are only half empty at last. Believe me, they contain so much tasty water of life…

8 *The Unity of Mankind and the Plurality of States*

JÁNOS KIS

Cosmopolitanisms

1. Does the principle of the unity of mankind allow the division of the world into a plurality of states? Cosmopolitans hold that this question is relevant for the assessment of the claims that states make against individuals and their groups. Most notably, states claim to have legitimate authority, which those within their jurisdiction must obey and those outside of it must not subvert. According to cosmopolitanism, no state whose jurisdiction ranges over a population smaller than humanity at large can be legitimate in this sense unless the restriction of its range is shown to be permitted by the principle of the unity of mankind. Let us call the test which assesses particular institutions or personal conduct towards those institutions against the principle of the unity of mankind the *cosmopolitan test*.

Classical or world-state cosmopolitans maintain that the plurality of states is incompatible with the unity of mankind. All human beings are moral equals, so the argument goes, and their moral equality cannot be done justice by political organization unless any two individuals are citizens of the same state. The only morally acceptable government is a world government.[1]

Enlightenment or nation-state cosmopolitans deny the classical statement. A cosmopolitan world order can exist, they maintain, without it being the case that any random pair of individuals are subjected to the authority of one and the same government. Moreover, the separate governments can be sovereign over an exclusive jurisdiction without diminishing the cosmopolitan virtues of the international order.[2]

The folk view on Enlightenment cosmopolitanism is different. It classes Enlightenment philosophers with world-state cosmopolitans. Minor figures in eighteenth-century political thought did in fact cherish the idea of a global government.[3] Leading cosmopolitan thinkers, Condorcet or Kant, for example, did not place themselves in this tradition, though.[4]

Kant's views are particularly telling. He believed that the world state is not an attractive idea in the first place: because the ability of laws to bind individual conduct is in an inverse relationship with the size of the government, a "universal monarchy" would oscillate between soulless despotism and anarchy.[5] More importantly, Kant believed that world government is not even needed for a cosmopolitan order to obtain. It is sufficient, he claimed, that the international regime is subjected to three "definitive articles of eternal peace": namely, all states adopt a republican form of government, all of them join a peace federation, and, finally, visitors from a foreign country enjoy general hospitality everywhere (i.e., they are not met with hostility by local residents).[6] A regime of domestically sovereign nation-states is able to satisfy these requirements.

This essay will examine the implications of the cosmopolitan view that the plurality of states needs to be justified against the standards of the unity of mankind. Its main argument will develop around the question of whether nation-state cosmopolitanism is defensible.

2. A nation-state regime is an international order which consists of states and states only. State sovereignty seems to be a logical consequence.

A state is *sovereign* if neither its supreme instance nor any of the inferior instances are liable to obey any instance beyond the state's own organization. In a world where the only units with international standing are states, no state can be subordinated to any other authority but (some instance of) another state. Being subordinated to another state entails that the putatively separate state is nothing else but a sub-unit within a larger state's hierarchy. In order to be separate, nation-states must be sovereign.

Sometimes states interfere with the domestic competencies of another state without having the right to do so. A formally sovereign state may depend on another state as a matter of fact. The international order was never one of fully sovereign states, at least not in the de facto sense. But sovereignty even as an ideal suffered a dramatic setback in the last half-century or so. The discrepancy between state sovereignty on the one hand and the progressive melting away of the boundaries between domestic policy and foreign policy is an uncontested fact of the contemporary world. Economic activities run within the jurisdiction of one state have effects of ever larger significance for activities in other states. The rise of transnational corporations exposes the regulatory and taxation capabilities of states to a severe test. The expansion of the financial markets reduces the ability of domestic governments to pursue social policies on their own. Modern technologies, such as informatics, defy localized control. Environmental effects of economic activities (ozone depletion, acid rain, deforestation, etc.) defy state frontiers. The increase in labor migration makes the binary division between citizens and non-citizens, an important feature of the traditional concept of citizenry, more and more obsolete. Humanitarian disasters in one region of the world trigger a flood of refugees towards another. The growing interdependence seems to make the nation-state regime obsolete.[7]

Still, political philosophy continues to be dominated by the image of isolated, more or less self-sufficient states. The discussion of subjects as widely varied as that of political obligation and distributive justice takes it for granted that the unit of analysis is "a society". The society in question is accepted to be congruent with the subject population of a state. And the state is tacitly understood to be an organization, which is sovereign over an exclusive jurisdiction. Political philosophy is still relying on these unexamined background assumptions. The only context in which the question of the legitimacy of state authority is being raised is that of the relationship between the state and its members. The only individuals to whom a state is presented as owing justification for its claim of authority are its own citizens. The conditions under which a state's claim to authority over its domain can be legitimate from the point of view of non-citizens is left unexamined, as if it were natural that if a state is legitimate inwardly, it automatically commands legitimacy outwardly as well.

It is not natural, though. The criticism of nation-state cosmopolitanism will help to establish, or so I hope, some of the standards of external legitimacy a state must meet in order for its authority claim to be fully justified.

3. If nation-state cosmopolitanism proves to be untenable, does it follow that cosmopolitans have to embrace, as a fallback position, the world-state view? The answer is "no". The world-state regime and the nation-state regime do not jointly exhaust the class of possible global orders.

Both world-state and nation-state cosmopolitanisms assume that the global order includes no members of separate standing other than states. The difference is in the numbers: one or many. There is a large number of alternatives to these states-only regimes. Setting aside the no-state option defended by anarchists, one can easily conceive of a global order where, besides states, non-state organizations also have public international standing. Suppose that some of these organizations have authority to issue binding instructions and to enforce compliance with them. They lack, however, certain characteristic features of states. The jurisdiction of some of them may not be defined territorially but functionally (think of an international tribunal on war crimes). Others may have only states among the addressees of their instructions; they might lack any reach to private individuals or organizations (think of an international body supervising state policy on trade or state compliance with international norms of environmental protection or arms production). And so on. Suppose, finally, that such supra-state institutions are not united under one central organ but, rather, that they draw crisscrossing lines of authority. Such is the international order we are witnessing emerging since about the end of the Second World War.

In a regime like this, a state can share its sovereign powers with political organizations of international standing and, as a state, remain separate nevertheless. Let us call an international order consisting of separate but not sovereign states, for better or worse, a *supranation-state regime*.[8]

4. The Kantian view of a cosmopolitan order relies on a very weak definition of the cosmopolitan test. The "definitive articles of the eternal peace" do not transform an international regime into a cosmopolitan one unless it is the case that the unity of mankind confronts a state and its citizens with negative duties only, such as not to kill, not to torture or maim human beings, not to destroy or carry away their property, and so on. These are the kind of requirements to which a state will conform by committing itself not to wage wars of aggression and not to deny protection to foreigners who enter its territory against hostile treatment. Positive demands, those of maintaining distributive justice, of providing humanitarian assistance to the needy, and of intervening on behalf of those suffering severe rights violations beyond a state's jurisdiction cannot be satisfied by simply imposing non-aggression and non-hostility. The Kantian international order cannot meet the cosmopolitan test, unless it is true that the principle of the unity of mankind, at least when addressed to states, does not include positive requirements.

This is not a natural view. The unity of mankind is not about the content of general morality but about the range of people to whom its principles apply. It states that human beings are members of the same moral community. Membership in the moral community is said to be based on non-relational properties such as rational agency, personhood and the like. These properties count as reasons to treat their bearers as proper objects of concern and respect. In other words, these properties are claimed to confer moral standing on their subjects. And because they are shared equally by (virtually) all human beings, they confer equal moral standing or equal membership in the moral community on (virtually) all humans.

Thus, the principle of the unity of mankind amounts to saying that whatever we owe to each other as a matter of general morality, we owe it to all human beings equally. But general morality is not reduced to duties not to hurt. It includes demands of benefiting fellow humans as well. The suggestion that states are not subject to requirements of beneficence in their relationships to outsiders requires an explanation.

5. The explanation, if there is any, must flow from a theoretical account of what states are supposed to do and why: What is the point of, and the justification for, their existence? Now, all viable theories assume that states are providers of public goods such as peace, security, economic prosperity, education, or welfare. The goods in question are public in the sense that their provision requires cooperation, and often in the further sense that once they are available, nobody can be excluded from their benefits, not even those who did not pay for them. Non-excludability will enter my argument somewhat later. At this point, I would like to focus on cooperation.

State-run cooperation has distinctive features. States issue rules for cooperation, which are part of a *legal system*: where there is a state, there are higher-order rules which apply to the adoption, recognition, interpretation, amendment and revocation of the first-order rules. In a state, a first-order rule exists if, and only if, a higher-order rule identifies it as being part of the legal system.[9] Second, states claim authority for their rules over a population, which is *territorially* identified.[10] The jurisdiction of a state is the territory to which its legal system applies. Third, within that territory, the state claims *supremacy* for its legal system over any other system of rules.[11] Fourth, states back their rules by the threat of using *force* against those who do not comply with them and, moreover, they claim a monopoly over deciding, who can apply force, when, and against whom.[12] For various aims, further properties such as direct access to subjects, reliance on bureaucratic apparatuses and centralization have importance. For the aims of the present discussion, however, it is the capacity and the right to issue binding instructions (the existence of a legal system, territorial jurisdiction and supremacy), and the monopoly of force which matter.

Theories of the state are expected to show that an organization endowed with these properties is needed in order to coordinate action for the provision of public goods that are important enough to justify the burdens of legal restrictions backed by coercion.

One way these theories differ from each other derives from the fact that they strike a different balance between the range of public goods provided via state coordination and the powers of the state over its subjects. Defenders of a minimal state believe that legal regulation and coercion are not justifiable unless they are applied in the interest of protecting the life, liberty, personal security and property of individuals and of enforcing the agreements they voluntarily enter with each other. Others argue for larger government and more ample provision of public goods.

But there is a more basic distinction. Whatever the aim of state-coordinated action, individual participation in it can be understood in two different ways: either as a matter of agreement or as a matter of prior duty. In the first case, coordination by the state is claimed to serve what John Rawls called a "cooperative venture for mutual advantage". In the second case, the point of cooperation is not mutual advantage but satisfying a normative requirement. This distinction plays a central role in any theory of political obligations.

The Mutual Advantage Account

6. The mutual advantage conception goes like this. Whatever the demands of general morality, they leave room for people to pursue their personal aims, severally and in cooperation with others. So long as the costs of the cooperative venture are not displaced onto outsiders or the latter are not harmed in other ways, non-participants have no valid claims against the cooperating agents.

Suppose the responsibilities of states are exhausted by their role in coordinating joint action for mutual advantage. Suppose, furthermore, that citizen A draws on state-regulated cooperation for benefits (for example, he lives in a district where public security improves dramatically as a result of the government raising additional taxes to fund a larger police force). Then, the duty of fairness demands that A takes his part of the burdens rather than taking advantage of the efforts of others.[13]

The duty of fairness is owed to fellow citizens. But the duty to fellow citizens translates into an obligation to the state. This is because cooperation is rule-based, and the sacrifices undertaken by others are imposed on them by the rules made and enforced by the state. The fact that a sufficiently large part of the citizenry does indeed abide by the rules, combined with the fact that A himself accepts the benefits of their cooperative efforts, puts A under the obligation to abide by the rules himself. "[W]hen a number of persons engage in a mutually advantageous cooperative venture according to certain rules and thus voluntarily restrict their liberty, those who have submitted to these restrictions have a right to a similar acquiescence on the part of those who have benefited from their submission."[14]

To be sure, everybody is supposed to contribute his fair share to the joint efforts, and the benefits are supposed to be allocated in a fair manner, too. Therefore, the state, insofar as it is responsible for the distribution of burdens and benefits, is itself subject to an assessment against the standards of fairness. Citizens stand under the obligation to comply with its rules only if it is just. This is why Rawls states explicitly that "a person is required to do his part as defined by the rules of an institution when *two* conditions are met"[15]—the fact of having accepted benefits from the joint efforts of others being only one of these, the other being that "the institution is just (or fair)".[16]

Some of the benefits provided by state-regulated cooperation, such as protection of life, liberty, and bodily integrity consist in preventing action which is morally wrong. General morality demands refraining from such action in the first place. But the mutual advantage conception does not justify the existence and workings of the state or the obligations citizens owe to it by the moral duty not to engage in this kind of action. Rather, it argues from the benefits which make engaging in the cooperation advantageous. Once people do cooperate, they stand under a duty of fairness towards each other and under an obligation to comply with the law towards their state. But they have no prior duty to cooperate. Nor are they burdened by any duty of fairness towards such individuals who are not party to the cooperative venture.

The mutual advantage conception, if true, successfully explains why a nation-state regime which is subjected to the definitive articles of the eternal peace can pass the cosmopolitan test. This is because, according to this conception, states are nothing but instruments of cooperation among a limited group of people. Their responsibilities are to their own citizenry. The rest of humankind has no other claims against them than those embodied by the duties of not harming. And those duties are well covered by the articles of peace federation and of general hospitality.[17]

This result is independent of the way we want to determine the scope of the public goods which state-regulated cooperation is permitted and required to provide for citizens. Whether we do believe that only minimal states can command legitimate authority or that we are partisans of a more extensive state, the mutual advantage conception will restrict the duties of the state and of its citizens towards outsiders to the minimum of not doing harm to them. So if the mutual advantage conception is true, nation-state cosmopolitanism is true as well.

7. But this conception has serious defects. First, it fails to account for the fact that states do not claim authority over a human population as such but over a population in its relationship with a territory. There is no state without a territorial jurisdiction, and sovereign states claim exclusive authority over their jurisdiction. They claim the right to decide who is allowed to enter their territory. They claim the right to decide what kind of natural resources within that territory can be privately owned. They claim the right to determine, through a system of taxation and redistribution, who else besides the owners should benefit from the fruits of the productive uses of property, and so on. By carving out a territorial jurisdiction for themselves, states withdraw part of the surface of the earth from free access to outsiders. So if the state is a set of institutions which regulate cooperation for mutual advantage, then its members are to be seen as agreeing to carve out a territorial unit for themselves, and to monopolize, through their state, the right to decide who is allowed to enter that territory, to settle on it, to use the resources available within it, and to stand to benefit from the cooperative venture going on inside of its boundaries. Such an agreement directly affects the legitimate interests of outsiders. If states have the right they claim to possess to their territory, then, of course, outsiders are under the obligation not to interfere with the exercise of that right. But outsiders, by definition, are not parties to the cooperative venture. Nor are they supposed to enjoy its benefits. Being in need of some concept of agreement in order to explain political obligations, the mutual advantage account cannot explain why they are duty-bound to refrain from interfering with the cooperating group's control (exercised via its state) over its territory.[18]

A further difficulty is related to the idea of the duty of fairness as Rawls explained it in his early article. The mere fact of deriving benefits from the cooperative efforts of others is not sufficient to establish such a duty. Suppose A did not ask for the benefit she happens to enjoy. Had she the liberty to refuse the benefit and to divert efforts and resources needed for reciprocating to some other aim, she would be better off. Obviously, those who made her a beneficiary of an advantage she disprefers to something else, have no right to enforce reciprocation. A is not bound by a duty of fairness towards the participants of a cooperative venture unless she agreed to join that venture. Rawls is explicit on this. He says that only someone who "has *voluntarily* accepted the benefits of the arrangement or taken advantage of the opportunities it offers" is duty-bound to do "his part as defined by the rules" of cooperation.[19] But the rights and obligations of a citizen are not something most people have voluntarily accepted. Suppose our state recognizes the right of its citizens unilaterally to resign from their citizenship. It does not follow that if they do not do so, by this they have expressed their agreement to stay. We might have a preference for membership in another state which, however, denies us the status of citizen. Actually, most people are deprived of choice in this matter. They simply find themselves, at the age when they start giving reflexive thought to their own person, being citizens of a particular state, without ever having the opportunity for change. Thus, the mutual advantage account fails to meet what A. John Simmons calls the condition of generality: except for a very small minority, it cannot explain why people do stand under the obligation to abide by the law of their state.[20]

By the time he published his *Theory*, Rawls had come to the conclusion that if political obligations are indeed grounded in the duty of fairness, then only office-holders can bear political obligations. "There is, I believe, no political obligation, strictly speaking, for citizens generally", he says.[21]

This sounds odd. Citizens at large are claimed to be morally required to abide by the law of their country. Rawls does not deny this. What he comes to deny is that the requirement of compliance can be based on voluntary commitment. And because he sticks to the definition of obligations as normative demands incurred voluntarily, he maintains that the requirement to obey the law is conceptually different from what we call political obligation. He looks for normative demands which are, according to an expression I borrow from George Klosko, "functionally equivalent to political obligations",[22] and identifies these as the "natural duty of justice".

The "natural duty conception" is a non-voluntaristic account for the requirement to obey the law. It is not the only such account. It has a popular competitor in what we could call, following Ronald Dworkin, the "associative obligations conception".[23] The two accounts go in opposite directions. The natural duty conception, as the term indicates, is universalistic, while the associative obligations conception is particularist. The natural duty conception ties political obligations to the requirements of general morality, while the associative obligations conception ties them to the requirements embodied by special ties between individuals. A brief discussion of the second will shed light, by way of contrast, on the character of the first.

The Associative Obligations Account

8. Associative obligations are part of the role we fulfill as participants in social practices such as those of friendship, family, and the like. For an associative obligation to hold, it is not necessary that the individuals related to each other by special bonds consent to fulfilling their role. The newborn cannot possibly choose to be a role-bearer within a parent–child relationship, nor can it choose to be a child of particular parents. Nevertheless, the child has a role in a family, a web of special role relationships burdens it with obligations, and those obligations are owed not to any adult person who could qualify to be a parent but to the actual parents.

Let us call groups of individuals which are tied together by bonds of reciprocal obligations communities. The family is a community. Having filial obligations is just part of what it means to be a member of a family. A citizenry is a community, too. What is true about filial obligations applies to citizen's obligations as well.

Thus, according to the associative obligations account, individuals are bearers of obligations towards their fellow citizens and their state by virtue of finding themselves to be citizens of a particular state. Or at least such is the case if their state satisfies some further conditions of fairness or justice which make the citizenry a true community tied together by the bonds of reciprocity.

If the associative obligations account works, it does the same job for nation-state cosmopolitanism as the mutual advantage conception would have done. Because these obligations tie community members and only community members to each other, the only kind of duties the political community is supposed to bear towards outsiders, under this conception, are duties to refrain from harming. The "definitive articles of the eternal peace" take care of these duties sufficiently. So again, whatever the scope of the public goods which the community is allowed or required to secure for its members by means of state-regulated cooperation, the collective duties towards outsiders are restricted to a minimum, and nation-state cosmopolitanism is vindicated.

9. However, the associative obligations conception is no more successful in resolving the difficulties that the mutual advantage conception failed to resolve. First, it is no better at coping with the problem of showing how outsiders can be obligated to respect the state's claim to its territory. Given the reliance of the associative obligations conception on special ties among community members, this should not surprise us. It is surprising, however, that it is not a genuinely non-voluntaristic conception. Or, more exactly, it either implies that citizens have the obligation never to relinquish their citizenship of origin (not even in the rare cases where they have both the opportunity and the desire to do so), or it is not a genuinely non-voluntaristic conception.[24]

For suppose the theory does not imply that obligation. Then a person who in fact did relinquish his citizenship in his country of origin does not stand under any special political obligation towards the citizenry and the state of that country any more. The claim of associative political obligations must be formulated in such a manner as to give room to this fact. It must include the rider that citizens are bound by associative political obligations so long as they do not dissolve the bond of citizenship which ties them to their political community and its state. But, then, the fact of obligation depends on the citizen's choice not to disallow it. And the fact that the majority simply do not have the choice will not play any role in justifying the claim that they are politically obligated. It will only explain why their failure to depart is not evidence for their consent to remain.

To sum up, defenders of the associative obligations conception face the following dilemma. Either they allow for unilateral, voluntary relinquishing of citizenship and, then, they return to the family of voluntaristic theories of political obligation. Or else they want to save the non-voluntaristic character of their theory but, then, they have to assume that citizens are "owned" by their state and their political community. If they take the first option, they are back with the difficulty that voluntaristic accounts are unable to meet the condition of generality. If they take the second option, their theory will not qualify as cosmopolitan.

We need an alternative non-voluntaristic theory which is capable of explaining how individuals who have the right to alienate their status of citizen can still bear political obligations towards their state so long as they have not done so. Rawls' conception of the natural duty of justice is such a theory.

The Natural Duty Account

10. The natural duty of justice, Rawls maintains, "requires us to support and to comply with just institutions that exist and apply to us". [25]

Natural duties are our pre-institutional duties which are rooted in general morality. Thus, "they hold between persons irrespective of their institutional relationships; they obtain between all as equal moral persons".[26]

Furthermore, a natural duty "requires no voluntary acts in order to apply".[27] If so, then the natural duty of justice "binds citizens generally".[28]

But, then, we are left with an account of political obligations which is radically different from the one provided by the mutual advantage conception. The natural duty conception implies that the cooperation to provide public goods, at least in some important cases, should not be treated as a venture for mutual advantage (which one either joins or not, depending on one's preferences) but as cooperative action demanded by morality (which those under the duty should join, irrespective of their preferences).

Incidentally, Kant himself was closer to this view than to the mutual advantage account. Unlike Hobbes, he did not understand the original contract as an optional agreement which the parties join for the sake of personal benefit, but as a matter of duty which they are required to accomplish.[29]

Once a just institution exists, and once it is the case that we are within the purview of its authority, we have the duty to support it and to comply with its directives, Rawls maintains. Political obligations need not be incurred by giving voluntary consent (or by belonging to an ascriptive community). They flow from the existence of a general duty to support and comply with institutions which 1. exist; 2. are just; and 3. apply to the person who is claimed to stand under an obligation, combined with the facts that 1. the institutions in question do indeed exist; 2. they are indeed just; and 3. they do indeed apply to the person in question.

However, there are a number of questions the natural duty conception has to answer before it can claim success. First and foremost, how can there be a natural, that is, pre-institutional, duty to support and comply with any institution? Second, how can a natural duty (that obtains between all as equal moral persons) bind individuals to institutions which range over a population smaller than humanity at large? Third, how can a duty which is supposed to hold "between persons irrespective of their institutional relationships" bind a particular individual to a particular institution rather than binding individuals in general to institutions with the requisite general properties including that of being just?

The first question is the hardest one. It seems to me that if we find a satisfactory answer to it, the remaining two will be easy to handle. So let us address the first question first.

11. I suggest approaching the problem from the perspective of the determinacy of general moral duties.

Some of our moral duties are sufficiently determinate in themselves. Duties of forbearance of the "You shall not kill" type are of this character. We can tell without any hesitation who are the persons burdened by the duty (everybody) and who are the persons to whom the duties are owed (everybody else). In core cases we are also able to tell without hesitation what the person bound by the duty is liable to do (refrain from any acts of killing).

Duties of assistance of the "Save the life of the person in mortal danger" type are likely to be much less determinate. There are exceptions, to be sure, like the stock example of the drowning child. A small child is drowning in a pond. There is one single adult on the scene of the accident. One can tell without hesitation that he and only he is under the duty to come to the rescue of the child. But suppose the scene of the accident is a crowded beach. Among those lying on the sand there are many capable of rescuing the child. All of them stand under the duty to help. But they cannot help at the same time. If all wade into the water, they might do harm to each other without succeeding in saving the child's life. On the other hand, if, fearing the danger of such an outcome, they all vacillate between action and inaction, the moment when the child still could have been rescued might be lost.[30]

The difficulty stems from the fact that, unlike in the original case, in the crowded beach case the duty of rescue is spread over many people. In order for it to be executable, a small number of individuals (possibly one) need to be identified. In other words, a *selection rule* is needed to pick out those who will be charged with the responsibility to act on behalf of the rest. The moral demand that people in a position to help come to the rescue of a person in mortal danger does not include any rule like this. It is underdetermined.

Sometimes the situation is such that it is natural for everybody to act on a particular selection rule. Suppose one and only one adult is conspicuously closer to the scene of the accident than anybody else. Then, a natural proximity rule applies: it is the person nearest to the drowning child who should run to its rescue. Everybody can safely expect everybody else to follow this rule. But suppose those on the beach are all at an equal distance from the drowning child. Then, the proximity rule cannot possibly apply. There are many other rules which compete for application but none of these has natural salience. The duty to save the life of someone in mortal danger cannot effectively guide action in such situations, unless one of the competing rules is made salient by institutional convention.[31]

In other cases, the duty cannot be executed by the action of one single individual. It demands, for its satisfaction, cooperation by many. Beyond selecting the participants of the collective venture, their action needs to be concerted. Think of the case of rescuing the inhabitants of a burning house or of defending a settlement against flood. Effectively concerted action again necessitates rules. And again, more than one set of rules might offer itself without any of these enjoying natural salience. Institutional convention is needed to make determinate the moral duty applying to many people at the same time.

12. The natural duty to support and comply with just institutions (that exist and apply to us) is based on this relationship between moral duty and institutional rules. Some of our duties are collective in the sense that, although they apply to individual members of a group severally, the number of those who are burdened by them is significantly larger than the maximum number of those who can effectively discharge them, and/or they require for their execution concerted action by a number of people. In the absence of coordination by selection rules and concertation rules, such duties cannot be successfully met. Often, those rules must be established by institutional convention. This is what makes compliance with institutions an obligation for those to whom the institutions apply. If a moral duty which applies to us depends, for its execution, on the existence of institutions, then that moral duty requires us to abide by the appropriate institutional rules.

There is an unavoidable element of contingency in this: other rules could do as well, and different rules could have a different scope of application, so that individual A, to whom institution i_1 does apply, might have found herself beyond the scope of an alternative institution, i_2. However, once it is i_1 rather than i_2 which exists, the moral duty demands that A supports i_1 and complies with it whether or not she has chosen to be within its jurisdiction. Institutional obligations are entailed by an underdetermined moral duty supplemented by conventional rules which provide the duty with the requisite determinacy.

In order for an institution to impose genuine obligations on those to whom it applies, it is not necessary that they join the institutional convention voluntarily. It is sufficient that they share with others a general duty which the institutional convention makes determinate for them.

The natural duty account is compatible with the idea that citizenship is alienable in principle. On the one hand, it is not the fact of belonging which explains, by itself, the obligation to abide by the institutions of one's state. It is this fact coupled with the general moral duties which those institutions make determinate for particular individuals. The fact that we have no opportunity to choose our citizenship does not diminish the normative force of the duty to comply with institutions which make the demands of morality determinate for us. On the other hand, the natural duties do not require that we remain within the scope of application of our particular institution even if we have the opportunity and the desire to change allegiances. It only requires us, under such circumstances, to join *a* system of (just) institutions which is capable of specifying our duties for us. In a world where individuals were completely free to change their citizenship whenever they so wanted, their choices would determine which institutions applied to them. But the duty to comply with the institutions which do indeed apply to them would not need, for its justification, any reliance on the fact of choice and acceptance. It would be sufficiently explained by the pre-existing natural duty.[32]

13. Let me summarize. The demand made by a state that its citizens support and comply with its institutions is justified if the state in question is ordered by natural duties.

This condition might sound excessively demanding. No existing state seems to come close enough to it. Therefore, one might make the objection that no existing state can expect its citizens to abide by the law as a matter of obligation. So the natural duty account seems to be vulnerable to an objection different from those which have been raised in response to the mutual advantage and the associative obligations accounts. But consider the following.

Our argument started from the observation that some of the general moral duties require, in order to become sufficiently determinate, institutions, and that more than one institutional scheme is capable of doing the job. This makes the selection of the particular scheme in force a matter of convention. Different schemes may distribute burdens and benefits differently. They also may circumscribe (partly) different groups of benefactors and beneficiaries. Individuals are duty-bound to support and comply with that particular institutional scheme which is capable of coordinating collective action with the aim of securing the morally required benefits. An institutional scheme which is inherently ineffective does not morally bind individuals to support and comply with it.

But effectiveness is not a characteristic fully internal to institutional schemes. It also depends on the readiness of the individuals within the scope of those schemes to follow their directives rather than those of an alternative scheme. Imagine a situation where two schemes compete for my loyalty. And suppose I can be sure that a large majority of the others who find themselves within the scope of the two schemes are disposed to comply with Scheme One rather than Scheme Two, so that the first but not the second has a chance of being effective. Then I have the obligation to follow the directives originating with Scheme One.[33] Suppose Scheme Two is, in principle, more nearly just. Still, my obligation is to comply with Scheme One. An institutional scheme which is less nearly just than some of its conceivable rivals can still impose genuine obligations on individuals within its scope. I presume Rawls had something like this in mind when he stated that "if the basic structure of a society is just, or *as just as it is reasonable to expect in the circumstances*, everyone has a natural duty to do what is required of him".[34]

Or at least this is the case whenever an attempt to abandon Scheme One for Scheme Two involves the risk of a breakdown in coordination and a return to the state of nature—a state full of injustices and other bad features and carrying the danger of ending up with a Scheme Three, much worse than even Scheme One, emerging as victorious. But suppose there is a way to change Scheme One, without running the risk of destroying it, towards a morally superior Scheme Two. In this case, the duty imposed on people under the authority of Scheme One to support and comply with its institutions is coupled with another requirement embodied by the natural duty of justice, which is also discussed by Rawls. This complementary duty consists in the demand that "we assist in the establishment of just arrangements when they do not exist, at least when this can be done with little cost to ourselves".[35] We have to support the institutions which exist and apply to us, provided they are "as just as it is reasonable to expect in the circumstances", but we also have to work towards their reform.

In a word, the theory suggested by Rawls is realistic enough but its realism does not deprive it of critical potential and normative force.

14. Let us now address the question I mentioned as second: How can a natural duty (that obtains between all as equal moral persons) bind individuals to institutions whose range is smaller than humanity at large?

One possible answer would be that a state whose central institutions would range over the entire human population is simply unfeasible. This is not the case.

World government would be an unfeasible option if it were the case that the growth of states unavoidably reached a ceiling long before a merger into one single organization could occur. Some institutions admit of such a ceiling to their size. The family is an obvious example.

The family is in deep trouble in contemporary society, and we simply do not know how it will evolve. But one thing we can know for sure: it cannot evolve towards significantly increasing its size. This is because the family has, among its points, that of maintaining intimate relationships between the family members. Intimacy, affectionate ties and caring are among the values which give us reason to continue to cherish the family. No institution devoid of these features would be an acceptable alternative. Thus, the family cannot possibly meet the challenge of its social environment by substantially increasing its size.

There is no such ceiling for the growth of citizenries. Citizenries are communities adapted to the conditions of anonymity and impersonality. If a state's expansion admits of a limit, that limit cannot be absolute. It will reflect and, therefore, it will change with the costs and benefits of organizational scale.

The costs are partly of a technological and economic nature. The larger a state's territory and population, the more information needs to be collected and processed for the government to be able to deal adequately with its tasks, the more complex its bureaucratic apparatuses need to become vertically, etc. The growth might reach a limit beyond which the state is not sustainable in the absence of dramatic technological development, or beyond which the economic costs of maintaining the state surpass its taxation capacity.[36]

Not all costs are technological or economic. Societies which are very far from each other in terms of economic development are much more difficult to unite than those at comparable levels of development. Distances between public cultures, traditions, and historical memories matter, too.

Some of these obstacles are likely to become less significant over time. The spectacular development of informatics and of transportation seems to eliminate the technological limits to the size of states, and to reduce dramatically the economic burdens of their maintenance. Although the experiences of the last fifty years or so are mixed as to the changes in the gap between the developed and the underdeveloped worlds, there are reasons for moderate optimism in this regard, even if not in the very short run.

Cultural change seems to be a less promising factor, though. We can expect the rise in the level of education, its progressive standardization over the world, and increasing cross-fertilization of everyday cultures, perhaps combined with a tendency towards secularization, to contribute to diminishing the cultural distance between societies. But there is no linear relationship between cultural proximity and mutual acceptance. Often, nationalist movements are not mobilized against groups which are very far from them on the cultural scale but rather against communities with which they share common history, customs, and in certain cases even language and/or religion. The conflict might come first and cultural divergence follow, rather than the other way round.[37]

Thus, the various impediments to a radical reduction in the number of states do not submit themselves equally well to changes conducive to improving the chances that a world state might become feasible at least in the distant future. This is sufficient to defend the claim that general morality can demand, as a matter of natural duty, that we support and comply with institutions whose jurisdiction ranges over a population smaller than mankind at large.

15. The final question regarding the natural duty account is: How can a duty which is supposed to hold "between persons irrespective of their institutional relationships" bind a particular individual to a particular institution rather than binding individuals in general to institutions with the requisite general properties, including that of being just? This is the problem A. John Simmons identifies as the problem of particularity. While voluntaristic theories are unable to meet the condition of generality, Simmons maintains, non-voluntaristic theories (including the natural duty account) fail to meet the particularity condition.

True, Rawls states that we have a natural duty to support and comply with just institutions that "apply to us". This is not an appropriate way to meet the particularity problem, Simmons responds, because the idea of "application" is hopelessly vague. Any institution might claim that it "applies to us". Any institution might want to extend its authority over us, and we have no way of refusing allegiance, on the grounds of the natural duty account, provided that the institution in question distributes burdens and benefits in a just manner. But we simply cannot be duty-bound to join an institution on the mere grounds that it is just.

However, the natural duty account does not maintain, in the reading I was giving to it, that we have the duty to pay allegiance to any institution which is just and which claims to apply to us. The natural duty of justice binds us towards those just institutions which serve to make general moral duties which we already have but which, left alone, are hopelessly indeterminate, determinate for us. Most of the existing (and possible) institutions fail to display this character. States do not, provided that they are "as just as it is reasonable to expect in the circumstances".

16. If we have a reason to believe that the natural duty account is the correct theory of political obligations, then we are invited not to take the correctness of nation-state cosmopolitanism for granted. Unlike its rivals, the natural duty account is not committed in advance to the view that a political community and its state do not have duties to outsiders other than those of not doing harm. On the one hand, this is a clear advantage it has over its rivals, because it makes it capable, in principle, of accommodating the issue of territory. On the other hand, it makes further investigation to see whether there are, in fact, positive duties to outsiders unavoidable.

Suppose governments have no other legitimate functions than those of a night-watchman state (Kant himself shared this view). In that case, it might seem plausible to believe that the same reasons which prohibit the state from taking up any functions more extensive than this might justify the restriction of its responsibilities towards outsiders to those of refraining from doing harm (and preventing their citizens from doing harm to them). But suppose the ideal of the night-watchman state is untenable. Suppose states are required, beyond protecting the rights of their citizens, to maintain distributive justice and provide humanitarian assistance to the needy within their boundaries. If this is the case, then we need a separate argument to establish whether governmental responsibilities can extend beyond the borders of the country. Nation-state cosmopolitanism cannot be true unless we find that the answer is negative.

Consider first the issue of transnational distributive justice.

Transnational Distributive Justice

17. Distributive justice is a controversial field. But there is a general principle to which few, if any, would deny validity. It claims that each agent should bear the costs of his or her activities or, to put it differently, nobody should be allowed to displace those costs onto others.

Sometimes, establishing the fact that an agent has shifted the costs of his activities onto others is a relatively unproblematic task. For example, industries which contaminate rivers may be able to cash in the full income of their production without shouldering the full costs of it: the harm caused to others remains uncompensated. This is a clear case of displacing costs onto others. The explanation for it is that there is no market for the quality of the water. Suppose we are able to simulate the way such non-existent markets would price river contamination. In this case we can find out how large a burden has been shifted by the producer onto the consumers of fresh air and water. No further inquiry is needed.

In other cases, the investigation cannot stop at this point. One simply cannot tell, in the absence of an answer to further questions, whether the agents have displaced costs onto other individuals. Consider the alternative of erecting a public building with or without ramps and other facilities needed by people in wheelchairs. A representative of the group of disabled might claim that if the investors are free to take the second option, that allows them to displace some of the construction costs onto his constituency. A representative of the investors might claim that if the first option is enforced, some of the costs for the moving around of the disabled are shifted, coercively, onto his constituency. Which of the mutually exclusive claims is valid? This answer to this question depends on how we assess the initial situation. Is it the case that people cannot be held morally responsible for redressing some disadvantage unless its occurrence is correctly attributed to their own action or unless they have voluntarily accepted benefits related to the fact of the disadvantage in question? If the answer is "yes", then the representative of the investors is right. If the answer is "no", then the disabled people's representative is right.

Let us call the issue of assessing the initial distribution the issue of basic distributive justice. Basic distributive justice is about those background conditions against which we assess the way human action changes the distribution of costs and benefits.

Basic distributive justice, however, raises a further problem—that of the scope of the population to which the principles of justice apply. When we are interested in activities, the costs of which are claimed to have been displaced onto others, the relevant population is determined by the very activities under discussion. It consists of the agents (e.g., the factory which contaminated a river and the firm which owns and manages the factory) and of those who suffer harm as a result of the activities (inhabitants of settlements along the river, fishermen, etc.). When it comes to an inquiry into the background distribution, though, actions and their effects do not help to draw the scope of the relevant population. We will depend on other criteria.

The choice of these auxiliary criteria might have a momentous impact on both the volume and the direction of transfers required by justice. Suppose we agree that something like Rawls' difference principle holds for background justice. In this case, the poor in Bangladesh will expect, as a matter of justice, much more massive transfers in their favor if the criteria of scope determine a relevant population extending far beyond their country to include the United States, rather than restricting the relevant population to Bengali citizens only. Middle-class families in the United States will have to expect much heavier redistributive taxes under criteria which merge their relevant population with that of Bangladesh, rather than separating the two. Welfare recipients in the US might be transformed into net welfare contributors by a criterion under which the relevant population includes both American and Bengali citizens, and the same criterion might make earlier welfare contributors in Bangladesh into welfare recipients.

The consequences are significant for the controversy over nation-state cosmopolitanism. Some of the criteria of scope would leave nation-state cosmopolitanism intact. Others would make it untenable. So it is of great importance to know which are the appropriate criteria.

18. A criterion potentially favorable to the nation-state view is suggested by communitarian authors. Communitarians maintain that the population relevant to the aims of basic distributive justice must coincide with the membership of a particular community, national or other. If justice demands that an initial distribution is transformed into another one, that means that human beings are made responsible for offsetting disadvantages not due to their own responsible action but to sheer luck. In itself, this demand is not plausible, communitarians argue. In a population whose members are not connected to each other by special bonds, harms are allowed to be left with the persons who suffer them, except when there is somebody else who is responsible for their occurrence. The relationships between two randomly selected members of a large-scale population cannot be personalized. They must be such that people who are strangers to each other could still recognize the existence of a special relationship between them. The bonds of community do satisfy this requirement. Justice demands that people share in each other's misfortune if they are members of the same community. It does not demand sharing between strangers who are not related to each other by communal bonds.[38]

If the communities in question are citizenries of particular states or their subgroups (an assumption generally held by communitarians), then the communitarian criterion for the scope of basic distributive justice does not damage nation-state cosmopolitanism. And if the principles of basic distributive justice do not apply to any populations other than those which qualify as communities, then nation-state cosmopolitanism is so far justified.

Even so, it would not follow that there are no demands of justice beyond borders. As we have seen already, the demands of justice are not exhausted by those relative to initial distributions. Justice imposes requirements on the way human action allocates its costs and benefits. The effects of many activities do not stop, however, at the boundaries of states. Negative environmental effects, for example, fail to respect frontiers. The larger the dimensions of industrial production, the greater the risk that activities run in one state will have significant harmful impacts on the environment of human life in another. If this is true, then there is at least one requirement of distributive justice, that of fair compensation and of taking reasonable precautions to prevent harm in the first place, that seems to conflict with the principle of national sovereignty.

19. More importantly, communities are not the only candidates for defining a population to which principles of basic distributive justice apply. Social and economic cooperation creates yet another framework within which principles of basic justice have authority, whether or not the cooperating population forms a community. Society, understood as a "cooperative venture", is identified by Rawls as the domain of distributive justice. True, for the aims of his *Theory*, Rawls identified the cooperating unit as a more or less closed "national society" coinciding with the jurisdiction of a nation-state. And one can argue, as Brian Barry did, that it is not the mere fact of cooperation but the fact of special kinds of cooperation—collective provision of public goods and quasi-insurance schemes of mutual aid—which triggers the considerations of basic distributive justice. Such special kinds of cooperation do, however, rely on the institutions of the state. So even if we agree that the principles of basic distributive justice are activated by cooperation, the kind of cooperation which transcends national boundaries—cooperation coordinated by trade and the market—does not give rise to more than principles of justice as requital (as fair exchange rates).[39]

Yet Barry's argument seems to be hasty. Any set of market exchange rates depends, for its fairness, on background conditions of initial distribution. Horizontal systems of exchange involve, too, an underlying scheme of basic distributive justice. Participation in cooperation not coordinated by any institution other than the market is sufficient to make one part of a population to which the demands of basic distributive justice apply.

If this is so, then the scope of the principles of basic distributive justice cannot be restricted to the nation-state. Since its very rise, the nation-state has found itself embedded in a wider network of social and economic cooperation called by social historians a "world system".[40] And the modern world system is notoriously characterized by continuous shifts in the advantages and disadvantages of economic growth, technical evolution, and social development between its center and the peripheries. Often, one can observe without further inquiry that such shifts consist in an unjust displacement of the costs of evolution from the center to the peripheries. At other times, however, the judgment about the fairness or unfairness of the exchange between developed and underdeveloped regions depends, for its truth, on a prior judgment about the fairness or unfairness of the basic distribution across the populations integrated by the market.

Moreover, there is a potentially still wider context within which the principles of basic distributive justice can apply even in the absence of division of labor and exchange. Imagine that the international order is the same as it is now, the whole inhabitable world being divided up among territorial states, the only significant difference consisting in the total absence of cooperation across frontiers. Isolated as they are from each other, the separate national societies still remain connected by one fact of major significance: the territory of the earth and its resources are scarce factors, and those scarce factors are somehow distributed among the existing countries. Whatever amount of resources one country has, it is withdrawn from the inhabitants of other countries, and the latter have pro tanto fewer means to pursue their aims. Those better endowed are in a more advantageous position than those worse endowed, and the advantages and disadvantages are mutually related. Because human societies compete for the same natural resources, the dividing up of the earth among the territorial states is in need of justification. Scarcity is a circumstance of justice, as we know it at least since David Hume; it mandates that the initial distribution of resources among societies be equal unless there is some special justification for inequality. Thus, considerations of basic distributive justice apply to the entire human population, whether or not there is cooperation between the more limited national societies into which it is divided up.[41]

Let us consider now the case of humanitarian assistance.

Humanitarian Assistance

20. Suppose extending help to a distant people in great distress is an act of supererogation rather than that of discharging a duty. If this is so, then no erecting of supra-state institutions to coordinate benevolent action is required by morality. Like engaging in the action itself, engaging in supra-state coordination will be at the discretion of particular communities.

To be sure, the very assumption seems insulting in our world where, year by year, entire societies are ravaged by earthquakes, droughts, floods, and manmade disasters. Yet these are contingent facts which could be otherwise. We could inhabit a different world where no single human being has worse expectations than the worst-off inhabitant of a very developed country. I believe that even under the assumption of such a world the argument would fail, and it is instructive to see why. So I begin by identifying the additional fact which, together with the division of the global population into distinct citizenries, is supposed to provide justification for the claim that there are duties of assistance up to the borders of one's state but no duties beyond those borders.

Ordinary morality holds that duties of assistance depend on proximity between the needy person and the potential helper. If you are walking along a beach where a child is drowning, you are under a near categorical duty to come to its rescue. If you are miles away from the beach and you hear about the accident, your duty to hurry to the scene to rescue the child is much weaker. Peter Singer denies the ordinary view. According to him, distance is morally irrelevant. Other things being equal, it does not matter whether the accident occurs next to you or thousands of miles away from you. We should not discriminate against a needy person on the grounds that she happens to be at a great distance from us.[42]

This seems to me true. But it is also true that some other factors are near to impossible to hold constant if distance varies. And some of the variations correlated with distance are morally relevant. As we have seen earlier, it is not the same whether you are the only person who could possibly do something about the drowning child, or you are just one among the many on a crowded beach. In the first case, the duty is assigned to you without ambiguities. Suppose you are on your way to the Academy of Science to give your inauguration talk—still, you have no morally defensible option other than to come to the rescue of the child. But suppose many adults happen to be on the scene. Then, I think, you are permitted to continue your way to the Academy, unless you have good reasons to assume that nobody else will come to the child's rescue. You have no grounds to believe that you are specifically designated to discharge the duty of rescue which applies to everybody on the scene.

Now, one of the consequences of the increase in distance is that the likelihood that you are *not* the unique bearer of the duty to help in the particular case tends to increase as well. If there are others conspicuously closer to the drowning child than you are, and if you have no grounds to believe that none of those people will run to its rescue, then you are permitted to continue on your way to the Academy. Thus, although distance in itself is morally irrelevant, other factors associated with it are not.

21. The above argument relied on the hidden premise that the person in distress and the potential helper are complete strangers. If we change this assumption, significant consequences follow. At least some of the special responsibilities are resistant to the corrosive effects of distance.

Suppose the drowning child is your daughter: would it be all right for you to continue your journey to the airport and leave the other adults on the scene to take care of her rescue? Of course, you will be satisfied by the knowledge that someone or other will save her life. But satisfaction about the outcome will not suffice. The fact that she will be rescued is not the only thing that matters to you. It also matters that you are the one who actually does the job of saving her life. Or that you at least have your try. Or that you are part of the rescue team. As a parent of the child, you have good reason to believe that it is wrong for you to walk away and leave others to do the job.

Or suppose you are informed that your daughter is drowning on a beach miles away from the place where you are staying: would it be all right for you to go on with your activities in the (well-founded) expectation that other people will save her anyway? If the answer is "no" in the case when you are near the accident, it will remain "no" in the case when you are at a distance from it. You ought to rush to the scene in order to do for her what you can.

The upshot seems to be this. Duties of assistance fade away with distance, unless the needy person and the potential helper are related in some specific, obligation-generating manner. Whenever an individual bears a duty to aid another individual far away from him, it must be the case that the two are bound to each other by special ties. Common humanity is not a sufficient ground for the claim of duty in such cases, particular bonds must intervene as an additional factor.

Suppose common citizenship is a special relationship which, like that between parents and children, gives rise to obligations that are resistant to the effects of distance. If so, then we have an explanation as to why strangers who are nevertheless related to each other by the bonds of common citizenship are obligated to accept sacrifices for each other even if they are separated by a great distance, while strangers unrelated by any bond other than that of common humanity are not.

22. But is this in fact so? Those who think it is not may try to show that common citizenship is not like family roles, in the relevant respect that its capacity to resist the corrosive effects of distance is no greater than that of common humanity. Or, alternatively, they may try to show that there is an important class of cases (and the typical issues of international assistance belong to this class) in which the effects of distance on duties of assistance are not dramatic, not even in the absence of special relationships. In what follows, I will take the second way.

Distance matters because the number of individuals simultaneously burdened by duty varies with it, and because it matters whether that number is small or large. Yet we have seen already that numbers have a corrosive effect on duty only where, in the absence of social rules, the duty-bearers cannot possibly know whether they are among those selected for performing the required action, or they cannot know what they should do in the event that they are among those selected. Let me further elaborate on this point.

The situations in which assistance is demanded differ according to the number of potential helpers that matter in them. In some cases, the required assistance is indivisible. The number of those who can participate in the beneficent action cannot increase indefinitely. Such is the case of the drowning child. As soon as one of the potential rescuers wades into the water, no contribution towards the rescue remains to those who follow suit. And so the decision of one person to hurry to the rescue of the child releases the others from their duty to help. Whoever takes up the responsibility for the rescue takes it up completely; whoever is released from the duty is completely released.

In other cases, the assistance is divisible. Given appropriate coordination, the number of participants can increase. The fact that one person engages in the beneficent action does not release the others from the duty to provide their own contribution. Consider the case of a starving child. There are three strangers in its proximity, each capable of helping. Even if one of them is willing to provide a meal to feed the child without the contribution of anybody else, it would be unfair on the part of the remaining two to leave him to take up the whole burden alone. The duty applies to all of them, and the task can be divided up into equal shares. Other things being equal, each one is duty-bound to bear one-third of the burden.

23. Imagine now a large population of adults divided up into groups of three in such a manner that, for each group, the habitat of the nearest other group is at a great distance. And let children in great distress be distributed unevenly over the territory of the entire population: there is one in some habitats, two in others, and so on up to a number at which the local group is incapable of saving all the children in their habitat, while there are a very large number of habitats where there is no single child in distress. Are those living in habitats free of children in distress justified in disclaiming responsibility for children in distant habitats?

I believe not. Proximity and distance are not absolute properties. For a single individual, given the costs of transport, the distance from a starving child might be very great. It might be very great for a small group of people. But it diminishes dramatically with a significant increase in individuals who pool their resources. Where significant help can be delivered by joint action, the relevant distance is relative to the cooperating group. A group with a capacity to expand and to take up a more complex organization may come into the proximity of needy people who, originally, were far away from it.

This has consequences for individuals. In judging whether we stand under a duty to assist needy people far away from us, we are not supposed to measure their distance from us severally. The distance from one individual to another is not the relevant distance. The question we have to ask from ourselves is whether we are potential members of a cooperative group which, as a whole, finds itself in the proximity of the needy;

whether that group does already exist or can be created or enlarged at no prohibitive cost so as to reach the needy people. In the same manner, in judging what burden the assistance to the needy would impose on us, we have to ask questions about the capacities of the maximum mobilizable group and the fair share we have to assume from the general burden.

The upshot is that in cases where the required assistance is divisible, the needy person and the potential helper must not be tied by special relationships (political or other) in order that the corrosive effects of distance are mitigated. It is sufficient that institutions are available or feasible, at no prohibitive costs, to coordinate the action of the potential helpers. Insofar as the nation-state regime depends, for its moral defense, on the assumption that the duty of humanitarian assistance vanishes with distance unless supported by obligations towards fellow citizens, that defense relies on shaky grounds.

Humanitarian assistance to societies in great distress is not a responsibility for the citizenry of *one* particular state but for *all* who are in a position to help. It is the entire community of the economically developed nations which bears responsibility for preventing famine in the underdeveloped regions of the world, for absorbing the flood of refugees from countries visited by natural or social catastrophe, for securing justice in access to natural resources, etc. Both efficacy in helping and fairness in distributing the burdens of help require supra-state coordination.

To be sure, states might attempt to resolve the coordination problem without surrendering any part of their sovereign powers. The alternative consists in entering into international treaties. However, in the absence of a higher instance vested with the authority to determine each party's share, the negotiations are likely to result in extremely biased agreements. The bargaining force of the more developed countries being far superior to that of the countries dependent on help, general underprovision of assistance is a likely result. The bargaining force of the more developed countries being very unequal among themselves, unfair distribution of the burdens across those providing assistance is another likely result. Moreover, in the absence of some higher power of enforcement, the already highly imperfect treaties are likely to erode due to mutual expectation of non-compliance by the signatories. Sharing state sovereignty with supra-state organizations vested with authority and enforcement powers seems to be the right answer to the problem.

The Politics of Human Rights

24. Humanitarian assistance and transfers required by global distributive justice are different in the following way. The demands of distributive justice are independent of any expectations regarding the capacities and conduct of the target country's government. Transfer is due to the target country even if its government works in a satisfactory manner. Humanitarian assistance, on the other hand, is not required unless the government of the target country cannot be expected to deal by itself with some serious problem. The cases where the classical functions of the state, those of protecting rights, are at stake in the international arena, are analogous, in this respect, to delivering humanitarian assistance. International action in the defense of human rights is demanded when a government is either incapable of doing the job by itself or when it is the main agent responsible for massive rights violations. In a way, the politics of human rights can be seen as a special case in the politics of humanitarian assistance. What is special in it is the nature of the bad to be averted. If sufferings caused by natural disaster trigger the duty of international humanitarian assistance, and if sufferings caused by human rights violations are comparable to those caused by natural disaster, then human rights violations trigger a duty of international action in the defense of human rights. Or so it seems at first glance.

But there is a problem. Consider the cases where there is a causal connection between the two kinds of bads. The disaster which humanitarian assistance is supposed to mitigate is not always due to nature alone. It is not always the case that the government has no organizational or material resources to meet the dimensions of a terrible catastrophe. The government might display reckless disregard for the suffering of its people. Or it might provoke, by its very action, the disaster which it is then unable or unwilling to avert (as when famine follows internal war or forced relocation of an ethnic or social group).

Whenever a disaster is (partly) due to human rights violations on the part of the government, humanitarian assistance cannot be delivered without interference, sometimes military, in the domestic sovereignty of the receiving state. Humanitarian aid, in itself, does not necessitate interference. The politics of human rights always does. Herein lies the problem.

Sometimes the need for intervention is created by the collapse of the local state: in order to save the country from chaos and anarchy, other states must send forces to take care of elementary police and administrative functions. This case seems to me unproblematic as a matter of principle (although it might raise serious concerns of feasibility). There is no conflict with sovereignty when the sovereign state is not there any more. At other times, the government, rather than being unable to protect human rights within its territory, is itself the agent which should be stopped. Far from collapsing, it mobilizes a highly efficient coercive apparatus to oppress and persecute its subjects, and to systematically eliminate its opponents. But because the government is there, intervention conflicts with its claim to sovereignty. Therefore the question is not simply whether states have a *duty* to come to the defense of oppressed and persecuted people abroad, but whether they have the *right* to do so. If they cannot possibly have such a right, they cannot stand under the duty either.

This is the problem I want briefly to address in the following sections.

25. There are three types of principled objection to human rights interventionism. The first is raised by the realist theory of international relations. Realism holds that the international order is based on the sovereign independence of states and that the participants should maximally respect this fact. Non-interventionism follows.[43] This argument seems to me question-begging. It is not obvious that sovereignty must always enjoy priority over the life, security, dignity, and well-being of human individuals—the opposite seems to be much more plausible. Thus, the idea of the strict priority of sovereignty needs to be defended rather than merely voiced.

In *Just and Unjust Wars*[44] and in articles responding to its critics, Michael Walzer put forward a moral argument in favor of state sovereignty. This represents the second type of objection. The root idea is this. When a government violates human rights, internal and external perspectives on the facts of violation are significantly different. The oppressed and persecuted citizens face a government. Foreign agents face a state. The government is the organization vested with authority and coercive power over the territory of the state. The state is the unity of this organization and of the citizenry. Under certain conditions, the citizens form a historical community. Members of communities have, collectively, a right to be self-governing. Self-government has two separate aspects: internal and external. A state is a self-governing entity, internally, when the powerholders are elected by (and from among) those subjected to their rule and where they find themselves under the control of the latter. Despotic governments violate the internal self-government condition. The state is a self-governing entity, externally, when it is ruled from within, not from a distant imperial or colonial center. Alien rule, whether direct or exercised through puppets, violates the external self-government condition.

Both aspects of self-government matter in their own right. And each can be preserved in the absence of the other. Alien rule can allow wide room for democratic practices. Domestic rule can be utterly undemocratic. So long as the attack on internal self-government does not go so far as to disrupt the unity between government and community, that is, so long as members of the community can consider themselves as oppressed by their own government, foreign states have a strong reason to refrain from intervention. Non-intervention, in this case, is not due to the government but to the community. The conditions which make it permissible for a community to resist its own government are not the same as the conditions which make it permissible for foreign governments to intervene on behalf of the community. "[S]tates can be presumptively legitimate in international society and actually illegitimate at home."[45]

Walzer's argument does not aim to establish an absolute principle of non-intervention. On the contrary, Walzer defends the possibility of intervention against absolute non-interventionists. But he sets the threshold very high and makes the task of justification extremely difficult. External agents, he says, must accept a "presumption of fit" between domestic government and domestic community. To be sure, this presumption is open to rebuttal, but it needs positive evidence to be rebutted. In the absence of sufficient evidence, intervention is not permissible.

Why the "presumption of fit" rather than its opposite? Walzer's answer is complex but his key reason is simple. Foreigners do not know enough about the history and culture of the community in question, they are not in a position to form concrete judgments "of the conflicts and harmonies, the historical choices and cultural affinities, the loyalties and resentments that underlie it".[46] Now, information on these matters is generally badly needed for assessing correctly the community preferences on the alternative of intervention or non-intervention. But it is the latter which is relevant for the claim of self-rule, not the former. Respect for self-rule is obligatory so long as members of the community, no matter how oppressed, prefer the risk of the persistence of domestic dictatorship to foreign intervention. The problem is that they might be no less in the dark on this than foreigners are.

Absence of a free press and of public discussion, and pervasive official propaganda are not the right conditions under which people can form accurate judgments on what they really want. Suppose the majority of the oppressed and humiliated people believe that it is better for them to live under the bloody domestic dictator than to face foreign intervention. If we have good reasons to assume that this belief is blatantly erroneous and that it would be quickly corrected under the conditions of unimpeded public deliberation and a free flow of information, would their actual desires have authority against the hard evidence of the suspension of basic rights, of kidnappings, torture, killings, and intimidation? Under the conditions of democracy, the actual choices of the community, as aggregated by the collective decision-making system, have ultimate authority. But the background assumption is that democracy is a system with powerful mechanisms for the self-correction of erroneous choices. Dictatorship is not. So it is unclear why a decision on intervention ought to be predicated on the actual, potentially distorted, desires of the people rather than their hypothetical, informed desires.[47]

All this does not amount to debunking the claim that there is such a thing as the right to self-rule and that this right sets obstacles to foreign intervention. But it amounts to suggesting that, whenever it comes to massive violations of human rights, the presumption must be reversed. Walzer does not deny this. He says that under certain conditions "we must assume either that that there is no 'fit' between the government and the community or that there is no community".[48] The first assumption holds when the government engages in internal war against its entire population. The second holds in cases of ethnic cleansing.

26. The third objection to human rights interventionism goes like this. Perhaps there are cases where intervention to defend human rights is justified in principle. But strong governments are likely to use a righteous cause as a pretext to promote self-seeking purposes by means of subverting weak governments. Moreover, the nature of the intervention-justifying conditions is open to controversy, and so is the evidence for their presence in particular situations. This makes even greater the danger that the rhetoric of human rights serves as a mere means to cover up action aiming to maximize the power and advantage of the intervening state. There is a very serious possibility that, rather than contributing towards making the international order more moral by raising protection of the life, liberty, and security of human individuals and their groups to the level of supra-state politics, human rights interventionism will actually serve as a means to make the international order less moral by allowing strong governments to use force against their weak competitors. This argument is sympathetically related by Stanley Hoffmann in his *Ethics and Politics of Humanitarian Intervention*.[49]

Hoffmann himself is explicit, however, on the point that the objection based on the possible misuses of human rights interventionism does not really affect intervention in general but only unilateral intervention. Upholding the principle of non-intervention is not an appropriate answer to the facts of grave domestic violations of human rights, he says. What are needed are adequate rules and procedures for collective intervention, prominent among them being the creation of an impartial supra-state body with the right to license coercive international action, whether by one single state or by many, so that no intervention shall be legitimate in the absence of the endorsement by that body.[50]

This argument again points towards supra-state coordination. But, as we can see, the reason why the nation-state regime is insufficient in the domain of the international protection of human rights is different from that which supports supra-state coordination in the domains of international distributive justice and humanitarian assistance. In the latter, authoritative coordination is needed because, in its absence, states might defect from delivering their fair contribution to the common cause. In the former, authoritative coordination is needed because, in its absence, strong states might engage in unilateral self-seeking action disguised as a crusade for human rights.

We are now in a position to summarize the results of our argument.

Summary and Conclusions

27. We started from the assumption that, in order to be morally acceptable, international regimes must pass what we called the cosmopolitan test. The background idea is that some of the duties individuals bear jointly and discharge with the help of governmental coordination are owed to individuals who are outsiders to their state. Some of these duties are duties of refraining from harmful action. If this is all that general morality requires with regard to outsiders, then the cosmopolitan test is rather weak and even a nation-state regime is able to meet it. Other duties, however, demand positive collective action to ensure that the distribution of advantages and disadvantages at the international level conforms to the requirements set by the principles of distributive justice, to guarantee that humanitarian assistance is available to the needy in proportion to the capabilities of the better-off nations, and to protect human rights against abuses by national governments. In this case, the cosmopolitan idea gives rise to a much more demanding test. Given that the positive duties beyond borders spread over a population which is significantly larger than the citizenry of any particular state, they require, in order to be adequately discharged, supra-state authorities. In the absence of coordination at the supra-state (sometimes global, sometimes regional) level, they either remain unsatisfied, or if they are met, the burdens of contributing are distributed in an unfair manner, or both. To put it briefly, nation-state regimes do not meet the more demanding version of the cosmopolitan test. Nation-state cosmopolitanism is untenable.

Its failure leaves us with the alternative of world-state cosmopolitanism and supranation-state cosmopolitanism. The first seems to be an implausible idea in the historical perspective of the present. Whether or not the number of existing states can be significantly reduced in the distant future, we have good reasons to believe that this is not a realistic objective for the next century. But there is a functional alternative to it: the growth of supra-state organizations with overlapping jurisdictions which share with states the authority to issue binding instructions and the right to mobilize coercive action to enforce them, but which are dissimilar to states in many other respects. It is this trend which I described as the rise of a supranation-state regime.

28. The supranation-state regime is a functional alternative but not an exact equivalent to the world state. The ultimate source of the American constitution is "We the People of the United States", not "We the States United under a Federal Government". In a similar manner, the world state, if created by federate states, would have as the ultimate source of its constitution "We the People of the United Globe". However, the ultimate source for the authority of the supra-state organizations, whose growth in number and competencies is currently transforming the international order, is not the will of mankind but the concurring agreement of the citizenries of the particular states. In the regime which is unfolding before our eyes, states do not preserve their separate existence only but their privileged status as well.

Herein lies the most portentous answer to worries that interference with domestic sovereignty undermines the claims of political communities to self-government. The fact that a state shares its sovereign powers with supra-state authorities does not amount to eliminating self-government. First, the state is not assimilated, by such a move, to a larger state. Second, its consent to share its sovereign powers with supra-state instances remains the source for the authority of the latter. Instances outside of it cannot issue binding instructions to it, nor can they enforce these except according to rules it endorsed; they derive their authority from its agreement; and they are not at the level of its competitors, that is, they are not states.

To be sure, large and strong states have an exceptionally powerful voice in the processes of deliberation and bargaining which shape the policies of supra-state authorities. Small and weak states are facing the danger of being subjected to higher-level decisions which they are not in an equal position to influence. But this danger is not due to the change in the structure of the international institutional order. It is a result of the progressive integration of social and economic activities in the world. The spontaneous processes of globalization are not an arena where struggles for consolidating the position of small states can be led, if at all. Only the conscious elaboration of the rules and procedures of supra-state cooperation can serve as such an arena.

29. Some of the results of our argument affect political philosophy. The analysis of the cosmopolitan test showed that the usual treatment of the problem of state legitimacy and political obligations is defective. States are not self-sufficient, closed systems. They are part of an international regime. They divide mankind into insiders and outsiders. The project of justifying their claim to authority usually disregards this circumstance. It asks how the belief that a state has the right to issue binding instructions can be justified to the insiders. The conditions under which such a belief can be justified to (and with regard to) outsiders remain without discussion. The question of the duties that a state has to recognize and discharge towards outsiders so that they can consider its claim of definitive control over its jurisdiction, is not asked. Nor is the question regarding the structure of a legitimate international regime.

Generally, it is taken for granted that if a state is legitimized to the insiders, outsiders stand under the duty not to violate its right to control access to its territory and to the resources within it, and not to try to carry away some of that territory by force. It is also taken for granted that if a state is legitimized with regard to the insiders, then the latter are not allowed to balance their obligation to obey the law against duties of their community towards foreigners (as when they decide that, all things considered, it would be better for them to withdraw some of their taxes and to send the money to a very poor, distant country). These claims cannot be taken for granted. It needs to be shown why they can be true and under what conditions they are true indeed.

This approach to political obligations is compatible with one particular analytic conception of them, the natural duty account. Cosmopolitanism and the natural duty account are theoretical allies. And so are the strong reading of the cosmopolitan test and the interpretation I suggested of the principle of the natural duty of justice as a requirement to comply with institutions which make jointly held and therefore indeterminate moral duties determinate for those to whom they apply.

Notes

1 Zeno the Stoic was reported by Plutarch to have written, in his *Republic*, that "our household arrangements should not be based on cities or parishes, each marked out by its own legal system, but we should regard all men as our fellow citizens and local residents, and there should be one way of life and order, like that of a herd grazing together and nurtured by a common law". See A.A. Long and D.W. Sedley, *The Hellenistic Philosophers* I. Cambridge: The University Press 1987, 439. For a modern version of world-state cosmopolitanism, see Kai Nielsen, "World Government, Security, and Global Justice". S. Luper-Foy, ed., *Problems of International Justice*. Boulder, Col.: Westview Press 1988.

2 I take sovereignty and exclusive jurisdiction as the defining features of a nation-state. This essay will focus on the problem of sovereignty. I discuss the problem of exclusive jurisdiction in another paper: "Nation-Building and Beyond". In W. Kymlicka, ed., *Western Political Theory and Ethnic Relations in Eastern Europe.* Oxford: The University Press (forthcoming).

3 E. g., the Prussian ex-baron von Klotz (deputy of the French revolutionary Convent under the name Anacharsis Cloots) was a dedicated partisan of world government. See R. Pomeau, *L'Europe des Lumières*. Paris: Stock 1966, 205.

4 For Condorcet's position, see his *Esquisse d'un tableau historique des progrès de l'esprit humain*. Paris: Flammarion 1988, 288 ff. Kant developed his views at various places, such as "Über den Gemeinspruch: Das mag in der Theorie richting sein, taugt aber nicht für die Praxis" and "Zum Ewingen Frieden". Both in Kant, *Werke* 9. Darmstadt: Wissenschaftliche Buchgesellschaft 1964.

5 "Zum ewigen Frieden", 225. "Gemeinspruch", 169. John Rawls agrees with Kant on this point. See "The Law of Peoples". Rawls, *Collected Papers*. Cambridge, Mass.: Harvard University Press 1999, 539.

6 For the three conditions, see "Zum ewigen Frieden", 204–217.

7 For a balanced summary of these (and opposite) trends, see E. Hobsbawm, "The Nation and Globalization". *Constellations* 5 (1998): 1–9.

8 Thomas Pogge suggests, in his "Cosmopolitanism and Sovereignty", *Ethics* 103 (1992): 48–75, that the cosmopolitan order should evolve in this direction.

9 For the concept of a legal system, see H.L.A. Hart, *The Concept of Law.* Oxford: Clarendon 1961.

10 For the transition to the territorial principle, see C. Tilly, "On the History of European State-Making". Tilly, ed., *The Formation of Nation-States in Western Europe*. Princeton, N.J.: The University Press 1975. See also R.T. Ford, "Law's Territory". *Michigan Law Review* 97 (1999): 843–930.

11 For the supremacy of law within its jurisdiction, see H. Kelsen, *The General Theory of Law and State.* Cambridge, Mass.: Harvard University Press 1943.

12 This formulation originates with Robert Nozick. See his *Anarchy, State, and Utopia.* Oxford: Blackwell 1973.

13 J. Rawls, "Legal Obligation and the Duty of Fair Play". S. Freeman, ed., *John Rawls' Collected Papers*. Cambridge, Mass.: Harvard University Press 1999, 117–129.

14 Rawls, *Theory*, 343.

15 Ibid., 111 (italics added).
16 Ibid.
17 The role of the republican form of government is dual. First, by guaranteeing that all individuals enjoy the same liberty and the same status of equality within their respective states, its universal spread makes all human beings bearers of the same basic legal rights, even if they remain subject to different governments. Second, by tying succession in government to election, it greatly reduces the propensity of the rulers to go to war.
18 This difficulty is discussed in the recent literature on secession. See L.A. Brilmayer, "Secession and Self-Determination: A Territorialist Reinterpretation". *Yale Journal of International Law* 16 (1991); and A. Buchanan, "Self-Determination, Secession, and the Rule of Law". R. McKim and J. McMahan, eds., *The Morality of Nationalism.* Oxford: The University Press 1997.
19 Rawls, *Theory*, 112 (italics added).
20 See A. J. Simmons, *Moral Principles and Political Obligation*. Princeton: The University Press 1979.
21 Rawls, *Theory*, 114. Later, Rawls adds to the group of "those who assume public office", another group of "those who, being better situated, have advanced their aims within the system". This is a much larger category, but the denial of generality remains. See ibid., 116.
22 For the "functional equivalent" formulation see G. Klosko, "Political Obligation and the Natural Duties of Justice." *Philosophy and Public Affairs* 22 (1994): 251–270 (251).
23 See R. Dworkin, *Law's Empire*. Cambridge, Mass.: Belknap 1986, 196.
24 See J. Hampton, *Political Philosophy*. Boulder, Col.: Westview Press 1997, 119–130.
25 Rawls, *Theory*, 115.
26 Ibid.
27 Ibid., 116.
28 Ibid.
29 See his "Gemeinspruch", 145. See, for this interpretation, J. Waldron, "Special Ties and Natural Duties". *Philosophy and Public Affairs* 22 (1993): 3–30.
30 See R.E. Goodin, "What Is So Special About Our Fellow Countrymen?" *Ethics* 98 (1988): 663–686.
31 J. Feinberg, "The Moral and Legal Responsibility of the Bad Samaritan". Feinberg, *Freedom and Fulfillment*. Princeton: The University Press 1994, 175–196.
32 The natural duty account, however, is not sufficient to account for the entire web of political obligations we deem justifiable. States do deliver functions for their citizens which have no background in natural duties. For example, they pursue economic policies to maintain high rates of growth. Suppose, for the sake of argument, that a one percent increase in GDP improves the general position of the citizenry without changing any member's relative position. Still, the state might be required to strive to secure it, and its citizens might stand under the obligation to abide by the rules which make this possible. In order to cope with such cases, the natural duty account needs to be combined with a complementary account. I will not expand on the question of how this can be done. For the aims of this essay it is sufficient to show that at least for some aims, the natural duty account offers an indispensable and true theory.

33 I have borrowed much of this argument from Jeremy Waldron's "Special Ties and Natural Duties".

34 Rawls, *Theory*, 115 (italics added).

35 Rawls, *Theory*, 115.

36 For an elegant formulation of this idea with respect to the traditional empire's capacity to expand, see M. Elvin, *The Pattern of the Chinese Past.* Stanford: The University Press 1973, 17–22.

37 Think of the enmity between Serb and Croat nationalisms, or of that between Bosnian Croats and Muslims (the latter having considered themselves mostly as Croats with Islamic religious affiliations—in a highly secularized society). For an illuminating discussion see N. Miscevic, *Nationalism and Beyond.* Budapest: Central European University Press (forthcoming).

38 See M. Sandel, *Liberalism and the Limits of Justice.* Cambridge: The University Press 1982, 77–82; and M. Walzer, *Spheres of Justice*. New York: Basic Books 1983, 64 ff.

39 See B. Barry, "Humanity and Justice in Global Perspective". J.R. Pennock and J.W. Chapman, eds., *Ethics, Economics, and the Law.* Nomos XXIV. New York: The University Press 1982, 219–252.

40 For the world-system paradigm see I. Wallerstein, *The Modern World-System* I. New York: Academic Press 1974.

41 This paragraph relies, for its main idea, on Charles Beitz's *Political Theory and International Relations.* Princeton: The University Press 1979, 136–143.

42 See P. Singer, "Famine, Affluence, and Morality". *Philosophy and Public Affairs* 1 (1972): 229–243.

43 For the realist paradigm of international relations see H.J. Morgenthau, *Politics Among Nations.* New York: Knopf 1949.

44 New York: Basic Books 1977.

45 M. Walzer, "The Moral Standing of States". C.R. Beitz et al., eds., *International Ethics*. Princeton: The University Press 1985, 222.

46 Ibid., 220.

47 In my country, a substantial majority favored one-party rule at the beginning of 1989. Within six months, multiparty democracy had majority support.

48 "Moral Standing", 225.

49 With R.C. Johansen, J.P. Sterba and R. Väyrynen as contributors. Notre Dame, Ind.: The University Press 1996, 18–21.

50 Ibid., 22. Hoffmann agrees that this body should be the UN Security Council.

III The Legal Dimension

9 *Human Rights and Sovereignty*

ARYEH NEIER

Most ideologies that rose and flourished during the last century had declined and been discredited by its end. An exception is the belief in universal human rights: the idea that all are entitled to enjoy certain liberties, not because they are nationals of a particular state but because of their humanity. Proclaimed at the end of World War II and accepted officially by the nations of the world through their ratification of the United Nations Charter and their adoption in 1948 of the Universal Declaration of Human Rights, it may be the only secular faith that is growing in strength and in the number of its adherents worldwide at the beginning of the twenty-first century. By definition, the concept of universal human rights is a limitation on sovereignty.

One reason why belief in the human rights cause is getting stronger is that ideologies that are about the exercise of power are suspect. In contrast to the faiths that caused so much strife and suffering in the past century, a commitment to human rights is about placing limits on power. Sovereign states may undertake policies that address the needs and desires of their people in many ways, but they may not limit peaceful inquiry or expression; they may not deprive their nationals of their freedom unfairly, without the protections provided by the rule of law; they may not punish cruelly; and they may not deny each person, regardless of race, religion, sex, or national origin, his or her right to count equally under the law. Other ideologies prescribe what should be done. A belief in human rights—to the extent that the concept is limited, as I believe it should be, to civil and political rights—is more modest. It is mostly about what may not be done.

As yet, unfortunately, a significant part of the commitment to human rights worldwide is only rhetorical. Large-scale abuses of rights persist in many countries and these often are the cause of internal strife and take extreme forms when armed conflicts break out. Some conflicts, such as those in Afghanistan, Burundi, Colombia, and Sudan, have endured so long that the vast suffering they cause attracts our attention only sporadically. We take them for granted. Severe violations of rights are not incidental to the conduct of the combatants. They are, rather, the main way that they strive to gain the upper hand. As I write, a low intensity war continues in the Northern Caucasus between Russian troops and Chechen guerrillas. As is now customary, the vast majority of the victims are civilians. During a period of several months when the war was more intense, Russian aerial forces and ground troops again destroyed Grozny and other civilian towns, as they had done a few years earlier, killing large numbers indiscriminately and causing the flight of hundreds of thousands of refugees in reprisal for terrorist bombings allegedly committed by Chechens. If any of those who were involved in the bombings in Moscow are among the victims, it is purely by chance. It is a great paradox that crimes against humanity are committed in so many parts of the world during the era of growing faith in the human rights cause.

During most of the period that the human rights movement was becoming an important force internationally, its main ways of responding to abuses were to campaign on behalf of individual victims of abuses and to compile detailed reports pointing out the discrepancies between what governments and guerrilla groups say about their support for human rights and their actions. The purpose is to embarrass those engaging in abusive practices and their supporters internationally and, thereby, to change the behavior of those violating human rights. In the last decade of the twentieth century, however, two other ways of protecting human rights also attracted support. One was the establishment of international criminal tribunals to prosecute and punish those who commit the gravest crimes. The other is international military intervention to protect the victims of great abuses. Both of these responses to extreme violations of human rights have gathered momentum recently. Their significance is profound. It indicates the emergence of a global consensus that international responsibility to halt certain abuses of rights takes precedence over national sovereignty. The opening sentences from the Annual Report of Human Rights Watch for 1999 are a clear statement of this trend:

> Sovereignty loomed less large in 1999 as an obstacle to stopping and redressing crimes against humanity. Governmental leaders who committed these crimes found a greater chance of prosecution and military intervention. The lesson sent is that leaders risk their freedom and control of territory if they commit the most severe human rights abuses.

The speed with which the human rights cause is transforming international affairs is breathtaking. In common with most committed proponents of human rights, I have espoused intervention. At the same time, I recognize that profound questions are raised by this development. Among those I will try to address in this essay are the criteria for interventions; the relative merits of legal and military intervention; and the unintended consequences (*pace* George Soros) that may result from the declining significance of sovereignty that is the corollary of intervention.

Though they are widely familiar, it is worth enumerating the dramatic events of just the past two years with respect to both international legal and international military intervention to protect rights. They should be seen in the context of developments earlier in the last decade of the twentieth century.

The establishment of a permanent International Criminal Court was approved at a United Nations sponsored conference in Rome in July 1998. It may prosecute genocide and crimes against humanity whether committed in times of war or peace; and it may prosecute war crimes committed in accordance with a policy or a plan, or on a substantial scale, whether in international or internal armed conflicts. The statute for the tribunal leaves open the possibility that it may also prosecute aggression, but delegates to the Rome conference did not agree on a definition. Once the International Criminal Court is established, seven-eighths of the countries that have become parties to it by their ratification of the treaty establishing it must agree on a definition before prosecutions against aggression can take place, a prospect that seems remote—and vanishing. Most likely, therefore, the Court will confine itself to prosecuting violations of international humanitarian law that were the main focus of efforts to establish it by the human rights movement: genocide, crimes against humanity, and war crimes.

In a bow to sovereignty, the Court will have automatic jurisdiction only over crimes committed by nationals of a state that has ratified the treaty establishing it or on the territory of such a state. This will deny it authority on its own initiative over crimes by Saddam Hussein's Iraqi regime or by the military rulers of Burma (Myanmar) against their own people on their own territory, as there is no chance that the leaders of rogue states will expose themselves to prosecution by becoming a party to the treaty. In such circumstances, the possibility remains for the Security Council of the United Nations to authorize a prosecution. However, the Council's actions are subject to veto by any of its five permanent members. Crimes committed on its own territory by a state that has not ratified are immune to prosecution and punishment if that state has a determined protector among the permanent five. Also, of course, if any of the permanent members do not ratify, and themselves commit crimes on their own territory—such as those by Russia in Chechnya—it can bar prosecution of its own officials and troops by the International Criminal Court by exercising its veto power on its own behalf.

Over time, the inability of the Court to prosecute crimes in certain states while exercising jurisdiction over similar crimes in other states will, no doubt, prove intolerable. Predictably, a moment will arrive when a state protected by a permanent member of the Security Council commits horrendous crimes on its own territory. A demand for prosecutions will be blocked by the exercise of the veto power. A cure for this deficiency in the treaty establishing the International Criminal Court can be expected only when there is worldwide outrage over such a situation.

In Rome, 120 countries supported the establishment of the International Criminal Court, 7 were opposed, and 21 abstained. The United States joined Iraq, Qatar, Libya, Yemen, Israel, and China in opposing the treaty. As with the earlier international treaty banning land-mines, the Clinton administration allowed military opponents in the United States Department of Defense to determine American policy. The publicly stated rationale is not sovereignty *per se*, but apprehension that the treaty does not guarantee that a politically motivated prosecutor would refrain from malicious prosecutions against American soldiers stationed in other countries that have ratified the treaty or consent to prosecutions of crimes committed on their territory. In fact, however, the treaty is filled with protections against any such possibility. These include: definitions of the crimes that may be prosecuted, limiting them to those committed on a large scale; a provision for "complementarity", requiring the Court to defer to good faith prosecutions in national courts; a requirement that two separate panels of judges must authorize prosecutions, one at the investigation stage and another before an indictment is issued; the opportunity for the UN Security Council to defer prosecutions in certain circumstances; provisions allowing the prosecutor and the judges to be removed by the parties to the treaty for misconduct; and the provision that the appointment of the prosecutor and the judges will be decided by the parties to the treaty, which will be those countries most supportive of human rights and, therefore, least likely to support malicious prosecutions. Ironically, by not becoming a party to the treaty, the United States is depriving itself of one further means to avoid unwarranted prosecutions of its troops: the right to participate in the selection of the prosecutor and judges.

Securing ratification of the treaty for the International Criminal Court is difficult. Sixty countries must ratify before the Court comes into existence. Many governments that support the establishment of the ICC are slow to act because their constitutions must first be amended. Provisions that conflict with the treaty in some countries include prohibitions on the extradition of their own nationals, immunity for officials, and limits on the terms of imprisonment. Some conflicts may be more apparent than real. For example, a typical constitutional provision barring extradition refers to trials before the courts of another country. It may be argued that surrendering a defendant to an international criminal tribunal is not prohibited. Even where no revision of the constitution is required, however, such questions must be examined with care by ministries and parliaments. As a consequence, though it seems almost certain that the ICC will be established, getting sixty countries to ratify will probably take another two years. As I write, only seven countries have ratified. It seems unlikely that the first trial before the ICC will take place before 2003.

In the interim, the *ad hoc* criminal tribunals for ex-Yugoslavia and Rwanda are making headway. The tribunal for ex-Yugoslavia has indicted President Slobodan Milošević and four of his top associates for their crimes in Kosovo. At the very least, this means that if they fall from power their chances of obtaining asylum in another country are severely reduced. Few states, if any, will risk becoming a pariah or hardening their pariah status by sheltering them. Milošević's fate and the fate of his associates will be in the hands of their successors in Yugoslavia, who will face pressure to turn them over for trial as a price for restoring the country's international status. More than half of those publicly indicted for crimes in Bosnia and Croatia are now in the tribunal's custody, including a number of high officials, and several have been tried and convicted. They still do not include Radovan Karadzic and General Ratko Mladic, the architects of ethnic cleansing in Bosnia, but they are now in jeopardy. NATO troops have grown more aggressive in making arrests and it seems only a matter of time before they are apprehended and brought to trial. Karadzic is particularly vulnerable, as he is believed still to be in Bosnia, though he stays out of sight. Mladic, who remains close to President Slobodan Milošević, has taken refuge in Serbia where he makes occasional public appearances at events such as soccer matches. His chance of remaining free is tied to Milošević's retention of power.

The tribunal for Rwanda has about three-quarters of those it has indicted in custody. The defendants detained at Arusha include those accused of principal responsibility for the 1994 genocide. The Rwanda tribunal has handed down the first convictions by any international tribunal for genocide. Among those convicted for this crime is the prime minister of Rwanda at the time of the genocide, Jean Kambanda. Trials of lesser figures accused of complicity in the genocide are proceeding in the domestic courts of Rwanda. At the time of writing, a few hundred have been brought to trial, while more than one hundred thousand are still in prison awaiting trial.

The progress made by these two *ad hoc* international criminal tribunals has spurred proposals for other such bodies. Their establishment has been discussed in connection with the crimes of the Khmer Rouge in Cambodia, of Saddam Hussein in Iraq and Kuwait, and of the Indonesian military and militias in East Timor. As I write, some are calling for a tribunal for Sierra Leone. The main obstacle to the establishment of additional international tribunals is not sovereignty. Rather, the issues are whether the United Nations has the resources to operate such bodies and whether the international community has the political will to proceed. Their establishment does not conflict with the creation of the International Criminal Court, as they have jurisdiction to deal with past crimes or crimes committed currently. In contrast, the International Criminal Court will only have jurisdiction over crimes committed after the Rome treaty has been ratified by sixty countries.

Another dramatic recent development limiting sovereignty was the October 1998 arrest in London of General Augusto Pinochet to face charges in Spain for crimes during his more than sixteen years as dictator of Chile. Though he escaped trial for reasons of age and infirmity, the decision by the British law lords to permit his extradition greatly advanced the cause of international justice by accepting universal jurisdiction for crimes such as torture, and by holding that Pinochet's status as a former head of state does not provide immunity. The symbolic significance is even greater. In his resplendent military uniforms and cloaked with the protection of the posts he provided for himself in the constitution he promulgated in 1980, as senator for life and as the commander of the Chilean army who could not be removed from office by the country's elected officials, he appeared invulnerable. His arrest and the judicial determination that held he could be extradited and brought to trial signify worldwide that a new era of accountability is at hand. These have led in the short term to Senegal's decision to prosecute another former dictator, Hissein Habre of Chad, for his many crimes during his years in power. In combination, the Pinochet and Habre cases make clear not only that sovereignty is outweighed by universal jurisdiction, but also that there are diminishing opportunities for those who commit crimes against humanity to obtain sanctuary.

As a consequence of the Pinochet case, the Chilean judiciary is now actively pursuing prosecutions against other officials shielded previously by the amnesty issued by the former dictator in 1978. The courts in Chile are ruling that disappearances are continuing crimes until a death is proven. Hence, those responsible may be tried for holding the disappeared and not disclosing their whereabouts subsequent to the period covered by the 1978 amnesty. More than thirty military officers have been imprisoned since Pinochet's arrest in London. Also, Italy is attempting to extradite Pinochet's chief of secret police, General Manuel Contreras, for the attempted assassination and the critical wounding of two Chileans in exile in Rome, Bernardo Leighton and his wife Anita, a quarter of a century ago. Contreras is already serving a prison sentence in Chile for the assassination in the same era of another prominent exile, Orlando Letelier, and an American associate, Ronni Karpen Moffitt, by a car bomb in Washington, DC in 1976. Their murders were exempted from Pinochet's amnesty decree under pressure from the United States, which was outraged that such a crime should be committed on its territory.

Heightened public attention to war crimes, largely as a consequence of the work of the tribunals for ex-Yugoslavia and Rwanda, has also helped to produce a new round of national prosecutions for crimes during World War II. This suggests that the exercise of universal jurisdiction is persuading states to take more seriously their sovereign responsibilities. Perhaps the most significant example was the prosecution in Croatia of Dinko Sakic, then seventy-eight years old, the commander of the Jasenovac death camp. His conviction in October 1999 and the imposition of a prison sentence of twenty years—the maximum permissible under Croatian law and effectively a life sentence for someone his age—are noteworthy because these took place during the rule of President Franjo Tudjman who was, at best, grudging in acknowledging the crimes at Jasenovac. In a country where some leaders of the fascist Ustasha regime that ruled Croatia during World War II were celebrated as national patriots, Sakic might have expected to be welcomed home as a hero when he was discovered in Argentina and returned to his native land. That did not happen, because international prosecution of the war crimes committed by some Croatians during the past decade made it impossible to cover up the crimes by the previous Croatian state more than half a century ago. Britain, France, and Italy are among other countries where prosecutions have recently taken place for crimes during World War II. The flight of eighty-nine-year-old Maurice Papon in an attempt to evade the prison sentence imposed on him in France, and his speedy apprehension in Switzerland, further increased public awareness of war crimes and crimes against humanity and the importance of ensuring that states should punish those responsible.

The most dramatic international military intervention to protect human rights, of course, was NATO's war with Yugoslavia that began on March 24, 1999. For seventy-eight days, the most powerful military alliance the world has ever known bombed targets in Kosovo and in Serbia proper in an effort to halt attacks by Serb forces on Kosovar Albanians that began in February 1998. During the thirteen months prior to the NATO bombardment, about two thousand Kosovar Albanians were killed, some two hundred villages were destroyed, and approximately 300,000 civilians were forced to flee their homes and became internally displaced persons within Kosovo, crowding into the towns, or living without shelter and with inadequate food and water supplies in the woods and the hills. Military intervention by NATO was precipitated by the forced withdrawal, under harassment from Serbian troops, of a two-thousand-member unarmed Kosovo Verification Mission sponsored by the Organization for Security and Cooperation in Europe; by President Milošević's rejection of a peace accord proposed by a six-nation "Contact Group"—the United States, Britain, France, Germany, Italy, and Russia—accepted in February 1999 by Albanian negotiators at Rambouillet outside Paris; and by increasing violence by Serb forces against Kosovar Albanian civilians, such as a massacre of about forty-five people at a village called Racak. Much of the impetus came from human rights advocates who argued that NATO should have intervened earlier in Bosnia, or even in 1991 in Croatia when Serb forces bombarded Dubrovnik and laid siege to Vukovar.

The contemporary era of military interventions by Western powers to protect human rights began in summer 1991, a few months after the Gulf War for the liberation of Kuwait from Iraq. Immediately after the war, Iraqi Kurds rebelled, taking advantage of what they thought was the weakness of Saddam Hussein's forces following their expulsion from Kuwait. The Kurds, who had been severely oppressed for many years and who were the victims of poison gas attacks and mass slaughter in 1988 at the conclusion of the Iraq-Iran war, were briefly successful. They overran important cities such as Mosul, Kirkuk, and Suleimaniyah. However, Saddam Hussein's forces rallied and quickly overwhelmed the Kurds. Millions of Kurds fled to Turkey and Iran. To repatriate them, the Western allies that fought the Gulf War established a security zone for the Kurds in northern Iraq, prohibiting Saddam Hussein's forces from entering the area and barring his air force from flying over it. Ever since, Iraqi Kurdistan has been autonomous. The territory remains part of Iraq and no government recognizes it as an independent state. To safeguard the human rights of the Kurds, however, it is a military protectorate of the West. In practice, Iraq has lost all sovereignty over Kurdistan as surely as Serbia has lost authority over Kosovo.

A year and a half after a security zone for the Kurds was created in northern Iraq, UN-sponsored forces entered Somalia. The purpose was humanitarian, and intervention averted the death by starvation of many Somalis. It could also be considered as intervention to protect human rights because famine was a product of the indiscriminate warfare waged by rival clan leaders. Unfortunately, US troops in Somalia and troops from a few other countries involved themselves in the strife between clans. The intervention was discredited. One consequence was that the United States strenuously opposed the use of United Nations troops already present on the scene to stop the 1994 genocide in Rwanda which began just six months after eighteen American soldiers were killed in the streets of Mogadishu. Televised images of an American pilot's naked corpse dragged through the streets of the Somali capital profoundly shocked public opinion in the United States, making the Clinton administration eager to avoid involvement in another African conflict. The disaster in Somalia also played an important role in delaying decisive action by NATO to halt the war in Bosnia. It took the massacre of up to 8,000 Muslim men and boys at Srebrenica in July 1995, and the bombing of the Sarajevo marketplace, to create the resolve in Washington and other Western capitals to intervene militarily in a manner that brought an end to the war after it had gone on for three and a half years.

Another military intervention to protect human rights took place in 1994 when a US-led multinational force under the auspices of the United Nations occupied Haiti. Three years earlier, the elected president, Jean-Bertrand Aristide, was overthrown in a military coup. The Haitian armed forces then engaged in a reign of terror, killing as many as three thousand presumed supporters of Aristide and other opponents of military rule. In a December 1993 episode they set fire to a Port-au-Prince shantytown, leaving thousands homeless. Though a factor in the Clinton administration's military intervention was concern about thousands of boat people seeking refuge in the United States and claiming asylum because they were fleeing political persecution, the underlying purpose was to protect human rights. Ending the abuses that forced Haitians to flee was more attractive to Washington than turning back the fragile boats in which they fled.

The intervention by West African forces under Nigerian leadership in two internal armed conflicts in that region—in Liberia at the beginning of the decade and in Sierra Leone at its end—were also intended largely to protect human rights. Unfortunately, in the Liberian case, ECOMOG (Economic Monitoring Group) forces sometimes sided with those responsible for severe violations and were themselves accused of significant abuses. Nevertheless, they did ultimately restore peace to a country from which two-thirds of the entire population had fled, thereby permitting refugees to return to Liberia, and enabling rebuilding to begin.

Similarly, in Sierra Leone, ECOMOG's role was crucial in restoring a fragile peace and in curbing ghastly violations of human rights, including the mutilations of thousands.

The most recent example of military intervention to protect human rights is the deployment of Australian-led forces in East Timor, under United Nations auspices, to end the crimes by militias opposing the overwhelming vote for independence in a UN-sponsored referendum. Though many East Timorese who fled to the jungle and to West Timor have still not returned to their homes several months after the arrival of the multinational troops, and although rebuilding is slow, the intervention was a success. It halted the violence and is permitting a transition to the independence sought by the large majority of the population.

Looking back on the last decade of the twentieth century, the advance of global responsibility to respond to state terror seems one of its defining characteristics. From the standpoint of an advocate of human rights, there are circumstances, as in East Timor, when it appears that nothing other than military intervention can halt the committing of terrible crimes. If anything, the intervention should have been more speedy. On the other hand, there is a possibility that, as in Kosovo, intervention will result, at least in the short term, in a sharp escalation in the crimes it is intended to stop. Also as in Kosovo, those making war themselves may commit abuses. While great care was taken by NATO to comply with international humanitarian law, as the war proceeded the definition of military targets became broader, great damage was done to the civilian infrastructure in Serbia, and bombing mistakes resulted in the deaths of about five hundred Serb and Kosovar Albanian civilians. By its nature, military intervention to protect human rights transforms the human rights cause. It makes it far more than a way to limit power. War making is the ultimate exercise of power. Its use, even to protect human rights, may have unintended consequences that exacerbate violations of rights, as in Kosovo; or those who intervene to protect rights may themselves commit severe abuses, as in Liberia.

The experiences in Kosovo, East Timor, and other places where military intervention has taken place to protect human rights, suggests that several factors should be considered in decisions to intervene. Those that seem most important are: the nature, gravity, and scale of the crimes committed; whether alternative means are available to halt those crimes; whether the powers intervening have the capacity to do so effectively; whether there is a strong likelihood that intervention can take place in a manner that does not make a bad situation worse; whether intervention enjoys the legitimacy that derives from multilateral sponsorship; and whether intervention is proportionate and conducted in compliance with international humanitarian law. On such grounds, for example, there should have been military intervention in Rwanda. Certainly, the crimes committed there were of enormous magnitude. Once the killing started in April 1994, there was no way to stop it other than by military force. The means were at hand as a UN force was in Rwanda. Its Canadian commander, General Romeo Dallaire, insisted then, and has insisted ever since, that if he had obtained the requisite orders he could have stopped the genocide. It is inconceivable that the situation in Rwanda could have been made worse; on the contrary, timely intervention would not only have halted the genocide or, at least, greatly reduced the carnage, but it would also have prevented the flight from the country of millions of Hutus would have averted the wider conflict in Congo tied to their presence there. And, were it not for the opposition of two permanent members of the Security Council, the United States and France, both susceptible to embarrassment by a determined UN secretariat, intervention could have been authorized by the United Nations.

In contrast, one can look at the intervention in Chechnya or Kashmir. The crimes committed in both places are severe. Yet when the other criteria are considered, it is apparent that military intervention is unwise. The international community has other means to influence those committing crimes against humanity. Significant economic pressure should be tried before resorting to military force. The geography makes it difficult for any outside force to intervene effectively. In both cases, the probable consequence of intervention would be a wider war, perhaps involving nuclear weapons. Sponsorship of military intervention by any relevant multilateral body is out of the question. Inevitably, because the crimes committed in Chechnya are greater than in Kosovo and because India's conduct in Kashmir is comparable to what Indonesia did in East Timor in the period leading to intervention, questions arise about the evenhandedness of the international community's response to crimes against humanity. Yet if other factors are taken into account, non-intervention in Chechnya and Kashmir seems appropriate. In contrast, if military intervention is warranted anywhere, there is no valid excuse for the international community's dereliction in Rwanda.

Without ruling out military intervention, it is obvious that it would be far better for the human rights cause if the other means of responding to the great crimes that have secured support and made headway during the past decade were a more significant deterrent. In Kosovo and East Timor there are signs that many who murdered civilians went to some lengths to dispose of the bodies of their victims in ways designed to impede identification and prosecution. This suggests an awareness of developments in international law. It will take a long time, however, before the prospect of prosecution and punishment for genocide, crimes against humanity, and war crimes becomes a substantial factor in preventing such crimes. Regrettably, the prospect is remote in important countries such as Russia, India, and China. Yet looking back on the achievements of the decade that has just ended, it is apparent that great progress has been made. If momentum is maintained in the first decade of the twenty-first century, we could well be entering an era in which what governments say about their commitment to human rights more closely matches their practices.

My espousal of legal and, at times, military intervention is not without concern for the unintended consequences. These go beyond the possibility that those intervening may themselves commit abuses or trigger increased abuses. A further concern is that the erosion of sovereignty could impair the capacity of states to protect rights.

In an earlier era, as Stephen Holmes has pointed out, we thought that danger to rights emanated primarily from states that are too powerful. Today, threats to rights are also attributable to state weakness. In his essay[1], Holmes focused on Russia. He pointed out that Russia collects about 10 percent of GNP in taxes, whereas in the United States it is about 30 percent and in Western Europe about 45 percent. As a consequence, the Russian state is too weak to care adequately for the million persons confined in its prisons, subjecting inmates to the epidemics of tuberculosis and multi-drug-resistant tuberculosis that are centered in these institutions. Indeed, a factor in the high rate of incarceration is that the state also lacks the personnel needed to process criminal cases, leaving a large number in extended pre-trial detention. Because the state is too weak to collect taxes from many people who have become wealthy by stealing or privatizing state assets, it lacks the revenue to administer a criminal justice system effectively.

What has sovereignty to do with this? Perhaps a lot, if sovereignty carries with it the sense of community or solidarity at a national level required to maintain the strength of a state. Machiavelli pointed out that only a vital state can survive not only changes in government but also radical changes in the form of government.[2] Neither the Soviet Union nor Yugoslavia was such a vital state, as neither survived a change in the form of government. These federations were lacking in *res publica*, or civic spirit.

The process underway in the Soviet Union/Russia, and also in Yugoslavia, appears to be the reverse of that described by Eugen Weber in his classic *Peasants Into Frenchmen.*[3] In France, between 1870 and 1914, citizens who previously identified with their village, their commune, their town, or their region, gradually came to think of themselves as

French. They created a nation out of people of diverse ethnic and linguistic origins. In the former Soviet Union and in ex-Yugoslavia, on the other hand, the trend has been towards tribalism. The protection of rights in such circumstances is exceedingly difficult.

This trend is not limited to the former communist countries. Today, the most volatile states in the world include Indonesia and Nigeria. They are beset by ethnic, religious, and regional conflicts. Ironically, these two states are now led by individuals whose personal histories suggest that they are dedicated to the protection of rights. The difficulty they face is that their governments seem too weak to safeguard rights. Indonesia and Nigeria each experienced decades of corrupt, brutal, military rule that destroyed civic spirit. The possibility of fragmentation—and the potential for human rights catastrophes—is a direct consequence. In such circumstances it is crucial that the state should inspire loyalty and be able to count on the feelings of community and solidarity that it needs to survive. Unfortunately, this is in question in both Indonesia and Nigeria.

Is there a connection between the decline of sovereignty and the weakness manifested by multiethnic, multi-religious states such as the Soviet Union/Russia, Yugoslavia, Indonesia, and Nigeria? Certainly the diminishing significance of sovereignty is far from the main cause of their weakness. Yet it seems unwise to dismiss completely the possibility that there is a link between two phenomena that have marked the past decade: the enfeeblement of states and their loss of a measure of sovereignty.

For those preoccupied with protecting rights, it is inconceivable to give up the hard-won legal victories for universal jurisdiction to bring to justice those who commit the kind of crimes that will be subject to the jurisdiction of the International Criminal Court. And, in extreme circumstances such as Rwanda, military intervention must be an option to stop genocide. Yet as the main responsibility to protect rights rests with states, sovereignty—at least to the extent that it is one of the forms through which a commitment to *res publica* is expressed—is also a concern. Where possible, it seems incumbent on human rights advocates to reconcile our commitment to global responsibility for the protection of human rights with state responsibility. An example is the complementarity provision of the treaty to establish the International Criminal Court. It places primary responsibility to prosecute in the hands of national authorities. Trial before the ICC is only possible if a state evades its duties. This is the opposite of the requirements in the statutes for the tribunals for ex-Yugoslavia and Rwanda. These *ad hoc* international courts have primary jurisdiction. By bringing pressure on states to carry out their responsibilities, the ICC treaty can assist in promoting civic spirit. Far from undermining sovereignty, the ICC may strengthen states.

The growing willingness of the Chilean courts to deal with the crimes of the Pinochet era in the wake of legal proceedings against Pinochet himself in Britain is another example of the connection between global responsibility and state responsibility. Opportunities to promote national efforts to protect rights by international intervention will not arise in all circumstances. Yet as we must rely on state authority to safeguard citizens in most circumstances, it is essential that proponents of rights should not undermine sovereignty needlessly. Where it is consistent with our mission, we should design our strategies to reinforce sovereignty.

Notes

1 Stephen Holmes (1997). "Weak States, Weak Liberties". *The American Prospect.* July-August.

2 Niccolo Machiavelli. "States and Their Transitions". *The Discourses:* Book One, Discourse Two.

3 Eugen Weber (1976). *Peasants Into Frenchmen: The Modernization of Rural France, 1870–1914*. Stanford University Press.

10 *The Constitutional Honeymoon Is Over. The Paradoxes of Post-Communist Constitution Making*

WIKTOR OSIATYŃSKI

East European transitions are ten years old. They continue to be as surprising today as they were at the beginning. The very collapse of communism was not predicted, except by Adam Michnik, whom no one treated seriously in that respect. After 1989, political analysts continued to miss reality. The possibility of a simultaneous triple transition to market, democracy, and the rule of law was ruled out. The chance of adopting new constitutions was doubted. No one suspected that in countries which had developed alternative non-communist political elites—Poland, Hungary, and Czechoslovakia in particular—the former communists would return to power as fast as they did. Finally, in those countries where triple transition was successful, people who had dreamed about democracy and human rights were surprised to find out that, while economic reforms did change for the better the lives of common people, the transition to constitutional democracy did not bring major improvement. Many surprises and paradoxes of post-communist transitions call for explanations.

1

The possibility of simultaneous triple transition was first questioned by Jon Elster at the conference in Pécs, Hungary, in 1990. The essence of his argument was, that since the high costs of economic transition would be distributed unequally, the majority, which in the short run would be worse off, would use its newly won democratic powers to stop reforms.[1]

In the West, modernization took place in two separate stages: first the market and the rule of law (offering protection to markets and property rights) were established, and much later, when markets produced enough goods to be shared more evenly, democratization followed. Simultaneous transition was unknown and improbable.

Elster's reasoning proved right but his conclusions were wrong. Despite the popular economic hardships and the longing for the former security, and despite electoral support for the parties of the former communists, in Central Europe triple transition seems successful. In the mid-nineties a group of German scholars, joined by Jon Elster, looked at the development of democracy in Bulgaria, Hungary, Slovakia, and the Czech Republic.[2] They used, as the criteria of consolidated democracy, respect for democratic rules upheld by constitutions and statutes, as well as the institutional separation of such centers of power as the state, political parties, property, investment decisions, social services, the media, and other institutions of power and influence on society. Since, under communism, all these powers were confused and controlled by the party, the creation and separation of new institutions was the main task of a state in transition.

Elster, Offe, Preuss, and their young colleagues claimed that the most consolidated democracy exists in the Czech Republic followed by Hungary, while Slovakia and Bulgaria are pretty far behind. The main reason for the delay in the two latter countries is that in Bulgaria and Slovakia, communism did not involve cultural and political modernization. In the behavioral patterns, values, and world-views of the communist era, the basic concepts and perceptions of an agrarian society survived. Such ideas could coexist with coercive industrialization and communist ideology but they cannot be reconciled with a market economy and constitutional democracy. The authors suggested that transition will not be complete until these values, attitudes, and behavioral patterns change.

Having read their convincing book I would be depressed about the fate of Slovakia and Bulgaria had I not witnessed myself how the centuries-old, seemingly impenetrable anti-bourgeois values which dominated the minds of Poland's nobility and intelligentsia, and which pervaded the nation's literature and culture, its schools and media, vanished almost overnight. This is what happened in the early 1990s, when a number of bold decisions and laws, introduced by Tadeusz Mazowiecki and Leszek Balcerowicz, opened up opportunities for enrichment for those who had preached traditional values and condemned capitalism before such a possibility arose.

The reasons for the relatively successful transition to a market economy and democracy in Poland, Hungary, and the Czech Republic require some comment. Although transitions differed to a significant degree in each country involved, everywhere the social aspects were similar. The main beneficiaries of transition turned out to be primarily former communists and their relatives who used political power and appropriated state resources and connections in order to dominate the newly emerging capitalist class. Political parties made up of former communists channeled the anti-reform sentiments of the masses, securing for themselves a stable place in the new democracies and, to their own surprise, returning to power at least once in each country.[3]

Here lies the solution to the "Elster paradox". The impossible became possible because the post-communists, who were elected by the majority to stop reforms, had already become capitalists. It was in their interest to continue market reforms while using the power they had regained to strengthen their own control over the privatized companies, the banks, and the market. Social programs and rhetoric were insufficient to retain mass support and they were defeated in the next elections by the right-wing parties which are now creating their own capitalists and continuing reforms while losing support, once again. Thus democracy facilitated market reform rather than prevented it. By offering alternative governments, democratic institutions helped to keep social tensions from eruption. This is one of the main functions of democratic institutions in any consolidated democracy.

2

Elster also warned that if a democracy cannot deliver the goods in the economic sphere, "calls for an authoritarian regime will be made, and ultimately heard".[4] To make such authoritarian temptation more difficult, the third element of transition was necessary. Constitutions were to be enacted, and the rule of law established. The experience under communism proved that constitutions, even if not observed by the regime, can provide justification for claims for better treatment on the part of the opposition and the public. To be really meaningful, constitutions should separate the state from society. They should divide the powers of the state and assign competencies to each branch of government in such a way as to foster cooperation, while preventing the abuse of power or the emergence of destructive conflicts between the centers of power. Constitutions should also limit the power of a government, not merely by declaring the rights of individuals and minorities, but by providing accessible enforcement mechanisms and remedies for the protection of such rights. It was the lack of such remedies and the ability of state powers arbitrarily to limit the rights proclaimed in communist constitutions that made them useless.

Constitutions bring order and limit the power of the majority as well as the discretion of state officials in all democracies. In post-communist transitions there existed additional reasons why constitutions seemed particularly needed.

With economic crisis, growing unemployment, and unfulfilled expectations, those who are weaker—particularly national, ethnic, and religious minorities—can become scapegoats for the frustrations and fears of the majority. One of the first decisions made by a democratically elected local authority in an affluent suburb near Warsaw was to ban all HIV-positive people from their community.[5] From this and many similar experiences it is obvious that limited democracy cannot be learned from books or from models developed in older democracies. It has to be learned by each society through its own trials and errors, with inevitable mistakes and costs. Constitutions were desperately needed to limit the scope of the entire experiment so that mistakes would not involve too many victims and too high personal costs.

I presented these—and other—arguments in favor of creating constitutions in the post-communist world, during the debate that took place at the Cordozzo Law School in New York City, in November 1990. My adversary was András Sajó, a Hungarian professor of constitutional law, who, at that time, was just putting together the legal studies department at the Central European University funded by George Soros in Budapest and Prague.

Sajó agreed that constitutions were necessary. The problem was that they were not feasible. Constitutions were not attractive to the very people who were to prepare and adopt them, that is, to the political elites, including elites that had originated as anti-communist opposition. The power of all post-communist elites is based on the state and its role in the economy and society. National, regional, municipal, and local officials are as powerful as the state property they control. Thus bureaucracy and political elites will oppose any limitation of the state and its powers, whether constitutional or not. They find arguments in the needs of the transition itself (the state, as the main agency of reforms, should not be constrained in the fulfillment of its tasks), in the etatism that dominated the region before communism, and in popular expectations with respect to state protection and benefits. With a weak civil society, no one will be able to force a constitution on reluctant politicians, concluded Sajó.

Sajó's reasoning proved correct, but his conclusions were wrong. New constitutions were enacted in almost all post-communist states, although not in Hungary. Political elites did want constitutions, although for reasons other than those we had discussed. In Bulgaria and Romania communist-dominated parliaments passed new constitutions as early as 1991, in order to limit or prevent revolutions that never really took place.[6]

Many constitutions were adopted between 1992 and 1994 in the former Soviet Union.[7] They were, most often, variations on the old Soviet constitutional theme that paid lip service to human rights and a new power system, usually favoring those institutions which asserted domination during the transition itself—parliaments in the Baltic states and the president in Central Asia, Ukraine, and Belarus. Their primary goal was not to establish a culture of constitutionalism, but to ensure a new basis of legitimacy for predominantly old elites and to create the foundations for new states.

The case of the former Czechoslovakia is a good example of this. For three years the country struggled unsuccessfully with its new constitution. Inability to divide powers between the two republics was one of the reasons for the split in the federation. However, once a decision about the separation had been reached in the summer of 1992, each newly emerging country had a new constitution hastily drafted and adopted by the end of the year.

In the former Soviet Union, Yugoslavia, and Czechoslovakia, constitutions were prompted by an abrupt change—most often by the fragmentation of larger units and the emergence of new states. In Poland and Hungary, by contrast, there was no abrupt change: transitions were negotiated and new elites had to find a compromise with strong elements of the old system that remained in place. In such a situation it is very difficult to enact a new constitution since every player in the game resists any reallocation of power that might diminish his position.

Unaware of the difficulties, Poland's new leaders decided to pass a new constitution. It was hoped that this constitution would become law on May 3, 1991, to celebrate the two-hundredth anniversary of its first constitution, which was also the first modern constitution in Europe and the second in the world after that of America. In this they failed, and for eight years Poland was torn by constitutional trauma.

Hungarians were less romantic. They did not even try to write a new constitution. In October 1989, the still communist parliament adopted drastic changes that affected approximately 90 percent of the Stalinist constitution of 1949. In December 1990 a new parliament introduced further changes. The amended constitution created a very powerful

Constitutional Court that could invalidate all acts it held unconstitutional, and the procedure could be initiated by a single citizen. In addition, between 1989 and 1990, the Hungarian parliament passed by a two-thirds majority a number of separate constitutional acts that regulated basic human rights (to assembly, association, freedom of conscience, and religion, as well as an act on the status of churches and the modification of the act on the freedom of the press). In 1993 the act on the rights of national minorities was adopted and the institution of the ombudsman was created.

Thus the Hungarians created their constitutional order by installments. They exploited the brief constitutional momentum at the beginning of the transition when the communists were demoralized and ready to adopt any measure that would increase their legitimacy in an inevitably approaching democratic order. While changing the constitution and introducing new laws the Hungarian constitution framers looked into the past, at its abuses and violations. They first established democracy, then limited it, giving immense powers to the Constitutional Court so that similar abuses would not reappear in the future.

András Sajó came to believe that this is the way in which constitutions are created. "Constitutions do not reflect the wisdom of the Fates; they reflect fear, originating in, and related to, the previous political regime", writes Sajó in his most recent book.[8] They are written "out of fear of an earlier despotic power", and the freedoms they guarantee are seen as "the institutional negation of the oppression recently endured".[9] Constitutions also reflect another kind of fear—the fear of oneself. The constitution framers know that a moment will come when they themselves will be tempted to act on the basis of interest or passion, so they make a constitutional pre-commitment in the present. This situation is described well by Jon Elster's metaphor of Ulysses binding himself to the mast because he is aware that when he hears the song of the sirens he will be unable to resist temptation. Similarly, in a democracy we realize that we may desire more power than we should have, and therefore we need to "increase resistance against the dictates of the actual moment" in the future. Constitutions are written after the fall of an oppressive regime and before its atrocities have been forgotten, in order to prevent history repeating itself, according to Sajó.

I disagree. While I think that *Limiting Government* is one of the best books on comparative constitutionalism recently written, I do not believe any longer that constitutions are created as pre-commitments. At the beginning of transition I shared Sajó's idea. In 1989, I wrote in *Gazeta Wyborcza*, a high-circulation daily in Poland, an essay called "The Constitution Is a Marriage", in which I advocated a constitution as a self-limiting commitment by the ruling elite. This was at the very beginning of my personal journey as one of the constitution framers. This ten-year journey saw me acting as advisor to a number of constitutional committees in the Polish parliament; co-authoring, in 1992, a draft Bill of Rights; helping to broker a number of deals between major players in constitution making; and actively advocating a far from ideal, but at least acceptable, final product before the popular referendum in 1997. I also observed and helped to record the process of constitution making in the region as a whole; I wrote and taught about it, and, on occasion, advised constitution framers in other countries. The journey was full of hopes and frustrations, trials and errors. Eventually I came to believe that the concept of a constitution as a commitment based on fear and on the desire to learn from past mistakes is far from the reality. The Polish case suggests that when a brief momentum is missed, constitution making is subject to passions, interests, and base emotions similar to those that constitutions are supposed to limit.

3

Three major reasons for this are people, institutions, and parties. It is not surprising that politics, being about power and the allocation of scarce resources, everywhere attracts more psychopaths and thieves than do other professions. Their aim is to keep the state powerful and rich so they can feed themselves and their cronies, precisely as described by Sajó in our 1990 Cordozzo debate. However, I am more interested here in the honest, highly motivated people who had been engaged in risky opposition activities under communism. After 1989, when they first came to power, they still wanted to change society for the better and to create new rules which would prevent the abuse of power. With time, they came to see how difficult social change is, how powerful are the forces of social inertia, how many people oppose change. Faced with responsibility and difficulties it was quite natural for them to come to think that the limitation of state powers, necessary for the completion of reforms, was no longer wise.

I have encountered liberals, who, soon after being appointed to office, sought greater power for the state and began to oppose constitutional limitations. I have also met former human rights activists, who, after being promoted to an official position, began to say: "Yes, human rights were worth fighting for under communism, but now, when we have a democratic government which needs to implement important changes, when we face the breakdown of state authority, rising crime rates, and the need to restore law and order, we should not insist on human rights any longer."

Difficulties reinforce a tendency towards increased control. "Power spending in order to maximize control, rather than power investing in the interests of devolution, institution building, and eventually power sharing is the order of the day", write Elster, Offe, and Preuss.[10] Each state institution wants to increase its own power. No wonder that, at the beginning, transitions were marked by conflicts between institutions. Legislators fought with the executive and with other legislators. In Poland, the war between the Senate and the Sejm resulted in the failure to enact a new constitution by the 1991 deadline. Even more visible were conflicts within the executive. In Hungary, the war between Prime Minister József Antall and President Árpád Göncz marked the early period of transition, although it never reached the intensity of hatred displayed by Slovak Prime Minster Mieczyslav Meciar towards President Michal Kovacs. In Poland, the national hero Lech Wałęsa, unable to resist surges of adrenaline, fought with all prime ministers, including those whom he had appointed himself. His creative legal minister, Lech Falandysz, believed that in the early stages of institution building, competencies are not clearly defined. If an institution does not hesitate to grab new powers they will eventually be accepted. Falandysz helped Wałęsa to amass incredible power by the use of bold—most often dubious—constitutional interpretations. Since that time, the Polish language has a new verb: "to falandize" means to stretch the law beyond its intentions and limits in order to foster the interests and power of an institution.

Even the newly formed constitutional courts took part in the fight for power. Zorkin's court in Russia fought openly for power with the president and was dissolved after a coup in 1993. In other countries, these courts, among their first decisions, usually attributed to themselves greater power than was given to them in the constitutions. I remember a meeting in 1991 in Kiev with the late Professor Juskov, who was appointed by President Kravchuk as the first chairman of a newly elected constitutional court. Associate judges were to be elected by the parliament, which was not able to obtain the majority needed to elect them. For over a year Juskov sat alone in his office and thought about the cases he hoped would be brought to the court, in which he could assert the court's power.

Similarly, institutions oppose changes that can limit their power. The human rights community in Poland was shocked when the draft Bill of Rights, submitted in October 1992 by President Wałęsa to the parliament, was fiercely attacked by the ombudsman for citizens' rights. The bill offered everyone direct access to a court, and the ombudsman feared he might lose his monopoly on doing good.

Thus the constitutions, at least in the sections defining the machinery of government, do not reflect wisdom learned from the lessons of the past or any theoretical considerations. They primarily reflect the power interests of the players—their actual power at the beginning and in the course of the transition, and calculations which aim at the limitation of competitors' power. Sometimes such calculations misfire. For example, before the first free elections in Bulgaria and Hungary the anti-communist opposition imposed a relatively weak presidency, in the false expectation that the office would be given to a communist.

With time, conflicts between institutions were overshadowed by wars between parties. At that point, two of the goals of transition became contradictory. For those who take constitutional democracy for granted, it may be surprising to realize that if the constitutional momentum was missed, the transition to constitutionalism was undermined rather than helped by the simultaneous transition to democracy.

Transition to democracy implies the creation not only of representative institutions, but also of a mechanism for selecting the representatives. Although initially there were ideas to base post-communist democracy on national fronts or citizens' committees, very soon it turned out that political parties were indispensable. Such parties had not existed, except for the former communists and their allied "parties" of peasants and the communist-controlled intelligentsia. Non-communist parties had to be formed from scratch, and with little tradition in the representation of social and economic interests most of them emerged by way of splits in anti-communist fronts. In Poland the story was quite simple: in 1990, Lech Wałęsa came into conflict with Prime Minister Tadeusz Mazowiecki, and as a result Poland had two non-communist parties. A year later Wałęsa fired his new allies and there were three parties. Around the same time the left-wing caucus split from Mazowiecki's party to join one small party of former communists, and then there were four parties, and so on.

New parties were formed around ambitious leaders whose position was based not on their contribution to transition as such but on their claims to merit in the fight against the communists before the changes. The leaders needed to attract followers and tried to do so by fighting among themselves; with these roots the war soon focused on proving past merits and on blaming others for not being "clean" enough. In this phase of democratization the first post-communist elites were attacked as traitors, *collaborateurs*, or agents of the secret services by those who were still in line for power.

One is unlikely to attract supporters to a particular party by describing the ways in which one agrees with other parties. Conflicts are necessary; they have to be public and visible. In young democracies the most visible places were the parliaments, which began to serve two contradictory functions. As the institutions where governments were to be selected and supported, policies established, and laws made, parliaments needed a significant dose of consensus. As places where party systems were being formed, parliaments resembled battlefields. In this situation, it was almost impossible to obtain the clear majority that was required for the enactment of a new constitution. Moreover, constitution making itself was a much more rewarding area for the inter-party war than "regular" politics, since conflicts over identity, religion, social justice, and national or class symbols were safer for the politicians than economic reform and the distribution of a shrinking pie. A party that advocated certain economic measures and made social promises could be held to account after elections. This was hardly the case, however, when a party promised to care about Christian values or national treasures and labeled their adversaries as atheists, fundamentalists, or cosmopolites. Sajó shows that the best constitutions were written in secret by small groups, quite often in violation of the original ground rules, and subsequently legitimized in a democratic ratification process or in a national referendum.[11] In Poland, however, it was useful for most players to have a constitution prepared—and fought over—in a democratic process that attracted public attention.

As a result, politics dominated the rule making. Instead of being immune from political conflicts, constitutional rules were the main object of those conflicts. Between 1989 and 1993, the political scene in Poland was like a football field on which the players were simultaneously playing the ball and arguing about the rules—even occasionally changing teams. After 1993, when the warring right-wing parties failed to pass the threshold in the elections, a more unified anti-constitutional coalition was formed against the parliamentary majority of post-communists and peasants. In the war over the constitution, its actual content began to count less and less. The desire to avoid repeating past mistakes, consistent constitutional ideas, successful examples from other countries—all such considerations were secondary to the one, overriding factor: who had come up with a given proposal. If it was "our" proposal it was to be supported, while "their" suggestions were to be rejected, regardless of their content and merit. In December 1994, the four great political authorities in Poland—that is, the then president, Lech Wałęsa; the Catholic Church; the Solidarity trade union; and the extra-parliamentary right-wing opposition—called for the rejection, in a popular referendum, of the draft constitution which was being prepared in the National Assembly. No one yet knew what they would be rejecting, since at that time only seven draft articles had been agreed upon by the Constitutional Commission. However, the battle lines had been drawn. By the time of the national referendum in May 1997, the war over the constitution consisted of misunderstandings, simplifications, and simple lies.

The adoption of a new constitution became possible in Poland primarily because of the results of two subsequent elections. After the parliamentary elections in 1993, the socialists were facing the liberals in the Constitutional Commission so a compromise on social and economic issues could be reached without having simultaneously to address the problems of identity and ideology.

In 1995 the election of Aleksander Kwasniewski as president of Poland helped to deal with a second controversial constitutional issue, that is, the division of powers between the president, the parliament, and the prime minister. Having served between 1993 and 1995 as the chairman of the Constitutional Committee, Kwasniewski regarded the passing of the constitution as proof of his personal success. He agreed to give away some presidential powers and to shift the political system in Poland from the semi-presidentialism of Lech Wałęsa towards a cabinet-dominated system modeled on Germany.

The third major controversy initially concerned relations between the church and the state. With time, it came to encompass a whole range of philosophical and ideological problems. The right wing, supported by the Catholic Church, wanted to include in the constitution a reference to God, to subordinate the constitution and statutes to natural law, and to ban abortion in the constitution. These and many other demands by the right were included in the citizens' draft constitution submitted to the National Assembly by the Solidarity trade union in 1994. Having collected close to two million signatures under its draft, Solidarity wanted it to be put to a national referendum as an alternative to the constitution adopted by the National Assembly. When this demand was rejected, Solidarity and the right-wing extra-parliamentary opposition refused to negotiate with the National Assembly. The latter, faced with a national referendum, nonetheless made a compromise "with itself", adding to the draft constitution certain changes demanded by the opposition and by the church. This action, while it failed to win the support of opponents, meant that the final document better reflected the heterogeneity of society and resulted in the constitution being confirmed, by a slim margin, in the national referendum on May 25, 1997.

While an open style of constitution making increased the legitimacy of the constitution, it had an adverse effect on the content of the new constitution. Compromises made in the daylight can be perceived as the betrayal of one's constituency. A preferred mode of compromise was to add to the draft more and more new provisions to satisfy the demands of all. As a result, Poland's constitution is a patchwork which includes, on the one hand, such clearly liberal measures as the independence of the Central Bank and the limitation of the state deficit, and, on the other hand, the recognition of the family farm as "the basis of the agricultural system", a concession won by a populist peasant party which wants to petrify the extremely backward structure of Poland's agriculture in order to retain a large electorate. Socialist and peasant constitutional majorities also secured vast scope for positive social and economic rights in the final text of the constitution.

This blurs the distinction between constitution and politics. Democratic politics is primarily about the allocation and redistribution of inadequate resources. In the political process various interests, social goals, and visions of the future are discussed, weighed against the available resources, and eventually put together in a compromise which is reevaluated every year in the state budget. Constitutional rights, in contrast, are not a matter of democratic compromise. They take precedence over "normal" political processes in which a society defines its priorities. If a constitution is to be treated seriously, regardless of the actual economic situation—prosperity or crisis—when preparing the budget, a government needs first to put aside the resources needed to fulfill constitutional obligations. The choice of priorities in the political process is limited to what is left over. It also means that when a constitution is protected by the courts, power over the part of the budget needed to secure constitutional rights moves from the parliament to the courts, which distorts the separation of powers. For these reasons the majority of Western democracies do not include social rights in their constitutions. Nevertheless, this did not prevent Sweden, Germany, and France from creating extensive welfare states, usually on the basis of one general provision in the constitution, or even in its preamble. For reasons of legitimacy post-communist constitution framers could not follow this pattern and are learning, at present, about another paradox of constitutional democracy: the more democratic the process of constitution making, the less room there is for democracy under the new constitution.

4

After a recent lecture on constitution making in Eastern Europe, given at the Central European University in Warsaw, an American student asked: "What are you going to do about the rule of law now that the constitutional honeymoon is over?" This question penetrates to the core of otherwise successful transitions. Democracy and constitutions can make governments more accountable and prevent gross violations of rights, but by themselves they do not change people's lives. Even if they protect people from the state they do not necessarily protect the weak from the strong, nor the state from falling into the hands of the strong. Democracy and constitutions do not automatically bring with them individual freedom, dignity, equality before the law, and protection from abuse. Today in Poland, the Czech Republic, and Hungary people have learned that they can have some control over the economic conditions of their lives. But in political and social dimensions most people still feel almost as powerless as they did before. Being at the mercy of the state bureaucracy, local administration, and organized crime, they are unable to secure for themselves the protection of the police or the courts.

In 1998, some 250,000 people in Warsaw, out of a population of 1.3 million, filed complaints and appeals against official decisions or inaction. The ombudsman for citizens' rights stated in his annual report that public administrators are arrogant, that they disregard citizens, and do not have a clue about the rule of law. This applies equally to the old administrators with roots in the communist system and to the new administrators who came with the Solidarity governments and who have traded the zeal of the first generation of reformers for corruption, clientele systems, and the building of their own little fiefdoms.

Administrative reforms do not help much, since they focus primarily on making the administration more effective—which may well mean more efficient in the service of their own, or their party's interests, and more effective in exploiting the population. This is becoming particularly visible at the local level. In Poland, the introduction of local self-government was perceived, just a few years ago, as the most successful element of the changes. Today, this enthusiasm is vanishing as new local elites are being formed that are greedy, selfish, and controlled by local market powers often linked to the mafia. Outraged by inefficiency, high salaries, and the unending growth in the number of local positions handed out to the cousins and friends of influential local politicians, the Poles are rediscovering the old truth that the decentralization of power, without the prior establishment of the rule of law and a system of effective remedies, ends up as the unlimited power of local cliques which control political organizations and foster their own interests at the expense of the population.

Although the judicial review of administrative decisions has been introduced, it takes years to get to a court. Officials have at their disposal thousands of technicalities that help them either to avoid issuing a final decision or to delay a complaint on its way—via the administration—to a court. Instead of the mandatory sixty days, it takes the Central Housing Office in Poland two years, the Ministry for Environmental Protection fifteen months, and the Ministry of Health or the Central Customs Office a full year to send the documents needed by the administrative court. There is no mechanism to enforce their compliance with the law. In Hungary, the Supreme Court, overloaded with administrative cases, ruled that the administration can suspend the case and that the party has no right of appeal, even if the suspension lasts years.

In civil cases, it takes a long time to get a hearing in a court and much longer to get a final court decision, which is not usually executed. Money awarded in such cases has already been consumed by inflation anyway, if it is ever recovered at all. Under communism there were no contracts between private individuals and not much room for private law. Such basics of the market economy as credit, the delayed delivery of products, and compensation for damage scarcely existed. No mechanism for the enforcement of private contracts by the state was developed. After 1989, new governments seemed not to realize the crucial importance of this fact for the market economy. And into this void entered the mafia.

As a result, more and more people are turning their backs on democracy itself and ceasing to take part in elections. After all, why should they bother to replace one elite with another, which will be as selfish and as remote from people as the previous one. People are starting to think that all reforms have just one purpose: to create lucrative posts for the families and friends of the ruling elites. The division, only too well known, between "us", the people, and "them", the rulers, is reemerging.

One dramatic and painful lesson of the transition was the discovery that a market democracy does not solve many important problems and, by itself, cannot be a remedy in individual cases. Democracy responds to money and numbers, that is, to powerful interests or large groups of potential voters (or protesters). However, it easily overlooks a small majority or an individual whose interests have been encroached upon or whose rights have been abused. One person will not mobilize a social movement or an electoral block to protect his or her rights or interests. Therefore a democracy, even a constitutional democracy, without a legal culture and the rule of law, is meaningless.

5

There is nothing particularly new here. Constitutions have usually served the strong and powerful. After every radical social change a new elite has emerged. Everywhere the first capitalist fortunes were built on pilfering, fraud, wars, and corruption. Everywhere the state and party structures, constitutions and legal systems, have served new elites rather than the masses of people left behind with unfulfilled expectations of the revolutionary period.

The French Revolution not only ended in terror but also banned, for almost a hundred years, freedom of association and other civil liberties; even well into the Fifth Republic an individual was almost as powerless vis-à-vis the state bureaucracy as individuals are today in Hungary and Poland. In the United States the Supreme Court, for its first 150 years, protected property and freedom of contract, benefiting the rich and ignoring other constitutional rights. In the 1930s some 90 percent of all rights-related decisions by the Supreme Court involved the protection of property rights. By the late 1960s, 70 percent of its decisions concerned individual rights other than property rights. During that period the Supreme Court created and extended freedom of speech and freedom of the press, rights against discrimination based on race and sex, as well as expanded rights in relation to criminal and administrative procedures. This represented a true revolution in terms of rights.

There is an important lesson in this revolution. The reasons for it have conventionally been seen in the existence of constitutional guarantees of rights, in the leadership by independent courts, and in the growth of the consciousness of rights among the population. Charles Epp, a professor of government at the University of Kansas, having compared rights revolutions in the United States, England, Canada, and India, added a fourth element to the rights revolution.[12] Epp claims that the initial stimulus for such revolutions came from outside the judiciary, from civil society, and particularly from organized rights advocates. The Free Speech League, the NAACP, the ACLU, the American Jewish Congress, the Jehovah's Witnesses, International Labor Defense, and many other organizations which embarked on constitutional litigation, had been laying foundations for the revolution since the early twentieth century. Initially, litigants everywhere faced unsympathetic, if not hostile, judges. But they persisted all the way to the Supreme Court, and, when the time was ripe, eventually succeeded.

As distinct from political upheavals, rights revolutions are slow and incremental; in order to bring about durable results steady support is far more important than one-off revolutionary mobilization. Epp analyses the case of India, where the rights revolution took off after the introduction of emergency rule in 1975. At that point, the middle and upper classes embarked on constitutional litigation against abuses of rights by the regime. However, in 1977, with the end of the emergency, the opposition withdrew its support for the rights revolution and returned to the policy of trading privileges between themselves. Even though the Supreme Court attempted to continue the rights revolution through a burst of judicial activism, it collapsed because it lacked broad and deep support in society.

In the US and, later, in Canada, it was when the rights advocates began to mobilize the necessary resources—from foundations, from members of affected groups, and eventually from state-provided legal funds—that the constitution could be taken away from the rich and powerful. In short, the new constitutional rights have developed "out of a democratization of access to the judiciary".[13] The prerequisite for such democratization is the existence of a support structure in civil society. "Without a support structure, even the clearest constitutional rights guarantees are likely to become meaningless in the courts; but a vibrant support structure can extend and expand the feeblest of rights. Participants in constitutional democracy would do well to focus their efforts not only on framing or revising constitutional provisions, not only on selecting the judges who interpret them, but also on shaping the support structure that defends and develops those rights in practice."[14]

Even though Charles Epp believes that rights revolutions can be learned, he is skeptical about the impact of support structures in civil-law systems where the role of precedent in the judicial system is very limited. I am more optimistic and strongly believe that Epp's conclusions are relevant in the context of Central European transitions.

True, common law is more open to experiments and change than a civil-law system where any novelty requires the permission of the central legislator. But the introduction of powerful constitutional courts, as well as the possibility for judges to use the constitution directly, have somewhat blurred the difference between statute-dominated civil-law systems and common law. Constitutional claims accessible to all citizens open the road for litigators. This road may be different and longer than in the common-law countries, but nevertheless it now exists. Moreover, decisions by constitutional courts have universal validity and thus are even stronger than common-law precedents. Access to European courts can also make up for any reluctance on the part of national courts. Rights to justice, to due process, and to a fair trial have already received strong support in the decisions of the court in Strasbourg, which has been open to the citizens of Central European states since their states joined the Council of Europe.

One important task is to overcome a cultural heritage that suggests revolutions, rebellion, strikes, demonstrations, and road blockades rather than the use of law in pursuit of social goals. Perhaps a new definition of civil society may also be needed—one that will no longer focus on a mere opposition to power but that will put more emphasis on the common interests of civic groups and on practical goals which can be reached not only by political but also by legal means. Perhaps a new theory of government, which would include non-governmental organizations in the very separation of powers, is called for.

It is well known that democracy, by itself, is insufficient to protect the rights and interests of individuals and minorities, particularly when they clash with the interests of the majority. Individual and minority rights are protected by constitutions. Constitutional rights are meaningless without the division of power. Whenever a claim is directed against the state, state officials should be removed from the final decision. This situation is guaranteed by the independence of the judiciary.[15]

What we have learned from experience is that access to the judiciary is the key to individual rights and to the legal protection of legitimate interests. An individual needs help in accessing the judiciary. As Epp's book shows, various social groups need resources and assistance in persuading the judiciary to apply constitutions and laws to the benefit of weak minorities and individuals. If an individual belonging to a socially vulnerable group has no other choice but to turn to such public officials as prosecutors or to the police for help to access the court against other public officials, we remain within the vicious circle of the state. It is therefore most desirable that an individual, in his or her pursuit of rights, should be supported by an organization that does not form a part of the state—for example a firm involved in law for the public interest, an advocacy NGO, or a legal-aid organization. Legal help, representation, and strategic litigation are as important to the existence of a constitutional democracy as freedom of speech, of association, and of assembly. They can become effective tools in East European civil society to the same extent as has happened in the West over the last fifty or so years. New constitutions open up such possibilities and constitutional theory can provide arguments for necessary state support for rights activism by non-governmental organizations.

It is unlikely that post-communist states will create and support such organizations. As in the West, the initial stage is left to private charity: the Council of Europe, European accession funds, and American private foundations are already planting seeds for the protection of rights through strategic litigation. Recently, they have replaced with a much more consistent effort the wave of Western constitutional advisors who took part in designing new constitutions. The movement is still young but is gaining momentum. It will speed up and generate local support when litigation brings its first results. I do believe that this movement will bring constitutions closer to the homes and lives of East Europeans.

6

In 1992 I took part in designing the law that was to define the way in which a new constitution should be prepared and adopted in Poland. I prepared my proposal on the basis of my knowledge of comparative constitutionalism, a subject I had taught at a number of renowned universities in many countries. I looked into the experiences of older democracies, as well as countries that have launched transition to constitutional democracy relatively recently, like Portugal or Spain.

I believed that the very process of constitution making should help bring about consensus within the elites, and between the elites and the people. Therefore, the constitution adopted by the parliament should be submitted for ratification by a national referendum. The ratification process itself should be difficult, long, and painstaking. Its purpose should be not merely the approval of the constitution, but primarily the constitutional education of the nation. Aware of the absence of a constitutional culture, I hoped that those drafting the new constitution would carry its ideas over to the people once the constitution had been agreed.

My reasoning and my conclusions were mistaken, and I have regretted many times what was left in the final law out of my original proposal. My 1992 ideas were naive, and my thorough education in comparative constitutionalism turned out to be of limited use. The idea that constitution making can be an educational process was vain and wrong. I looked at *The Federalist,* a primer on constitutionalism used in every course on the subject, and thought it to be as important a contribution to constitutionalism as the US Constitution itself. But this is how we see *The Federalist* two hundred years later, while during the ratification campaign it was as divisive as the constitution itself.

It was particularly naive to assume that politicians, once they had learned about constitutionalism themselves, would educate the people. Today, I am afraid that the majority of politicians, in any system, are hardly able to learn anything, and that they are virtually unable to teach anyone else. We should not therefore burden them with educational tasks.

Being a scholar, I believed that we should learn before acting. The lesson I learned is that practical skills—life skills and political skills alike—are learned in action rather than in theory. No nation has ever learned constitutionalism in theory, and a transition to constitutional culture may take place only when there is a constitution and when that constitution is used. If it is used against the people, there will be no constitutional culture. If it gives individuals and social groups tools that they can use for their own protection and benefit, successful transition to constitutional culture is only a matter of time.

Today, I still read constitutional treatises and teach constitutionalism. But I try to spend at least as much time helping non-governmental organizations to use constitutions in the pursuit of their own goals.

Notes

1 See Jon Elster (1993). "The Necessity and Impossibility of Simultaneous Economic and Political Reform". In *Constitutionalism and Democracy. Transitions in the Contemporary World*, ed. Douglas Greenberg, Stanley N. Katz, Melanie Beth Oliviero, and Steven C. Wheatley. Oxford University Press, pp. 267—274.

2 Jon Elster, Claus Offe, and Urlich C. Preuss, with Frank Bonker, Ulrike Goetting, and Friedbert W. Rueb (1998). *Institutional Design in Post-Communist Societies. Rebuilding the Ship at Sea.* Cambridge University Press.

3 In 1990, John Davis, the US ambassador to Poland, asked a new post-communist leader, Aleksander Kwasniewski, when his party would be able to return as a major force. "In twenty years", was the answer. Kwasniewski's party won the parliamentary elections in 1993, and in 1995 he was elected president.

4 Elster (1993), p. 271.

5 According to the law then in force, a decision by a local self-government which violated laws or the constitution could be nullified by the president of Poland. One of the many paradoxes of transition was that the ex-communist president, General Jaruzelski, did render the act invalid, and thus became the first protector of a vulnerable minority oppressed by the tyranny of a local majority in Poland.

6 Elster, Offe, and Preuss write that some provisions of the Bulgarian constitution were "directly inspired by the desire of former communists to protect themselves against criminal prosecution and demands for the restitution of property". Elster, Offe, and Preuss, p. 74.

7 Estonia adopted its new constitution in June 1992; Lithuania in October 1992; Kazakhstan in January 1993; Kyrgyzstan in May 1993; Russia in December 1993; and Belarus in March 1994.

8 András Sajó (1999). *Limiting Government. An Introduction to Constitutionalism.* Central European University Press, p. 2.

9 Idem, p. 13.

10 Elster, Offe, and Preuss, p. 33.

11 See Sajó, p. 21.

12 Charles R. Epp (1998). *The Rights Revolution. Lawyers, Activists, and Supreme Courts in Comparative Perspective*. The University of Chicago Press.

13 Idem, p. 202.

14 Idem, p. 205.

15 "Under constitutional law, rights bring the power of one branch of government to bear upon wrongdoers from other government agencies", write Stephen Holmes and Cass Sunstein in their recent book. "This is exactly what Montesquieu had in mind when he asserted that freedom can be protected only if power checks power." Stephen Holmes and Cass R. Sunstein (1999). *The Costs of Rights. Why Liberty Depends on Taxes*. W. W. Norton & Company, p. 55. Similarly, the 1789 French Declaration of the Rights of Man and of the Citizen stated, in article 16, that a society "in which the separation of powers is not defined, has no constitution."

11 *Affordable Shame**

ANDRÁS SAJÓ

I. What Is There to Be Ashamed Of: Blushing at the Holocaust

What should a society's proper moral attitude be toward genocide, if its majority previously victimized a group within the society? I will argue that it is both morally correct and useful in practice if the majority (and the whole country) feels shame,[1] discussing the problem in the context of the discrimination and extermination of Hungarian Jews during World War II. Hungarian authorities were active participants in the Holocaust, in Hungary. My proposition is that Hungarians and the Hungarian nation should feel ashamed of having participated in the persecution of Jews. This is a moral obligation on the part of the political community.

I take it as fact that the Hungarian state was responsible, in the strictly legal sense, for the racist discrimination against, and the persecution and extermination of, the majority of Hungarian Jews. The death toll was roughly 600,000. Beginning in 1920, the Hungarian parliament enacted a series of laws restricting the rights of Jews. An overwhelming majority of parliamentarians adopted these laws, without foreign pressure, meeting with very little public resistance or criticism. In 1944, Jews were deported upon the lawful order of government officials acting within

* I am grateful to Renáta Uitz for her assistance in preparing this essay.

their jurisdiction and competence. (State authorities carrying out such orders often acted with excessive brutality.) Even the 1944 decisions to deport Jews to Germany for extermination and forced labor cannot be explained by irresistible German pressure.[2]

There is a special problem with the moral obligation of shame for the Holocaust. The obligation is understood here as a kind of *collective* moral obligation, which is satisfied by institutional and collective action. Most moral theories posit the autonomy of the individual's conscience, and I have no reason to consider them otherwise. In applying this approach, a community or group cannot be a moral entity and cannot be the subject of moral obligations. Hence the above assumption regarding the moral obligation of the collective makes sense only as shorthand. This means that all members of a community must have the obligation *specifically because of their belonging to the community.*[3] Morality remains a matter of individuality, even if the source of the moral obligation resides in community membership.

There is a second preliminary objection regarding shame as a moral obligation stemming from the Holocaust. Is it meaningful to speak of shame as part of the collective consciousness? After all, shame is a psychological category. Is it permissible to treat a moral emotion as a feature of collective consciousness? Silvan Tomkins emphasizes that shame has its own physiological foundations (blush). Although collective bodies are not organic, collective representations are capable of inducing individual emotions. Shame in the collective consciousness stands for collective representations capable of inducing shame in the individual. Closely related to this meaning, collective representations personify the community and may attribute moral emotions to it.

Many psychologists agree with Broucek, who claims that shame is felt if someone is exposed. This understanding of shame is found as well in moral philosophy. Gabriele Taylor relates shame to those aspects of the self that "do not fit the sort of person" one thinks one ought to be. "Revelation of this position...will cause him to experience shame."[4]

One feels shame if a hidden or disguised feature or trait of the self becomes visible to others. The individual is seen as being something different from what he or she intended to expose. In the context of genocide-related shame, the members of the community are revealed as persecutors of Jews. We argue that even those members should, and indeed psychologically may, feel shame, who actually have (or had) nothing to do with the persecution. Indeed the high morality of many Hungarians is related exactly to their individual feelings of shame in the face of the persecution. This attitude is even more remarkable as their emotion of shame occurs and is expressed in a community that fails to share, or is hostile to, moral sentiment.

It may well be that revealing what the observers believe to be shameful is not shameful for the actual actors, in our case the persecutors of Jews. Indeed, the amorality of those who participated in genocide is partly the result of their lack of shame. At this point they may cease to be moral beings. A soldier who executed Jews on the order of his commander may feel shame or even guilt. He has probably committed a crime but remains a moral being. The torturers managed to find their crimes completely normal. The readiness to murder Jews might have been grounds for shame for Hungarian fascists before the Arrow Cross Party took power; but it became a deliberately accepted characteristic for anti-Semites at the moment when they had been engaged in hunting Jews. For the anti-Semite there was nothing morally wrong with massacring Jews. If a murderous racist is exposed as such, he will not feel shame for this predilection. A community of such racists is neither a moral nor a decent society.

Members of the community (the citizenry), whose earlier members were exposed as being involved in genocide and discrimination, should feel shame for the misdeeds of their forefathers. Otherwise, the community will seemingly identify itself with the earlier generation of murderers. Those who look at past genocidal actions as acts exposing a profoundly negative trait of a society do not need Holocaust victims and survivors in order to feel shame for living in the community of the exposed. With the presence of Jews among the population, or with their ghosts in the minds of the morally sensible members of the community, the conditions for feeling shame are given at the national level. Exposure is perpetuated and, therefore, the precondition for shame is present. Of course, it is possible that the majority continues to agree with the persecution; hence there is no shame. The shameless society, in this case, is amoral.

Holocaust survivors are actual victims; and contemporary Hungarian Jews are potential victims. Both groups qualify as victims, by being persecuted or respectively endangered under the original criteria. In their eyes, the others (the nation, the society, the community), as a group, are historically exposed as perpetrators of crime. This perspective might be shared by large numbers of morally sensitive people. As long as the community does not feel and, more importantly, does not *express* shame, both through the acts of its individual members and as a collective, the shameful conditions persist. Expressions of shame may/should include begging for reconciliation and leniency through legislation; at a minimum, some symbolic compensation to victims; and spontaneous local action to restore and maintain abandoned Jewish cemeteries at the community's, or an individual's, expense.

The absence of shame must be interpreted in the context of historical experience. It is not enough that victims and potential victims perceive today that the majority of the population shows no sign of outrage when confronted with racism. The growing visibility of recurrent anti-Semitic atrocities in Hungary is reinforced by the insufficiency of *collective* responses to such actions. The lack of any firm collective and governmental condemnation of, and sanctions against, racism, allows anti-Semitism to become increasingly and openly admissible.

In the absence of condemnation anti-Semitism is normalized. In an earlier time, men and women blushed when confronted with obscene language. Likewise, one might blush, or at least feel embarrassment, when one overheard anti-Semitic statements on the subway. Lack of shame for the Holocaust leaves very few people blushing. The normalization of racism goes even further. Disclosed anti-Semitism is not a reason for shame. Moreover, it is less and less a view to hide. The majority and the institutions of the community are not ashamed even of the fact that such shameful openness is possible at all. Of course, the more common and normalized anti-Semitism becomes, the less shameful it is in the prevailing socio-psychological context.

Week after week, year after year, the mob praises pogroms at soccer games. *The Protocols of the Elders of Zion* and other officially banned publications are on the shelves of bookstores. Jews and non-Jews request state intervention, so far largely in vain. Requests for special official concern are met with surprise and little understanding. As to breaking the image of continuity, the deputy prime minister stated that it was time to discuss the *Judenfrage*, in order to "clarify the situation of the Jews". He was incapable of grasping what was wrong with his statement, even after repeated criticism. Ironically, the leader of the extreme right-wing (pseudo-opposition) parliamentary faction claimed that allegations of anti-Semitism in Hungary were simply part of a campaign to discredit Hungary abroad.

Anti-Semitism has become accepted as one of many views, although racist political remarks are rare. Circumlocution remains the language of political anti-Semitism. Open racism would antagonize potential victims too much. The government avoids radicalism as it can easily spin out of control, or at least it would result in embarrassment to the government in the international arena. If there is anti-Semitism in Poland it is directed against a nonexistent community. In Hungary, anti-Jewish sentiment is palpable; yet it is vehemently denied.

The government's official position makes clear that it does not share the above sentiments (or sensibilities, according to some). The problem—according to the government—is only a product of excessive Jewish sensitivity. In a more conciliatory tone this is referred to as the understandable ultra-sensitivity of the Jews. In any case, the accusation that Hungarian society is anti-Semitic is unfounded, and this is documented by public-opinion surveys. As a result, there is nothing to expose; hence there is no place for shame. But the issue is not whether there is anti-Semitism. We are talking about shame. The issue, here, is the moral obligation of shame. The absence of shame reinforces anti-Jewish patterns (and racism in practice), especially where structured, traditional anti-Semitic prejudice exists. Fear of persecution may be reinforced without encouraging racism directly.

II. The Moral Foundations of Shame: Guilt

What are the moral foundations of the claim that the Hungarian public consciousness should contain shame for the persecution and overwhelming extermination of Hungarian Jews? Shame is felt for the deportation of Gypsies and for the level of collaboration with, or lack of resistance to, Soviet rule.[5] The claim to social shame might be justified (1) as settlement for injustice to victims, or (2) in terms of social decency. The victims' claim is based on corrective (restorative) justice. Some currently prevailing intellectual trends of sensitivity and equality lend special support to the justice claim. The social-decency argument is based on moral claims of the community. Here, the members of the community feel they have an obligation to themselves to remedy injustice. The need to undo injustice is related to the actors' dignity. The individual has an obligation to him- or herself. Or, at least, shame is to be felt if people would like to live in what Avishai Margalit calls a decent society.

II.1 The victims' claim

I begin with the victims' claim to justice, as this is the politically sensitive and prevailing approach with practical implications. To what extent do Jews living in Hungary (as well as those who suffered injustice as Jews in Hungary and those citizens who identify themselves with the sufferings of the victims[6]) have a claim vis-à-vis contemporary Hungarian society and its institutions? After all, the majority of Hungarian Jews living today were never subject to persecution, and with every passing day their relationship to actual victims is increasingly more remote and abstract. For the majority of Jews, historical injustice is fading into nothing more than mere statistics on victims. They may know relatives "who were there". Owing to the desire to assimilate and the need for Jewish self-protection, their experiences were seldom discussed within their families. "Fourteen uncles and aunts of mine were gassed." This is the standard expression of their relationship to the Holocaust. Turning victims into statistics is the ultimate cruelty of a history whose first chapter was written by the Nazis.

The problem with the outraged rejection of accusations of anti-Semitism (as demonstrated by leaders of extreme-right parties in Hungary and France) is that the silence concerning the Holocaust is not surrounded by shame. (Of course, shame-dictated openness would be convincing evidence.) For potential victims, it is an unconvincing argument that there is nothing to expose and thus no grounds for shame. In the authentic historical context—given the Holocaust as it truly happened—the absence of shame cannot be interpreted as a genuine and credible sign of a clear conscience. Here, silence is interpreted in the context of the unfinished business of restoration and reparative justice. Even retaliation was carried out rather capriciously and against only a few. In 1945–46, verdicts were reached hastily as acts of political justice. The court proceedings followed the worst traditions of Hungarian political justice as administered in the pre–1945 authoritarian regime. In the felony cases of the various Hungarian prime ministers, the presidents of the panels acted as if they were prosecutors; the defense counsels' rights were restricted (for neither good nor pragmatic reasons). To the extent that legal retaliation was initiated by the Soviets and their communist puppets, the entire administration of justice lost its sincerity and authenticity.

Anti-Semitism, to be sure, was strictly prohibited in communist times. A repetition of the persecution of Jews was firmly rejected. But the prohibition itself was without authenticity, again, as far as public opinion was concerned, as there was no public opinion. The rejection of anti-Semitism was not a genuine act of the community's consciousness. Moreover, anti-Semitism was neither less nor more prohibited than any other independent view; hence the recurrence of persecution was not authentically rejected. There was nothing in the system that would have recognized Jews in their Jewish capacity—quite the contrary.

Do (potential) victims have special grounds for the above mistrustful interpretation of silence and lack of shame? On what compelling moral grounds should the victims' expectation of shame be granted? Is it reasonable for the generation of descendants to address the snow of yesteryears? The past cannot be changed, but its recollection can be. This is crucial for the way the past is continued. It is indeed a feature of the community that it acts along the patterns of its own past. This is the community where the descendants of Holocaust victims live. If certain patterns of the past are repeated they will be in great trouble. This past is not a straitjacket, however; and history is not fate. The past can be the subject of collective reorganization, for better or for worse. Shame may act as a catalyst in this process. The individual living in a historically determined society lives along patterns and meanings that historically constitute society. The past is responsible for the life of the individual. Life plans include plans regarding descendants. Past life plans are lived by future generations. Hungarians participating in, or accepting, racial discrimination planned for their descendants a Hungary free of Jews. Today, Jews live in this partially successful life plan. Further, the present life of the individual and his or her future lies in the past of the community, or, better put, in forward-looking visions of that past. Past events have moral content for the present, to the extent that the present was shaped by this past.[7]

A perverse pastime of the survivors and concerned victims (including other potential victims) is to search the present for analogies and signs of the Holocaust. It is a perversion of our times that concern is interpreted as perversion. After all, in light of neurophysiology, this is a rational strategy to the extent that memory is nothing but the search for consistency. It is perverse, too, that rationality leads to perversion. If a person's concern is the repetition of the Holocaust, he or she should look for patterns of Holocaust preparation. The brain constructs consistency; therefore, the occurrence of events leading to the Holocaust are construed as the actual preparation of a new holocaust. Anti-Semitic slogans were often chanted in 1944 and the authorities could not have cared less. If similar songs go unprosecuted in 2000, for the mind construing consistency this means the repetition of the Holocaust.

I am not arguing that the repetition of the Holocaust is a realistic assumption in the current Hungarian and international situation (although one cannot rule out lesser atrocities). I am arguing, however, that given the history of the Holocaust and the lack of its proper treatment, and given certain similarities between 1938 (the year before the First [anti-] Jew Act)[8] and our times at the level of visible public (community-based) attitudes, the historically impregnated mind cannot disregard the similarities and the consequences.[9] I am also arguing that one could easily erase such similarities with public and governmental acts dictated by, and expressing, shame. István Bibó, in his second classic study on the Jewish problem (1949),[10] offers a whole typology of Jewish attitudes to the environment. Some of these attitudes are based on suspicion. Bibó found these attitudes dehumanized because they are based on suffering.

He explained that once such deformed attitudes prevail they become permanent in the interrelation with anti-Semitism.

II.2 Structural victims

Victims' claims are part of a broader contemporary argument. Cultures of complaint have become popular, and even irresistible, in affluent Western societies. Culture has become narcissistic and, therefore, feminine. This is partly due to the demise of the masculine heroism of World War II and the emergence of a troubled conscience among citizens of former colonizing countries. The change in public mood has created an opportunity for victims. With pictures of horror coming from Auschwitz *ad nauseam*, the moral supremacy of victim-martyrs has become difficult to resist. At least victims have been liberated from the stigma of being losers.

While the discrediting of masculine heroism created the proper intellectual atmosphere, the culture of complaint owes its political success to the advance of democracy and democratic egalitarianism. Interest assertion increases the chances of single-agenda victim groups in egalitarian-democratic regimes. It is much less risky, and it is more legitimate, to organize around victimization in a more sensitive social and political environment. To a considerable extent welfare states legitimize themselves by providing services and aid to their system's victims. During the Cold War, ideological warfare emphasized that the superpowers felt sympathy for the victims of the other's system. This explains the interest in one's own victims, as is clearly exemplified by the *amicus* briefs and secret memos of the US State Department during the desegregation cases. In our age, past suffering becomes the founding justification of new constitutional regimes. The preamble to the Constitution of South Africa provides the following: "We, the people of South Africa, recognize the injustices of our past; honor those who suffered for justice and freedom in our land..."

Victims' rights pervade international relations. In our international system, which finds pleasure in calling itself global, sympathy toward victims—and their rescue—has become a new legitimization for international intervention. Its limited and ambiguous status is exemplified in Somalia and Kosovo. In a post-colonial world, interventionism and penetration cannot be justified by any self-declared "*mission civilisatrice*" as it was in the first half of the twentieth century. The intervention must serve the protection of victims.

Eastern Europe jumped very late onto the victim bandwagon. Genocide victims could not voice their complaints under communism because this was a genuine initiative of those concerned and not the product of a Communist Party central-committee decision. Victim status could not be accepted as a source of rights before the collapse of communism.

After the collapse, public concern for victims was partly genuine. After all, the delegitimation of communism required proof of the injustice of communism, and victims of communism fit well into this picture. But this public interest—as the lack of any serious compensation in Russia proves—faded quickly, and most victim movements were and are simple and faded copies of their Western counterparts. The absence of genuine, homegrown victim patterns contributes to the disheartening landscape of victims' rights, where self-declared representatives are elbowing their way to the limelight and collecting benefits. Even worse, the increased sensitivity to victims was not the result of any long-held self-assertion. The public did not grow into the habit of increased sensitivity to victims' causes; thus victims' claims meet less favorable reactions. People in Eastern Europe have not yet learned to cope with victim issues.

Increasingly sophisticated victim groups often compete against one another for compensation or for other advantageous social positions in the West as well as in Eastern Europe. But in most societies, at least at the time of the victims' revolution (why not another one?), the groups tacitly agreed not to challenge each other's victim status so as not to undermine the legitimacy and hence the success of victim movements.

Under the circumstances of partial self-liberation after communism, and partly because of international interaction, many among the Hungarian Jews decided to come out and stop looking with shame at their victim status. Some of them have self-consciously opted to play on their victim status in their interest representation. Of course, they had to accept that they would compete with other victim groups.[11] Ironically they must compete among those who were involved in the extermination of Jews. Hungarian Jews had to live for the day when they became players in a revisionist quiz, competing for compensation, among others, against the members of the gendarmerie, who held the lion's share of the responsibility for the deportations.

Victim interest groups, of course, are no better than their social environment. Suffering at an earlier stage does not guarantee moral improvement. Selfish self-interest, myth making, and internal oppression within the victim groups are also part of this history. These unpleasant features do not delegitimize victims' moral claims to justice. Victim groups, like the Hungarian Jews, were subjected to extreme, unheard of, obvious, and undeniable injustice,[12] the sole reason being that they belonged to a so-called race. Such injustice triggers restitutive, restorative, and compensatory justice. The case of Hungarian Jews (like that of a few similar genocides) is made compelling by the full-scale involvement of their state in the persecution. Moreover, the authorities violated their own preexisting moral and legal norms.

To the extent that victims' claims fit into restorative justice, the claims correspond with an emerging contemporary socio-legal paradigm, which combines restoration as justice with equality/equalization. The new paradigm is exemplified in numerous judicial decisions around the world. The Canadian Supreme Court, expressly followed by the South African Constitutional Court, concluded that historically created disadvantages, consisting in the deprivation of fundamental human needs, create the likelihood of continued discrimination.[13] Hence, such traditionally discriminated groups are to be provided special protection in order to enable them to participate fully in social life.

The human need disregarded by genocide is the most fundamental one: *the security of life and existence*. Due to the already mentioned mechanisms of construing consistency, when authorities tolerate racist attacks this gesture immediately reminds potential victims of the earlier deprivation of security. The Hungarian rules of compensation for persecution discriminate against Jews. When the Hungarian Constitutional Court found these measures of compensation reasonable, the Hungarian Jews were reminded once again of the earlier existential menace. This is not an instance of excessive sensitivity on the part of the victims. Recall the reasoning of the Canadian Supreme Court, which concluded that victims were historically deprived of a fundamental need and then concluded that this results in structural, lasting injustice. The legislation and court of any decent society should also comprehend that need.

The survivors of genocide and their descendants (and as a rule all communities surviving the genocide) have become *structural victims*. The victim status of survivors is reproduced by the existing social and psychological structures, which originate in the historical moment and the aftermath of the genocide. Without special measures, the disadvantageous social position of the victimized will persist. The collective victim status of a given moment creates special social relations and psychological predispositions on both sides, resulting in inherited poverty or health conditions.

Restitutive justice dictates, at least, the compensation of victims. Injustice is aggravated if a perpetrator continues to enjoy the advantages of his unjust act. The victim should be brought into a situation as if the injustice had not occurred. In addition, retributive justice is generally interpreted as a form of proportionate punishment. Corrective justice, as translated into the theory of punishment, operates on the basis of individual responsibility and punishment. Victims' claims tend to disregard these features. Individual responsibility is extended, and its borderlines are diluted. Hence the preconditions of individual responsibility are undermined. This makes claims of punishment difficult to satisfy. Victims' claims are intellectual parasites of the concept of corrective justice. Their claims do not fully meet the traditional requirements of justice, as justice is a concept that takes interpersonal relations into consideration. It should be noted that the extension, and the problems related to it, inevitably follow from the fact that the injustice is committed, in essence, by the state, and that individual injustice is only secondary.

Individualized responsibility cannot satisfy the claims of structural victims. It does not follow that individualized punishment does not satisfy the needs of justice. Lack of punishment for genocide increases the sense of abandonment among survivors. Claims to restoration are also hard to meet in a system of individual responsibility and rights, although there might be identifiable groups that collectively (structurally) continue to benefit from the past injustice. This is the case when a group's assets are confiscated and distributed among the members of another group, or if the second group collectively shares the benefits of the booty. The land and houses of the *Sudetendeutschen* were distributed exclusively among Czechs. For practical reasons, and for the sake of social peace, the diffuse claims of structural victims can be satisfied only at the level of a virtual victim group. Of course, the more intact and identifiable the victim group is, as is the case of the Maori, who continued to live together as a community after they were dispossessed of their land, the more specific their compensation or restoration might be. On the other hand, potentially accountable beneficiaries of past injustice cannot be identified and grouped with sufficient certainty. This diffuseness limits the chances for restoration and contributes to injustice. The broader the circle of victims (in regard to the actual sufferers of the primary injustice, e.g., the Holocaust or slavery), the more diffuse the group of those to be held accountable, the more time that has elapsed since the injustice occurred, and the more collective the attempt on both sides to restore justice, the more uncertain are the means of rendering justice. It is exactly among these conditions of uncertainty and danger of additional injustice that shame in the public consciousness might play an important instrumental role. Shame does not necessitate singling out individuals. It is cheap, as it does not require burdensome or alienating efforts from the individual. Nor does it endanger social peace.

II.3 The responsibility of the "innocent generation"

It is often stated that the present generations cannot be held responsible for the past. This position is as comfortable as it is immoral. Moral positions, of course, often tend to be uncomfortable. Who cares about morality, especially if it is something different than the foggy motto of Christian morality? "Morals are hypocrisy" is the slogan of the technicians of power, who honestly misunderstand Nietzsche. They seem to forget that morality today has become of pragmatic importance even for the power technicians. Welfare and extended democracy made it affordable in the uni-polar world to grant a limited, pragmatic role to morality. The disregarding of the moral sensitivities of democratic public opinion may result in self-isolation. A country that excludes itself from the world causes itself harm. Moreover, a total abandonment of morality undermines the very power of the dominant immoral group, as they must rule without the help of moral legitimation.

The objection to the above claim is that victims' claims are addressed to the members of contemporary society, to people who might not have even lived when the persecution occurred. Those who are not responsible for the past may still be responsible for the present as the continuation of the past, as part of the past. In more pragmatic terms, individuals do have a special responsibility for preventing the repetition of the past. The duty of care is that of potentially responsible beings. The more the past is present, the more likely it will repeat itself in the future. It is quite reasonable, therefore, that potential victims feel actual menace or even emotional distress with regard to that possibility of events. A reasonable expectation of humiliation is reasonable grounds for distress, hence the responsibility to prevent repetition. In order to determine present responsibility, original responsibility must be determined as precisely as possible, particularly as it relates to the state and to non-governmental institutions (e.g., churches). Original responsibility is a function of the original sin and the result of guilt. The sin can be assessed by determining the extent of suffering and the moral relation to it (initiation, actual murder, complicity, tacit support, and the like) at the time of its commitment.[14]

Anti-Semitism remains popular, and this is by no means attenuated by the discovery that xenophobia and anti-Gypsy sentiments are stronger (or, at least, that they are being disclosed more openly). It is not surprising that the feeling of recurrence and of the potential for repetition is not fading, given the absence of any clear-cut resolution of a certain kind of murderous history. The sense of continuity sealing the walls of silence results not only from the above mentioned discriminations in compensation.

The potential victims are bound to remain in their victim status and hence retain their victim attitudes and reactions, which further increase victimization. To break the vicious circle, the government should unequivocally, systematically, and continuously reject the possibility of a repetition of the Holocaust. In order to satisfy the needs of restorative justice, the structural elements that prepared the Holocaust or that resemble them should be clearly rejected. This is the state's special obligation to Jews. One may disagree with the strictly punitive and interventionist German attitude, but the moral foundations identified by the German authorities for such active prevention are applicable in Hungary, too. The Hungarian authorities (like any post-genocide government) should be reminded of what the German Supreme Court wrote about these duties:

> The historical fact itself, that human beings were singled out according to the criteria of the so-called Nuremberg laws and robbed of their individuality for the purpose of extermination, puts Jews living in the Federal Republic in a special, personal relationship vis-à-vis their fellow citizens; what happened [then] is also present in this relationship today. It is part of their personal self-perception to be understood as part of a group of people who stand out by virtue of their fate and in relation to whom there is a special moral responsibility on the part of all others, and that this is part of their dignity. Respect for this self-perception, for each individual, is one of the guarantees against repetition of this kind of discrimination and forms a basic condition of their lives in the Federal Republic. Whoever seeks to deny these events denies vis-à-vis each individual the personal worth of [Jewish persons]. For the person concerned, this is continuing discrimination against the group to which he belongs and, as part of the group, against him. [15]

It is simply wrong to assert that Hungary has less to do with the Holocaust than Germany, that the perpetration of genocide by the country should play a lesser role in Hungarian consciousness than in Germany. This is true irrespective of the impact of Hitler on the actual fate of Hungarian Jews floating in the Danube, gassed at Auschwitz, or beaten to death by Hungarian troops near the Russian front line. That Hungary needed a Hitler for its genocide only exposes how limited the small European nations were in fulfilling their history and mission on their own. The genocide in Rwanda is perhaps (hopefully) the last instance of self-determination of people living in relative isolation. But even in the Rwandan case the owners of the machetes needed the encouragement of the cynical idleness of the French and Belgian governments.

Indifference to the past is more than mere moral debasement; it excludes the possibility of morality and moral discourse. Where there is simply no chance for shame and shaming—as such emotions are seen as irrational and irrelevant—and morals are superfluous, it is not surprising that countries such as Hungary are leading in racism and xenophobia in Europe.

In Hungary, as in most East European countries, public reflection on past crimes is not part of discussions shaping national identity. Reference has been made already to the hasty and compromised nature of postwar justice. Jews were not fully compensated; their property was not restored. All that was secondary, as most of them were murdered and the survivors lived on with lasting mental and physical sufferings. Not only was that injustice not undone, but also, with the quick advent of communism, even the possibility of any justice became illusory. History froze once again in lies. Generations grew up without understanding their intimate relation to history. The latest generations may have learned only delusions of grandeur from the doctored pages of what is offered to them as history. History is perceived as a continuum of events sealed for good and, therefore, devoid of relevant problems. Indifference to history is believed to be a pragmatic-rational handling of the past. After all, as history (in all East European nations) is full of so many tragic victims there is no other way to handle them except through oblivion.

A modestly voiced but morally strong claim from Hungarian Jews now confronts this prevailing attitude. Although there are many claims by many victims the Jewish claim still towers above them. By its mere magnitude, the overwhelming tragedy of the Hungarian Jews dominates the public perception of persecution. This does not diminish the suffering and dignity of others who were persecuted. It neither denies their sufferings nor diminishes them. But one should not hesitate to assert that the magnitude of the Holocaust and the direct participation of the Hungarian state in the persecution will, and should, determine the priorities of social consciousness in our time. Therefore, if Jewish justice claims are disregarded, any other compensation aimed at rendering justice to other victim groups will remain problematic and immoral.

Once again, it is the Hungarian Jews whose overwhelming majority was annihilated. It was the Hungarian Jewry that was objectively incapacitated in reorganizing its communities, distorting the collective mentality of Jews for fifty years after the Holocaust. The point of reference of Hungarian–Jewish identity remains the Holocaust. The "Jewish mentality" is fixed and constantly struggling with the possible recurrence of persecution. Hungarian–Jewish identity remains crippled and schizophrenic. While the Jews were persecuted by their compatriots in violation of the prevailing and known norms of the twentieth century, István Nemeskürthy, a conservative historian, assumes that 80 percent of the population found the discrimination against the Jews "natural" in the 1940s. Jews have witnessed little public or official systematic condemnation of that attitude. To find the community responsible for, or associated with, the genocide is different from ex post condemnation of murders. Announcing that what was done to Jews was outrageous is unsatisfactory. It must be made clear who committed the crime. However, as István Bibó demonstrated, Hungarian public reactions to the Holocaust did not go beyond the mere condemnation of anti-Semitism. The idea that the Hungarian people might be responsible or should assume responsibility was rejected as self-debasement. When an unofficial assembly of pastors asked the Jews for forgiveness in 1945 this was rejected by "a very noticeable" irritation.[16] Has anything changed?

In 1995 the Constitutional Court said that after the transition the democratic Hungarian state is under no obligation to compensate victims for personal injuries caused by the conduct of state officials in previous regimes. Compensation for personal injuries, loss of life, and suffering is based mostly on an *ex gratia* gesture of the democratic government.[17] This official denial of continuity in terms of state responsibility is especially bothersome, as in other regards legal continuity is the core concept of the self-legitimation of the new, democratic regime. The Hungarian state missed another crucial opportunity to clarify its position vis-à-vis the murders committed with its assistance a few decades ago.

Crimes without perpetrators remain unsolved mysteries. The community and its institutions should openly admit complicity, institutionalize shame, and ask honestly for forgiveness. Repentance is a different story. This is not a matter of nuances. It is quite telling that Pope John Paul II, who laudably asked for forgiveness for the crimes committed against Jews, admitted only the sins of the sons and daughters of the church. The church itself remained beyond the reach of repentance—preserving continued discontent and suspicion.

III. Shame in a Decent Society

We now turn to the second ground of the moral obligation of shame for genocide. Here the justice claims of victims become immaterial. Now the concern is that all members of society become moral beings or at least live in a decent society. Lack of shame for the earlier denial of the human dignity of Jews amounts to actual denial of their dignity. It is highly unlikely that one can remain a person with, or worth, dignity, if one denies the dignity of other beings or of whole (race-based) classes.

The conditions for a decent society cannot be met without the condemnation of the Holocaust by the majority and by the state. Condemnation is authentic if it is accompanied by the moral sentiment (emotion) of shame. Decency is not satisfied when social institutions force members of a legitimate social group to feel ashamed and live in fear just for having a given legitimate personal identity.[18] Hungarian society is not a decent one so long as Jews are forced to feel humiliation because of their Jewish identity, because the Holocaust happened and could happen again.

Why should Hungarians feel shame about the Holocaust if they want to be moral beings? Obviously, most Hungarians living today had nothing to do with the persecutions. They were born innocent. But as the Holocaust was not adequately stigmatized and justice was rendered improperly, the moral obligations continue to exist and have been inherited by the new generations. Someone must undertake the moral task of cleaning the residue of past brutalities. Current generations must make it clear they are not following the bad traditions of their ancestors, that they refuse identity with the society and state that committed or assisted genocide. Virginity of the mind can be lost by omission. The innocence of the late born is unsustainable as it is insufficient to create trust under an unsettled score of the past. Those who claim the benefits of innocence should recall that their collective identity is determined by collective memory. The claimants of innocence create their identity selectively. The selection of historical memories is a moral act, a matter of moral responsibility. "But remembrance in this sense is equally important to communities—families, tribes, nations, parties—that is, to human entities that exist often for much longer than individual men and women. To neglect the historical record is to do violence to this identity and thus to the community that it sustains. And since communities help generate a deeper sense of identity for the individuals they comprise, neglecting or expunging the historical record is a way of undermining and insulting individuals as well."[19]

Such insulting neglect of the historical record can be prevented by collective shame. This moral emotion dictates tact and sensitivity. Collective shame, once institutionalized, will quickly make the potential victims feel secure and integrated. It would also improve the moral qualities of Hungarian society by opening up a learning process. It is only through collective learning that the past can be intellectually processed and neutralized. Shame—even collective shaming—is not humiliating. Rather, shame for genocide—mere recognition in the collective consciousness—enables people to recognize themselves as moral beings. Shame is relevant for Jewish moral rehabilitation, and it is crucial for the Hungarian nation as a community of moral beings (agents). Shame is indispensable for the moral rehabilitation of the society.

Every society is a historical community: its relation to history structures the community. The collective consciousness of moral agents should address shameful events as shameful: they should handle it. Disregard or whitewashing of shameful events is a lie, and dismissing lies is not conducive to morality.

A paper on the incomplete handling of past genocides and current racism cannot avoid some variations on Emerson. An indifference to history brings us closer to suffering again the same history, or at least its variation. There are many countries that would be better off without repeating their infamous and cruel histories. Their repetition would make suffer even those who otherwise are the victors of history. Accepting shame means taking responsibility for past crimes committed by the state and other social institutions. Such a responsibility dictates that a society must dispose of the falsifications present in its history. When a society ignores this responsibility, falsified patterns of behavior determine the shaping of its future. The falsified (assumed) scheme of earlier events will shape the future.

Indifference to the past is a well-known recipe for future repetition. In addition, selective historical memory aids in consolidating the position of the victors (in this case that of the "victors" of genocide). It contributes in building (or maintaining) false self-confidence. If historical injustice is not visible, it never occurred. Hence there is no need to restore justice. Living in a lie makes moral action difficult. The late born cannot hope for happy innocence as there is no innocence in self-imposed ignorance. Those who refuse to face genocide contribute to preserving the sense of continuity with the inheritance of the persecutors. Those who claim to be innocent refuse to take a stand in this matter and fail to reject revisionists.

Oblivion with respect to genocide denies the grounds of self-confidence and pride as it does not allow for all the individual heroism of saving the lives of the persecuted. Of course, the heroes created additional problems.[20]

IV. The Good Works of Shame

We concluded that, given the difficulties with other forms of responsibility, shame is the proper contemporary reaction to the Holocaust in countries where the past has not yet been adequately treated. Shame, as defined above, is the emotion generated by exposure. Denial of shame implies there is nothing to be exposed. Shame prevents identification with what one feels ashamed about. Where negation, silence, and indifference surround genocide in a community, its members and past members are left with nothing to prevent identification with, and repetition of, evil. This identification is facilitated by the shameless position that declares its lack of interest in an unpleasant past.

Noticing the violation of the moral code triggers shame. "Feeling ashamed" has been related to the persecutors, at least for being part of the community and being unable to halt or to prevent them.

What would shame dictate under the circumstances? Of course, shame does not dictate positive or compelling solutions, only tact and honesty. Standard legal solutions of individualized justice cannot apply where victims and those seeking some kind of compensation cannot be identified with sufficient certainty.

Personally, as a closet First Amendment liberal, I find little sympathy with turning anti-Semitic rubbish into pulp as an official policy. A ban on Nazi commemorative meetings or the imprisonment of football hooligans for incitement is not an adequate policy for breaking with continuity. Shame dictates different, less authoritarian, behavior. Decent people simply do not buy the *Protocols* (certainly not under the circumstances). Moreover, decent people boycott bookstores where such rubbish is available. The state should not subsidize publishers of Keats if they happen to publish *Mein Kampf.* Decent people avoid interesting soccer games where the mob urges fast trains to leave for Auschwitz. Television producers and program directors should refuse to consider the broadcast of such games as a matter of principle; networks should not be interested in their broadcast regardless of the audience rating. Decent people should not subsidize teams with racist fans. If I were the club management I would never allow such mobs in the stadium. If I were a player at a game where racist slurs were heard all the time, I would not kick the ball.

Assuming a weak responsibility for a historical sin requires modest courage, but "without courage, there cannot be truth, and without truth there can be no other virtue" (Wavell, Viceroy's Journal). This attitude of moral bravery does not demand serious sacrificial efforts. It requests only a psychologically and socially manageable and, therefore, affordable shame.

The original sin of the Holocaust is different from the additional injustice of the recent compensation laws. This recent and actually effective injustice requires a more demanding material remedy. Shame in the current Hungarian situation would be insufficient to resolve the injustice of past genocide and current racism. Discrimination in the current compensation and rampant racism require special governmental and societal action. Hungarian legislation, supported by the Constitutional Court, concluded that it was enough to pay about 98 percent less to relatives of other groups of Hungarians murdered by the state.[21] These Jews were murdered with the active complicity of the Hungarian authorities, while most of the other victims passed away in Russian camps as prisoners of war. Not only is shame not working here, but the solution itself is a source of additional national shame.

This lack of governmental sensitivity is even more blatant as it violates not only victims' justice-based rights but equality, too. Adding insult to injury, once again the equal dignity of citizens was disregarded in the compensation legislation. It is difficult to resist the drift of continuity where freely elected representatives of the nation repeat an injustice by casting their votes for discrimination. Shame would have been able to break this continuity. This is not what happened. Instead, members of the government mumble about *Judenfrage* and the need to extricate oneself, as if on a Freudian couch, from the Jewish issue.

All this exhibits a lack of sensitivity—at best. The society is silent. In the best case this silence reflects a lack of interest and understanding. In the worst it denotes casual agreement.

The prime minister, who offered 98 percent less compensation, might have admitted that a fully equal compensation would have been just but impossible in fiscal terms due to inflation, a lack of funds for orphanages, or whatever—he should know. He should have suggested still a higher amount, one that required a certain minimal sacrifice from all members of the society. This nominal effort—perhaps ten fewer bottles of beer per person annually—he would continue, was to express the need for compensation with an official and collective act. He would also emphasize on behalf of the community that he felt shame that the country and its economy could not afford more *at the moment*. In other words, imperfect and unequal compensation is not the norm; it is abnormal. Better years might yield better opportunities for compensation and the like.

Once again, and apart from the special story of the current discriminatory legislative compensation (see *supra*) very little specific action or actual claim is dictated by the Holocaust. Expectations of shame dictate symbolic actions (like, at least, a formal attempt to find the living perpetrators of genocide). Symbols, if applied honestly, are sufficient to break the image of continuity. The simplest act of discontinuity is simply the institutionalized expression of shame both at the governmental (public) level and in social action. Shame should be made part of official politics. As Christopher Lasch would put it, where society is the patient, politics and therapy are indistinguishable. Official statements (not only at small-scale Holocaust memorials but also at every national holiday) time and again should emphasize the collective shame of society that its ancestors participated in what should never ever have happened. Further, shame should be expressed for being so late with such admissions. The story of the Holocaust should be a key component of public and private education. A few recent, tentative steps point in this direction. So far, no large-scale non-governmental initiatives have followed.

IV.1 Why is it so difficult to inculcate collective shame into the collective consciousness?

According to a popular but contested view, whole societies operate on fundamental assumptions of shame. Ruth Benedict suggests that Japan is a shame culture, and entire European cultures are based on guilt. Genocide (against other ethnicities) did not result in shame in Japan; it did not result in guilt in most other countries either. It seems to be the case that one needs active victims to undertake the representation of either cause. Indeed, sympathy with victims and the acceptance of parts of a history tainted with shameful injustices are perhaps more common where victims have openly accepted their victim status and advocated their cause along those lines. The votes of African Americans made their victim strategy more successful than that of American Indians, who chose (were forced into) isolation.

The best and most important example of assuming collective shame for genocide is found in Germany. This case is of limited use, however, as it is the result of continuous external pressure, which sometimes insisted on collective guilt. It is quite possible that many Germans are fed up with the continued evaluation of German acts from the perspective of being non-Nazi. But it is clear that turning anti-Semitism into a taboo did and does work. Without external pressure and monitoring it is more difficult to assume shame. In Vichy France, the French authorities were responsible for deportations and killings. French collaborators were everywhere in the country. Many were held accountable in summary proceedings. At the same time, however, de Gaulle declared that France and Frenchmen had nothing to do with Vichy. Thus Vichy simply disappeared from the landscape of French memory. In order to glorify the grand nation, one needed amnesia. French Jews participated in building the wall of silence in exchange for relative protection. Of course, here victims are silent—and ashamed for that reason. It is unlikely that those responsible for deportations and their accomplices will ever be brought to justice. At least since the beginning of the eighties, French legislators have been ready to criminalize all sorts of racial slurs, so at least assurances about the future have been given, although still without serious soul-searching. Only President Chirac has asked for forgiveness.

The Soviet-dominated states of Eastern Europe have never had an opportunity for soul-searching. When rejecting national responsibility, the post-World War II regime avoided any serious public scrutiny of past genocide. Interestingly enough, the dictates of communist power and ideology also reflected this attitude. In the years of Stalinism it was strictly forbidden to present contemporary history free of indoctrination. Communists relied on the services of many Hungarian Nazis. The democratic governments of France did the same. And for about forty years Austrian and German politics were tainted by the disclosure of former Nazi and SS members in high government positions. Rákosi, the Stalinist ruler of Hungary, made remarks about a "guilty nation", but again not for the sake of rendering justice. His interest was only in making the population even more frightened and submissive. This kind of handling of the past, in a mental tradition that used to glorify its past, resulted in an even firmer rejection of responsibility or even of recognizing that something wrong had happened to the Jews during the war. The public's need for historical justice was satisfied by the cheap slogan that the Hungarian people "have already atoned for their past and *future*".[22] This line exonerates Hungarians from all soul-searching. It would be unfair to state that the majority of the Hungarians were involved in the genocide; it is fair to say what István Bibó said in this context: the Hungarian peasantry (the majority of the population in 1944) was neither for, nor against, such "faraway things".[23] This lack of condemnation itself amounts to moral wrong and creates lasting moral obligation.

In light of the above tradition that refuses considerations of responsibility it is not surprising that in most former communist states there was no serious calling to account for crimes committed under communism. Denunciators and spies could not be held accountable where there were no clear expectations of morality and where it had become impossible and irrelevant to differentiate between sinners and victims—although, paradoxically, the perversion did not go as far as saying that good and bad made no difference in the past or that these are completely meaningless categories. Handling the problem in this way reinforced the tradition that even if there are wrongdoings in the past, they are not to be related to perpetrators. The prevailing attitude suggested that Hungarians had suffered enough for everything, and since individual responsibility was not practiced, there were no patterns for introspection or for collective introspection. The issue of morality was not on the agenda at the time of the transition of power. Of course, one cannot just blame the lack of a historically conditioned moral sensitivity on the absence of collective soul-searching. Most people made their small immoral bargains with the oppressive regime, at least in Hungary. The bad consciousness of "dirty togetherness" (Adam Podgorecki) did not help moral scrutiny. Once again, this made morality as a category of collective consciousness dubious, even frightening, nonsense. As there was no genuine self-respect, there was no sense of shame. The result is another round of indifference to the victims of history. The pattern repeated that of 1945. In Romania, some people simply butchered the dictator, and that was all that was done about responsibility for the past. But contrary to the post-war period, the transition offered genuine democratic opportunities. Discontent with the insufficient treatment of the past was openly voiced, and some people tried to engage in serious study of the past in order to create some kind of memory. One could no longer blame Soviet oppression for suppressing memory.

IV.2 Is shame conducive to positive morality and social peace?

A person who is ashamed for an act (not necessarily for her own act) is most likely a moral being. According to the German proverb, so long as there is shame there is hope for virtue. Members of a society where genocide occurred are not required to be moral virtuosi or acrobats in order to admit that a terrible crime was committed in and by the society. Nor does one need heroic qualities to recognize such sad truths. Admitting a crime is nothing more than denying a lie. Shame is the emotional recognition of the violation of a norm. It is the acknowledgment that we who were born innocent are not free of blame for the crime. And it follows from our shared history that we must prevent anything like it from occurring in the future. This is by no means a serious burden on the collective moral consciousness. Moreover, this responsibility is even less of a burden on the psyche of the individual, as in normal times the obligations of the individual are satisfied by the proper functioning of institutionalized public consciousness. The citizen should follow his or her shame-dictated sense only when the authorities fail to act according to personal sensitivities dictated by shame. Under ordinary circumstances one need not devote time to the maintenance of Jewish cemeteries as long as the local government considers this a public duty.

Shame is sufficient in mobilizing against lies, but it will not generate feelings of guilt because it is mediated through public institutions. There is no need for living in permanent individual (psychic) shame as long as the shame functions are taken over by the collective memory. Hence there will be no aggression, and shame will not have paralyzing or self-destructive effects. Collective actions dictated by shame should send reinforcing messages to actual and potential victims, and, at the same time, they should make clear for both potential victims and ready-to-act perpetrators that any attempt to assert racial discrimination will meet firm social condemnation. If shame is activated it will direct the individual to report racism and to testify against racists. A community of honestly ashamed citizens does not tolerate the humiliation of any minority. (I hope.)

The sense of shame (*pudeur*) bars the hidden glorification of the shameful. Often this is a matter of good taste. Tactfulness dictated by shame makes evident what is wrong (indecent) and disgusting about the rehabilitation of the Hungarian gendarmerie. Tact could tell what is wrong with a commemorative marble plaque that immortalizes the "glorious memory" of the Hungarian gendarmerie. The historical investigator deprived of shame will become distasteful. Truth can be cruel, and it may hurt, but it should not be indecent. Lack of taste carries the historian away from fact-finding. One should never forget when one undertakes to rewrite the history of the gendarmerie that a certain Colonel Finta committed his crimes mostly within the organizational rules and code of ethics of the gendarmerie. The gendarmes were not collectively responsible for the Holocaust and other persecutions, but the Hungarian Royal Gendarmerie as an organization committed heinous crimes, acting within its mandate.

Shame is triggered by appearance. We are ashamed because we are seen as something different from what we pretend to be or what our social status would require. If seen in the company of "deviants", I am ashamed because I assume that being seen in the company of despicable people will lead to the conclusion that I am one of "them". As a Hungarian I feel uncomfortable in the company of racists. I am afraid people will consider me a racist. As a Hungarian I feel ashamed that there are active racists in our society. I am ashamed of being classified as one of them, even in the absence of the disapproving glances of observers. One does not need actual observers (like the EU) for such a moral feeling to occur.

The observer is within me. The anticipation of the shame helps me to avoid awkward situations by preventive distancing. The stronger the feeling of collective shame, the less the individual must feel ashamed. The individual may rely on the fixed institutions of the community as (and as soon as) they address the issue of past, never settled injustices.

Appendix I. On Shame-Induced Sensitivity

Quite by accident I stumbled upon what is missing if there is no shame-dictated sensitivity. Egyed Hermann was the dean of the Faculty of Humanities at Szeged University during the war. He was among the six professors who decided to stay in Szeged when the Soviets occupied the town in late 1944. Hermann was also a member of the Race Protection Society, a radical racist association. Nonetheless, he was willing to sign two proclamations, at the request of the Red Army, testifying that the Russians were not deporting the city's youth.

His biographer notes that despite this move a politically biased action was initiated against him by the organization of students, a body closely affiliated with the Communist Party. He was supposed to attend a public hearing of the de-Nazification clearing committee. Hermann refused to do so. According to him, most of the conspiring communist students were Jewish youths who had just returned from the forced-labor battalions. He was particularly upset because these youngsters "were welcomed with sympathy and indulgence upon their return to the *Alma Mater Szegediensis*", the university under Hermann's guidance. [24]

I have no information regarding Hermann's pro-Jewish acts, other than the above indulgent understanding. It is obvious that for the returning survivors the racist dean, who was known for being the creature of a proto-fascist minister, must have been suspicious. Hermann and his biographer, in particular, have no sense of national shame for what happened a couple of months before and fifty years earlier. They sense only ingratitude. This is not to admit that there might have been some injustice in the official treatment of Hermann. The dean and his biographer have both forgotten that something else must have happened to the Jews and other victims, something that would make the forced-labor survivors suspicious. The surviving students had every good reason to be suspicious of a high exponent of a racist Hungarian regime. If Hermann had been someone of demonstrated antifascist feelings, his disappointment and resentment would have been fully justified. But for our understanding of insensitivity the case of the author of the above biography is the one who is exemplary.

Appendix II. On the Specificity of the Holocaust

It has been argued that the long-lasting obligations towards the Jews as victims that encompass the present generations are related to the magnitude of the crime committed against the Holocaust victims. Obviously, this resembles the favorite game of the revisionists. The revisionists would like us to believe that policies and morality depend on the magnitude of suffering (operationalized commonly as the number of victims). We are not interested in this numbers game. It is irrelevant here what level of sacrifice one or another group was forced to assume. Such comparisons are inhuman and unnecessary as they destroy the unity of the victims, which is crucial for effectively formulating and presenting their interests.

The revisionists' primary concern is to so manipulate appearances as to turn the responsible majority into a victim. This is an old trick: the persecution of Jews often began with accusations that they were engaged in conspiracy, to the detriment of the majority. Blood libel is a typical victimization myth.

In the revisionists' world the victims scramble for martyrdom, and the banality of being victimized makes their status a matter of majority recognition. The non-compensation incident, in Hungary, indicates that the majority may successfully shelter itself from responsibility by transforming persecutors into victims. According to the immorality of the majority, victims should not compensate other victims. The cosmetic surgery that turned persecutors into a sacrificial lamb helps to hamper all scrutiny regarding the responsibility of the majority for the Holocaust. After all, such scrutiny would jeopardize the moral merits of the sufferings of the majority. The Holocaust remains the sin of a handful of select, evil men. The entire culture of victims is full of similar irrational and demoralizing games.[25]

As mentioned above, a common way to identify the size of sacrifice and compassion for the Holocaust requires looking at some quantitative (proportional) indicator, like the percentage of the murdered out of the total victim population, or the impact of the genocide on the biological reproductive capacity of the population concerned.[26] These indicators might be decisive for the victims, but it aids in determining suffering and, as a result, reduces responsibility. A study of responsibility should focus on the causation and on the party who caused the damage. One should look at the systematic or nonsystematic nature of the persecution and the official sanctions and public support of the persecution. One should also put persecution in its historical context.

The meaning of racial persecution or prejudice may differ, depending on the normative and cultural context and, more specifically, on the violation of the norms of civilization at the time the murders were committed. There is a fundamental difference between the seventeenth-century slave trade resulting in partial depopulation in Africa and the genocide of Armenians and the Jewish Holocaust. Notwithstanding or in any way diminishing its cruelty, in the seventeenth century slave trade was not perceived as a violation of existing standards. Indeed, for many Africans slave hunting and trade was business as usual. Genocide against the Armenians occurred in then semi-civilized Turkey, where the dominant religion perceived Christians as lesser beings. Armenians in Turkey were always second-rank subjects. Germany, on the contrary, was proud of its high culture, and Jews had been guaranteed equal civil status for a century. Other ethnic persecutions were carried out without the desire for systematic annihilation (e.g., the expulsion of Germans from various East European countries). When conceptualizing past instances of genocide the observer should be sensitive to the historical and moral context within which the murders took place. It makes a difference whether the murders constituted a violation of an existing norm at the time they were committed. The perception of genocide, the level of shame, and the legitimacy of justice claims today depends on the classification of the murders at the time they were committed.

To demonstrate the practical consequences of the above distinctions, one must look at the national actions that resulted in genocide. The Armenian genocide in Turkey was presented as the inevitable consequence of compelling military exigencies fueled by religious teachings.[27] Genocide was "accidental" to the extent that most of the killings were due to bad weather and lack of food. The Stambul massacres were the result of mob action incited by the authorities. The brutalities were criminal even by the standards of the law in force, as a Turkish military court recognized right after the war. Nothing of this recognition became public, and nothing of it became part of the Turkish collective consciousness. No element of collective shame emerged, simply because the facts were denied. Compensation is unheard of, and the falsification of history prevails. The consequences are well illustrated in the totally insensitive and aggressive handling of the Kurds. There is no place for repentance where collective denial prevails. Of course, undigested history is to be blamed in this case, too. The mutual Turkish–Greek genocides immediately following World War I created the well-founded conditions for feeling oneself a victim of genocide. Mass-scale victimization, per se, absolved the collective consciousness from self-reflection.

Notes

1 National shame of this kind is also justified in cases where the acts of genocide were directed against groups in other countries. Such acts have specific legal implications. This paper will not discuss the specific problems of international (transboundary) genocide.

2 There were additional killings after the Hungarian Arrow Cross Party came to power in the fall of 1944. The Nazi government in Hungary was clearly a German puppet. But in Budapest, where many of the murders occurred, the Arrow Cross government had at least some legality and broad discretion to act. It is fair to say that, during this period, many of the murders were committed under the colors of the flag.

3 The obligation applies, therefore, to Jews as members of the community. "Jews" are not a homogeneous class. Relations among various groups of Jews differ. Some are Holocaust survivors; others are descendants of the persecuted. Many people refuse to be identified as Jews. They should be treated, nevertheless, with the same specific shame attitude as people with victim identity.

4 Gabriele Taylor (1985). *Pride, Shame, and Guilt, Emotions of Self-assessment.* Oxford: Clarendon Press, p. 83.

5 The Soviet score might be seen as settled because of the 1956 uprising.

6 As a matter of principle, all moral agents may equally and legitimately formulate claims that injustice should be undone. To the extent that a specific remedial action is directed towards the victims themselves, pragmatic authenticity favors that the victims' voices be heard. A person who has suffered or is in actual danger may know better and argue more authentically in favor of a preferred remedy. Claims made on behalf of victims by other moral agents are inherently suspicious and have an air of paternalism.

7 Jeremy Waldron (1992). "Superseding Historic Injustice". *Ethics* 103 (October): 7

8 Act No. 15 of 1938 on the more efficient guarantees of equilibrium in social and economic life.

9 István Bibó (1986). "Zsidókérdés Magyarországon 1944 után" (The Jewish question in Hungary after 1944). In István Bibó, *Válogatott tanulmányok*, Vol. 2. Budapest, p. 632. Bibó was of the opinion that an anti-Jewish mob sentiment, if left on its own, may very easily turn into persecution and murder. "Such historical experience was built into the nerves of the Jews in the thirties."

10 István Bibó (1986). "Néhány kiegészítô megjegyzés a zsidókérdésrôl" (Some supplementary remarks on the Jewish question). In István Bibó, *Válogatott tanulmányok*, Vol. 2. Budapest, p. 807.

11 Compare, for example, with Afro-Americans. This is a risky strategy as these Jews control only a few votes as a block; thus their political weight is limited.

12 Only a handful of the revisionists claim that millions of European Jews would have survived World War II. The mainstream revisionist claim is that Jews did not perish in the gas chambers.

13 Egan v. Canada (AG) (1995) 2 SCR 513; and President of the Republic of South Africa v. Hugo (1997) CCT 11/96. The position of the Canadian Supreme Court on the significance of reviewing past discrimination was expressed recently in an even stronger form in Law v. Canada (Minister of Employment and Immigration) (1999) 1 SCR 497.

14 This is not to argue that the special obligations are related to the *uniqueness* of the Holocaust. See Appendix II.

15 Holocaust Denial case 90 BVerfGE 241 (1994), translated in Donald P. Kommers (1997). *The Constitutional Jurisprudence of the Federal Republic of Germany*, 2nd

ed. Durham: Duke University Press, p. 386. In the case the Constitutional Court quoted the Supreme Court approvingly.

16 István Bibó (1986). "Zsidókérdés Magyarországon 1944 után" (The Jewish question in Hungary after 1944). In István Bibó, *Válogatott tanulmányok*, Vol. 2. Budapest, pp. 624–625.

17 1/1995 (II.8.) AB decision, J. Lábady, writing for the court.

18 Avishai Margalit formulated the above criteria for the decent society. Avishai Margalit (1996). *The Decent Society*. Cambridge, Mass.: Harvard University Press, p. 133. Isn't it a violation of this criterion that we insist on shaming generations of Hungarians who had nothing to do with the Holocaust? Isn't it the case that we advocate that belonging to a legitimate group (the Hungarians) becomes the source of shame?

19 Waldron, loc. cit., p. 6.

20 Probably the most successful Hungarian savior, Pál Szalai, was a long-time, committed member of the Arrow Cross Party. Indeed, it was his relatively high position in that party that enabled him to act on a broad scale.

21 Act No. 32 of 1992 provided for compensation for unjust deprivation of life and liberty for political reasons. This compensation did not cover loss of life during deportation to Germany or in Russian camps, except if unlawful deprivation of life occurred on the basis of a judgment of a Hungarian court. Jews who served in forced-labor battalions on the front but "not on the front line" (in so-called non-combatant units, i.e. as if they were ordinary soldiers), were excluded from compensation. The Hungarian Constitutional Court found these provisions discriminatory and, therefore, unconstitutional in 1995 (1/1995 [II.8.] AB decision). The Court ordered that a new law be enacted providing compensation for those who were discriminatorily disregarded by the 1992 act.

In 1996, Parliament submitted a bill to the Constitutional Court for preliminary review. The bill provided HUF 300,000 to the descendants of those deported to Germany as well as to those whose relatives perished in Soviet labor camps (typically prisoners of war). The Court found that although there can be no discrimination among the various groups of victims, it is up to the legislation to determine the level of compensation, taking into account what is feasible given the state of the national economy. This meant that the higher compensation paid to certain groups of victims under the 1992 act was left out of consideration.

In 1998 the new conservative majority adopted a government-sponsored bill. The new scheme offers HUF 30,000 as compensation, although those who qualified for compensation under the original law have received HUF 1,000,000.

22 This sigh is the closing phrase of the Hungarian national anthem. The verse was written in the early nineteenth century, and this line is known by all Hungarians as the simplest truism.

23 Bibó, loc. cit. p. 631.

24 Words of Hermann quoted in István Kertész (1998), "'Iparkodtam jó magyar emberré lenni', Hermann Egyed életpályája" (I strove to become a good Hungarian. Hermann Egyed's carrier path). *Historia* 20 (9–10): 57.

25 Another pet-argument of the revisionist-victim game concentrates on the responsibility of the victims. Even if Bruno Bettelheim and Primo Levi are absolutely accurate

regarding the behavior of concentration-camp prisoners, one should reject morally and simply as a factual statement that victims and perpetrators are both responsible, although to differing degrees. (This view was presented by the first post-communist minister of culture, in Hungary, when he was a university professor.) Whatever one believes of victimology it is simply ridiculous to look at the Holocaust as if it were a simple case of pick-pocketing where theft is facilitated by the carelessness of the victim, an elderly passenger.

26 The reproduction depends on post-Holocaust developments, too. Here, the attitude of second- and third-generation majorities matters considerably. The majority may influence reproductive attitudes by rehabilitation programs and with reinforcing attitudes, including shame.

27 The internment of Americans of Japanese descent was likewise legitimized as dictated by military exigencies. It must have been obvious, in 1942, that the commander followed only his racist whim as there was nothing in the military situation that would have made such action reasonable (or even less, legitimate).

IV The Economic Dimension

12 *Hidden in an Envelope: Gratitude Payments to Medical Doctors in Hungary*[1]

JÁNOS KORNAI

An ethnographer from a faraway land who visited Hungary these days carrying a hidden camera would notice a strange tribal custom when medical doctors and patients meet. The conversation often ends with the patient bringing out a plain envelope and handing it to the doctor with a grateful smile: "Thank you so much, Doctor, for your kind attention", the patient will say. Then the doctor makes a dismissive gesture: "No, I can't accept that." "Oh do, Doctor, I beg of you!" The exchange may continue for a while longer, but in the end the physician pockets the envelope after all. Alternatively, the ritual may take place silently: the patient slips the envelope onto the doctor's desk surreptitiously, but to a place where it will soon be seen and opened when the patient has gone.

Inside the envelope there is money, often with a line or two of thanks. The phenomenon of such payments, known in Hungarian as "gratitude money", is the subject of this study.

The Economic Significance of Gratitude Payments

Some Hungarian physicians conduct regular private practice, in which patients pay for the provisions in the normal way. No one would call these payments gratitude money, even if words of gratitude are spoken.

Most of Hungary's health provisions are offered by institutions in public ownership—hospitals and outpatients' clinics in most cases. The doctors working in these institutions are employed by the hospital or clinic concerned, or, if formally self-employed, under a contract to them that resembles employment, and as such they receive an official salary for their work. Patients are entitled to free medical care by Hungarian law.[2] The expression "gratitude money" customarily refers to cases where the patient, more or less illegally, gives money to a state-employed doctor for a provision for which the doctor is not entitled to a direct payment, according to the regulations.[3]

What is the economic significance of this curious type of payment? Let us look at the question first from the angle of the consumer of medical provisions, the "buyer" in this unusual market transaction.

Gratitude money can be seen as a *wage supplement*. The buyer (the patient) makes a voluntary contribution to the wages that the seller (the hospital or outpatients' clinic) pays to the doctor, thereby raising that employee's total earnings. This concept of gratitude money points to the resemblance it bears to the tips given to waiters, hotel porters, or taxi drivers. Employers in such trades calculate in advance that their employees will receive regular tips in addition to wages, and set their wages accordingly.

Gratitude money can be seen as a *bribe*. The idea of bribery may remind many Western readers of the scandalous occasions when private firms pay huge sums to civil servants or politicians in return for a fat contract or order. The advantage that the buyer gains here is more paltry: a little extra attention, a move up the queue, a shorter period of waiting, a better bed in a crowded hospital, or simply receiving treatment from a chosen doctor instead of the one assigned.

Now let us look at gratitude money from the "seller's" side. The phenomenon of *rent seeking* is well known in economics.[4] Typically, the provision of some kinds of service is contingent on a state permit, which makes that service scarcer than it would be under balanced market conditions. Those in possession of a permit have a chance of adding a rent to the price they collect from those availing themselves of the service. Ultimately, this rent goes to the bureaucrat who issues the permit, or to the provider, or it is shared between them. A good example would be an immediate referral for hospital treatment, with a bed in a single room. The gratitude payment made for the referral to a single hospital room can be classed as a rent pocketed by the treating physician or his or her superior, the senior physician in charge of the ward, or shared between them.

The same example suggests another interpretation as well. The patient is paying an extra fee for immediate referral to a bed in a single hospital room. However, the payment is not going to the owner of the bed, the publicly owned hospital, but to the doctor, the owner's employee. This *"black" rent* resembles the "black taxis" found in the socialist economy. The drivers of cars belonging to state offices would "taxi" private passengers, but the passenger would pay the driver, not the state, for the use of state property.

These four interpretations of gratitude money are closely allied. One type of phenomenon can shade into or coincide with another. They certainly have one important feature in common: gratitude payments are earnings that are concealed. The recipients avoid paying tax and other compulsory deductions (such as social-insurance contributions) on them. The secrecy may apply not only to those who receive the gratitude payments but to those who make them, who are ashamed to be seeking advantages in such a way. Concealment is also encouraged because the transaction is illegal, although it is not an offense punished in practice. Neither has anyone ever been prosecuted for accepting gratitude money or for the associated tax evasion. Since the law is not applied in this area, perhaps it would be more appropriate to describe such transactions as semi-legal.

The Extent of Gratitude Payments

Since gratitude payments are concealed transactions there are obviously no accurate statistics about their incidence or volume based on direct observation. Nonetheless, there are ways of gaining a numerical picture of the gratitude-money syndrome. As mentioned in note 1, the author was involved in designing a broad survey carried out in 1998 by TÁRKI, in which two samples were asked for information about gratitude payments in a detailed oral interview. One sample of about 1,400 persons represented the adult Hungarian population, while the other, of about 1,000 persons, represented the medical profession. This empirical research is the main source to which the following refers.

The extent of gratitude payments is shown in table 1. The sample of the public was asked whether it is customary to pay gratitude money for the fourteen medical acts taken as examples. The majority of the respondents answered in the affirmative for eight of the fourteen acts. Even for a simple injection, every third patient makes a gratitude payment.

It is worth noting that the incidence data estimated by doctors are lower than the estimates by the public. Respondents were asked "How many patients out of ten give gratitude money to an obstetrician, in your opinion?" The average figure in responses by the public was 9.2, and in those by the medical sample, 8.5. The difference was greatest in the case of a district pediatrician: 6.5 according to the public and 4.6 according to the medical sample[5] (BGK 2000b, table 4 on p. 301). The doctors were also asked what percentage of certain types of doctor accept gratitude money. The average figures given by respondents were 94.4 percent for obstetricians and gynecologists, and 89.9 percent for surgeons. The lowest percentage was 78.5 percent for psychiatrists (BGK 2000b, table 6 on p. 305).

Table 12.1 *The Frequency of Gratitude Payments for Various Kinds of Medical Intervention, in the Opinion of the Public (Percentage of Those Who Named a Figure Higher Than Zero)*

Question: "*In your opinion, how much gratitude money is it customary to give for the following health-care provisions?*"	Answer
An X-ray examination	8
The taking of a patient's blood pressure	12
An injection	31
Radiotherapy treatment	35
Physiotherapy, per treatment	48
A routine gynecological examination at a specialist clinic	48
A therapeutic massage	51
Compulsory inoculations given by a pediatrician on a house call	51
Regular home visits by a pediatrician or family doctor	75
A tonsillectomy	77
House call at night by a duty doctor	86
An appendectomy or gall-bladder surgery (to the surgeon)	87
Childbirth (to the obstetrician)	92
A heart operation (to the head surgeon)	92

Note: For instance, the figure 8 in the first row means that 92 percent of respondents think nothing need be given for an X-ray examination and only 8 percent that some payment should be made. The proportions given ignore the "don't know" responses.

Source: BGK (2000b), table 3 on p. 300.

An attempt was made to arrive at a numerical estimate of the proportion of Hungarian doctors' total earnings that gratitude payments represent. Here just the result is given. Taking net official income (after the deduction of tax and compulsory contributions) and gratitude money together to equal 100, only 38 percent consists of official income and 62 percent of gratitude money (BGK 2000b on p. 312).

The gratitude-money phenomenon is not confined to Hungary. According to expert opinion, semi-legal payments to doctors are widespread in Romania and Poland as well, and it seems likely that they are made in other post-socialist countries too. Research in Poland found that the gratitude money paid in 1994 about equaled the amount that doctors were receiving in official net income (Berman 1998). This is an extremely high proportion, although it is still less than has been found in Hungary. Without any national pride, it can be said that the gratitude-money syndrome, as a sickness of the health-care system, occurs to the most serious extent and exhibits the most acute symptoms in Hungary. The conclusions in the rest of the study are based throughout on the experiences in Hungary.

The Motives behind the Spread of Gratitude Payments

The rather pompous expression *paraszolvencia*, now a synonym for gratitude money current among Hungarian doctors, dates back to the period before the Second World War. However, *paraszolvencia* at that time had a different meaning from the one it acquired later. Senior doctors would put an appreciable proportion of the rather high fees they received from private practice into what was known as a petty-cash fund. This they distributed from time to time among the subordinate doctors and assistants working for them. It was a redistribution of fees from *private* medical provision. It differed from the gratitude money of the socialist and post-socialist periods in having no connection with free provision funded out of the public purse.[6]

Gratitude payments in today's sense began to spread when the provision and financing of health care were completely nationalized after the introduction of the socialist economic system. In the initial, Stalinist period, when the dictatorship was at its most brutal and repressive, there were greater risks attached to making, and still more receiving, illegal payments, which kept gratitude money within relatively narrow bounds.

The phenomenon of gratitude money really began to flourish in the Kádárite period of "soft" dictatorship. What induced patients to resort, voluntarily, to a procedure that was unpleasant and costly for them?

The Kádár period brought some loosening of the command economy and attempts to introduce "market-socialist" ideas into industry, agriculture, and commerce. The same did not apply to the health system, where the system of bureaucratic allocation remained unchanged. Patients who submitted themselves to the rules did not have any real choices. Administrative regulations decided which doctor they consulted when they were ill—that is, the "district physician" for their place of residence. That doctor prescribed the treatment or referred them on to a specialist or a hospital. There they were passed from hand to hand in a similar way, and in each case the patients had to submit. Gratitude payments alleviated their defenselessness to some extent: it bought them a little freedom. It could influence which doctor treated them, how attentively they were nursed, what tests were done on them, and so on. In a distorted way, it slipped a little of the market into a realm of bureaucratic constraints.

The doctors' motives were similar. The centralized command economy strictly controlled wages in every branch of the economy, including the health system. The supply and demand for highly qualified work had little effect on relative wages, since the centralized command economy also disabled the labor market. Wages in health care were set according to the importance that the central decision makers attached to its activity, compared with other sectors. Medical work, like most intellectual activity, received little financial reward, so that doctors' pay hardly exceeded the average pay for employees. However, doctors could soar above that depressed standard of living through the gratitude money they were given.

Through this concealed market, patients and doctors, as buyers and sellers, became accomplices in breaking the regulations of the state. Unauthorized transactions took place and the flows of money were concealed from the tax authorities.

Of course, the financial and health authorities were not stupid. They knew very well that gratitude payments were being made, but they tolerated this happening over a wide area. They saw it as a cheaper solution than raising doctors' official pay. Furthermore, there was a political gain to be made. It reduced the tensions in society to some extent. Perhaps citizens would grumble less if they felt they could purchase a little privilege with their money. So the state leadership connived with those who cheated the state, in what became a general characteristic of society in the Kádár period.

The same kind of connivance with those who infringed the rules allowed semi-legal, concealed, informal economic transactions to develop in every sector of the economy, as the "second economy" or "shadow economy".[7] Gratitude money is the specific manifestation of the informal economy found in the health sector.

The Kádár period ended in 1989, when the change of system began. This covered the political sphere, where a one-party system gave way to a multiparty system, and dictatorship to democratic government based on free parliamentary elections. Within a few years the change of system had also extended to the narrowly defined business sphere (industry, agriculture, transport, commerce, etc.), as private ownership and market coordination became dominant. Despite all these changes the phenomenon of gratitude payments obstinately survived and perhaps even expanded, appearing in even more perverse forms than it had before the change of system.

The survival of gratitude money is connected with the fact that the health sector belatedly began to undergo, in the 1990s, a process of reform of the kind that the business sphere of the economy had undergone in the Kádár period.[8] The changes display a strong ambiguity: bureaucratic and market coordination, and public and private ownership combine in a sometimes healthy and sometimes distorted way. Gratitude money fits into this ambiguous environment.

To take one form as an example, many more doctors have a legal private practice these days while remaining full-time employees of the state health organization. Many of them keep up a private clinic for the purpose, in their homes or elsewhere. A patient calling at a doctor's private clinic is given a preliminary examination, or may simply have a conversation with the doctor. The patient is charged for this private provision. Then the sequence of events becomes more problematic, legally and economically. The same doctor goes on to treat the same patient in the state hospital where he or she works, as his "own" patient, but of course on state premises, using state equipment. The doctor does not pay any fee to the state for using its capital assets or for the work done for the patient by colleagues and subordinates. How can the payment this patient has made to the doctor be classified? Nominally, it is nothing other than the market price for a private provision. In fact, much of it is a tacit form of gratitude money, for the "extra attention" given to a favored patient by a doctor in state employ. All four explanations of gratitude money given above apply here. The inclusion of a private practice, or the fact that the patient pays the money openly in the private clinic instead of tucking it into the doctor's pocket in the hospital corridor, makes the transaction easier. Whatever kind of inspection is attempted, it is legally impossible to say where the regular market price of a provision ends and gratitude money begins.

The Economic Consequences

Gratitude money has several harmful effects from the economic point of view.

The incentive effect. Patients, in their own way, are giving the doctor a financial incentive. They hope this will encourage the doctor to give them privileged treatment. However, the chance of the incentive being effective is not great, for several reasons.

The doctor is bound by professional standards. These preclude making the care given to patients dependent on the size of a gratitude payment. One of the questions put to the physicians in the survey was "What percentage of doctors, in your opinion, do their duty only for the money?" The average given in the responses was 9.1 percent (BGK 2000b, table 9 on p. 306).[9]

There is confusion about what the customary "price" in gratitude money is for various medical actions. According to the survey, only about a third of patients have previous information about what it is customary to pay (BGK 2000b, table 15 on p. 316). That is one of the drawbacks of a quasi-market transaction that does not take place under transparent circumstances. The patient may have "underpaid" and the doctor be disappointed, or he or she may have "overpaid", meaning that the same incentive effect could have been obtained for a smaller financial sacrifice.

According to Walrasian theory, a process of "groping" *(tâtonnement)* takes place in a normal market—repeated collisions between supply and demand prices lead ultimately to an equilibrium price that harmonizes supply and demand. On the kind of concealed market in which gratitude payments are made, the lack of transparency means that the process fails to converge on an equilibrium price. Instead, the "buyers" bid each other up, sending the price higher and higher. Once the price has risen, a new patient immediately feels called upon to give what the others usually do. Ultimately, the price can only go up and never down.

Furthermore, gratitude money is not the only incentive force in this distorted coordination mechanism. At least as weighty a consideration are the patient's connections with the medical network; their power, position, and prestige; the extent to which a doctor can expect reciprocal favors from the patient or the patient's circle; even the degree to which the patient is to be feared. The doctors' views on this are shown in table 2. The two incentives (gratitude money and connections) work together, which in itself means it is problematic to decide what role to ascribe to gratitude money in this complex of effects.

Patients are unable to judge what contribution various people make for their treatment. According to table 3, the size of the gratitude payment tends to depend on the "assertiveness" and the grade of the doctor, rather than the actual performance or the degree of experience. The bluntness of gratitude money as an instrument is also apparent in its uneven distribution between medical fields. The most gratitude money goes to those whose contribution is most felt by the patient: the obstetrician at childbirth or the surgeon directing the operation. Yet the correctness of the diagnosis may depend largely on how conscientiously those working in the laboratory or on the X-ray or other diagnostic appliances perform their tasks. The lives of patients undergoing surgery are not only in the hands of surgeons, but in those of their assistants and the anesthetists.[10] Nonetheless, the latter fall outside the sphere of gratitude payments. Gratitude money, which is based on superficial impressions, represents an extremely clumsy means of giving incentives.

Table 12.2 *Opinions on the Usefulness of Gratitude Money and Connections (Responses As a Percentage of the Sample of the Public)*

Question: *"In your opinion, which achieves more: gratitude money or connections?"*	Answer
Gratitude money	19
Personal connections	41
They achieve the same	35
Neither achieves anything	5
Total	100

Source: BGK (2000b), table 17 on p. 317.

Table 12.3 *Factors Influencing the Size of Gratitude Payments, by Medical Specialty*

Question: *"In your opinion, what decides whether a doctor receives more or less gratitude money?" (The relative frequencies with various factors are cited.)*

Factor/Informant	Family doctor	Pediatrician	Medical specialist	Surgeon	Psychiatrist	Total
Specialty	85.3	87.6	89.1	82.9	91.6	86.8
Rank	66.1	72.6	79.3	84.9	80.4	75.6
Reputation	68.3	70.0	77.2	84.4	67.3	74.0
Length of service	19.8	24.7	28.7	27.1	14.9	23.6
Whether able to decide on referral	24.7	53.4	50.0	42.2	44.9	45.3
Assertiveness	53.3	60.3	50.4	55.3	49.5	53.0
Performance	35.3	28.8	36.9	33.2	32.7	34.6
Other responses	3.3	2.7	2.5	4.5	0.0	2.9

Note: The question was posed only to the doctors' sample.
Source: BGK (2000b), table 8 on p. 306

The distributive effect. Another damaging economic effect of gratitude payments is an added distortion introduced into a distribution of income and expenditure that already contains many injustices. Many poor, or even destitute, patients feel they have to give gratitude money. The gratitude "price" of a childbirth averages between HUF 19,000 and 23,000 (BGK 2000b, table 10 on p. 307), while the net monthly average earnings by employees in the survey year was HUF 45,162 (KSH 1999 on p. 93). This is an enormous burden on a lower-income family.

The survey does not support the optimistic supposition that wealthier patients are more likely to make gratitude payments than poorer ones. In a regression analysis explaining the frequency and incidence of gratitude payments, the variable representing income did not prove significant (BGK 2000a on p. 25).

Health-care expenditures impinge on people's lives unexpectedly and unpredictably. A patient may pass from being healthy to being seriously ill in a matter of moments. This certainly places a great financial burden on the patient and his or her family, especially if the patient pursues paid activity that has to be suspended or reduced for a longer or shorter time. As a consequence, medical care is among the classic fields of insurance, both as social insurance covering large groups of the public, and as private, commercial insurance. Gratitude payments fall outside the sphere of institutional insurance. The extremely large, unexpected costs of an illness cannot be turned into a regularly paid premium of a supportable size. Individuals or families are obliged to make gratitude payments when the illness has already placed them in a worse financial situation.

The Disruptive Moral Effect

Many doctors are aware of how unfairly the costs of illness become distributed among patients through the system of gratitude money. The survey showed that more than half of doctors consider case by case whether to accept a gratitude payment (BGK 2000b, table 9 on p. 306). One criterion is the patient's financial situation, although the doctor, too, may be in need of the money. Doctors may accept gratitude money from wealthier patients, but not from poorer ones. It is good to know that many doctors score well on this moral test. But what sort of system is it that sets a test of this kind to its doctors, day after day? Along with the difficulties of making professional decisions, they have to deal with many psychologically demanding ethical problems in any case when they weigh risks and face the many dilemmas related to prolonging life and the quality of life. How can it be permissible to burden them also with the problem of assessing their patients' financial means and promoting an equitable distribution of income?

Table 12.4 *Opinions on Medical Gratitude Money, among Doctors and among the Public*

Opinion	Wholly	Partly	Wholly	Partly
	agree		disagree	
Giving gratitude money reassures patients, because they feel they are buying extra attention.				
Physicians	19.4	44.2	19.5	16.9
Public	26.1	28.4	19.8	25.7
Gratitude money makes no difference.				
Physicians	32.0	17.6	23.7	26.7
Public	14.4	17.1	30.0	38.5
Gratitude money erodes the confidence essential in the doctor–patient relationship.				
Physicians	17.8	17.6	31.9	32.7
Public	15.1	21.7	33.2	30.1
Gratitude money is a necessary evil.				
Physicians	58.0	22.2	9.8	10.1
Public	52.3	30.1	9.2	8.4
So long as the state does not pay them properly, doctors have a right to accept gratitude money.				
Physicians	54.4	27.5	11.0	7.1
Public	39.1	28.4	17.5	15.0
It is morally reprehensible for doctors to accept gratitude money.				
Physicians	3.6	7.5	29.4	59.6
Public	16.6	17.7	33.3	32.4
Gratitude money is unpleasant and demeaning to both doctors and patients.				
Physicians	68.0	21.8	7.1	3.1
Public	30.0	32.4	22.6	15.0
The existence of gratitude money shows that society considers doctors to be underpaid.				
Physicians	72.6	17.5	6.7	3.2
Public	41.6	28.1	17.0	13.3
Gratitude money is not a moral issue.				
Physicians	42.2	29.1	18.1	10.7
Public	33.5	29.3	19.4	17.8

Note: The average values are the arithmetical means of the values obtained on a four-point scale (wholly agree=4, tend to agree=3, tend not to agree=2, wholly disagree=1).

Source: BGK (2000b), table 1 on p. 295.

The mechanism of gratitude money spreads moral disruption, the effects of which become more harmful as the phenomenon spreads and becomes more deeply rooted. It institutionalizes falsehood. The official rhetoric, under the socialist system and in the self-promotion of the "social market economy", states that citizens have a right to free health care, while everyone knows that most patients are taking gratitude money out of their pockets and putting it in a plain envelope for the doctor. The rhetoric states that everyone shall have equal access to health-care provisions, while everyone knows that people are trying to buy themselves unequal access more favorable to themselves.

The survey sought to probe into opinions on gratitude money, among the public and among the medical profession. Nine strong statements were formulated. Respondents were asked to express a view on each, using a four-point scale: 1 for complete agreement; 2 for stronger agreement than disagreement; 3 for stronger disagreement than agreement; and 4 for complete disagreement. The distribution of the responses, which appears in table 4, clearly reflects the moral discomfiture. In the bottom row, only 37 percent of the public and only 29 percent of the doctors were prepared to admit that there is a moral problem involved here. The others dismissed the idea. The strong statement that accepting gratitude money is morally reprehensible was accepted by only a tenth of the doctors. Indeed, only a third of the public identify with it wholly or partly.

Karl Popper contrasted the "closed" and the "open" types of society, giving several criteria for distinguishing them (Popper 1962). Although it does not feature on Popper's list of distinguishing marks, there might be arguments for including a sense of transparency as a sign of "openness". The gratitude-money phenomenon is alien to a truly "open society". It riddles the society with hidden, secret relations. It is impossible to fathom, under these circumstances, what the relationship between doctor and patient is. Is the doctor serving the patient as an agent of the caring state? Or are the doctor and the patient accomplices in cheating the state? Does the seller stand in a money–goods relation to the buyer? What is the relationship of the patient who makes a gratitude payment to the other patients? Is it one of solidarity, or are the secretive envelopes intended to ensure that he or she can cut in before the others?

Contemporary sociology and economics pay great attention to the problem of social confidence. The weaker it becomes, the more needful it is to govern personal interactions by legal prescriptions and economic incentives. Gratitude money undermines social confidence, day after day. Table 4 shows that more than a third of respondents sense this confidence-destroying effect.

Why is the System of Gratitude Money So Firmly Rooted?

The gratitude-money phenomenon is economically and morally damaging. So why does it survive so obstinately?

The answer, according to the first approach, is that society has fallen into a trap. Economists are aware of many states of equilibrium that are sub-optimal or even expressly harmful to the long-term interests of most of those involved, but that maintain a kind of balance among the interactive participants. A harmful equilibrium may be stable in that it recovers from slight oscillations. The gratitude-money syndrome seems to be one of these. There are strong vested interests in retaining it.

Before analyzing these conserving forces, it is worth considering what structure the health system would have if there were no gratitude money. Rather than taking an abstract system, let us look at three structures that function without it (OECD 1993 and 1994; Saltman and Figueras 1997; Fuchs 1996; and Newhouse 1996). One is Britain, which has a strongly centralized, nationalized system, in which the state pays the National Health Service doctors respectable salaries out of taxpayers' money. They do not receive gratitude payments. Another is Germany, where the core of the health sector is provided by a social-insurance system grounded on traditions dating back to Bismarck. There is periodic wage bargaining between the medical associations and the health-care funds, leading to agreement on medical pay. This turns out to be three or four times the average earnings, not between 1.3 and 1.5 times as in Eastern Europe. There is no gratitude money. Finally, there is the United States system, where most of the financing comes through decentralized, private insurers. This market form provides doctors with high earnings, as open, commercial income. There is no system of gratitude payments.

This study is not intended to take sides on the question of which example, or combination of examples, Hungary might follow. What is common to all three structures is their *transparency*. If the health sector is financed out of taxation, taxpayers can see how much they are taxed and on what legal basis. If there is a market-based structure in which the financing comes from insurance premiums, the insured can see what premium they will have to pay for what cover.

It would be naive to expect Hungarian society to stand up and sing in unison, like the cast of *Hair*, "Let the sun shine in!" Far from it. There are strong vested interests in maintaining the opaqueness. Many prefer a situation in which they can conceal from others the advantages they have gained.

The medical profession is divided, for some are receiving a lot of the gratitude money and some little or none at all. Let us assume that gratitude payments are abolished in a way that provides enough compensation to maintain *average* medical earnings. Even then there would be winners and losers and the distribution would depend on the extent to which the compensation was proportionate to the official salaries so far. The gains and losses would be widely dispersed. Furthermore, many of the probable losers who receive large amounts of gratitude money at present would be among those in the main positions of power and influence, although the two spheres would not entirely coincide.

The medical profession is not only divided but ambivalent on the question of eliminating gratitude money. On the one hand, there are doctors, even among those who win by the present arrangements, who find the system problematic and demeaning. According to table 4, the vast majority of doctors share this feeling. On the other hand, even doctors who initially shrank from accepting gratitude money have built these payments into their household earnings and could not do without them. They have calmed their consciences over the moral objections by arguing, in the words of one of the statements featuring in table 4, "Until the state pays doctors properly, doctors can justifiably accept gratitude money." The survey showed that 82 percent of doctors fully or partly identified with this view and that two-thirds of the public accepted it more or less.

That leads to the other group with an interest: the general public, the actual or potential patients. People regard the gratitude-payment mechanism as a burden, but at least they know it to some extent. They feel (rightly or in some illusory sense) that this is an expenditure over which they have direct control. Many people see the connection they have built with a doctor through the payment of gratitude money as an important investment, since it makes it possible for them to continue to rely on him.

A sizable proportion of the population is averse to change, because the alternatives to the present system are not clear. Will people have to pay higher taxes and health contributions so that doctors can legally receive higher pay? Will this extra deduction be voted for in parliament? Or would the public be willing to take out voluntary private insurance to finance the higher earnings of doctors? In another survey carried out by TÁRKI, people were asked if they would be willing to take out auxiliary, private medical insurance. The response was affirmative from 48.7 percent of the respondents (unconditionally, or with certain conditions attached), while 41.6 percent definitely rejected the idea.[11] This latter group may well be large enough to block any change.

The question of change depends primarily on the political sphere. The progress and specific outcome of reform does not depend on rational arguments. It depends on the "political economy" of the process and the power relations among political parties, parliamentary blocs, and political pressure groups and lobbies. It is precisely the politicians who appear to be shrinking from the transparent solutions. It is easy to talk of the need for health reform in general terms when addressing political rallies or parliamentary debates. The phrase has never been absent from the arsenal of slogans among government or opposition parties. It is another matter to know which party will dare to address the matter outright and when, saying who is to pay for a radical increase in the *legal* pay of doctors and how. For that is ultimately the question. Gratitude money cannot be abolished by the stroke of a pen, by passing a law or issuing a directive. The concealed, semi-legal gratitude payments have to be *replaced* by extra legal, taxable earnings. Ultimately, politicians will have to decide how and when the trade-off should take place. Is there to be a drastic rise in social-insurance contributions for health care? Should some other kinds of tax be raised and the extra revenue diverted to raising the pay of doctors employed in publicly owned institutions? Should more be spent for this purpose from existing revenues, while reducing other types of expenditure?

No one in Hungarian public life has yet made a clear, numerical proposal. The government parties have not made a commitment and the opposition parties have not promised to do anything specific if they come to power.

If the political sphere does not prepare to replace gratitude money by fiscal means, there is no other way left than to legalize the market transactions. A way has to be found to finance the increase in legal medical pay through private insurance under commercial conditions. This will not only have to be permitted, it will have to be admitted to the public that the change will increase the inequality of access to health provisions. It will not be possible to take this course while blandly talking of equal access and stirring up feelings against the market and the profit motive.

The political moves required to replace gratitude money are certainly unpleasant ones. For the time being, politicians prefer the twilight zone in which gratitude payments remain, in which mutually inconsistent statements, promises, and arguments can coexist.

If the distorted gratitude-money system had never emerged in Hungary and other Eastern European countries in the first place, it would now be easier to arrive without it at a more favorable combination of public and private ownership and bureaucratic and market coordination. As people say ironically, it would have been better to have started from somewhere else. However, that is the initial situation. The habits and the economic and moral consequences of the gratitude-money system have penetrated deep into every participant in the Hungarian health system.

I cannot make a forecast, only outline a scenario. Perhaps the strongest hope is that the private sector will spread on the supply side of the health service. Private enterprise, by its nature, adjusts to the situation on the labor market, and so it will offer steadily higher wages to its employees than the public sector has. To be able to finance this, it will press for the appearance of private insurers and impartial treatment for all sectors from the social-insurance system. In other words, it will insist that the social-insurance system be willing to finance all providers on equal terms, irrespective of whether they are publicly or privately owned. These developments will also force an increase in legal medical pay in the public sector, so as to prevent a flight of the best doctors to the private sector. Thus earnings will steadily rise and gradually supplant the semi-legal gratitude money. That in turn will bring about alterations in household budgets, to varying extents for different families and individuals.[12] This may take place without any great upheavals, provided the transition coincides with a general, steady rise in real incomes.

This scenario fits into the Hungarian tradition of gradual transformation. It does not call for a brave stand by politicians. They will simply need to be willing to accept an organic growth of the private sector in the health-care system and provide for periodic codification of de facto institutional changes that have occurred. Of course, the long, slow, painful period of transformation could be radically shortened by a charismatic reforming government prepared to let society out of the trap rapidly, even at the price of initial unpopularity.

However, let me repeat that this is not a forecast. It is not possible to guarantee that there will be either a slow, gradual transformation or a bold breakthrough. There are traps from which societies do not succeed in escaping for long, long periods of history.

Gratitude Money As an Emblem of the Post-Socialist Transformation

Gratitude payments in the health sector are an important problem. Their survival or elimination affect the lives of almost all Hungarian citizens. However, their significance goes beyond this, which is one reason why they are worth examining closely. Gratitude payments are symbolic of the remnants of a closed and opaque society, or new variants of this in

Hungarian society. They represent, in an extreme and blatant form, a twilight in which public affairs are hidden from the public, personal relations are sullied, mutual confidence is undermined, the state is outwitted by collusion, moral values are impaired, and plain, honest speaking is absent.

The incidence and size of gratitude payments, and the progress made in eliminating them, can serve as a yardstick. They make a good proxy for where the health reform stands. More importantly still, they indicate where Hungary stands with the structural transformation and moral purging of its society and its political sphere.

References

Ádám, György (1986). *Az orvosi hálapénz Magyarországon* (Medical gratitude money in Hungary). Budapest: Magvető Kiadó.

Berman, Peter (1998). *National Health Insurance in Poland: A Coach without Horses?* Cambridge, Mass.: Harvard; and Warsaw: Jagellonian Consortium for Health.

Bognár, Géza, Róbert Iván Gál, and János Kornai (2000a). *Hálapénz a magyar egészségügyben* (Gratitude money in the Hungarian health sector). TÁRKI Társadalompolitikai Tanulmányok No. 17. Budapest: TÁRKI.

Bognár, Géza, Róbert Iván Gál, and János Kornai (2000b). "Hálapénz a magyar egészségügyben" (Gratitude money in the Hungarian health sector). *Közgazdasági Szemle* 47: 293–320.

Buchanan, James, Robert D. Tollison, and Gordon Tullock (eds.) (1980). *Toward a Theory of the Rent-Seeking Society*. College Station, Texas: Texas A and M University Press.

Dallago, Bruno (1990). *The Irregular Economy: The Underground Economy and the Black Labor Market.* Aldershot, England, Dartmouth and Brookfield, Vt.: Gower.

Ékes, Ildikó (1993). *Rejtett gazdaság — láthatatlan jövedelmek tegnap és ma* (Hidden Economy—Hidden Incomes. Past and Present). Budapest: Published by the author.

Friedman, Eric, Simon Johnson, Daniel Kaufmann, and Pablo Zoido-Lobarton (1999). *Dodging the Grabbing Hand: The Determinants of Unofficial Activity in 69 Countries*. Paper prepared for the Fifth Nobel Symposium in Economics: The Economics of Transition. Stockholm, September 10–12.

Fuchs, Victor (1996). "Economics, values and health care reform". *American Economic Review* 86: 1–24.

Gábor, István R., (1979). "The second (secondary) economy. Earning activity and regrouping of income outside the socially organised production and distribution". *Acta Oeconomica* 22: 291–311.

Gábor, István R. and Péter Galasi (1985). "Second economy, state and labour market". In *Labour Market and Second Economy in Hungary*, ed. Péter Galasi and György Sziráczki. Budapest: Campus.

Havasi, Éva and Róbert Schumann (1999). „A rejtett gazdaság a lakossági vélemények tükrében" (The hidden economy in the reflection of public opinion). *Statisztikai Szemle* 77: 952–65.

Janky, Béla and István György Tóth (1999). *Adótudatosság, fiskális illúziók és az egészségbiztosítás reformjával kapcsolatos vélemények* (Tax awareness, fiscal illusions and opinions on the reform of the health care sector). Budapest: TÁRKI. Mimeo.

Keszthelyiné Rédei, Mária, Judit Lakatos, and Zsuzsanna Szabó (1999). „A rejtett gazdaság kiterjedése 1997-ben" (The expansion of the hidden economy in 1997). *Statisztikai Szemle* 77: 913–31.

Kornai, János and Karen Eggleston (2000). *Choice and Solidarity: Reforming the Health Sector in Eastern Europe*. Cambridge University Press. Forthcoming.

Krueger, Anne O. (1974). "The political economy of the rent-seeking society". *American Economic Review* 64: 291–303.

KSH (1999). *Statistical Yearbook of Hungary 1998*. Budapest: Központi Statisztikai Hivatal.

Lackó, Mária (1999). *Hidden Economy—An Unknown Quantity? Comparative Analysis of Hidden Economies in Transition Countries in 1989–1995*. Working Paper 9905. Vienna: Institut für Volkswirtschaftslehre.

Newhouse, Joseph (1996). "Reimbursing health plans and health providers: Efficiency in production versus selection". *Journal of Economic Literature* 34: 1236–63.

OECD (1993). *OECD Health Systems*. Vol. 1: *Facts and Trends 1960–1991*. Health Policy Studies No. 3. Paris.

OECD (1994). *The Reform of Health Care Systems. A Review of Seventeen OECD Countries*. Paris.

Popper, Karl R. (1962). *The Open Society and its Enemies*. Vols. I–II. New York and Evanston: Harper and Row Publishers.

Saltman, Richard E., and Josep Figueras (eds.) (1997). *European Health Care Reform: Analysis of Current Strategies*. Copenhagen: WHO Regional Office for Europe.

Tullock, Gordon (1967). "The welfare cost of tariffs, monopolies, and theft". *Western Economic Journal* (now *Economic Inquiry*) 5: 224–32.

Notes

1 In writing this paper I have relied extensively on research into the medical gratitude system conducted by TÁRKI, an independent Hungarian social research institute. This research was directed by the author in conjunction with Dr Géza Bognár, MD and the sociologist and economist Róbert Gál. I would like to take this opportunity to express thanks to these two colleagues of mine and to István György Tóth, director of TÁRKI, for their inspiring cooperation. The numerical findings of the research are reported in the studies Bognár, Gál, and Kornai (2000a and 2000b), to which I refer in the abbreviated form BGK (2000a and b, respectively).

My research has been supported by Collegium Budapest, the Central European University, and the National Scientific Research Foundation (OTKA programmes T 018280 and T 30080).

The study was written in Hungarian. I am grateful to Brian McLean for his excellent translation and to Julianna Parti for her editorial help, and to both for their helpful comments.

2 In recent years patients have had to contribute to the cost of certain services, but these co-payments are not great relative to the total cost.

3 For simplicity's sake, the payments are considered in this study to come from patients, although in many cases they may be made by a relative on the patient's behalf.

4 See Buchanan et al. (1980); Krueger (1974); and Tullock (1967).

5 We were careful not to put the question to the doctors in the form "How often do you personally receive gratitude money and how much?" We were afraid that medical respondents would decline to answer and would lose their confidence in us. Instead, we asked "In your opinion, how often on average do doctors (or doctors in a specific field) receive gratitude money, and how much?"

6 See Ádám (1986), p. 57. This book gives an excellent account of the history of gratitude payments in Hungary.

7 This behavior is known in English-speaking countries as moonlighting.

The most important works on the second economy in the Kádár period are Gábor (1979); Gábor and Galasi (1985); Ékes (1993); and Dallago (1992). The latest studies on the hidden economy in post-socialist Hungary are Mária Rédei Keszthelyi et al. (1999); and Havasi and Schumann (1999).

Turning to the size of the post-socialist informal economy, several authors have tried to give a comparative quantitative estimate for several countries. The most reliable results have come from the investigation by Mária Lackó (1999). These suggest that the output of the informal, officially unrecorded economy in 1997 added 25.5% to the officially recorded GDP in 1997. Another quantitative comparison is described in a study by Friedman et al. (1999).

8 For more detail, see the author's book on the Eastern European health-care reform (Kornai and Egglestone 2000).

9 In 1998 the Central Statistical Office asked a representative population sample of 2,500 to what extent they agreed with the following statement: "There are circumstances in which tips have to be given, like it or not." There was complete agreement by 59.6% of the respondents and strong rejection by 9.5%. The rest agreed with the statement to some extent (Havasi and Schumann 1999, p. 953).

10 Interestingly, anesthetists in the United States are among the best-paid medical professionals, while in Hungary they are paid no more than the average for doctors and receive no gratitude money.

11 This research was headed by the author and István György Tóth. For the numerical findings, see Janky and Tóth (1999). The proportions quoted in the text appear on p. 64 of the report.

12 If one of the main sources for the increase in medical earnings became voluntary private insurance, this would make the financial burdens on a family easier in a year in which a family member fell ill. However, the premiums would also have to be paid

at other times, when no member of the family happened to be ill. On the other hand, the long-term cost of private medical insurance may be greater, or it may be less, than the long-term cost of making gratitude payments. It will probably be greater (i) because the extra pay, however generated, will affect all doctors, not just those receiving gratitude money, which increases the costs that private insurers have to meet; (ii) private insurers may allow cross-subsidy of the relatively sick by the relatively healthy; and (iii) private insurance will be costlier to administer than gratitude money.

13 *What Could the West Have Done to Help the East?*

ANDERS ÅSLUND

In 1989 the collapse of communism and the Soviet bloc was the dominant theme in the world. It penetrated all discussions about society. Immediately, 1989 was seen as one of the great revolutionary years in history, and was most often compared with 1848 (Ash 1990; Dahrendorf 1990). It was the dominant theme of all international discussion. Views about what should be done and by whom differed, but the importance of these events was beyond dispute. All issues were discussed at length and with unprecedented public attention. The whole range of social scientists were suddenly preoccupied with post-communist transition to democracy and a market economy.

This raises a plethora of issues. What kind of assistance did these societies need? What could they absorb? What could the West do for them? What organizations or forms of cooperation should be used? How much money was needed, and was the West prepared to put it up?

In this paper we shall first consider the extent of the resources that the West could possibly have put up. We shall then examine the major potential tasks of the West that are often suggested, namely, support of macroeconomic stabilization, foreign direct investment, technical assistance or consulting, trade access, and education. We shall also consider the role of private assistance.

The Peace Dividend Did Not Require Any Contemporaneous Action

When the Soviet Union collapsed, the Soviet military threat disappeared. As a result, the West was able to undertake a radical reduction in its military expenditures, and this it has done, although gradually. As the

US spent the most, the cuts it has made have been greatest. Between 1982 and 1989 the US spent 6.0 percent of its GDP on defense, but in 1998 and 1999 this share had fallen to 3.2 percent of GDP. If we accept 6.0 percent of GDP as the peacetime standard imposed by the Soviet threat during the Cold War, this means that the US benefited from a peace dividend of no less than 2.8 percent of GDP in 1999—that is, $242 billion. If we calculate the whole US peace dividend from 1992 to 1999, we obtain almost $1.4 trillion in current US dollars (see table 1).

Table 13.1 *The US Peace Dividend*

Year	% of GDP	Current Dollars (in billions)
1992	1.1	68.7
1993	1.5	98.4
1994	1.9	132.0
1995	2.2	159.9
1996	2.5	191.5
1997	2.6	210.9
1998	2.8	238.3
1999	2.8	257.6 (est.)
TOTAL		1,357.3

Source: US Census Bureau (1999), p. 368.

These are huge numbers. As the US budget deficit used to be approximately 3 percent of GDP, it turns out that it is not President Clinton alone, but primarily Presidents Gorbachev and Yeltsin who have eliminated that deficit. Arguably, the US could have restructured its defense much faster, making the peace dividend considerably larger. However, this huge gain went largely unnoticed, as nobody had any interest in claiming it.

However, for the contemporaneous Western governments, the peace dividend was for free. Regardless of what the West did, the peace dividend obtained. As gratitude is not a force driving world politics, few felt any need to undertake any real serious measures. The West saw little threat from the former Soviet Union and little possible gain.

Nor was there much urge in the West to give monetary assistance to anybody at this time. Development aid to the Third World had been widely discredited as ineffective, and as corrupting rather than helping. Therefore, most of the free-market Right, especially in the United States, was against most government assistance at home and abroad. In Europe, left-wingers had advocated large government transfers of money both at home and abroad, but they were not very enthusiastic about a right-wing transformation of the former communist world. Thus the Right liked what it saw happening in the East, but it was against spending government money on principle. The Left favored government largesse but it was against what happened in the East. The obvious consensus was to disagree on the substance and spend a minimum.

Therefore, some loose talk in the debate about a Marshall Plan was never taken seriously. The Marshall Plan had amounted to 2 percent of US GDP, that is, some $180 billion in current dollars. Instead, limited amounts of money were disbursed for accepted purposes through largely traditional channels.

Macroeconomic Financial Support Led the Way

The great early need for external financing was for macroeconomic stabilization. Most post-communist countries suffered from rampant inflation, large budget deficits, excessive foreign debt servicing, and plummeting exchange rates. The only exceptions were Hungary and Czechoslovakia, and partly Romania. Here there was a broad Bretton Woods consensus that international financing was needed.

The need for external financing was of two kinds. First, the nearly depleted international reserves needed to be replenished. Second, in some cases foreign debt servicing had to be restructured or even partly written off. The first of these tasks was a standard IMF assignment. Characteristically, the IMF demanded that a country reduce its budget deficit both through expenditure cuts and increased revenues, in return for loans designed to replenish that country's international reserves.

An additional idea was to extend the international reserves through a stabilization fund that would guarantee a pegged exchange rate in the course of the financial stabilization. The pegged exchange rate would facilitate stabilization by providing a nominal anchor and enforcing monetary discipline early on. The great champion of stabilization funds was Jeffrey Sachs (1991a, 1993a). Institutionally, the problem was that the IMF did not usually provide such financing, thus direct bilateral financing was needed. This was much more difficult to mobilize politically since the parliament in each country involved usually had to make a special budget allocation for any stabilization fund.

Debt restructuring was a much more complicated matter, involving several bodies. Government debt to other governments was renegotiated in the so-called Paris Club, while government debt to commercial banks was discussed in the London Club. The basis of any debt restructuring was usually a functioning IMF loan program, and the Paris Club usually preceded the London Club. Poland desperately needed a reduction in its debt to Western governments, and Bulgaria a partial write-off of its debts to foreign banks. Russia could not manage without a restructuring of its foreign debt servicing as it was taking on the whole former Soviet debt.

The IMF is not supposed to finance the budget, although that does happen. The World Bank and bilateral donors, however, can and do provide so-called balance-of-payments financing, which means credits for the state budget. World Bank "adjustment loans" are provided to a government on condition that a number of systemic reform measures, often connected with deregulation, are undertaken.

To any standard economist it was obvious that these countries needed macroeconomic stabilization. However, in most post-communist countries, knowledge of standard economics was minimal and few understood this need. Worse, many thought that the issuing of money and high inflation stimulated production. In addition, the budget deficits tended to be huge—in the order of 20 percent of GDP in the former Soviet republics just after the collapse of the Soviet Union. Moreover, a few influential people made huge fortunes on inflation and arbitrage between state-controlled prices and free prices. This complicated the politics of financial stabilization.

Traditionally, the communist countries had looked upon the IMF and the World Bank as vestiges of capitalism and had refused to join them. Hungary and Poland had broken this ideological taboo in the 1980s and the Soviet Union had started cooperating with the IMF in 1990, although it did not formally join the organization. After the demise of communism the East Central Europeans swiftly joined the IMF, while most of the CIS countries were admitted in the spring of 1992 to both the IMF and the World Bank. Both the Bretton Woods institutions facilitated early and swift membership.

The international financial institutions and bilateral donors faced a sensitive dilemma. They could weigh in and change the politics of a country with relatively limited amounts of money, which were crucial for the countries in crisis; but at the same time they risked losing the whole amount offered. If they stayed away, financial stabilization was not likely to occur for some time and the social and political costs of transition would be far greater, but new credits would not be wasted. Arguably, the handling of this choice represented the most important international impact on the transition. Six of the early transition countries undertook early and successful transformations and gained adequate international support. However, the support they needed differed, and their experiences left different legacies.

Hungary, Poland, Czechoslovakia, and the Baltics Received Effective Aid

Hungary had already undertaken much of the transition to a market economy. It had already been a member of the WTO, the IMF, and the World Bank for some time. Its foreign debt burden and severe macroeconomic strains were considerable but manageable. Hungary received plenty of early credits from the international financial institutions and became their darling. The Hungarian lesson was that nothing very radical was necessary, either in economic policy or in international assistance. The international financial institutions could go about their business as usual and no dramatic emergency measures were necessary. That the Hungarian situation was peculiarly normal was played down.

Poland appeared to be the opposite of Hungary, with its rampant financial crisis. The Mazowiecki–Balcerowicz government committed itself to eliminating the budget deficit and the West promised to provide international reserves, a stabilization fund of $1 billion to facilitate the pegging of the zloty exchange rate, and eventually to write off half of Poland's foreign debts. The Balcerowicz reform program was published in mid-October 1989, and the last two months of the year were devoted to the twin tasks of pushing through the necessary reform legislation domestically and raising international financing for the reform efforts. Both were needed for success, and both were accomplished. The West displayed a broad consensus from the outset. They got together in the G-24, a group of the then twenty-four members of the OECD, and made bilateral pledges of financing to the stabilization fund. In parallel, the IMF and the World Bank provided substantial multilateral credits. All the assistance was based on strict policy conditions agreed with the Polish reformers. The parliament of each donor country then had to approve a specific budget allocation. This was done, but it was a tedious political process which was possible only because of great Western commitment to Poland's success. While the substantial Western financing was important for Polish success, the Western focus on sound economic conditions helped to guide Poland in the ensuing stage. A contributing factor in the strong Western support for Poland was that it was relatively cheap. The up-front cost was about $1.6 billion (Sachs 1993a). Poland stood out as an instructive example of what international support could mean in a real crisis.

Czechoslovakia was the simplest case. It had a government with a firm parliamentary majority strongly committed to radical economic reform and a sound fiscal policy all along. The country was only facing a liberalization shock, which it took in its stride. The West, in the form of the G-24, raised a stabilization fund that made the pegging of the Czechoslovak krona possible, but Czechoslovakia did not need, and did not request, any IMF funding until 1993. Similarly, the Czechoslovak government did not want much in the way of World Bank credits. With little regard for Czechoslovakia's very favorable initial financial conditions, the leading Czech reformer, Vaclav Klaus, went on to advocate that the outside world should not provide financing for any other transition countries either.

The Baltics offered a much more complicated situation. They emerged as independent states all of a sudden in August 1991, and they were simply not prepared to undertake early reforms. Their governments were intent on undertaking radical market economic reforms, but the competence of their policy makers was in doubt. Their parliaments had been elected in early 1990, and they were dominated by nationalists with vague economic views. As the Baltic states remained in the hyperinflationary ruble zone in early 1992, inflation surged and they did not control their monetary policy. Estonia set the trend by going for a very radical reform and introducing a currency board, with a firmly fixed exchange rate, a balanced budget, and a prohibition against monetary financing of the state budget in June 1992. Through its radical policies the Estonian government acquired international credibility, which was also lent to Latvia and Lithuania, who followed suit in the next few months. Again, the G-24 acted, identifying a financing need of $1 billion for the three Baltic states in one year. In contrast to Poland and Czechoslovakia, it was quite difficult to fill this financial gap, which was proportionately much larger than for Poland. The IMF and the World Bank provided only $400 million. The EU, the Nordic countries, and Germany saved the day with disproportionate bilateral contributions. The EU alone put up $300 million. The US, however, did not contribute at all. Estonia's early stabilization was, in effect, secured by Estonia's recovering substantial prewar gold reserves that had been deposited in the West (Citrin and Lahiri 1995).

Although the international aid effort to the Baltics was a success, it showed the limitation of the West. The IMF and the World Bank were not supposed to put up sufficient resources on their own. The Europeans could mobilize balance-of-payment support, but with considerable efforts, while far-away Japan did so with ease. The US, on the contrary, was not at all willing to do so. In effect, the US approach to the Baltics in 1992 marked the end of further major Western aid efforts to transition countries. For the future, the international financial institutions had to face the music on their own.

The West Did Not Support Russian Reforms

When the Soviet Union collapsed at the end of 1991, post-communist transition was already a well-established process, and the failed coup by communist hard-liners in August 1991 made it clear that the Soviet Union could not survive (Åslund 1991). Since the fall of 1989, the end of communism and the Soviet Empire had been a dominant theme in international discourse, and the importance of these events was never in doubt—as was made evident by enormous publicity and public discussion. The "Washington consensus" for Eastern Europe dominated in a vast economic literature.

The international community had geared itself up to handle market transition in the Soviet Union. In mid-1990 the managing director of the IMF flew to Moscow to launch a major study for the G-7 on how to reform the Soviet economy and on the criteria under which Western economic assistance could effectively support such market economic reform (Gould-Davies and Woods 1999). At the end of 1990, four big international economic organizations—the IMF, the World Bank, the OECD, and the EBRD—undertook a major study of the Soviet economy, which involved dozens of professionals from all these four organizations. The publication of the three-volume study was greeted as a major event, as the Soviet authorities had never before released so much information. The report advocated a radical and comprehensive reform program of the Polish type (IMF et al. 1991).

In June and July 1991 a Grand Bargain initiative was elaborated for the G-7 meeting in London in July 1991 by a number of prominent Harvard scholars and Russian economists on how to reform the Soviet economy with substantial Western support (Allison and Yavlinsky 1991). In spite of considerable Western sympathy the proposal was not accepted, because Soviet president Mikhail Gorbachev failed to make a sensible proposal himself, and his political control was obviously waning.

The aftermath of the August 1991 Soviet coup made clear that the Soviet Union was over and that the relevant entities were the union republics. It was also apparent that Russia had opted for democracy, and Boris Yeltsin had already been elected president of Russia with a majority of 59 percent of the votes cast in free and democratic elections in June 1991. On October 28, 1991, Russian president Boris Yeltsin made his greatest speech to the Russian parliament, presenting a comprehensive radical economic reform proposal and appealing for all kinds of Western support, though not mentioning numbers (Yeltsin 1991). His radical reform speech was overwhelmingly approved by a vote of the Russian parliament. A week later President Yeltsin undertook a radical government reform. He abolished almost all of the dozens of branch ministries, cut the government staff sharply, and appointed a completely new government of young reformers, largely drawn from economic research rather than from old political or bureaucratic cadres, with Yegor Gaidar as deputy prime minister and reform leader.

It appeared reasonable to expect the outside world to do whatever it could to support the Russian transition to a market economy. Seldom has a major event in history been so obviously positive and so evident in its coming. Seldom has such a great historical chance opened up. Alas, the West did not offer any significant support. Yeltsin's newly appointed young radical reform government was working night and day preparing its reforms, and a strong, informed Western opinion demanded action (Åslund 1995). In November 1991, for instance, the *New York Times* wrote in an editorial: "The challenge for the West is to encourage Mr. Yeltsin's real, radical program by giving attentive assistance now" (*International Herald Tribune*, November 13, 1991). On December 17, 1991, an editorial in the *Financial Times* stated: "Now is the first and, perhaps, the last chance for the West to promote radical economic reform in the former Soviet Union."

However, the leading Western governments revealed no intention of supporting reform in Russia. In mid-November 1991 the new Russian reform government received the deputy ministers of finance of the G-7. During four days of negotiations the G-7 deputies were only prepared to discuss one issue: the joint and several responsibilities of the soon-to-be former Soviet republics for the full Soviet debt. To judge by their actions, they seem to have been aware of the impending break-up of the Soviet Union, but their sole, short-sighted interest was in securing their claims on the Soviet Union. The young Russian reformers were shocked and dismayed by the G-7's total lack of interest in their reform plans.

The next Western initiative, a large international conference on humanitarian aid to the former Soviet Union, held in Washington, D.C. in late January 1992, was equally irrelevant to reform. Nobody from the former Soviet Union was invited. The obvious purpose of this meeting was to avoid any discussion of serious reform and macroeconomic stabilization. On April 1, 1992, US president George Bush and German federal chancellor Helmut Kohl had declared their intention of mobilizing a Western aid package of $24 billion for Russia, but this claim was never substantiated or rendered credible (Åslund 1995, pp. 214–7). In April the reformers faced a massive onslaught by the semi-democratic, and now anti-reformist, parliament, and by June 1992, President Yeltsin effectively gave up and appointed a number of reform foes, including Viktor Chernomyrdin, as deputy prime ministers. One of the reasons for the political failure of the Russian reform government was that it did not get any support at all for reform from the West.

It is difficult to comprehend how the leading Western policy makers could be so unwise. The only party that could have made significant decisions was the US president, but he did nothing. A number of factors seem to have contributed to this extraordinary passivity. The Bush administration seems to have been among the last to realize that the Soviet Union was breaking up, and it apparently wanted to shore up the Soviet Union until the very end, as evident from President Bush's "chicken Kiev" speech in August 1991, in which he told the Ukrainians to stay in the Soviet Union. Another reason was that the Bush administration was highly reluctant to provide any international financing, as later shown in the Baltics in 1992 as well, where the Europeans fortunately put up the money. The approaching presidential elections in November 1992 appear to have rendered the Bush administration totally ineffective, and a conviction prevailed that international assistance was unpopular with voters. The problem was that the Soviet collapse was so peaceful and democratic that it did not seem to require any urgent action. Personal factors were also relevant. Soviet president Mikhail Gorbachev was favored over Russian president Yeltsin, although only the latter was democratically elected. Gorbachev's aide, Grigory Yavlinsky, was preferred over Yeltsin's reform leader, Yegor Gaidar, who was not really known in Washington. In February 1992, the well-informed Washington Post columnist Jim Hoagland concluded that the US did not provide any support to Russia because President George Bush reckoned that Boris Yeltsin was a transitional figure (*International Herald Tribune*, February 12, 1992). As the *Financial Times* prophesied, this was the only big chance the West got to support reform in Russia. The responsibility must rest with President Bush and his closest aides.

The money discussed was insignificant in comparison with the benefits. The total request for financial assistance for Russian economic reform in 1992 was about $25 billion, of which $6 billion were meant for a stabilization fund. The bilateral US contribution desired would have been in the order of $3 billion, while the US gained some $69 billion in peace dividend that year alone (see table 1). In fact, the West gave over $12 billion to Russia in 1992, but against reform. This money was issued as commodity credits which merely benefited commodity traders and their corrupt conduits. These export credits were bilateral and not made conditional on any reform measures. Nor were they coordinated with any international financial institution (Åslund 1995). Thus Western policy was neither to support reform in Russia nor to use the international financial institutions for that purpose, while a substantial amount of bilateral money was spent.

The Other Former Soviet Republics Gave up on Reform

The other countries in the FSU all watched Russia and made adjustments accordingly. They saw a spectacular failure in Russia in early 1992, and they drew a number of important conclusions for themselves. First of all, financial stabilization and a return to economic growth were not in sight. Therefore, they could not see why they should challenge their own establishments and opt for an early radical reform. They preferred to wait and undertake minimal, gradual reform. Politically, this conviction solidified the standing of the old nomenklatura throughout the region.

Second, as the West was slow and niggardly in its financial support even to Russia, the other former Soviet republics realized that they had even less hope of economic support. They learned that essentially all international financial assistance would be provided by the IMF and the World Bank.

Third, in the short term one of the few factors that could mitigate their hard economic fate was the presence of Russian price subsidies and subsidized credits supplied through the ruble zone. Most former Soviet republics therefore supported the ruble zone more or less actively, and in effect preferred to extract the last Russian subsidies rather than trying to stand on their own legs. The result was hyperinflation in ten former Soviet republics in 1993.

It is difficult to apportion the blame, but it is clear that Western reluctance to engage early on and decisively in Russia contributed to the delay of reform not only in Russia but in all CIS countries. Stabilization was delayed not just by a little, but usually by three or four years. The frequent idea among Russophobes that the West should help everybody but Russia in the former Soviet republics was the worst disservice to those countries.

Investment Financing Has Been Over-Emphasized

A popular view, both on the Right and the Left, is that money should not be given to the government but to productive investment, which would return a profit. Such ideas inspired the establishment of the European Bank for Reconstruction and Development (EBRD) and a number of US Enterprise Funds for different countries. The World Bank has all along provided long-term investment credits, and so has the Asian Development Bank (ADB) for the Asian transition countries.

On the right wing, two kinds of argument have become popular. One argument is that foreign governments should help not states, but the private sector—but that is corporate welfare abroad, which is even more harmful to the economy than corporate welfare at home. Bearing in mind that post-communist countries have weak institutions and suffer from abundant rent seeking, any form of corporate welfare must be avoided. The state should not support private enterprises anywhere.

The other right-wing argument is stronger, since it is at least symmetric. It is essentially laissez-faire in its claim that all government aid is wrong and that only free-market forces should be permissible. This argument can be supported by the existence of both market failure and state failure, as well as a great shortage of information. With regard to international financing, the idea is that only private financing is permissible.

In the early stages of transition, economic conditions are highly uncertain and unstable. Few serious investment projects can be recommended as it is impossible to forecast relative prices, sales, profitability, or any market conditions. No enterprises in the region possessed standard audits at the outset of the transition. Legal conditions were even more uncertain, as little commercial legislation had been adopted and legal systems cannot be altered swiftly. Property rights in particular were not properly clarified. The only enterprises big enough to be worth the substantial transaction cost of an international investor or credit agency were state enterprises, and any investment in them was more likely to delay adjustment than to facilitate it.

For these and many other reasons, all kinds of investment financing tended either to be impeded or lost in the early stages of the transition. It was only later on that investment financing could become effective, but that meant that it was not much use in facilitating the actual transition. It was later that not only government agencies but private investors were prepared to provide substantial financing.

Today, there is virtual unanimity about the many positive qualitative features of foreign direct investment (FDI), but there remain problems with its quantity and timing. It comes very late in the transition process. By 1999 only the six most successful transition economies had substantial FDI. Rather than assisting the early transition, FDI comes as the proof of its success. It has thus been irrelevant for the success of a transition, with the possible exception of Hungary which received large early FDI and benefited from it.

The other form of private investment is foreign portfolio investment in bonds and equities, and it is difficult to say anything positive about it. It is characterized by four major flaws. First, like FDI, private portfolio investment does not come early, so it does not contribute towards financing the stabilization. Private investors are too averse to risk to substitute for the IMF and the World Bank. Even after stabilization they have demanded horrendous yields, often of more than 100 percent a year in domestic currencies. Second, unlike FDI this investment has been overwhelmingly oriented towards government bonds, mitigating the immediate need for fiscal adjustment but eventually leading to financial crises. Since portfolio investment is not connected with many macroeconomic conditions it weakens the conditionality of the international financial institutions. Third, when portfolio investment catches on it can swiftly reach tremendous and destabilizing levels. The case in point is Russia in 1997, which received $46 billion, or 10 percent of GDP, in foreign portfolio investment, while FDI was a moderate $6 billion (RECEP 1999). Fourth, the introduction of investment by minority shareholders on a large scale in countries with poor corporate governance implies a moral hazard to domestic businessmen. To steal this capital is so easy that those who do not do so are seen as stupid rather than moral. Thus, substantial early foreign portfolio investment has turned out to be of no benefit, but rather destabilizing and demoralizing. The Central Europeans and the Baltic states were wise in avoiding it, while primarily Russia, but also Ukraine, were hard hit. Borrowing in significant amounts through government bonds in particular, regardless of their denomination and maturity, should be discouraged, while it has generally been seen as a sign of sophistication.

We can conclude that foreign investment neither can nor should play a major role in the early stage of the transition, and that there is no replacement for the international financial institutions in financing stabilization. Financial destabilization is an ultimate market failure, when risks are perceived as excessive at any yield. Foreign direct investment is helpful, but it tends to come as a confirmation of success rather than as a catalyst. Significant foreign portfolio investment seems outright harmful in the early stage of the transition and should not be encouraged.

Advice/Technical Assistance Played a Significant Role

Whenever new thinking is required in a country, the natural instinct is to turn to the outside world. For outsiders, it is always exciting to be in demand. Countries and international organizations are mostly happy to provide knowledge and its human incarnation, consultants. Government advisors are supposed to work at a high level of government to transfer the new thinking. As the peak of the government is small, it makes sense to have only a limited number of foreign advisors. Foreign advice is therefore cheap, and many governments and organizations are happy to pay. The natural inclination of donors was to supply more technical assistance than was demanded; contributors found it difficult to identify sufficiently qualified consultants, and often the receiver was either not very interested, or simply unable to absorb the advice.

At the outset of the transition there was great demand for foreign economic advice. Liberalization and macroeconomic stabilization were well known in other parts of the world, and much of the knowledge could just be utilized. Very few consultants were required, as these needed to work directly with the minister of finance and the chairman of the central bank. This became the stage for considerable competition among donors, since a choice was being made between different ideologies and national schools. The independent advisors were largely academics, but many of them had government experience. The most famous economic advisor was Jeffrey Sachs, a professor at Harvard University, who worked at the outset of the transition primarily in Poland and Russia. If nobody else came forward, IMF and World Bank staff filled this role. Speed was vital in the introduction of outside economic advice since initial mistakes could not be unmade and the early reformers could not possibly grasp all issues.

Privatization was something completely new to the post-communist countries, and it is a large and complicated sphere of work. It involved multiple techniques and political traps. It was therefore marred with political controversy, but it also required far more consultants than any other part of government. The consultants were largely investment bankers and large consultancy companies, which can charge fantastic prices for their services. Fortunately, the post-communist governments did not have to deal with the procurement process on their own and using their own money, as this became a favored form of assistance for the US AID, the World Bank, and the EBRD. At the time, early advice seemed vital, but with hindsight it might not have been so important, as privatization proceeded in all reform countries sooner or later.

The drafting of new laws was an important part of transition. Much of the new legislation was commercial and in many countries had not previously existed. It was therefore natural to import legislation, and the best way of doing so was by inviting foreign legal consultants to draft new laws. While hundreds of laws needed to be drafted in each country, lawyers are actually quite productive and many existing laws in other countries were duplicated. Therefore, rather limited numbers of lawyers were needed. The agency that seems to have done most in this regard is the US AID. One drawback was that countries that had a body of law largely based on French or German law found themselves with somewhat alien Anglo–American legal acts. However, the work was done fast and with little commotion. The development of the legal system as such was also on the agenda, but much less could be done here as the demand from the receiving countries was much more limited. The legal establishment tended to be pretty conservative.

A large number of public and private organizations were interested in providing assistance in the development of constitutions and political systems. Although many contacts were established, most countries were reluctant to allow foreigners to play too great a role in the formation of their political system. Many understood that there were universal rules for economics but they found it difficult to believe that the same was true of political systems, which were widely perceived as very specific to each country. Another reason was, of course, that the political system had direct bearing on political power. The same was true of government organization, although available international assistance for rebuilding government does also seem to have been pretty weak.

All told, government advice did play a significant role. Economic and privatization advice was highly controversial, but it had an impact. In larger countries, the total number of consultants to the central government could exceed one thousand people. The expenditure on consultants was not all that great. The total cost of technical assistance in broad terms was slightly over $1 billion a year for the whole region. The US AID distributed a total of $8.5 billion, and the EU technical assistance organizations, PHARE and TACIS, distributed $7.9 billion between 1990 and 1998. The EU focused on the EU accession countries, Russia and Ukraine, while the US AID has increasingly focused on the CIS, particularly Russia and Ukraine. This was certainly more than could be absorbed, and many of the consultants were not good enough to be functional, as the pool of able and willing consultants was exhausted.

The efficacy of various advice is a hotly debated issue, as it involves so many of the people discussing the transition. There is usually quite a pool of advisors present, and an ambitious leader can easily extend it. In the end, it is the local politicians who have to make the decisions, and they know that they are responsible. Their political interests, as they see them, therefore tend to dominate in the longer term. At the outset of the transition, however, accidental advisors could play a significant positive or negative role. The main point is that there is only so much that technical assistance can do, and here the main problem was overshoot. The total resources used were really so small that they should not entice us into the scrutiny of efficiency.

Trade Access Is the Key to the Future

It is vital for emerging market economies to have access to export markets. Growth in all transition economies has been preceded by a substantial restructuring and expansion of exports. The openness of Western markets has been vital.

In this regard, too, the post-communist region can be divided into two parts. Poland, Czechoslovakia, Hungary, and Romania were already members of the World Trade Organization (WTO), while Bulgaria and the Soviet Union were not. The WTO functioned as the all-embracing international trade framework. Most international trade agreement required WTO membership. On the basis of WTO principles, the Central European Free Trade Organization (CEFTA) was formed by the Central European WTO members. It functioned as an antechamber of the European Union and facilitated the entry of Central European countries to the EU. Thanks to their adherence to the WTO, these Central European countries had a legal framework for their negotiations for trade concessions with all WTO members.

The situation for those countries that were not members of the WTO was far worse. Although the WTO is called an international organization, it is really only a conference organization and an arbitration court. The WTO has been very passive and it is likely to remain so. Although Bulgaria and most of the FSRs soon applied for membership of the WTO, the WTO dragged its feet, revealing no interest in recruiting new members. To begin with, two or three years were wasted on sheer formalities. Then, multilateral negotiations started at snail's pace. Only in 1996 did Bulgaria finally become a member of the WTO (Milthorp 1997). In 1998 Kyrgyzstan and Latvia followed, and in 1999 Estonia and Georgia. However, among the remaining countries only Lithuania, Armenia, and Moldova are likely to enter before 2002. In effect, the WTO has been absent from post-Soviet foreign trade policy. It has neither set standards nor provided technical assistance. No international organization has been preoccupied with international trade issues, which has been a serious void. To a limited extent, the World Bank and the IMF have functioned as substitutes. Being outside of the WTO, the post-Soviet countries were left as outcasts without any recourse to international trade law, and they could do little but submit to numerous anti-dumping actions.

The post-Soviet countries started off with such undervalued exchange rates that imports were very expensive. It therefore took a couple of years for significant protectionist pressures to emerge. This time could have been used to establish a framework of reasonably free trade. Unfortunately, nobody exploited that opportunity. Most post-Soviet countries developed substantial protectionist measures, mostly in the form of bureaucratic impediments rather than tariffs. The absence of an international trade organization that advocated free trade seems to be one of the greatest shortcomings in the international economic framework. While "trade but no aid" has become a right-wing slogan in both the West and the East, nobody is actually doing much about the liberalization of trade for the post-Soviet countries.

For the West, the opening of new countries for world capitalism can be perceived as both an opportunity and a threat, as new exchanges of goods, services, capital, and labor develop. Naturally, these effects have been most notable for their nearest neighbors in Europe.

Initially, many West Europeans feared that they would be flooded with émigrés. This had been their experience of previous upheavals in Eastern Europe—Hungary in 1956, Czechoslovakia in 1968, and Poland in 1968 and 1981, while the collapse of the German Democratic Republic had started with a mass exodus of East Germans. Moreover, the low standard of living in the East was evident. West Europeans did not welcome immigration as they themselves were suffering from significant unemployment of about 10 percent and there was growing support for nationalism. This fear of immigration led to a two-pronged approach, creating further division between Central Europe and the Baltics on the one hand, and the CIS on the other. West Europeans were anxious to help their closest neighbors with their economic development so that people would stay where they were, and they wanted to keep out those people who lived further away by the introduction of strict visa regulations.

A broader Western concern was that Western markets would be swamped with cheap products from the East. As the West did not think much of the production capabilities in the former communist countries they were primarily concerned with exports of steel and agricultural produce. At the beginning of the transition the output of machine building plummeted in the East, while metallurgical production kept up rather well and tended to lead the recovery. Because of the large numbers of old and inefficient steelworks in the West, increased East European exports of steel were badly taken. The EU and the US undertook repeated anti-dumping actions primarily against steel exports from Russia and Ukraine. West European agricultural protectionism was already so great that little agricultural produce from the East could enter Western Europe. While Western protectionism was hard on the East Europeans, the West could impose it with few restrictions. Size matters in trade policy. It is far easier to accept exports from small countries than exports from big countries, simply because small countries export less. This benefited the small Baltic states, and put Russia and Ukraine at a disadvantage.

Surprisingly, few Western businessmen saw the opening of the East as a business opportunity. Among big companies some did favor establishment in the East—ABB, Procter and Gamble, and McDonald's, for example, advanced on a broad front. Volkswagen undertook the biggest investment of all in the region in the Czech Republic. By and large, however, big business was not very aggressive. The new Eastern markets were small and uncertain. At the end of communism the Soviet bloc accounted for only 2 percent of world trade and 4 percent of EU trade. Another reason was that big Western enterprises were not very agile in the new post-communist economies, which required a great deal of management time. Much of this new business was developed by small entrepreneurs, and they did not have much political clout.

Trade liberalization is one of the big issues that remain on the agenda for the future.

Education Deserves More Attention Now

Strangely, little attention was given to serious education. The general view both in the West and the East was that socialist education was good, although slightly different from Western education. Certain holes in socialist education therefore needed to be filled with brief courses in transition lasting for a few weeks. Western support for post-socialist education was concentrated in brief courses and brief exchanges of academics and students.

This was a misperception of the task required. While the socialist countries had good education in general, especially in mathematics and physics, their education in economics and the social sciences was awful. What they called economics was closer to Marxist–Leninist exegesis, plus some vocational training. Education in economics needed to be built up anew, and the thousands of professors in the political economy of socialism represented an impediment to ordinary Western economics. One reason for this misperception was that three socialist countries—Poland, Hungary, and Yugoslavia—had maintained a much more Western system of education, and they were the most accessible. Another reason was that Westerners naturally knew the best scholars and tended to generalize in terms of those individuals. Moreover, the socialist universities had departments of social sciences and economics, and it was difficult to comprehend how difficult the task could be.

If a proper diagnosis had been made from the beginning, the approach would have been very different. Rather than sending faculty staff and students on brief exchanges, the West should have organized full degree courses for thousands of both undergraduate and graduate students. The ambition would then have been to build up new universities and research institutions rather than reforming the old ones. While the East Central European universities seem reformable, the CIS universities have proven harder nuts to crack. Most top education institutions in the region are new—such as the Central European University in Budapest, the New Economic School and the Higher Economic School in Moscow, the Kiev–Mohyla Academy in Kiev, and American Universities in Armenia, Bulgaria, and Kyrgyzstan. They are usually the result of foreign funding, and the main provider of funds for these new elite institutions has been George Soros (Pleskovic et al. 1999). Clearly this is an area in which an extensive Western engagement would be both welcome and fruitful.

Private Assistance Has Gained New Importance

The post-communist transformation offered non-governmental organizations (NGOs) a new opportunity to play a role in international affairs, which they seized with great energy and enthusiasm. From the very beginning, the foundations established in the region by the billionaire philanthropist George Soros became the pioneers and models.[1]

George Soros's aim, inspired by Karl Popper, was to build an open society (Soros 1991). He did so by spreading financing in the form of grants from his personal fortune to a large number of new NGOs in the region, starting with Hungary and Poland long before their actual democratization. He financed photocopiers and international exchanges, and he helped stimulate the development of local NGOs in one country after the other. As communism collapsed, George Soros expanded his activities to all post-communist countries, and the sphere of activities also expanded greatly. There were many reasons why his foundations became models that made both other foundations and governments appear to be playing "follow George". First, George Soros was personally involved, traveling extensively in the region, and he had an enterprising eye for what could usefully be done in the transition. Second, using his own money, Soros could put up substantial amounts for instant use. Soros's total funding rose to over $400 million a year by the late 1990s, making his foundations by far the greatest donors in the region. Third, by being fast, non-bureaucratic, and sensitive to local voices, Soros could thrive on the enthusiasm of activists. Thus, while generally paying lower salaries, he got better and more motivated collaborators than consultancy agencies. Fourth, with the strong idea of encouraging and thriving on local activism, Soros spent most of his money locally, where it gave much more than when spent on foreign consultants. He left real local NGOs behind. Fifth, Soros ventured into all kinds of activities that made sense but that were not undertaken by others. Sixth, because of the generally outstanding reputation of his foundations, others followed him with money and enhanced his initiatives. Finally, with as little bureaucracy as had been involved in the launching of a project, he cut financing when he realized that a project made little sense or that money was being embezzled.

The history of post-communist transformation is therefore, to a great extent, the history of the Soros foundations. They, and other NGOs, did a great deal to build civil society and many related things in the transition. Now, when the big tasks of government assistance agencies are largely over, the private foundations will remain and become all the more important, as they develop more of a domestic life and contribute to civil society.

The West Got What It Opted for

We may conclude that Western policy towards the former Soviet bloc became dualistic from the outset, and that the West got what it chose—although it seems slightly unaware of what it did choose. A broad Western consensus favored democracy and market economies in general. Germany and like-minded West European states reckoned that Central Europe should once again become a full-fledged part of Europe, and the Nordic countries adopted the Baltic states. However, nobody cared much about Romania and Bulgaria. Russia was regarded with palpable suspicion, and many wanted to keep it down and out. Asia did not play much of a role.

West Europeans were anxious to limit immigration from the East, which meant that they favored economic development in their nearest neighbors while wanting to raise visa barriers against those further away. For the same reason, West Europeans accepted the liberalization of imports from their closest neighbors while resisting any liberalization for those countries further away. In particular, the large metal exporters Russia and Ukraine scared protectionists.

The disappearance of the Soviet threat brought a huge peace dividend to the West, especially the US, in terms of lower military spending requirements. However, the peace dividend was automatic and countries give little money out of gratitude. The case for providing financing for the transition countries was politically complicated. Many on the Right who were enthusiastic about the transition to market economies, did not believe in government financing, while the Left, which favored government largesse, was not altogether happy about the disbanding of socialism. The natural consequence was that little Western government money was provided to support post-communist transition. A Marshall Plan was never a real option, and while it was discussed in public, it was never really considered seriously in any government office.

In practice, Western policy towards the post-communist countries became dualistic. The European Union embraced Central Europe and the Baltic states early on, while the West kept Russia, Ukraine, and the rest of the CIS out. Romania and Bulgaria were left as a rest post towards which the West had no policy in particular.

In most cases where the West provided significant early financing, reforms were successful. Bulgaria is the only case of a reasonably radical reform program that obtained IMF support early on and fell apart. The West did nothing for Russia, which severely hampered the Russian reforms. The absence of powerful Western support for the Russian reform and the reformers discouraged other countries from even trying for a couple of years. The frequently offered argument that the West focused too much on Russia and that it should have looked more on the other former Soviet republics appears insubstantial. As everybody in the region looked at Russia it was the obvious model for the region as a whole, regardless of how it worked out. Moreover, when not even Russia received significant international aid, that option seemed hopeless for others. In the absence of any prospect of early international financing, the CIS countries became all the more dependent on the ruble zone and Russian financial assistance connected with it.

Still, international support on its own is never enough. No reform has been carried out without a committed reform government. In some countries the international community has effectively trained some of the top policy makers and has helped to develop the domestic constituency for reform. Yet such people must come to power through their own political skills, even if a domestic preference for such policy makers helps.

References

Allison, Graham, and Grigoriy Yavlinsky (1991). "Window of Opportunity: Joint Program for Western Cooperation in the Soviet Transition to Democracy and the Market Economy". Cambridge, Mass.: Harvard University; and Moscow: Center for Economic and Political Research, 29 June. Mimeo.

Ash, Timothy Garton (1990). *We the People: The Revolution of '89 Witnessed in Warsaw, Budapest, Berlin and Prague*. Cambridge: Granta Books.

Åslund, Anders (1991). *Gorbachev's Struggle for Economic Reform*. 2nd ed. Ithaca: Cornell University Press.

Åslund, Anders (1995). *How Russia Became a Market Economy*. Washington, D.C.: Brookings.

Citrin, Daniel A., and Ashok K. Lahiri (eds.) (1995). "Policy Experiences and Issues in the Baltics, Russia, and Other Countries of the Former Soviet Union". International Monetary Fund Occasional Paper, No. 133. Washington, D.C.

Dahrendorf, Ralf (1990). *Reflections on the Revolution in Europe*. London: Chatto & Windus.

Gould-Davies, Nigel, and Ngaire Woods (1999). "Russia and the IMF". *International Affairs*, 75, 1: 1–21.

International Monetary Fund, IBRD, OECD, and EBRD (1991). *A Study of the Soviet Economy*. Paris, February.

Milthorp, Peter (1997). "Integration of FSU/Economies in Transition into the World Trade Organization". *Economics of Transition*, 5, 1: 215–223.

Pleskovic, Boris, Anders Åslund, William Bader, and Robert Campbell (1999). "Proposed Strategy to Address Critical Economics Education and Research Needs in Transition Economies". Open Society Institute, Eurasia Foundation, Starr Foundation, and the World Bank, March. Mimeo.

Russian European Centre for Economic Policy (RECEP) (1999). *Russian Economic Trends*.

Sachs, Jeffrey D. (1991a). "What Is to Be Done?" *The Economist*, 13 January.

Sachs, Jeffrey D. (1993a). *Poland's Jump to the Market Economy*. Cambridge, Mass.: MIT Press.

Soros, George (1991). *Underwriting Democracy*. New York: Free Press.

Yeltsin, Boris N. (1991). "B.N. Yeltsin's Speech". *Sovetskaya Rossiya*, 29 October.

Note

1 From 1992 to 1994, our economic advisory project to the Russian government was financed by the Swedish government and the Ford Foundation. From August 1994 until the end of 1997, I was advising the Ukrainian government on economic reform, financed by the Open Society Institute (the main Soros foundation).

14 Financial Crises, Exchange Rate Arrangements, and the IMF

RUDIGER DORNBUSCH

George Soros has been on two sides of international financial battles: as an important protagonist in bringing down currencies, as in the case of sterling or the ruble; and as a commentator reflecting on existing arrangements and their shortcomings. In this volume honoring his accomplishments as a philanthropist, a world financial personality, and a thinker on issues of the market and the open society, it is appropriate to comment on current issues in the very fields in which he has taken an interest. Leaving philosophy per se to others, comments here will focus on several topics in the area of international financial institutions and markets.

Emerging Market Financial Crises

Among developing-country currency crises another useful distinction is that between the old-fashioned, slow-motion current account crises of the 60s and 70s, and the new ones that might be called fast-motion balance sheet crises.

The old-style crises involved misaligned exchange rates and spending levels. With spending high relative to income and the currency appreciating in real terms, in time financing runs out. When capital inflows no longer finance the current account deficit, reserves start running out. And once that process gets moving it is only a question of time. With finite reserves and borrowing facilities, deficits are unsustainable and hence must one day end. Of course, governments can invent extra lives for an overvalued currency by introducing exchange restrictions, trade restrictions, restrictions of all kinds. But even these cannot add much time, even though they come at a great cost to economic efficiency. In the end the devaluation comes and a new chapter is opened.

In the old-fashioned world in which capital flows and balance sheets play no role, the run-up to devaluation, and the actual event, are thoroughly uneventful. They do not really deserve the name "crisis", except that devaluation does offer a resolution, at least until further notice. Today it would seem to provide a candidate for such a crisis. In most emerging economies capital markets have been liberalized, both within and cross-border, and hence the sheer thought of forthcoming devaluation creates havoc. But the best candidate today is probably Egypt: the country keeps appreciating in real terms, reserves keep falling. Everybody waits for the government to make up its mind that devaluation is desirable, necessary, and inevitable, and that it is only a question of time. Everybody knows it is some 10 percent or so, not much more, and God only knows when.

In other words, a very dull situation for everyone except a handful of people who will lose their jobs when it happens simply because someone has to get the blame. In the meantime, somewhat increased interest rates restrain imports and the little capital that might leave. Repressed finance, to use the technical term describing a bankrupt and government-controlled financial system, is mostly untouched by what is going on.

The difference between this and the new, fast-motion crises could not be more marked. The background here is one of a certain vulnerability in the domestic banking system, in the government debt market, or on the external front in the form of misaligned exchange rates and out-of-line current accounts. The problem can be inside or on the external front, there is little difference. The next point is the understanding that if anything goes wrong, everything will go wrong. Why? A default risk in the banks means a domestic financial collapse, and the wise preemptive move for foreign lenders or domestic residents is to get their money offshore. The same is true if there is a question about domestic public debt, foreign debt, or the exchange rate. Whatever weakness is expected, it deeply undermines the national balance sheet. And when, in the end, one, and hence all, of these vulnerabilities come into play, the blow-up is enormous.

But let us get somewhere midway into the story. The country has been discovered, it is a miracle country with growth success and bold reforms, not least the opening up of financial markets. The exchange-rate system is predictable and offers a vast excess return on borrowing offshore to make loans at home, real estate and all. No questions are asked, and where necessary envelopes change hand to grease the wheels of easy credit.

The next phase is a question about sustainability: Can the exchange rate last? Are the loans made with borrowed money sound? Will money keep coming? At this stage there will be a difference of opinion: those who believe the government has no alternative but to continue the Ponzi game of borrowed prosperity will accept to borrow more, in dollars and at shortening maturities. Those who believe they have seen it all before will take their money out. The central bank will be caught in between: raising interest rates might keep the money in but will worsen the balance sheets of financial institutions and the prospects for growth. Lowering interest rates helps growth and the balance sheets but it also means that money will leave more plentifully. We are already in the last phase, which has one certain outcome: the currency, the banks, and many companies will go. That might only come a year later, or even two, but it always happens. And the longer it takes to get there, the more betting will have taken place and the worse will be the balance sheets of those who believe that ultimately everything will work out.

When the crisis does come—in Mexico, Russia, or Asia—the result will be a formidable mismatching of maturities and of denominations. Banks may have borrowed in dollars and lent in dollars, but to customers who do not earn dollars. Or they have lent in local currency and are broken for that reason. Or they get caught by the short maturity of their liabilities relative to the long, illiquid, and often impaired credits on their books. They experience a sudden ending to the rollover of their funding—"it is not speed that kills, it's the sudden halt", the bankers' saying goes, and the rest is history.

Two summary points in these crises are worth bearing in mind: first, it does not really matter where the misalignment is; in the end, everything goes. In Korea it was the banking system and the Chaebols; in Indonesia it was everything; in Russia it was the public debt and the banks. The reason is that soundness does not exist, the entire balance sheet is vulnerable, the value at risk is formidable. Even though the country may have functioned with the system for years, the decisive shock of the cutting off of funding or of a massive capital outflow followed by currency collapse brings down *everything*. And because everything goes, the benefits of a sharp, real depreciation are little solace because the costs of a destroyed financial system are formidable. The second point is about timing: financial crises, even when they are quite obviously in the making, take longer to come than you think; and then they happen much faster than you would have thought. A good chance for economists to be wrong twice.

With these characteristics in mind, what is the recommendation for avoiding crises in the first place? The answer surely comes in two parts. First, emerging market economies should not have exchange rates. Their institutions are far too weak for the enormously difficult task of managing sound money. Even Italy and France surrendered in a merger with the German Bundesbank; alone they could not deliver good money! Emerging market economies should have a rigid currency board arrangement. Eastern Europe should be on a currency board with the euro and, ultimately, be part of monetary union. There can be no reason to wait even a day.

Latin America, obviously, should be on the dollar. This is most obvious in Mexico, where, once again, the real exchange rate is under discussion and it is conceivable, though unlikely, that the typical sixty-year cycle will once again deliver a collapse. And what goes for Mexico also holds for the rest, from Central America to Brazil and Chile. Argentina does not have an easy time given its credit history and debt overhang, but at least it has the confidence that stems from a decade of sound money. In Asia the pattern of trade makes it harder to select, but even here, rather than the current undefined regime, a dollar currency board would be a great advance pending the arrival of China as the center country in the next decade or two.

The second critical element for financial stability is a sound banking system. Given institutional weakness and the politics of banking as a preferred agency of political loans and the parking lot for dead credits, the banking system should be sold to offshore sound banks. They, in return, would have to provide the lender of last resort function which central banks and treasuries are too weak to do effectively. That means good banks—and this is, of course, a prime ingredient for growth.

The IMF

In the aftermath of the Asian crisis, the IMF has become the focus of widespread criticism and of a call for reform. Some, like former secretary of state George Shultz, propose its abolition. Others, including some members of the Meltzer Commission, look for radical reform. Still others, including the US Treasury, seek the moderate refocusing of goals and operating procedures. And yet others, most prominently Joseph Stigliz's the former World Bank chief economist and distinguished academic, see nothing right about the IMF and merely offer scathing (ignorant and misdirected) criticism.

There are three sets of overlapping issues in IMF reform: how to make the IMF better prepared to anticipate/prevent crises; what remedies to apply when a crisis does occur, that is, are IMF programs right; and how to restructure the IMF as part of the international financial architecture.

Let us consider first the crisis prevention issue. In health care it is widely accepted that preventive care vastly lowers the costs of the system by both avoiding the buildup of crises in the first place, and by early detection. Much the same surely applies in international finance. The interesting crises in this perspective are of course the ones that are large, that have spill-over potential, and that bring down regions and perhaps even the international economy. Clearly, these are balance sheet crises and the appropriate prevention must focus just here. As I have argued elsewhere (Dornbusch 1998), the IMF should conduct systematic *value at risk* analyses of client countries' financial systems.

Such analyses are complicated; there is no unanimity about appropriate models, and it is often a scenario issue rather than a daily risk measurement. While all this is true, responding by doing nothing is absurd. Yet until very recently the very notion of value at risk was alien to IMF country inspection. Even today, now that it is recognized that the fact and magnitude of the crises is a reflection of balance sheet vulnerability, value at risk scenarios have not yet become routine. There is a focus on data dissemination but not on risk measurement.

What would such analyses reveal? They would have shown the exposure of Korean investment houses to Russian and Brazilian debt financed with short-term dollar or yen loans. They would have revealed the exposure of Thai and Indonesian banks to a funding run. They would have exposed the maturity and denomination of Mexican funding and the resulting explosive vulnerability of the entire national balance sheets. Of course, that issue continues to be live in many countries.

The second issue that attracts very lively criticism is the particular form that IMF programs take. Why so much austerity? Why high interest rates? Why fiscal contraction in the midst of what is already a crisis? This range of criticisms became most vocal in the Asian crisis, unlike during the Mexican events. Countries were indignant about the fact of a crisis—they had been stars and now they were goats. They were hit by the balance sheet collapse and could not fathom why the way out was high interest rates. Their questioning was reinforced by Japanese criticism of IMF programs and, most vocally, by the ex-chief economist of the Word Bank, Professor Stiglitz. In a lead article in the *New Republic* he lambasted the IMF and the US Treasury for their alleged mismanagement, for poor economics, and for their unqualified professional staff.

The criticism was misdirected. When a crisis does occur, the hemorrhage must be stopped and there are only two ways to do this: by disrupting a commitment to an open capital market in the manner of Malaysia, or else by a demonstration of an unwavering commitment to financial stability. When countries are carried into the IMF, as it were on a stretcher, and into the emergency room, it is a poor time to try cute ideas. Basic trauma treatment is appropriate and niceties must be set aside in favor of basic survival treatment (see Dornbusch 2000c). The latter route worked in Mexico and Brazil and in all those Asian economies, notably Korea, that signed on to full and unqualified IMF treatment.

The remaining issue is the reshaping of the IMF. A survey by Williamson (2000) reviews the various headlines, from lending policy to conditionality, from transparency to governance. At one extreme there is an attempt to obtain unlimited support for pre-qualified customers. This is the view of the Meltzer Commission that wants to narrow IMF rescue down to having countries pre-certified on their policies so that any crisis situation is an "honest mistake". That leaves open the question of limits on bailouts and, more importantly, the question of how to look after the system when a big debtor, or a group of big debtors, goes into crisis, whether honest or not.

At the other extreme is the IMF's deputy managing director's position (Fischer 1999). He makes the case for the IMF, as a formal lender of last resort, an important stepping up from the current ad hoc role. Neither of the extreme proposals will go anywhere. The IMF remains the policy tool of the major economies in the world: it will operate—principles or no—in their interest and, at best, it will improve its surveillance and transparency.

The right focus, in any event, should not be the bailout function, but rather the preventive role. That could be done in a minor way with transparency but it is much better accomplished by having currency boards and offshore banking guarantees. That direction of reform would abolish amateur central banking in emerging economies and it would make crisis prevention market-based by enrolling the self-interest of the private offshore lenders of last resort.

The Euro

Among the current issues in international finance, the creation and the early performance of the euro has rightly drawn important attention. This has been a once-a-century audacious step. Its success remains to be seen, but there is no lack of conjecture. Among its chief critics have been Soros (1997) and Feldstein (1997).

The euro raises three important questions. The first is surely whether the European Monetary Union in some significant way improves on the preceding arrangements of a Bundesbank-led hard money zone. That, indeed, had been the prior arrangement, although the ability to temporarily opt out had been used in 1992 by Italy, for example. The main conceptual idea in evaluating the usefulness of a monetary union goes under the heading of "optimum currency areas". This perspective, due to Nobel Laureate Robert Mundell, argues that, in principle, a world money is the best solution for minimizing information and transaction costs. But flexibility of relative prices is essential, too. To the extent that, within an economic region, wages and prices are inflexible, a flexible exchange rate toward the outside can make up as an adjustment tool. Hence the optimal domain of a currency union is the economically integrated region that experiences common shocks relative to the rest of the world. Europe pretty much meets that criterion.

There is also an entirely different and, probably more important, perspective in looking at the integration of capital markets. A monetary union can play an important role in creating a region of financial stability. Bringing under the same roof a stable core—Germany—and a more precarious periphery helps stabilize the latter, avoiding regional currency and fiscal crises. Surely Europe has accomplished that even before it started: Italy and France were house-trained, and Italy's looming fiscal crisis went away by the simple fact of common and low interest rates. The euro worked miracles.

The next question is whether the euro can last or whether the inherently divergent political objectives and monetary cultures must clash within and across the Atlantic. This point has been made by Feldstein (1997, p.60) in his comment: "If EMU does come into existence...it will change the political character of Europe in ways that could lead to conflicts in Europe and confrontation with the United States." Outside the United States this way of thinking has been widely interpreted as sour grapes in the face of a dramatic European quest for a role in world leadership.

It is hard to be impressed by the argument that the euro breeds conflict. For a decade or more, European central banks, notably in Italy and France, have pursued a follower-role to the Bundesbank, accepting its leadership even when Buba policy was not obviously in their interest. Today, money is managed jointly. A European focus is explicit and the role of the ECB is accepted in its commitment to price stability. (Remember Germany's finance minister, Lafontaine, falling from grace in no time after his attempt to usurp the independence of the ECB.) It is certainly true that Bundesbank policy, conducted with Europe in view, is not right for everyone—Ireland is experiencing a boom and Italy stagnates. But surely Italy would not prefer to devalue and it is not obvious that Ireland would want to appreciate. Yes, there are tensions, but it is also recognized that monetary policy cannot solve all problems. In fact, the very creation of the ECB makes it more apparent that it is a mistake to overburden the central bank and neglect a serious commitment to supply-side economics.

As to a conflict with the US, a more seriously managed European money, and seriously managed US money, surely are an expression of partnership. To argue that Europe grows stronger as a result of economic and monetary union is totally appropriate. It is also appropriate to note that precisely this has been the US objective for the past fifty years. The US has believed, and acted on the belief, that a strong Europe is good for the US in terms of both security and economic prosperity. Viewing it as a threat is confusing American interests with a soccer game.

The remaining issue is, in the perspective of mid-2000, the deep depreciation of the euro against the dollar, and especially against the yen. The euro, at least in the eyes of Europeans, was to take away the US hegemony in world finance. Massive portfolio shifts into the euro and out of dollars were to eliminate the "exorbitant privilege" that de Gaulle criticized and that has chafed the French ever since. Embarrassing as it is, we are on the verge of seeing the US Treasury having to bail out the euro. It has not come quite to that, and Europe's pride would suffer immeasurably, but here we are.

The euro depreciation surely won't last for much longer. The principal reason for it is that just as the euro was introduced, with unimpressive economic performance in Europe, the US unveiled a spectacle of super performance in growth, innovation, and financial stability. No way Europe could compare even with an upswing to 3 percent growth, which is called a boom in Europe but in the US would surely be seen as a slowdown. It will take seriously bad news in the US, and at least neutral performance in Europe, to see a major shift in currency values. Returning to the high opening quotation enjoyed by the euro any time soon seems hard to believe.

Surely there is no chance of the European Monetary Union breaking up or its commitment to monetary stability being undermined—with open capital markets undermining monetary stability is a luxury governments no longer have! Surely nobody can afford to opt out at the bottom because they would pay with formidable interest rates. Opting out at the top, as Germany did when it left the fixed rate system at the beginning of the 1970s, is indeed an option and it would mean a tendency towards currency appreciation. But Europe's supply side is so bad that this might be more readily an option for Ireland than for Germany. But what would Ireland do? Float freely? Surely that is an uncomfortable regime, too. For decades to come, the euro will be there and the interesting issue now is the widening of the euro area as Eastern Europe looks for rapid access.

Both breakdown of the monetary union or, even less plausibly, transatlantic war induced by Europe's new might, are far-fetched ideas!

G3 Exchange Rate Arrangements

After three decades of flexible exchange rates among major currencies, the discussion about international monetary arrangements for G3 remains alive. For some, the current plight of the euro is a case in point, as is the strong yen, or the overvalued dollar. Hard landing is always around the corner even though the US has not experienced it in a long time. It did not experience it in the aftermath of the 1985 overvaluation and it is unlikely to happen now.

The center of attention in the exchange rate discussion are the large swings in major bilateral rates, swings that are seemingly unjustified by commensurate swings in relative fundamentals. The accompanying table shows peaks and troughs in the yen/dollar rate in the past thirty years. An episode like 1995 to 1999 makes the point.

Table 14.1 *Yen/Dollar Exchange Rate (Nominal Rate, Monthly Averages)*

Date	Weak	Strong	% change
8–71	356		
5–73		265	–26
12–75	306		15
8–78		188	–39
4–80	252		34
1–81		202	–20
10–82	271		34
4–84		225	–17
2–85	260		16
6–88		127	–51
6–90	154		21
4–95		84	–45
8–98	145		73
12–99		102	–30

One answer, of course, is to recognize that there were, indeed, important swings in fundamentals. That is most conspicuously the case for Japan in the recent episode. From 1995 to 1998, Japan moved to the very verge of a depression with near-default of its banking and insurance system and a steep decline of activity. In the ensuing year dramatic policy guaranteeing the financial system and providing huge fiscal stimulus restored a measure of normality and certainly moved the country away from imminent depression. There is little doubt that a flexible rate should broadly exhibit the pattern it did show.

But there is the extra point that even if the broad outline is right, the extent of movement is far exaggerated. Why, for example, did the Japanese currency appreciate all the way to 84 yen/dollar in mid-1995. Sometimes there is nothing stark in fundamentals that might justify these movements and when that is the case, the discussion gets in no time to alternative exchange rate regimes.

At the intellectual level there is some progress in understanding why asset markets exhibit outsized movements. At this point, the best story is based on the "noise trader" model, in which a group of exuberant agents can, by their optimism or pessimism, dominate market trends *and* make money![1] Of course, the very basis of this phenomenon is the distinction between "fundamentals" traders who understand reality, and exuberant traders. Ex post, we know who is who; ex ante everybody believes they have the right judgment.

At the level of policy, there are two views. One is the recommendation of having a system of managed exchange rates with a specified band around declared target zones. The other is to live with what we have, including opportunistic intervention when the misalignment of rates is extreme and intervention is promising. The target zone view, most prominently held by the Institute of International Economics in Washington, D.C. (see Bergsten 1999) does not have a broad following. This is in part because identifying benchmark equilibrium exchange rates is hard. Models that focus on PPP or on equilibrium current account imbalances don't do very well. But more importantly, even if there were agreement on target rates, there is the formidable issue on making exchange rate targets the focus of policy. Would the Federal Reserve and the US Congress be willing, and would they be well advised, to make exchange rates the target of monetary and fiscal policy? Would Japan do the same, and the ECB and European parliaments?

Let us consider the simple case of the euro today. By any definition of equilibrium rates we have had from the target zone crowd, the equilibrium level of the euro is somewhere near 1.20 dollar/euro. How to get there? The US would have to cut interest rates in the midst of a super boom or Europe would have to hike rates in a non-inflationary mild upturn. There is no question that this will not, and should not, happen. And if there are situations like this, then target zones are not going to be persuasive as a policy regime.

Most observers will accept that large, and possibly exaggerated, swings in currency rates are regrettable, but that doing anything about the situation is even more so. That leaves them with the possibility of intervening at extreme points to help the realignment once it gets underway. Even here success may be elusive. In early 1995 the US Treasury tried on two occasions to reverse the extreme upswing of the dollar, but the market was not ready; only at the third attempt did it work. Similarly, for the euro today intervention would be very unpromising. While intervention remains part of the policy arsenal, just as central bank intervention to sustain financial stability in the face of an asset market collapse or credit market freeze, target zones for asset prices including currency are not going to happen.

References

Bergsten, F. (1999). "The Decline of the Dollar." Presented at the World Economic Forum, Davos, Switzerland. Available at http:/www.iie.com

Dornbusch, R. (1998). "Asian Crisis Themes". Available at http/web/mit.edu/rudi.www

—— (2000a). "Stiglitz and the IMF". *The New Republic*, May 21, and at http/web/mit.edu/rudi.www

—— (2000b). *Keys to Prosperity*. Cambridge,Mass.: MIT Press.

—— (2000c). "Stiglitz vs. the IMF: Another View. Letter to the Editor". *New Republic*, May 21 and at http/web/mit.edu/rudi.www

Feldstein, M. (1997). "EMU and International Conflict". *Foreign Affairs*, Nov–Dec.

—— (1999). "Focusing the IMF". *Foreign Affairs*, March–April.

Fischer, S. (1999). "The IMF as an International Lender of Last Resort". *American Economic Review*.

Shleifer, A. (2000). *Inefficient Markets. An Introduction to Behavioral Finance*. Cambridge: Cambridge University Press

Soros, G. (1997). "Can Europe Work". *Foreign Affairs*, Sept.–Oct.

—— (1998). "The Crisis of Global Capitalism". New York: *Public Affairs*.

Williamson, J. (2000). "The Role of the IMF: A Guide to Reports". At http:/www.iie.com

Note

1 For an excellent introduction see Shleifer (2000) and the evidence and references given there.

V The Historical Dimension

15 *Medieval Central Europe: An Invention or a Discovery?*

GÁBOR KLANICZAY

It has been nine years since the idea of creating a Medieval Studies Department at the recently founded Central European University first popped up. That specific historical moment, after the changes of 1989, had a specific agenda: work on the transition. Transition from dictatorship to democracy, from socialism to capitalism, from the Eastern Europe of COMECON and the Warsaw Pact to the European Union and NATO, from the sloppy despotism of "late socialist" regimes to the rule of law, from a "closed" society to an "open" one. The pathos of this rhetoric has been intensively felt by those intellectuals connected with George Soros and his foundation network which had been working for similar goals in various socialist countries already since the 1970s. Actually, we had little time to argue about this at any great length. It probably seemed self-evident to us that the fortunate coincidence of the historical changes with the availability of new, generous funding possibilities offered by Soros would allow the growth of any new intellectual enterprise that could convincingly argue its values and usefulness within the broader stream of transition.

The suggestion of promoting medieval studies in this context sounded rather surprising, and I sensed that it was far from convincing at first sight. While nobody doubted the importance of classical-type philological scholarship, and no one questioned the merits of diligent work on the maintenance of medieval historical tradition, the question must have been asked as to how the aims of the proposed "interdisciplinary medieval studies" related to the mission of the young CEU. Together with some colleagues who were allied to this project, we did our best to formulate a coherent reasoning to convince the Board and Soros himself.

Some of our arguments were of a historical nature: we referred to the fact that this region became European precisely in the Middle Ages. If it now wanted to become part of the new Europe it had to understand and reinvigorate the medieval foundations of this belonging: "the common roots of Europe", to quote the evocative title of a book published at that time by Bronisław Geremek.[1] Closer scrutiny of the medieval period could enable us to train a new generation of modern experts who could safeguard an institutional, cultural, and artistic legacy which had once been created precisely for the service of the first adhesion of this region, to *Europa Occidens*, or which had been the immediate result of this alliance.

Within this legacy one finds a number of political and cultural patterns which could be interesting models also for the future. One such example is the medieval duality of universal structures (empire, papacy, and various ecclesiastical institutions and orders, Latinity, Canon Law, and Roman Law, and, indeed, the universities) versus local or regional ones (kingdoms, territorial powers, immunities, monasteries, parishes, holy sites, vernacular languages, customary law, etc.). Another example could be the multiethnic character of medieval kingdoms. As St. Stephen, the founder of the Hungarian Christian state, said in his famous *Exhortations* to his son Emeric: "A country with a single language and a single custom is weak and vulnerable."[2]

The study of the medieval founding period could, at the same time, indicate a series of difficulties, of potentially explosive problems that we have to confront in the current new phases of transition and European enlargement. The conversion and "Westernization" of this *barbaricum*, by disrupting and destroying older social and cultural structures and creating a set of new dependencies, frequently generated lasting resistance to the West—from the first "pagan" upheavals to the preference given to Byzantine Christianity and the creation of *Slavia Orthodoxa* and the subsequent hostilities. Another deeply rooted and still relevant problem is the ethnic and territorial fight among the various peoples in this region. This was well addressed in 1994, two years after the foundation of the Medieval Studies Department, by a Croatian student of ours who was selected as Student Speaker for the first festive Commencement of the CEU held in Budapest City Hall. "Present political observers may be perplexed by the explosion of Yugoslavia, by the bitter and murderous hostilities, by the passionate fighting around tiny stretches of new borderlines", she said. "We medievalists are less surprised, and we could explain to them that these political, ethnic, religious, and cultural animosities, these contested, shifting boundaries, have been there for a thousand years; we could also continue to give warnings, indicate where are the tectonic cracks underneath the peaceful surface, where the future outbreaks and earthquakes are to be expected." Along these lines we added that medieval studies can help not only in the diagnosis, but also in the therapy: a common discussion of old conflicts and misunderstandings, the painstaking development of a common vision of the millennial history of the peoples of this region, developed in the seminars of an international community of young and committed academics, could lead to real and lasting change here.

Another part of our argumentation related to the academic innovation which could be brought to the CEU by an apparently traditionalist discipline such as medieval studies. With experience of the age when the institution of the *universitas* was created in Europe, medievalists, we argued, could provide many useful services for the building of a new university. They have a double commitment to maintaining the tradition of classical learning and rethinking its relevance in a modern context (as in the twelfth-century confrontation between *antiqui* and *moderni*, captured in the respectful yet self-conscious metaphor of Bernard of Chartres: "We are dwarfs perched on the shoulders of giants. We therefore see more and farther than they, not because we have keener vision or greater height, but because we are lifted up and borne aloft on their gigantic stature."[3]). The field of medieval studies was among the first to pioneer an interdisciplinary cooperation (history, art history, philology, linguistics, geography, anthropology, ethnography, archaeology, etc.), and in many countries medieval studies were in the forefront of methodological innovation within the humanities, with Marc Bloch, Percy Ernst Schramm, Erwin Panofsky, Ernst H. Kantorowicz, Georges Duby, and Jacques Le Goff, to name only a few examples from the West, a list that could well be supplemented by representatives of the East European tradition in these disciplines: István Hajnal, František Šmahel, Aron Yakovlevich Gurevich, Bronisław Geremek, Alexandru Duțu, Jenő Szűcs. The relative scarcity of historical documentation obliges medievalists to rely upon the skills of neighboring disciplines, to contemplate their data in a broad comparative context, and to combine erudition with inventiveness and modern techniques of computerization and digitalization. The past decades saw the old-fashioned archival scholars, library addicts, and philologists become the pioneers of giant database projects, CD-ROM editions, and sophisticated computerized approaches, without losing their original identity and predilection for classical erudition. Among the many desired transitions in the region, we argued, the CEU could help in bringing in the essential know-how of innovations such as these, which had been totally missing in past decades because of the prohibiting lack of the necessary infrastructure and academic communication. A new generation of erudite, digitally trained experts, able to cooperate on an international level, could help the rebirth of a whole institutional infrastructure of museums, archives, libraries, and heritage preservation institutes. Nor would the significance of such an innovation be restricted to classical learning—it would also be economic and political.

Finally, we did not omit a reference to the fact that classical and medieval studies suffered a serious disruption during the socialist regime and that there is much to rebuild here. Beyond the general distortions coming from the Marxist ideological sphere, archival resources and historical monuments tended to deteriorate under communism, mainly through neglect. The result of this situation was that classical scholarship fared worse than it should have done, its experts were left marginalized and devoid of possibilities to educate a younger generation to take over their tasks. While a few outstanding older scholars continued working under these difficult conditions, another group converted to Marxism and confirmed their position by paying due tribute to ideological commonplaces. But the essence of the situation remained the same: a disruption in the continuity of institutions, museums, academic traditions, intellectual schools, and scholarly craftsmanship. It is not always recognized that those representatives of the intelligentsia who were oriented towards the maintenance of classical culture (labeled significantly in Hungary as *Lateiner*) suffered nearly as much as outright political dissidents, and that the rebuilding of their subtle network is as indispensable for the reconstruction of a cultured European civil society as, say, that of the lawyers (who, incidentally, also belonged to this *Lateiner* class in Central Europe). This may perhaps also explain why some prominent political dissidents happened to come from the peaceful fields of classical and medieval studies.

Actually, they followed a dignified tradition of medievalist scholars here: Marc Bloch was executed for his participation in the French resistance in 1944; Johan Huizinga was interned in a concentration camp in 1942; two leading Polish medievalist scholars, Aleksander Gieysztor and Jerzy Kłoczowski, fought in the armed resistance against the Germans. In Czechoslovakia, post-1968 "normalization" pushed many leading intellectuals, with prominent medievalists among them, either into exile (František Graus), onto the margins (František Šmahel), or into silence (Dušan Třeštík). The famous seminar on Plato held in Jan Patočka's apartment in Prague became a symbol of intellectual resistance to communism. Another case in point is Bronisław Geremek's dual role as scholar and politician: even during his years of persecution as Lech Wałesa's chief adviser, he regularly held a semi-legal seminar on marginals and outcasts in medieval society. Karol Modzelewski, another Solidarity leader, studied medieval "state serfdom" after having spent several years in communist prisons. In Moscow, the circle around Aron J. Gurevich was not expressly politicized, but represented an alternative scholarly orientation, a link with French and Anglo–Saxon intellectual life. Jenő Szűcs, Hungary's most noteworthy medievalist historian in the past decades, became an important figure in the intellectual opposition through his contributions to the 1980 samizdat memorial volume dedicated to István Bibó. It was here that Szűcs's famous essay "The Three Historical Regions of Europe", first saw the light of day.[4] The piece is an attempt to probe the deficiencies of contemporary East Central European civil society through an examination of the medieval roots of the problem. In Hungary, another important group of dissidents were working, in cooperation with well-known émigrés, on the rehabilitation of 1956. Here again a medievalist, János M. Bak, played an important role. A one-time active participant in the 1956 revolution, who then emigrated and became one of the organizers of the Imre Nagy Institute in Brussels in 1959, he decided, after decades of exile, to come home to Hungary, with a double commitment to participation in two new foundations—the Medieval Studies Department at the CEU and the Institute for the History of the 1956 Revolution. If I may add modestly, I myself also had this dual belonging in the 1980s, and tried to participate both in the public activities of the professional circles of medievalists and historians, and in the semi-clandestine ones of the democratic opposition. This "resistant" record of classical scholars and medievalists in Central and Eastern Europe was not of course evoked for the purpose of asking for some kind of "compensation" for these "historical merits", but rather to illustrate the commitment of this large group of intellectuals to working for goals which should have their place when the future mission of the Central European University was being formulated.

Our arguments received unexpected additional support from the recent worldwide interest in the Middle Ages. These were the years of glory for the historical novels of Umberto Eco: *The Name of the Rose* and *The Foucault Pendulum*, and many French, Italian, English, and American medieval historians were able to achieve bestseller status with well-written historical narratives. This tremendous success was analyzed in 1991 in a historiographical bestseller, a book by the American medievalist, Norman F. Cantor, *Inventing the Middle Ages*.[5] By providing a rather controversial portrait of the life and work of twenty great medievalist scholars of the twentieth century, he argued with provocative flair that the medieval world was not simply being excavated by them through systematic research but was also being conceptually created and artistically modeled. In short, it had come to be invented. George Soros has a good eye for anything that produces an unexpected vogue, and he must have perceived this invention of the Middle Ages in France, England, Germany, or the US. In any case I was most happy to hear, in the summer of 1992, that George had accepted our proposal with the comment: "Let us now go ahead and invent medieval Central Europe!"

Those times indeed brought some significant investments in the invention of medieval Central Europe. In the Visegrád palace of King Matthias, archaeologists and art historians reconstructed, with record speed, a room commemorating the 1335 Visegrád meeting of the three Central European kings, Charles Robert of Anjou (Hungary), John of Luxemburg (Bohemia), and Casimir the Great (Poland). This rebuilt room was soon hosting the new, grand meeting constituting the post-communist alliance of the "Visegrád countries" that took place there, on February 15, in 1991, with the participation of Lech Wałesa, Václav Havel, Árpád Göncz, and József Antall. The political and cultural goals of this reconstituted Central European alliance (which had been at the roots of the foundation of the CEU as well) were supported by many intellectuals and institutions, but were becoming, at the same time, increasingly controversial from the point of view of the emerging new nationalist currents and their intellectual lobbies. The Central European Middle Ages, in particular, became a construct that conflicted with a number of reinvented "national" visions of this same period. It became once again a battleground.

During the past eight years of teaching students from all over this region and beyond at the Medieval Studies Department at the CEU, this question has frequently emerged: Is medieval Central Europe an invention, or is it rather an entity that we can try to rediscover and reconstruct? The obvious preference of the historian is for the latter, though it is a much more rewarding rhetorical exercise to demonstrate, in a self-critical but also self-congratulatory manner, that it has been a fascinating invention by us medievalist scholars. What I can report here, in this Festschrift for George Soros, is that we indeed discovered many vestiges of a once existent, flowering Central Europe.

We discovered them mostly during our academic excursions. After the year-long preparations of our international Excursion Seminars animated by József Laszlovszky, and under the guidance of a team of our "local" CEU students and professors, we could compare and closely examine the medieval cities of Sopron, Kutná Horá, Telc, Česky Krumlov (Krumau), Krems, Sandomierż, Levoča (Lőcse), Cluj (Kolozsvár, Klausenburg), Sibiu (Hermannstadt, Nagyszeben), Zagreb, Rovinj, Poreč (Parenzo); or medieval monasteries such as Pannonhalma, Pécsvárad, Zlatá Koruna, Sázava, Klosterneuburg, Heiligenkreuz, Tyniec, Koprzywnica, Moldovița, Sucevița, Voroneț; or splendid royal castles and palaces such as the Hradčani in Prague, the Karlštejn, the Přemysl Palace in Olomouc, the Wawel in Cracow, the Burg and its Schatzkammer in Vienna, and compare them with Buda, Esztergom and Visegrád, or those of the higher nobility, Hunedoara (Vajdahunyad), Suceava, Česky Šternberk, Spišsky Hrad (Szepesvár), Orava, Sárvár, Sümeg, Siklós. And one could continue with the frescoes in the village churches, the varieties of agricultural landscape, the system of plots, terraces, woods, archaeological sites. I must say, it was always an experience when this international group of students and professors took possession of, or rather enjoyed together, a piece of historical heritage that they could locate and interpret from their own specific tradition, and situate it also within a newly understood and explored regional unity. We not only learned a lot, we also caused significant surprise and wonderment among the local custodians, accustomed either to local patriotic school-classes or to curious and ignorant Westerners. A recently formed community was rediscovering its historical territory.

We also discovered many past treasures of medieval Central Europe in our seminar discussions, in our library research, in constructing our computer databases, and in coordinating an extended comparative inquiry among our students. Students and professors experience daily that there is indeed a lot to be discovered and understood from the common historical constraints of this region, formed in the Middle Ages.

In examining the medieval history of the region we have encountered, no doubt, much invention as well, and we certainly did add to this, consciously or unconsciously, our own set of inventions. But it must be said that what we discovered was more appealing and more exciting. Let me summarize now, in the second half of this essay, some of these findings. How can this rediscovered and reinvented medieval Central Europe be described?

***

"Where do the internal borders of Europe run?" The question with which Jenő Szűcs started his famous essay on the three historical regions of Europe twenty years ago[6] has been occupying the thoughts of historians ever since the notion of Europe was formulated in Antiquity: Tacitus was well aware of the North/South divide, and the bipartition of the Roman Empire (also based on the duality of Latin and Greek cultures) had made the East/West divide apparent at least since the times of Diocletian[7]. These European dividing lines subsequently became complicated and nuanced when *Europa Occidens* reasserted itself in Carolingian times[8], but they basically preserved their vitality up to our own times. The political and cultural geography of Europe seemed to be content with the repeated resurrection of this quadruple partition each time the continent was thought about in polar oppositions. Medieval Christianity opposed

Western Latinity to the Greek and Slavonic Eastern Orthodox Churches. The "barbarian" North was again opposed to the Mediterranean South in Renaissance times, and the Enlightenment merrily reinvented the exotic Eastern Europe.[9] Only much later, in the nineteenth and twentieth centuries, could one observe the gradual formation of the idea of the intermediary region of Central Europe. It was the noteworthy success of this modern *Mitteleuropa* which subsequently called forth the need to research the historical genealogy of this problematic geographic unit.

Polish, Hungarian, and Czech historians have been engaged in this regional inquiry since the 1920s. Among the Polish, one should mention the work of Marceli Handelsman and Oskar Halecki, who founded, in 1927, the Federation of Historical Societies in Eastern Europe, and dealt for decades with the definition of an East Central region throughout European history.[10] Let me quote how Halecki formulated the problem some decades later, in his synthetic work *The Borderlands of Western Civilization*.[11] He characterizes historical interest as either dedicating its attention to Western Europe ("frequently identified with the whole continent") or completing the vision of Europe as a whole by rediscovering Byzantium, the Ottoman Empire, or Muscovy. He then goes on to say: "There remained, however, a vast *terra incognita* of European historiography: the eastern part of Central Europe, between Sweden, Germany, and Italy, on the one hand, and Turkey and Russia on the other. In the course of European history a great variety of peoples in this region created their own independent states, sometimes quite large and powerful; in connection with Western Europe they developed their individual national cultures and contributed to the general progress of European civilization." Subsequently he points to the "difficulty of giving to that part of Europe a truly fitting name...If only two parts, Western and Eastern Europe, are distinguished, it is impossible to find a proper place for a territory which does not belong *in toto* to either part. If the conception of a Central Europe is added, it must be specified at once that there is an inherent dualism in that central region. Leaving aside its western, homogeneously German section, only the eastern section can be roughly identified with the 'new' or 'unknown' field of study which is being introduced here into the general framework and pattern of European history. For that very reason the name East Central Europe seems most appropriate."[12]

In Hungarian historiography it was István Hajnal who addressed, after the 1920s, the issue of distinguishing historical regions within medieval and early modern Europe, on the basis of the spread of the practice of writing.[13] Similar regional comparative attempts can be detected in the work of the two leading Hungarian historians of the same period, Gyula Szekfű[14] and Elemér Mályusz[15]. Between 1935 and 1944 Emil Lukinich published the review *Archivum Europae Centro-Orientalis*. The most important results of Czech historiography in the same field were the achievements of Francis Dvornik, which concentrated upon a comparative presentation of the processes of state formation and conversion to Christianity in the region.[16]

After World War II, the historical problem of Central Europe came to be reformulated by economic and social historians. In Hungary it was Zsigmond Pál Pach who raised the issue in agrarian history, positing a Central European "deviation" in the early modern period from European, Western patterns,[17] and Jenő Szűcs, in connection with the early modern "halt" of urban evolution.[18] Ultimately it was their colleague, László Makkai, who integrated the various regional indices into a coherent picture of the "caractères orginaux" of this region, and who built structurally similar modules from this very varied raw material.[19] This is the context in which Jenő Szűcs turned to another field of comparative regional history—to the problem of identity and national/tribal consciousness (*Gentilismus*). Here he could identify a neat Central European regional pattern: the common traits distinguishing Central Europe's freshly converted "New Barbarians" around the year 1000 both from the Germanic peoples that had converted centuries earlier, and, of course, from the Ottoman Southeast or the Russian, then Mongolian, East.[20] The long-term evolution of this Central European model was initiated by his studies on national consciousness, carried forward in his essay on the three historical regions.[21] He points out that after an initial similarity between the new East Central European states and Kievan Russia in the eleventh to thirteenth centuries, the Mongolian attack introduced a breach and pushed Central Europe towards more intensive assimilation to the West. Yet the hastened and centrally promoted modernization produced side-effects (e.g. the disproportionately large nobility, the comparative weakness of urban development), and allowed this Western orientation to be reversed several times subsequently, producing a pendulum swing (or, to echo the great Hungarian poet, Endre Ady, a "ferry-like" movement) of this region, now assimilating to the West, now to its eastern neighbors.

Medievalist and "modernists" found here a fertile territory for common discussion: in 1986 Jenő Szűcs debated the problem of the historical regions of Europe with the great expert on Austro–Hungarian Monarchy, Peter Hanák, whose fascinating researches on Hungary's place in this modern *Mitteleuropa* have been influential in the emergence of the idea of the foundation of CEU, and who founded, subsequently, its History Department, and directed it for many years.[22]

In Poland, historians started also with a new look at social and economic topics: Aleksander Gieysztor, Bronisław Geremek and Henrik

Samsonowicz wrote a number of studies on Polish and regional urban development and early state formation.[23] The model was set by the comparative economic studies carried out by Marian Małowist[24] and Witold Kula[25]. Meanwhile, many Polish medievalists tried to do their best to situate Polish history into a broad comparative European context: continuing the nineteenth-century tradition starting with the pioneering works of Joachim Lelewel[26], the studies and books written by Gieysztor,[27] Geremek[28], and Samsonowicz[29] were the most important.

One last significant group of historical investigations has to be added to this mainly Polish and Hungarian enumeration: that of German (and partially Czech) historiography and the series of investigations by Ferdinand Seibt concerning *Westmitteleuropa*.[30] Seibt, and the whole tradition of German and Austrian *Ostforschung*, coined this term principally to analyze the economic, social, and cultural influence of Germany upon this region in commercial contacts, urban structures, and religious orders. Exploring the explanatory validity of the term *Westmitteleuropa*, however, it seems that it can account for a number of important influences which reached these countries from the direction of Germany or the papacy. Since the times of conversion the spread of the forms of urban and rural social organization, the Benedictine, Cistercian, Premonstratensian and mendicant monasteries, the stylistic features of Romanesque and Gothic architecture, castle building, courtly societies, and social movements all testify to this modernizing impact coming from the Western and Southwestern neighbors.[31] At the same time, these influences mingled not only with local traditions in Central Europe, but constantly received stimulation from the other side, from Byzantium and from *Slavia orthodoxa*.[32] While frequently menaced with becoming the meeting place and the prey of the Western and Eastern grand powers (the Holy Roman Empire, Byzantium, the Mongols, the Osman Empire, Russia), in the Middle Ages this region was unique as a meeting place of Western and Eastern, Northern and Mediterranean cultures.

The last book of Aleksander Gieysztor gives an elegant synthesis of the recent research on the birth of this medieval Central Europe: *The new Europe of the year 1000. The Papacy, the Empire and the "Newcomers"*.[33] In his complex account one can rediscover his own favorite themes and the rich experiences of half a century's work among Polish colleagues, but at the same time one can also recognize the broadened perspective of comparative research that had been enriched in the past decade by his frequent stays in Hungary as guest professor, board member at the Medieval Studies Department of the CEU, and his service also as an academic board member at the Collegium Budapest. What he presents is a systematic comparative panorama of these transforming tribal societies, unified by emerging new elites and dynasties taking up the Christian faith. He describes in detail the emergence of the three Christian states of Central Europe—the Czech, the Polish, and the Hungarian—and then shows how the specific personal impact of some of the great historical personalities contributed to the reception of this region into the structures of Europe. He starts his book with a description of the Rome-based, all-European network developed by the martyr missionary bishop, St. Adalbert, who worked towards the better incorporation into the world of *Christianitas* of his native Bohemia and its two neighbors, Hungary and Poland. One also meets the learned pope of the year 1000, Gerbert d'Aurillac, or Sylvester II, who allegedly sent the crown to St. Stephen; and his disciple, the "marvel of the world", the grand emperor, Otto III, who decided to convert and co-opt this region rather than try to conquer it, but who left his utopian plan unfinished when he died at the age of twenty-two.[34]

Let me conclude on the basis of Gieysztor's book. Yes, Central Europe was an invention, but this invention occurred 1000 years ago. We might reinvent it again, but luckily these inventions can now rely upon an ever more complete rediscovery.

What we did invent, on the other hand, is the fact that this ongoing discovery can now rely upon the alliance and cooperation of a motivated, committed, internationally well trained group of young experts, sitting in all these countries in the various museums, archives, libraries, university departments, and cultural heritage offices. And I hope they will be able to invent a way to make good use of this favorable and unprecedented situation.

Two final paragraphs are in order here about unintended consequences. Inventing Central Europe in around 1000 allowed the extension of *Europa Occidens* towards the East and the constitution of the Holy Roman Empire as the center of *Christianitas*. What was unforeseen then, in the times of Emperor Otto III, was that this extension would soon hurt against various forms of resistance from the East, and the Eastern part of this "central" region would acquire its specific identity by remaining a conflictuous intermediary zone between West and East, an *antemurale*, a buffer region with recurrent existential insecurities and frequently resurgent split consciousness.

Reinventing Central Europe after 1990 has lead, at least at the CEU, to quite a different effect. University registrars had to recognize very soon the unintended consequence: as for the applying students, not only the representatives of traditional Eastern Europe and South-Eastern Europe showed up in this new Central European academic community, but students from the Caucasus, Central Asia or even South Africa as well. Medieval Studies Department had to open up its original interest in Latin Christianity towards a comparative examination of Latin, Greek, Slavic and Eastern Christianity. This was indeed a discovery for us: to recognize the various forms and limits of the gradual extension of European civilization to these regions already in the Middle Ages. And be part, at the same time, together with the whole CEU community, of the construction, indeed the invention of a new kind of Central Europe, which exists now as a possibility at least for a new generation of intellectuals. Central Europe as an open, inclusive, inventive laboratory for a large unlimited world eastwards from the West—a real utopia to inspire us and make us resistant to different, less welcome unintended consequences.

Notes

1 Bronisław Geremek (1991). *The Common Roots of Europe.* Cambridge: Polity Press. First published in Italy under the title *Le radici comuni dell'Europa.* Arnoldo Mondadori Editore.

2 Josephus Balogh (ed.) (1938). *"Libellus de institutione morum".* In E. Szentpétery (ed.), *Scriptores Rerum Hungaricarum,* Vol. II, pp. 614–621. Budapest: Stephaneum; Jenő Szűcs (1981). "König Stephans 'Institutionen'—König Stephans Staat". In idem, *Nation und Geschichte. Studien.* Budapest: Corvina, 245–262; idem (1988). "Szent István intelmei: az első magyarországi államelméleti mű" (The exhortations of St. Stephen, the first Hungarian work on the theory of state). In Ferenc Glatz and József Kardos (eds.), *Szent István és kora* (St. Stephen and his age). Budapest: MTA Történettudományi Intézete, pp. 32–53.

3 Cf. Jacques Le Goff (1993). *The Intellectuals in the Middle Ages.* Cambridge: Blackwell, p. 12.

4 Jenő Szűcs (1983). "The Three Historical Regions of Europe. An Outline". *Acta Historica Academiae Scientiarum Hungaricae*, 29, pp. 131–184; also published in *Civil Society and the State: New European Perspectives*, ed. J. Keane. London, pp. 291–332.

5 Norman F. Cantor (1991). *Inventing the Middle Ages. The Lives, Works, and Ideas of the Great Medievalists of the Twentieth Century.* New York: William Morrow and Company.

6 Szűcs, "The Three Historical Regions", p. 131.

7 On the evolution of the notion of Europe, see Federico Chabod (1958). *L'idea di Europa.* Bari: Laterza; Oskar Halecki (1963). *The Millennium of Europe.* Notre Dame, Indiana: University of Notre Dame Press; Jean-Baptiste Duroselle (1965). *L'idée d'Europe dans l'histoire.* Paris: Denoël; Denis Hay (1968). *Europe. The Emergence of an Idea.* Edinburgh: Edinburgh University Press; Robert Bartlett (1993). *The Making of Europe. Conquest, Colonization and Cultural Change 950–1350.* Harmondsworth: Penguin Books; Jacques Le Goff (1994). *La Vieille Europe et la nôtre.* Paris: Seuil; Brian Patrick McGuire (ed.) (1996). *The Birth of Identities.*

Denmark and Europe in the Middle Ages. Copenhagen: C. A. Reitzel; Peter Rietbergen (1998). *Europe. A Cultural History.* London–New York: Routledge.

8 Jürgen Fischer (1957). *Oriens–Occidens–Europa. Begriff und Gedänke 'Europa' in der Spätantike und im frühen Mittelalter.* Wiesbaden.

9 Larry Wolff (1994). *Inventing Eastern Europe. The Map of Civilization on the Mind of the Enlightenment.* Stanford: Stanford University Press.

10 All this is described by Jerzy Kłoczowski (1995). *L'Europe du Centre-Est dans l'historiographie des pays de la région.* Lublin: Institute of East Central Europe.

11 Oskar Halecki (1952). *The Borderlands of Western Civilization. A History of East Central Europe.* New York: Ronald.

12 Ibid., pp. 3–4.

13 István Hajnal (1993). *Technika és művelődés* (Technics and civilization). Ed. Ferenc Glatz. Budapest: História; idem. (1954). *L'enseignement de l'écriture aux universités médiévales.* Budapest.

14 Gyula Szekfű (1922). *A magyar bortermelő lelki alkata. Történelmi tanulmány.* (The mental habitus of the hungarian wine-grower. A historical study), Budapest: Eggenberger.

15 Elemér Mályusz (1933). "Árpádházi Boldog Margit (A magyar egyházi műveltség problémája)" (Blessed Margaret of the Arpad Dynasty. The problem of Hungarian ecclesiastical culture). In *Emlékkönyv Károlyi Árpád születése nyolcvanadik fordulójának ünnepére* (Árpád Károlyi Festschrift). Budapest, pp. 341–384.

16 Francis Dvornik (1949). *The Making of Central and Eastern Europe.* London: The Polish Research Centre; idem (1962). *The Slavs in European History and Civilization.* New Brunswick: Rutgers University Press.

17 Zsigmond Pál Pach (1963). *Nyugat-európai és magyarországi agrárfejlődés a XV–XVII. században* (West European and Hungarian agrarian evolution in the fifteenth to eighteenth centuries). Budapest: Kossuth.

18 Jenő Szűcs (1955). *Városok és kézművesség a XV. századi Magyarországon* (Towns and crafts in fifteenth century Hungary). Budapest: Művelt nép; idem (1963) "Das Städtewesen in Ungarn im 15–17. Jahrhundert" in György Székely (ed.), *La Renaissance et la Réformation en Pologne et en Hongrie.* Budapest: Akadémiai, pp. 97–164.

19 László Makkai (1970). "Les caractères originaux de l'histoire économique et sociale de l'Europe orientale pendant le Moyen Age". *Acta Historica Academiae Scientiarum Hungaricae,* 16, pp. 261–287.

20 This book, written in the 1970s, was only posthumously published: Jenő Szűcs (1992). *A magyar nemzeti tudat kialakulása. Két tanulmány a kérdés előtörténetéből* (The formation of the Hungarian national consciousness. Two studies from the prehistory of the question). Szeged: Magyar Őstörténeti Könyvtár; see also my review of it in *Budapest Review of Books* 4 (1994), pp. 25–29. Idem., Zwei Fragmente, in *Studien zum Nationalen Bewußtsein: Mittelalter und Gegenwart* (ed.) János M. Bak, Special Issue of *East Central Europe—L'Europe du Centre-Est Eine wissenschaftliche Zeitschrift.* Vol. 2023, pt. 2 (1993–1996), pp. 55–90.

21 Szűcs, "The Three Historical Regions".

22 Jenő Szűcs and Peter Hanák (1986): *Európa régiói a történelemben* (The regions of Europe in history). Budapest MTA Történettudományi Intézet; Péter Hanák

(1993), *Ragaszkodás az utópiához* (Insisting upon utopias), Budapest: Liget Könyvek (s.a.).

23 Aleksander Gieysztor (1957). "Le origini delle città nella Polonia medievale". In *Studi in onore di Armando Sapori*. Milan, t. 1, pp. 129–146; idem (1961). "Les stuctures économiques en pays slaves à l'aube du Moyen Âge jusqu'au XIe siècle et l'échange monétaire". In *Moneta e scambi nell'alto medioevo*, 21–23 aprile 1960, pp. 455–484. Spoleto: Settimane di studio del Centro italiano di studi sull'alto medioevo, 8); Tadeusz Mannteufel et Aleksander Gieysztor (eds.) (1968). *L'Europe aux Xe–XIe siècles. Aux origines des états nationaux.* Warsaw; A. Gieysztor (1987). "Trade and Industry in the Middle Ages: Trade and Industry in Eastern Europe before 1200". In *The Cambridge Economic History*, t. 2, ed. M.M. Postan and E. Miller. Cambridge, pp. 474–524, 912–917.

24 Marian Małowist (1972). *Croissance et régression en Europe XIVe-XVIIe siècles.* Recueil d'articles. Paris: Armand Colin.

25 Witold Kula (1970). *Théorie économique du système féodal. Pour un modèle de l'économie polonaise XVIe-XVIIIe siècle.* Paris–La Haye: Mouton.

26 Geremek, "Western Europe in the Middle Ages". In *The Common Roots*, pp. 17–19.

27 Aleksander Gieysztor (1968). "La Polonia medioevale tra Occidente ed Oriente europeo". *Studi storici*, 9, pp. 247–260; idem (1997). "L'Europe médiéval du Centre-Est: frontières mouvantes de cultures". In *Europa medievale e mondo Bizantino. Contatti effettivi e possibilità di studi comparati*, ed. Girolamo Arnaldi and Guglielmo Cavallo. Rome, pp. 213–220.

28 Geremek, *The Common Roots.*

29 Henryk Samsonowicz (1995). *Miejsce Polski w Europie* (The place of Poland in Europe). Warsaw: Bellona.

30 Ferdinand Seibt (1973). "Von Prag bis Rostock. Zur Gründung der Universitäten in Mitteleuropa". In *Festschrift für Walter Schlesinger*, ed. Helmut Beumann. Cologne–Vienna: Böhlau, pp. 406–426; Winfried Eberhard, Hans Lemberg, Heinz-Dieter Heimann, and Robert Luft (ed.) (1992). *Westmitteleuropa–Ostmitteleuropa. Vergleiche und Beziehungen. Festschrift für Ferdinand Seibt zum 65. Geburtstag*. Munich: Oldenbourg.

31 This systematic internal homogenization, the "Europeanization of Europe", is analyzed by Robert Bartlett in *The Making of Europe*, pp. 269–291.

32 Cf. Arnaldi and Cavallo, *Europa medievale e mondo Bizantino*.

33 Aleksander Gieysztor (1997). *L'Europe nouvelle autour de l'An Mil. La Papauté, l'Empire et les «nouveaux venus».* Rome.

34 Cf. also: Pierre Riché (1987). *Gerbert d'Aurillac, le pape de l'an mil.* Paris: Fayard; idem (1999). *Les grandeurs de l'an mil.* Paris: Bartillat.

16 *The Marginality of Totalitarianism*

ALFRED J. RIEBER

It has long been fashionable to seek the origins of totalitarianism in either or both of the great congeries of ideas known collectively as the Enlightenment and the Romantic movement.[1] This approach has much to commend, but only if we acknowledge and reconcile the paradoxical, contradictory, and deterministic elements that characterize it. Paradoxical in terms of their outcome, the Enlightenment and Romantic movement were inspired by, and directed toward, the liberation of man, but were then manipulated to subjugate him. Contradictory, because the rational and romantic concepts of man are opposed to one another and ultimately incompatible. Deterministic, when it preaches a direct, unbroken, lineal descent of ideas, whether from Luther to Hitler or Rousseau to Stalin. The historian who believes that ideas ought to be placed in the context of their time (the healthy and not apologetic side of historicism); that two opposite causes cannot produce the same result; and that politics, economics, and culture require a place at the table of causality along with ideas, will recoil from the genetic fallacy of totalitarianism as the product of the two main currents of Western thought in modern times.

The epistemological dilemma that confronts all theorists of totalitarianism is threefold. In the first place, there is the problem of cognitive dissonance between the phenomenon and the idea, between practice and theory. In the second place, there is the test of time: theories of totalitarianism have not worn well in the face of empirical studies. In the third place, totalitarianism is a construction of reality both by its practitioners in order to legitimize their power, and by its critics in order to delegitimize it.[2]

The present essay cannot claim to resolve these various problems. Rather it seeks to offer a point of departure for an alternative approach to totalitarianism. It takes as its central theme the marginality of the men, ideas, and circumstances that produced the two quintessential totalitarian regimes—Nazi Germany and Stalinist Russia.[3] What set these two regimes aside from all preceding and succeeding ones was a unique combination of factors reflecting a conception of politics, of the structure of power, and of the organization of society and the economy. An all-powerful leader, endowed with a quasi-mystical legitimacy and a monopolistic ideology that touched every aspect of human behavior, ruled through a single-party system and techniques of mobilization that relied upon massive doses of propaganda and terror. The prescribed aim of these regimes was to maximize central control over the economy and to create completely homogeneous societies through an ordeal of purification. Although the totality of control over thought and behavioral norms was never complete, even in the Nazi and Stalinist regimes, they came as close as any political system to approaching these goals.

The Men and Their Ideas

Hitler and Stalin were marginal figures in the societies they came to rule in several important ways: their place of birth, social origins, and cultural background led them to search for new identities, without which they could not play the political roles to which they aspired. Unlike almost all the national leaders of Central and Eastern Europe, and most of those in Western Europe as well until the early twentieth century and beyond, they did not emerge from the traditional ruling elites. Their obscure origins explain in large part the dearth of sources, their own reluctance to provide evidence, and consequently the mysteries of their early development. Their situation invited myth making and counter myth making. They did not seek to conceal their humble beginnings but turned them to advantage. In an era of mass politics characterized by growing literacy, the popular press, and extended suffrage, they could claim with some justification to be closer to "the people", a term which in both languages (*Volk* and *narod*) carries a deeper cultural, indeed mythical, significance than in English or French. In this way, and it was not the only case of inversion, they were able to convert their position on the margins to one at the center of society.

That both men were authoritarian personalities is clear enough, even if the sources of their early development are too scanty and unreliable to provide sufficient material for a convincing deep psychological portrait. Much speculation and no little nonsense has been written in a vain effort to unearth their personal abnormalities.[4] More fruitful, it seems to me, is to explore how the elements of their political style, as revealed in adult behavior, inclined them to authoritarian, indeed totalitarian, solutions. Both men were obscure figures even in the early histories of the parties they came to dominate until they discovered and perfected the peculiar skills that enabled them to outmaneuver or defeat their rivals in the competition for leadership. They were, to be sure, drawn to political groups—one hesitates even to call them parties in their earliest manifestations—which were contemptuous of liberal democracy in any form. But their rise to positions of unchallenged and dictatorial leadership introduced a radically new element into the politics of their group and ultimately of their societies at large. In form, their principle skills were quite the opposite of one another. Hitler's was the power of public speaking, Stalin's the power of bureaucratic organization. But they functioned in quite the same way as instruments of mass mobilization. Hitler exulted in the discovery of his power to sway large audiences. Stalin was less forthcoming as he quietly gathered the organizational threads of the party into his hands. The practice and fine tuning of these skills within an anti-democratic milieu led irresistibly to the monopoly of power in their hands and the emergence of the supreme leader—that is, "*Fuhrerprinzip*" in one case and the "*Velikii Vozhd*" in the other. This is not to suggest that Hitler ignored institutional questions. The process of *Gleichschaltung* was designed to eliminate most, if not all, organizations outside the party and its offspring. But the Nazi state was "a government without administration".[5] Similarly, Stalin did not neglect the massive use of propaganda and agitation. But the Soviet Union was a hypertrophied administrative state.

Hitler and Stalin were both men of the borderlands. Bohemia and Georgia were not only located on the periphery of the polyethnic empires to which they belonged. They were also frontier provinces, albeit of different types. In Hitler's Bohemia the German-speaking population was drawn in two different directions. The cosmopolitan center of the Habsburg Empire, politically ruled by an Austro–German monarch and bureaucracy, served as one magnet; the attractions of Pan-Germanism—the unification of all Germans in a great Central European state—the other. In Stalin's Georgia, the tension was between identification with the strong revival of indigenous national feeling, and association with an all-Russian (*vserossiiskii*) polyethnic state.

Hitler's quest for cultural self-identity took him first to Linz, the most German city of the Monarchy, then to Vienna, which he quickly came to detest for precisely its cosmopolitan character, and finally to Munich where he found his true allegiance. In these early years Hitler lived very much on the margins of society, an impoverished, quasi-Bohemian lifestyle with no regular work in hand. Even later in the twenties, as leader of the young, brash Nazi party, his appearance still defined him as a man at odds with the upper class or respectable burghers of Munich, with his gangster hat, trench coat over dinner jacket, sporting a pistol and a dog whip. He kept his Austrian accent and his bizarre mannerisms throughout his life. Yet he chose to link his destiny to Germany.

When the First World War broke out Hitler enlisted in the Bavarian Army, although as a citizen of the Austro–Hungarian Monarchy this was, strictly speaking, an illegal act. In fact, he only became a German citizen on the eve of his taking power as chancellor of Germany. But he never abandoned the aspiration of joining his two homelands. In *Mein Kampf* he spoke of how providential it was that he had been born on the border of two countries that it was his life's task to unite.[6]

Once in power Hitler proceeded to construct a new territorial Reich that did not correspond to the contours of any previous German state. It was Pan-German but within limitations. That is, he did not aspire to extend the boundaries of the Reich to encompass all the *Volksdeutsche*, but only those of the frontier areas, Austria, Bohemia (Sudetenland), Alsace–Lorraine, and the Polish border strip. There were many Germans left outside. Under certain circumstances they could be transported, either voluntarily or not, to the Reich, but the Reich would not be expanded to include them. To have annexed their lands would have involved absorbing large numbers of non-Germanic peoples, in other words creating another polyethnic empire, like the Habsburg Monarchy, which ran counter to Hitler's deepest instincts. The racial state was a totalitarian utopia; it meant the destruction or expulsion of all those who did not meet the standards—admittedly changing and not always consistent—that he established for racial purity.

By making race, or to be more accurate a spurious concept of blood descent, rather than citizenship, territoriality, or culture the essential quality of national identity, Hitler was able to carry out a remarkable change in his relationship to the rest of German-speaking society. His definition of what it was to be German was the only one that could possibly have included himself. At the same time, it allowed him to divert the highly assimilated German Jews, who had been an integral part of the various German states for a century, from the mainstream into a doomed tributary of that society. Thus, his definition of what it was to be a German was also one that fitted his hatred of the Jews.

Nevertheless, Hitler was not entirely consistent in applying his racial theory, one of many flaws in the totalitarian concept of the perfect state. For reasons of political advantage he often compromised his own racial ideals. For example, in order to placate Mussolini, he did not insist upon the resettlement of the Germans in South Tyrol; still less, to their great disappointment, did he demand their territorial incorporation into the greater Reich. He left the *Volksdeutsche* of Banat and Backa, and most of the so-called Danubian Swabians, under foreign rule, whether Hungarian or Romanian, rather than jeopardize his strategic relations with his allies.[7] Hitler, like Stalin, as we shall see, was not attached to ideas in the abstract but only in so far as they served to enhance his concept of self and the pursuit of power through mass mobilization.

Hitler was not content to limit the frontiers of the state to those areas adjacent to the Reich that were already populated by *Volksdeutsche*. His concept of *Lebensraum* was devised to make Germany largely self-sufficient in foodstuffs and raw materials so that it could never again, as during World War I, be forced to undergo the ordeal of the blockade, shortages, and hunger. But the mere conquest of territory, primarily in the East, would be an inadequate solution without an expansion of the racial order. Moreover, Hitler claimed, without much justification, that Germany needed an outlet for its surplus population. Possibly he was more concerned about the social advantages and military security that would be gained by granting his soldiers and their families substantial farms in rich agricultural lands. The creation of vast agricultural colonies fitted well into the belief that the independent German farmer was the *volkisch* ideal, the main guarantor of the longevity of the "Reich for a Thousand Years".[8] This massive resettlement of Germans would mean, of course, that the indigenous population would have to be expelled, its fate a matter of little consequence to Hitler and his subordinates. Thus, the racial myth that was central to Hitler's concept of self-identity with Germany spawned Pan-Germanism, anti-Semitism, and *Lebensraum*. What held them together was the final element in Hitler's system—the myth of the Judeo–Bolshevik enemy.

From the early twenties Hitler vigorously promoted the idea that the great external threat to Deutschdom, and at the same time the great potential for fulfilling Germany's destiny, lay in the East with Soviet Russia. Throughout the twists and turns of his foreign policy he never abandoned, but only postponed, the goal of destroying this his main enemy. In order to convince the Germans to embrace his cause and to follow him into the cauldron of defeat and destruction, he conjured up a nightmare so terrifying that it could only be banished by a war of annihilation. The Soviet Union was, as he portrayed it, the result of a Jewish conspiracy foisted upon a dull, inert, and inferior Slavic population that controlled the land and resources necessary for the survival and greatness of the German people. With such an enemy there could be no compromise.[9]

It was more difficult, indeed impossible, for Stalin to disguise himself as a transplanted Russian. Russian was not his native language, and he wrote and published only in Georgian until 1907 when he reached the age of twenty-eight. His strong Georgian accent, habits, personal associations, even his appearance betrayed his origins. His homeland had only been annexed to the empire in 1801; assimilation took longer. Although the Georgians initially regarded the Russians as defenders of the faith and liberators from the threat of the Muslim powers, the Turks and the Iranians, they soon learned to resent the bureaucratic-military domination imposed by their erstwhile saviors. This ambivalence carried over into Stalin's early years in the Tiflis Seminary. There he mastered Russian and read its literary classics, yet deeply resented the enforced russification that discriminated against his own language.[10] Consequently, Stalin's search for a new self-identity in the course of his political odyssey from revolutionary on the margins to statesman at the center was more complex than Hitler's.

For Stalin, experience taught him that if he was to play an important political role beyond his provincial location and at the all-Russian level then he would have to transcend his origins without denying them. This meant a search—surely as much sub-conscious as conscious—for some way to combine the three defining elements in his early life: his humble social background, his primordial Georgian culture, and his adopted Russian identity. To further his revolutionary career Stalin moved the center of his activities from the provincial capital of Georgia, Tiflis, to the industrialized oil town of Baku, where he found a receptive audience for his propaganda and organizational work among the Russian and Muslim labor force.[11] Stalin had already associated himself with that wing of the Russian Social Democratic Labor Party that placed the greatest emphasis on class over national identity—namely, the Bolsheviks. From the beginning of his revolutionary activities he had presented himself to the world as a true son of the working class, a proletarian. This was stretching the truth. With the possible exception of a few months in a leather factory he never engaged in manual work. But careless dress and coarse speech marked him off from most of his revolutionary colleagues. He expressed contempt for intellectuals as "soft" and "wavering". He preferred the practical revolutionary to the theoretician. In the first Bolshevik government he was the only figure who could have been considered, largely by dint of his own efforts, to be a man risen from the masses.

Writing in Russian and attending social democratic congresses as a Bolshevik, he distanced himself from the provincial Georgian scene, which was dominated by his bitter enemies, the Georgian Mensheviks. As he identified himself more with the all-Russian politics, he contemptuously dismissed the socialists of the borderlands as lacking in revolutionary zeal, reflecting the underdeveloped state of the economies of the periphery and infected with nationalist sentiments.[12] At the same time, he became one of the few strong voices within the Bolshevik ranks in favor of recognizing cultural differences, including the right to use local languages, within the party program and, more importantly, within the polyethnic revolutionary state that emerged in 1917.

Once in power, Stalin's approach to the nationality question was to distinguish himself from two extremes among the Bolsheviks as well as within the international socialist movement. He rejected the view of the radical internationalists who assumed that the abolition of classes would lead immediately to the rapid disappearance of all national and ethnic differences that were mere expressions of bourgeois consciousness. But he also resisted efforts to create a genuine federation of soviet republics each enjoying a high degree of autonomy from the (Russian) political center. His formula "nationalist in form, socialist in content" expressed the process by which he had integrated his own personality. In practical politics it meant, at least in the twenties, the carrying out of a kind of affirmative action policy at the republic and district level: promoting loyal, Bolshevik representatives of the indigenous nationalities, establishing schools and other cultural centers in their own languages, but maintaining strict ideological controls and concentrating real political power at the center in Moscow.[13]

Stalin's system, like Hitler's, had profound implications for his foreign policy. As a proletarian state, the only one to survive the revolutionary upheavals after World War I, the Soviet Union was confronted with the security nightmare of capitalist encirclement. The least "European" of the Bolshevik leaders, Stalin had always been the most skeptical of revolutionary help from the West. In consolidating his own power he reversed the original Leninist concept, shared by Trotsky and others, that the establishment of socialism in Russia ultimately depended upon revolutions in the advanced capitalist countries. Stalin's formula was that by building socialism in one country the Soviet Union would become the bulwark of international revolution. Like Hitler too, Stalin was not willing to allow wild ideologues to determine how and when his foreign policy aims would be carried out. Both Stalin and Hitler saw fascist and communist parties abroad as useful tools only if they were completely subordinated to the purposes of the totalitarian state. Like Hitler, Stalin alone would determine the tempo and direction of projecting the power of the state outside its boundaries. As Hitler was reluctant during World War II to permit fascist parties to take power in his satellites until and unless there was no alternative to maintaining his influence in those countries, so Stalin distrusted the independent activities of local communist parties and sought to delay or prevent the establishment of soviet regimes after the war for fear of antagonizing the Western powers and creating alternative sources of communist power that might one day challenge his own.

By adopting Russian, the hegemonic language of the empire, and by advocating the right to maintain cultural distinctions while giving precedence to class as the primary element in the revolutionary movement and the construction of a new socialist state, Stalin, like Hitler, was able to transform the disadvantages of his marginal existence into a political system which became the foundations of a totalitarian state.

Because of their sudden rise from obscurity to supreme power, Hitler and Stalin were never entirely secure on their lonely pinnacle. On their road to power they had ruthlessly eliminated any potential rival. After their conquest of power neither man was really intimate with any of his associates. Their disposition toward violent solutions intensified whenever signs of opposition to their policies or whims appeared. Their resort to repression and terror, which became one of the hallmarks of the totalitarian state, was in part a projection of their own fears and fantasies in response to what they imagined they would have done if they were still aiming for power or, knew they had done in achieving it. Beyond this mass terror was the only means of carrying out in their lifetime the radical transformation they set for themselves as the object of their rule: the racial state and the classless society. They had so completely identified their own radical transformation of selfhood with that of the societies they ruled, that they could not tolerate a failure to complete the process. They would turn a humiliated and powerless Germany, a backward and encircled Russia into world powers as they had brought themselves from obscurity on the margins of those societies to the center. Any obstacle, real or imagined, had to be swept away. The Holocaust and dekulakization were different in murderous intent and scale. But in the long run the human losses from the slaughter of the Jews and the famine brought on by collectivization of the peasants were frighteningly similar. To be sure, Stalin more than Hitler was endowed with a deeply suspicious nature. He repeatedly turned against his colleagues and even his own supporters in the party itself, while Hitler satisfied himself with one major purge in the Night of the Long Knives and then left his lieutenants to squabble among themselves for advantage in gaining influence with, although never over, him. It required military defeat, the destruction of the Nazi state, and the death of Hitler to end the terror in Germany and occupied Europe. Significantly, the death of Stalin was a sufficient cause to bring mass terror to an end in the Soviet Union as an instrument of rule, although police repression continued to be employed against political and religious dissidents. The totalitarian state, so much a product of the two men who had created it, died with them.

The Intellectual and Social Context

Hitler and Stalin may have performed prodigies of integration in their search for new self-identities, but this by itself could hardly have produced the totalitarian system which they designed and developed. Two questions remain. How did their ideas and politics, their systems if you will, fit within the main intellectual and political currents of their times? If—to anticipate—the climate of opinion, or if you prefer, the reigning paradigms of political culture, in late-nineteenth and early-twentieth-century Germany and Russia were not receptive to radical transformations of the kind associated with both men, then what combination of circumstances could have produced a situation in which they became so?

To argue that the political ideas and practice of the totalitarian utopias, as exemplified by Hitler and Stalin, lay at the margins of European thought and practice at the end of the nineteenth and beginning of the twentieth century is to enter a minefield of historiographical debate. There is firstly the methodological question that has exercised historians over the past twenty years, of what constitutes a suitable context in which to analyze the influence of ideas. Secondly, there is the even more formidable question of assigning relative weights to the elements of continuity and discontinuity in the totalitarian phase of German and Russian history. To clarify my own assumptions without claiming to contribute anything new to those debates, the parameters of context in the following section are set by the main intellectual currents in the lifetime of our subjects, as measured by the most recent investigations. The edge here is given to discontinuities without insisting upon the totalitarian phase as a rupture or complete break with previous social, political, and cultural forces present in the preceding period. The third section of the paper will take up the question of the reason for these discontinuities.

At the turn of the twentieth century the intellectual life and social structure of the Kaiserreich and Imperial Russia shared a number of salient characteristics. It is my contention that they can be combined in a single term that is both descriptive and analytical—fragmentation.[14] The intellectual spectrum in the two empires encompassed the broadest range of political ideas of any European state. To a large extent this was the result of historical peculiarities that emerged in the course of state building and economic change under the impact of industrialization.

Within the European state system both empires developed their national institutions, except for the monarchy, at a relatively late date—an all-German Reichstag in 1871, an all-Russian Duma in 1906. Regional identities and loyalties remained strong. Again relatively late and rapid, if uneven, industrialization and urbanization produced deep fissures in both societies and powerful reactions by elements of both the Right and Left which were attached to agrarian values. At the same time, the same two processes gave rise to radical labor movements on the Left. The monarchies and bureaucracies sought to stem the tide of rapid, and in their eyes disruptive, social processes by conserving as much as possible the traditional orders or estates (*Stande* or *soslovie*) which often gave these societies the appearance from the outside of museums of archaic social forms.

Understandably, the intellectual and artistic elites of Germany and Russia struggled to come to grips with the bewildering pace and uncertain direction of changes visible all around them. The epigones of Marx were thick on the ground of Central and Eastern Europe, from Bebel and Kautsky to Rosa Luxemburg, Struve, Trotsky, and Lenin. But so were the ultra-nationalists of the Pan-German League and Pan-Slavists. Anti-Semitism was rife; the spurious Protocols of the Elders of Zion were first published in Russia but found their most avid audience in Germany.[15] Yet, lest we forget, Zionism originated in Russia and was most ardently propagated by German Jews. Munich and St. Petersburg rivaled Paris and Vienna as centers of the modern movement, but were also more inclined to its mystical, even occult, dimensions. Overall, German and Russian artists and musicians powerfully expressed the fragmentation and dissolution of old verities and social identities. To be sure, other European states shared some of these characteristics, especially France, Italy, Spain, and above all the Cisleithian half of the Habsburg Monarchy. But nowhere else were the fissures so numerous, deep, and apparently irreconcilable. Nowhere else did the existing institutions or conceptual strategies appear increasingly unable to surmount or overcome the fragmentation and the hostility of one part of society or one ideology to another. Pluralism, the foundations of an open society, is one thing, but it must rest upon a common allegiance to the basic institutions and ideals upon which the society rests. Without this prerequisite the fragmented society may become, under conditions of extreme pressure, a recipe for conflict and chaos.

In this context, then, it is important to emphasize that what Hitler and Stalin represented on the eve of World War I was not in any sense a dominant or prevailing trend in their respective societies. The very nature of a fragmented society prevented the emergence of a consensus. In so far as the Kaiserreich is concerned, it is certainly possible to detect plenty of evidence of extreme nationalism, anti-Semitism, and a mystical notion of the German social order resting upon patriarchy, harmony, and hierarchy. But these elements, taken as a whole, constituted a distinctly minority position in German thought and institutions.[16] To be sure, there was a powerful illiberal tradition in the humanistic faculties of the universities, the legal system, elements of the business community, the court, and, above all, the army. But there were also countervailing forces. In the universities a rational and rigorous empirical approach to science predominated in the science faculties and had already produced a large number of Nobel Prize winners. Outside the admittedly privileged ranks of the army, the rule of law prevailed and the German legal system, while conservative, was grounded in Roman law. Liberal ideas still attracted about a quarter of the voting public (in 1912), and were undergoing a marked revival that aimed at modernizing and enlarging the liberal constituency. During the last quarter of the nineteenth century, the German burgher class had quietly achieved many of its social and economic aims within a highly conservative political atmosphere.[17]

In addition there was a strong social democratic tradition which was gradually shedding its revolutionary spirit, if not its rhetoric, and moving steadily toward notions of a peaceful, parliamentary road to socialism. It had survived the anti-socialist legislation of Bismarck's time and, by the turn of the century, had developed a distinct and legal sub-culture with its own press, trade unions, sports clubs, and women's associations. On the eve of World War I it was the largest political party in Germany, and growing; it already controlled the local government of Prussia, where two-thirds of the population lived. [18]

The Catholics in Germany, while remaining a minority religion still smarting from the assault upon them of Bismarck and the liberals (the *Kulturkampf*), were, like the socialists, beginning slowly to adjust, if not integrate wholly, into German society. They, too, had their own political party (the German Center Party), press, schools, and separate social life, although they were losing workers to social democracy by the turn of the century. The Catholics, like the liberals and the socialists, maintained their separate mental and social worlds, yet there was evidence that they were groping their way toward an accommodation with one another that might produce a consensus upon which a new Germany could be built.[19] The first significant sign that this might be so came at a most inauspicious moment during the height of the war in the summer of 1917, when the liberals (the Progressive People's Party), the Social Democrats, and the Center united to pass the Peace Resolution in the Reichstag. It was the same three parties that founded the Weimar Republic at a moment of national defeat and humiliation when the circumstances were also inauspicious. But there were still powerful obstacles yet to overcome and, above all, there was the need for a lengthy, peaceful, and stable environment in order that these tendencies could mature and flourish.[20]

In this setting, Hitler and those who formed the first ranks of the Nazi Party were entirely out of place. For all his sympathies with the anti-Semitic parties and movements like the Pan-German League, Hitler did not join any of them before the war. He was the first to recognize that World War I saved him from lifelong obscurity; he greeted it exultantly and for the first time in his life found a vocation as a front soldier.[21] Defeat in the war, the social turmoil that followed, and, for the Germans, the humiliating terms of the Versailles Treaty threatened to polarize Germany between extreme Right and extreme Left. It simultaneously introduced a level of domestic violence that Germans had not experienced since 1848. It was in these conditions that men who had been relegated to the margins of society found a new calling.

Imperial Russian social and intellectual life was rent by fissures similar to those in the Kaiserreich, but in addition there was a much higher level of social violence before the coming of the war. The strike movement, expressing both the economic and political aims of the small but highly conscious Russian working class, peaked in the 1905 revolution and rose again on the eve of the war to similar heights. In the early years of the twentieth century there was a revival of peasant rebellions, culminating in the mass agrarian disturbances of 1906. A more active national opposition to the sporadic, ineffective, but provocative government policies of russification also exploded in 1905 when the borderlands were the scene of some of the most violent clashes in the Empire between the revolutionaries and the police. Under the repressive rule of the autocracy there had been no opportunity for the creation and development of legal trade unions and national political parties. Consequently, outside the somnolent halls of provincial and local government, political activity was everywhere clandestine. This situation gave rise to endless quarrels over tactics, ideological hair-splitting, and bursts of individual terror—always the weapon of the weak. When parties were finally legalized in 1905 they continued to exhibit all the characteristics of their underground existence. Above all they were riven by internal splits. For example, the Russian Social Democrats were divided not only into Bolsheviks and Mensheviks, but subdivided into smaller factions. The Socialist Revolutionaries, the party of the agrarian socialists, was composed of at least three distinctive sections, none of which was very stable.[22] There was also a proliferation of parties, once they were permitted, each representing a particular interest group.

The fragmentation of political life was a reflection of the deep social divisions within Russian society. Although there were many voices claiming to speak for the peasantry, a great gap existed between the intellectuals and the toilers of the land. The peasantry itself—accurately dubbed the awkward class—shared only one aim, to secure more land. Otherwise they, too, were divided over issues of land tenure, ranging from those who embraced the Stolypin reforms in order to become individual landholders, to those who preferred to remain within the traditional but less risky confines of the commune. But the commune, too, contained a welter of social tensions between the rich peasant (*kulak*) who was an employer of hired labor, often a money lender and tavern keeper, and the so-called middle peasant and landless poor.[23]

The ruling classes were not immune to the bane of fragmentation. The bureaucracy had become largely cut off from its roots in the nobility and represented a distinct social group with its own ethos. The nobility itself had no common political aims, sense of purpose, or economic unity. A significant part of it had even become estranged from the monarchy and were, in the final analysis, unwilling to defend it. The outstanding Orthodox religious thinkers like Vladimir Solov'ev and Leo Tolstoy found themselves rejected or anathematized by the official church. The hierarchy was divided among those who followed the lead of the tsar in attempting to restore a version of pre-Petrine religious life, the small group of reformers, and the majority who stubbornly defended the status quo. There was a deep ideological and psychological gulf separating the professions from the commercial-industrial groups based mainly on the anti-capitalist mentality of the former.[24]

The signs of repairing the social and political fissures in Russia were fewer and weaker than in Germany. But, like Germany, they appeared during the war and immediately after the postwar changes in regime. The mismanagement of the war effort by the tsar and his leading bureaucrats brought together a brief coalition, the Progressive Bloc of center and center-left politicians, some of whom tentatively reached out to the representatives of the working class. But the attempt to form a government responsible to the elected duma met the resistance of the autocrat, Nicholas II. Following the revolution of February 1917 and the second failure of a similar coalition in May, there emerged a left-wing coalition of Mensheviks and Socialist Revolutionaries that appeared to rally substantial elements of the population around democratic and socialist goals. But it, too, collapsed in the face of military defeats and a rapidly disintegrating social situation. The Bolsheviks, including Stalin, occupying the left-wing margin of Russian politics up to mid-1917, held aloof from both efforts and roundly condemned them.

It should be recalled at this point that as late as the October Revolution in 1917 Stalin was completely unknown to the overwhelming mass of the Russian population, and that even Lenin, at least until his return to Russia in April 1917, after an absence of ten years, was still a little-known figure. As in Germany with Hitler, so in Russia with Lenin and Stalin it required the cataclysm of a lost war and massive social upheavals in order to propel the men of the margin to center stage.

The Circumstances

In the short period of fifteen years from 1914 to 1930, a series of seismic shocks profoundly altered the political and social landscape in Germany and Russia. On the eve of World War I, the Kaiserreich and Imperial Russia were clearly headed toward some kind of constitutional crisis. But it is hardly possible to imagine that the outcome would have produced anything like the radical transformation of those societies along totalitarian lines without the events that shattered their old elites, destroyed their established institutions, and plunged their populations into confusion and despair. Total war was the first step in that series of catastrophes.

Ever since the Thirty Years War had devastated central Europe, wars on the continent had been largely matters for professional armies fighting discontinuous, pitched battles or conducting long sieges. The civilian population had rarely been involved and there had been nothing approaching a large-scale mobilization of economic and technological resources. World War I changed all that. The German state and society was probably best suited to organize a total war which became, in any case, a matter of necessity once the enormous demand for men and materiel and the painful effects of the blockade were felt. Only the most extraordinary efforts of economic centralization and control over the allocation of raw materials, manpower, and food enabled Germany to survive four years of war.[25] On the eve of the armistice not a single square kilometer of German soil was occupied by the enemy. Nevertheless, the German army had been bled white, its last desperate offensive in the West (the second battle of the Marne) had fallen short but stretched its resources to the breaking point; the civilian population was exhausted and hungry but ignorant of the critical military situation and still resolute in expectations of victory. The admission of defeat came as a shock; the orderly return of the army in disciplined formations appeared to confirm the myth of the stab in the back. Then the harsh terms of the treaty, immediately branded a "*diktat*" by the Right, made a mockery of their sacrifices. The frontiers to the East were dissolving and the threat of Bolshevism imminent. The formation of volunteer units to defend the Fatherland, the *Freikorps*, signaled the debut of quasi-legal, paramilitary formations that presaged the destruction of German civil society.[26]

Hardly had the newly born Weimar Republic established its political control when it was deeply shaken by the devastating effects of rampant inflation. Following this, there were only five good years of stability before the first effects of the financial crisis and depression struck Germany. At the political extremes politics had become militarized and brutalized. The Nazis and Communists, even the Social Democrats, formed their own paramilitary guards. Assassination and intimidation, unthinkable in the Kaiserreich, had become part of German political life. The army, fearing above all to be involved in civil war, could no longer be relied upon. The political parties still loyal to the constitution were able, if barely, still to command the allegiance of the majority of German voters up to 1930. But they were insufficiently united and, more important, not constituted to compete with the politics of mass mobilization and organized violence that characterized their totalitarian rivals on the extreme Right and Left. This was the milieu in which Hitler, a virtual outcast in the prewar period, flourished as a political leader.

Russia was less well equipped to fight a long, to say nothing of a total, war. The bureaucracy placed obstacles in the way of the liberal industrialists and moderate socialists who had organized themselves in the War Industries Committees in order to promote a more efficient conduct of the war. It was the failure to organize the rear areas and to provide sufficient food and fuel to the cities, particularly St. Petersburg, that led to revolution, and not the military defeat of the army. Once the coalitions of the Provisional Government took power the democratization and decentralization of Russian politics proceeded at such a headlong pace that there was no possibility of imposing a total war program. The few feeble and tentative efforts in that direction by Kerensky, first as war minister and then as prime minister, led to increased strikes in the factories and mounting desertions in the army, culminating in the virtual collapse of public authority and the Bolshevik seizure of power.

Ironically, it was the Bolsheviks who became the advocates of total war, but not against the Central Powers with whom they signed the humiliating treaty of Brest Litovsk, surrendering almost all the territories acquired by Russia since the early seventeenth century. The total war was fought against the White Armies and peasant uprisings during the four-year civil war from 1918 to 1922. In opposition during most of 1917, the Bolsheviks had encouraged all the disintegrating forces of the social revolution: defeatism in the army, the seizure of factories by the workers and of land by the peasants. Once in power and fighting to stay there they sought to reverse the process. Armed with the Leninist doctrine of the centralized party, and imposing military discipline over the factories as well as the newly formed Red Army of Workers and Peasants, and ruthless in their collection of grain by armed detachments, their policies led to a militarization of the party, a return to archaic forms of rural life, and a hypertrophy of the state („statization").[27]

Stalin emerged as a political leader during the civil war. He played only a small role, subsequently vastly exaggerated, in the revolution itself. Although designated as commissar of nationalities, a minor post in the government, he neglected the job and devoted most of his time to serving as a military commissar and a political organizer where the real sources of power lay. At the front there were no constraints on his authority except for Trotsky's occasional complaints. His ruthlessness in a war without rules made him invaluable to Lenin.

A convinced centralist from his early days as a revolutionary, the civil war convinced him that "Bolsheviks could storm any fortress". He carried with him into the twenties and thirties the civil-war rhetoric and mentality that he would place at the service of the second revolution, the war against the peasantry.

Propaganda and terror were the twin instruments that Hitler and Stalin wielded in constructing their totalitarian regimes. The object was simultaneously to persuade and intimidate the population. But totally effective propaganda requires a set of simple propositions expressing an all-encompassing world-view and tolerating no alternative explanations. However, in regimes that stress dynamism and active responses to changing circumstances there are dangers in establishing a fixed dogma. To serve the needs of a mass revolutionary movement regime a sufficiently flexible ideological instrument is required. Hitler and Stalin responded to this challenge in similar ways.

We have already seen how the basic elements of Hitler's and Stalin's ideology reflected their personal experience as men of the geographical and cultural borderlands of their societies, and were largely in place by the time they came to power. For both, however, ideological maintenance was a more complex process than merely dictating new propositions. For Hitler it took the form of "working toward the Führer". For Stalin it was a matter of provoking intra-party "discussion" (*diskusiia*).[28] Hitler encouraged his subordinates to fill out his vague pronouncements, as in the case of the destruction of the Jews, by advancing radical proposals that he assured them in advance he was likely to support. This resulted in a good deal of confusion and conflict among his associates.

But that, too, served his purposes of freeing himself from dependence on one or several key advisers and keeping in his hands the power to make final decisions. Were the ends not so monstrous this might be called creative chaos.

Stalin's technique differed only slightly. Under certain conditions, such as those leading to collectivization and the blood purges, he also demanded radical solutions and expected his subordinates to carry them out without specifying just how this was to be done. He was then in a position to regulate the pace or intensity of the process: too fast, the comrades were "dizzy with success"; too slow, the party was "four years behind" in carrying out the purges. Under other conditions, requiring less drastic action perhaps, he encouraged public discussion by the appropriate group of experts within the party—say on the economic development of capitalism, the future of genetics, or the linguistic question—always reserving for himself the right to intervene at a crucial moment and declare as the winners those whose position corresponded to the outcome he sought. The losers might be arrested or lose their positions or be allowed to recant and remain where they were—in reserve, as it were, for the next discussion when they might, in altered circumstances, emerge as the new victors.

These ways of manipulating ideology were essential to the exercise of totalitarian power for they constantly reinforced the ability of the leader to resolve any controversy that arose within the system by interrogating the minds of others without admitting them to equal status in the decision-making process. It also minimized the risks of appearing to be mistaken. There was always a subordinate to blame for having misconstrued the outcome of the process. If things went wrong, it was always possible for the leader to initiate a new stage in the process. Where questions of doctrine were not involved, primarily in specific foreign policy decisions, both men took important decisions without resorting to the totalitarian techniques so carefully employed in domestic affairs. The reasons were clear. In matters of war and peace, timing and secrecy were essential for the success of their plans.

Conclusion

To return to the initial proposition on the widespread tendency to attribute a central role to ideas drawn from the Enlightenment and Romantic movements in the construction and maintenance of totalitarian regimes, Hitler and Stalin were eclectic, inconsistent, and primitive thinkers. Their writings are intellectually impoverished. Their few guiding ideas owed more to their personal experience as marginal men of the borderlands than to any other source. The scientific, rationalist foundations of Aryan race theory or Stalinist "planning" were hollow. Although they were both myth makers, they completely lacked the humanitarian ideals and individualism of the Romantic movement. To be sure, they picked up bits and pieces of the more extremist trends in the intellectual and cultural life of their respective societies: anti-Semitism in Germany, the collectivist tradition in Russia, authoritarian and hierarchical beliefs in both. In this sense they sought to root themselves in the culture of their adopted countries. But they so intensely radicalized these elements as to distort them out of all proportion to their original contexts. The appeal of their ideologies came from their claim to overcome the fragmentation of their societies and to build a new unified—indeed holistic—community out of the chaos of war, revolution, and economic crises. If there is any lesson to be learned from this exercise, it is that the power of ideas to radicalize and transform societies along totalitarian lines is directly proportional to the breakdown of institutional and economic norms that offer chances for the marginal men to represent themselves as saviors.

Notes

1 Early examples that established a model for this approach are J.L. Talmon. *The Origins of Totalitarian Democracy*, London, 1952; and William M. McGovern, *From Luther to Hitler. The History of Fascist-Nazi Political Philosophy*, London, 1946.

2 The literature is very extensive. A recent review of the uses of the term is Abbot Gleason, *Totalitarianism. The Inner History of the Cold War*, New York/Oxford, 1995. My own preference is for a narrow definition restricted to the Third Reich and Stalinist Russia.

3 There has been a growing tendency among political theorists and historians alike to draw conceptual and empirical distinctions among a variety of non-democratic forms of rule in the twentieth century. Max Weber has been the source for several of these, such as patrimonialism and sultanism. For a recent example see H.E. Chehabi and Juan J. Linz, *Sultanistic Regimes*, Baltimore, 1998. Thus, it is possible to set more precise historical and structural parameters to totalitarianism. Other communist regimes, particularly Maoist China, may be included in the category of totalitarian, but I consider them to be variants on Stalinist Russia.

4 Cf. Rudolph Binion, *Hitler among the Germans*, New York, 1976; Robert G.L. Waite, *The Psychopathic God. Adolf Hitler*, New York, 1977; and Robert Tucker, *Stalin as Revolutionary, 1879–1929*, New York, 1973. More persuasive is Philip Pomper, *Lenin, Trotsky and Stalin. The Intelligentsia and Power*, New York, 1990.

5 Jane Kaplan, *Government without Administration. State and Civil Service in Weimar and Nazi Germany*, Oxford, 1988.

6 Adolf Hitler, *Mein Kampf*, New York, 1939, p. 19. Hitler also proclaimed "...warm love for my German Austrian homeland, profound hatred for the Austrian [Habsburg] state", ibid. p. 30.

7 G.C. Paikert, *The Danube Swabians*, The Hague, 1967; Valdis O. Lumans, *Himmler's Auxiliaries. The Volksdeutsche Mittelstelle and the German Minorities of Europe, 1933–1945*, Chapel Hill, 1993.

8 Karl Lange, "Der Terminus 'Lebensraum' in Hitler's *Mein Kampf*", *Vierteljahrschaft für Zeitgeschichte*, 13 (1965): 426–37.

9 Geoffrey Stoakes, *Hitler and the Quest for World Domination*, New York, 1980; Woodruff D. Smith, *The Ideological Origins of Nazi Imperialism*, New York/Oxford, 1986.

10 V. Kaminskii, and I. Vereshchagin, "Detstvo i iunost' vozhdia. Dokumenty, zapiski, rasskazy", *Molodaia Gvardiia*, No. 12 (1939): 22–101 is the most frequently quoted source for Stalin's early years. It must be used with extreme caution.

11 Ronald Grigor Suny, "A Journeyman for the Revolution: Stalin and the Labor Movement in Baku, June 1907–May 1908", *Soviet Studies*, January 1972, 373–94; and Bala Efendiev, "Istoriia revoliutsionogo dvizheniia tiurkskogo proletariata", in *Iz proshlogo. Stat'i i vospominaniia iz istorii Bakinskoi organizatsii i rabochego dvizheniia v Baku*, Baku, 1923, pp. 39–40.

12 I.V. Stalin, *Sochineniia*, Moscow, 1946, II, 32–33, 49–51

13 Robert J. Kaiser, *The Geography of Nationalism in Russia and the USSR*, Princeton, 1994, pp. 124–35; and Roman Szporluk, "History and Ethnocentrism", in Edward Allworth (ed.), *Ethnic Russia in the USSR*, New York, 1980, pp. 41–54.

14 For the German case see Volker Berghahn, *Imperial Germany, 1871–1914. Economy, Society, Culture and Politics*, Providence RI, 1994; and especially Detlev J. K. Peukert, *The Weimar Republic. The Crisis of Classical Modernity*, London, 1991, who prefers the term "segmentation". For the Russian case, Alfred J. Rieber, "The Sedimentary Society", in Edith Clowes et al., *Between Tsar and People*, Princeton, 1991.

15 Walter Laqueur, *Russia and Germany: A Cultural Conflict*, London, 1969.

16 Ian Kershaw, *Hitler, 1889–1936. Hubris*, London, 1998, pp. 73–80, 131–36.

17 David Blackbourn, and Geoff Ely, *The Peculiarities of German History: Bourgeois Society and Politics in Nineteenth-Century Germany*, Oxford, 1984, pp. 1–35.

18 Carl E. Schorske, *German Social Democracy, 1905–1917. The Development of the Great Schism*, Cambridge, Mass., 1955.

19 W. Becker (ed.), *Die Minderheit als Mitte. Die Deutsche Zentrumspartei in der Innenpolitik des Reiches, 1871–1937*, Paderborn, 1986.

20 Larry Eugene Jones, *German Liberalism and the Dissolution of the Weimar Party System, 1918–1933*, Chapel Hill, 1988, especially the introduction and chapter one.

21 Hitler, *Mein Kampf*, p. 163.

22 On factionalism among the Bolsheviks see Robert Service, *Lenin. A Political Life*, Bloomington, 1985, I, 108–109, 176–78, 188–90; and for the Socialist Revolutionaries see Oliver Radkey, *The Agrarian Foes of Bolshevism. Promise and Default of the Russian Socialist Revolutionaries, February to October 1917*, New York, 1958.

23 Teodor Shanin, *The Awkward Class: Political Sociology of the Peasantry in a Developing Country. Russia, 1910–1925*, Oxford, 1972; and Leopold Haimson (ed.) *The Politics of Rural Russia, 1905–1917*, Bloomington, 1979.

24 Walter McKenzie Pintner and Don Karl Rowney (eds.), *Russian Officialdom: The Bureacratization of Russian Society from the Seventeenth to the Twentieth Century*, Chapel Hill, 1980; Alfred J. Rieber, *Merchants and Entrepreneurs in Imperial Russia*, Chapel Hill, 1982; Harley D. Balzer, *Russia's Missing Middle Class. The Professions in Russian History*, Armonk, 1996; Gregory Freeze, "Subversive Piety: Religion and the Political Crisis in Late Imperial Russia", *Journal of Modern History*, 68 (1996): 308–50.

25 Gerald Feldman, *Army, Industry and Labor in Germany, 1914–1918*, Princeton, 1966.

26 Robet Waite, *The Vanguard of Nazism. The Free Corps Movement in Postwar Germany, 1918–1923,* New York, 1969.

27 Moshe Lewin, "The Civil War", in idem, *Russia, USSR, Russia*, New York, 1995, pp. 42–71.

28 Kershaw, *Hitler*, chapter 13; Alexei Kojevnikov, "Rituals of Stalinist Culture at Work: Science and Intraparty Democracy Circa 1948", *The Russian Review* 57 (January 1998): 25–52.

17 *The Self-Not-Fulfilling Prophecy*

ISTVÁN RÉV

At around 15:20 on 19 August 1989, historical justice was done. Some 118 years before, the Habsburgs were denied the chance to play a decisive, constructive role in the process of German unification; Germany became unified in the "*kleindeutsch*", Prussio-centric way, by leaving Austria and the Habsburgs out. This time the process of German reunification started with the active participation of a Habsburg—Otto, the son of the last emperor of Austria and king of Hungary. On 19 August 1989, the Pan-European Union, under the presidency of Otto von Habsburg, organized a picnic near the border city of Sopron in western Hungary, to propagate the notion of a common Europe without borders. After 15 July 1989, large groups of East German citizens took refuge in the buildings of the embassies of the Federal Republic of Germany in Prague, Budapest, Sofia, and a few other East European capitals. On 13 August 1989, the overcrowded Budapest embassy building had to be closed with a few hundred East German refugees remaining behind the closed gates.

On the basis of a previous agreement between the Austrian and Hungarian authorities, the participants in the Pan-European picnic symbolically opened the border. At this moment, according to the testimony provided by the photographs of Tamás Löbenwein, exactly at 15:20, several hundred East Germans—who had most probably been tipped off by refugee workers in Budapest—broke through the gate: some 661 East Germans crossed the Hungarian–Austrian border. Not since the Berlin Wall had been built had such a large number of people escaped across the Iron Curtain at once. "The pulling down of the Berlin Wall began in Sopron", stated Lothar de Maizière, East Germany's last prime minister, later on. And at the celebration of the unification of Germany, Chancellor Helmut Kohl declared: "the soil under the Brandenburg Gate is Hungarian soil".

The Habsburgs managed to reclaim their share in the events that led to the latest unification of Germany. Although one cannot claim that this time a "*grossdeutsch*" solution was preferred, still it would be historical blindness to deny the Habsburg contribution, despite the fact that another *Anschluss* is not yet on the horizon.

Between 17 February and 15 March 1990, the German Institut für Demoskopie Allensbach, the large German polling organization, conducted a large, representative poll among the citizens of East Germany. The Institute tried to find out what percentage of East German citizens had foreseen what was coming, or, to be more precise, what percentage remembered that they had foreseen the future in retrospect? Although it is usual in such polls that people tend to remember that their past expectations were more in line with the outcome of events than was perhaps the case, only 5 percent of respondents claimed that they had been able to foresee what was coming. Sixty-eight percent answered that they had absolutely not predicted the fall of the Wall and of the GDR. The results of the poll are usually cited as proof of the *pre eventum* inability to foresee on the part of the people, who then became directly affected by the changes in which they had played no active part as a consequence of their blindness. The results might suggest that the end of communism just happened to the people without their having been able to participate in the historic changes.

Had the East Germans been able to foresee what was coming there would have been no need for them to flee to the West German embassies, to cross the "green border" during the night into Hungary, to make use of the Pan-European picnic, to resort to the helping hand of the successor to the Austro–Hungarian throne in waiting, to go into the streets, to demonstrate in Leipzig, or even, before all that, to be mortally wounded at the Wall while trying to flee in desperation from the so-called German Democratic Republic. It would have been enough just to wait at home for the end of the communist regime to come. But had they waited for the inevitable to come, sitting peacefully at home, looking forward to the fall, would the fall have come when it came, in the way it finally came? Are we in a position to say that the fall would in fact have come at all without the voice and exit of the East German citizens, without their participation in the form of flight to the West German embassies, which as we know—if from nowhere else, from the results of the poll—was the direct consequence of their inability to foresee? If, as a consequence of their accurate foresight (i.e., that the regime would collapse anyway), they had decided to stay home, and, as a result of this decision, the regime had not collapsed, their foresight would not have been accurate at all, and this amounts to saying that they would have been unable to foresee the future. In that case, accurate foresight would have prevented the desired event. This amounts to saying that the future would have been different from the foreseen outcome, that is, their foresight would not have been accurate at all; people would not have been able to foresee the future. We are back at square one. Or at least, so it seems.

However, we might draw the conclusion that—at least in certain cases—it is precisely the benign lack of foresight that makes it possible to bring about the desired future. Predictions by social scientists that become public knowledge might prevent the predicted outcome. In certain cases, far from the lack of it, it is foresight that can prevent certain events from happening. Sometimes, when something is foreseen and that foresight is made public, it acts as a prohibitive force that undermines the chances of the occurrence of the foreseen event. Had the Politburo of the Soviet Communist Party foreseen the consequences of Gorbachev's election to the post of secretary general of the Party, he most probably would not have been elected (he would probably have been immediately shot instead), and this in turn might have given a completely different twist to the history of the Soviet Union.

Unfulfillment is usually considered as the unproblematic, one might almost say natural, outcome of prophecies in the sphere of social life. If prophecies are not fulfilled, modern scholarship does not feel that there is anything that would warrant a scientific explanation: it seems obvious that usually there is no connection between prophecy, foreknowledge, foresight, and the later events at which the prophecy was originally directed. If there is a correspondence between a publicly known prophecy and the outcome in the social sphere, then scholarly analysis is usually interested not so much in how the prophet (the social scientist, the politician, the speculator on the stock exchange, etc.) was able to foresee the future, but much more in what the impact of public knowledge was on the behavior of the participants and in what way public knowledge could influence later events, irrespective of the ability of the prophet to foresee. The foreseen outcome does not justify the foreseer. In the case of the so-called nomological sciences we expect scientists to foreknow what is going to happen: we expect them to know in advance when a meteorite is going to strike the earth. But we also know that a car runs over another dog every day; so we do not expect the *ideographical* disciplines (like history) to give accurate projections. The incidents of yesterday (at least in the social sciences) are not coded information about the events of tomorrow.

Sober, careful social scientists take care not to make predictions publicly. And, *post eventum*, social scientists rarely take credit for the outcome, arguing that it was exactly their *silence* that significantly contributed to the end result. However, if publicly circulating foresight might prevent the predicted outcome, that is, might amount to a self-not-fulfilling prophecy, then there might be direct correspondence between silence and the occurrence of a specific event.

In what follows I would like to prove, with the help of archival documents, that lack of foresight could be *the* decisive factor in bringing about certain outcomes. After the fall of communism, the blindness of the kremlinologists was blamed for the surprise: they proved unable to foresee. In my view, the accusation was shortsighted: the blindness of the kremlinologists turned out to be one of the crucial contributing factors in the changes. I intend to prove that groups of central actors in recent major historical events have not been able to foresee what was coming; and that their inability to foresee turned out to be the crucial factor in the end. I would like to argue specifically—and, in a paradoxical way, this would confirm the wildest suspicions of certain political groups on the extreme right of the political spectrum—that members of the communist nomenclature and officers of the secret police in fact played an important role in bringing down the regime and in the process of transition.

After the unexpected and surprisingly peaceful historical changes in 1989, in almost all of the affected countries—where communism failed so spectacularly but without major bloodshed—suspicion has taken root about the role of the old communist nomenclature in the changes. The best known case is Romania, where different groups have tried to prove that what happened was not a genuine revolution, but rather a coup, a well-orchestrated show, in order to save certain groups of the old elite. According to a recent survey only 41 percent of the Romanian population continue to believe that what happened in 1989 was a revolution; 36 percent hold the alternative view that it was a coup d'état.[1] After 1989 a predilection for conspiracy theories among all sectors of Romanian society, combined with distrust and suspicion directed towards the former communists who ruled the country from December 1989 until 1996, contributed to the creation of the myth of the "stolen revolution".[2] According to the American political scientist Kenneth Jowitt, the vulnerability of Romanian society to rumor is a legacy of the secretive character of the Romanian communist elite that managed to survive and maintain its information monopoly.[3] Reports, and even best-selling fictional accounts, by former Securitate officers or individuals, who before 1989 had a close relationship with the Romanian Security Service, succeeded in substantiating the belief in a well-organized secret plot by implicating either Soviet or Hungarian secret agents or Arab terrorists in the overthrowing of the Ceauşescu regime.[4] Even Western analysts contributed to "the stolen revolution" thesis by emphasizing the alleged participation of foreign terrorists in the events, or by accusing the National Salvation Front of having invented a terrorist plot in order to cover up the coup or to legitimize its power.[5]

In Czechoslovakia, the new parliament was compelled to set up a committee to investigate alleged provocation and the role of the secret services during the Velvet Revolution. On 17 November 1989, student groups in Prague organized a rally to commemorate the fiftieth anniversary of the 1939 demonstrations, the brutal retaliation of the Gestapo, and the closing down of the Czech universities by the Nazis. The police forces of the communist regime attacked the demonstrators and the next day Radio Free Europe announced that the police had killed one of the students. The suppression of the demonstration, and especially the news of the killing of the student, acted as a catalyst that led to the mass protests that eventually brought down the communist regime. It turned out later that nobody had been killed during the police raid, that probably the news of the death of Martin Smid was a provocation spread by the secret services, and that it was most likely a police agent who lay on the ground pretending to be dead, etc. (Timothy Garton Ash later on met the man who purportedly played the role of the dead student.) In his study of the "second life" of 17 November 1989, Oldrich Tuma claimed that, with the exception of the fall of communism in Romania, one cannot find anywhere else such a broad scale of interpretations of events as in Czechoslovakia.[6] According to one of the members of the Commission of the Federal Assembly for the Supervision of the Inquiry into the Events of 17 November, there is a whole list of possible conspiracies behind the events and the false news of the death of one of the student demonstrators: a conspiracy by the secret police (StB) to strengthen the position of hard-line communists in the student movement; a demonstration of power to show the strength of the City Committee of the Communist Party and to intimidate the opposition; a demonstration of power by the Central Committee of the Communist Party; a conflict between liberals and hard-liners in the Central Committee; provocation by the hard-liners in order to strengthen their position before the party congress scheduled for December, etc.[7] Although the parliamentary investigation finally concluded that the speculation, according to which the demonstration was a well-organized provocation and a fraud, could not be substantiated, still the conspiracy theory and the questioning of the genuineness of the Velvet Revolution helped to undermine the authority of the post-communist regime and led to a widespread belief in the theory of the "stolen revolution".

The peaceful nature of the changes, which differed so much from the familiar notions of revolution (i.e., radical, sudden, often violent, led by a group of well-organized, usually conspiring cadres), made it difficult to believe that what had taken place in front of the eyes of contemporaries was real and not staged. Hungary was no exception: after the changes accusations arose about the "stolen" or "unfinished" revolution. In particular, groups from the extreme right of the political spectrum accused the post-communist elite of alleged collaboration with the communist secret police and the nomenclature. According to these accusations, the communists gave their consent to the peaceful transition in order to preserve their economic positions, to exploit the process of privatization, and to become "robber barons", the captains of the economy, in exchange for their lost political leadership. In what follows I will try to prove that in fact members of the secret police and the nomenclature of the Communist Party did play a decisive role in the peaceful transition in Hungary, and that there was a sort of tacit collaboration between members of the democratic opposition and the secret services. But I will argue that lack of foresight on both sides was at the root of the cooperation.

"Even funerals—in some instances *especially* funerals—can be considered not so much as due concern for the dead as a pretext for the seditious enterprises of the living. It can be the case that the most dangerous person at a funeral is the one in the coffin." Thus has Richard Cobb reconstructed the logic of the secret agent in his book on the French Revolution, written from the perspective of the informer.[8] The index of names at the end of the published minutes of the 1989 Central Committee meetings of the Hungarian Communist Party mentions the name of Imre Nagy, the executed prime minister of the 1956 revolution, on one hundred and fifty pages. He was reburied on 16 June 1989, and it is clear from the minutes that his ghost haunted the Party leadership throughout the year of transition. It was he who took the regime with him to the grave. (We know from the history of the transition in other former socialist countries that even without the reburial, something else would have brought the communists down.) But in Hungary, the history of post-communism starts with Imre Nagy's reburial, and its consequences still play an important role in the present.

From the moment in July 1988 when, at a press conference in San Francisco, the last Hungarian communist secretary general, Károly Grósz, casually answered a well-thought-out question by saying that the Party would allow the relatives to rebury the remains of Imre Nagy, there was no longer any chance for the Communist Party to find a firm foothold anywhere. From that moment there remained nothing else for the communists but continuous withdrawal. Communism did not function according to the logic of civilized common sense, which takes it for granted that families have the right to bury their dead. Under communism, the dead, especially the dead who lost their lives as a consequence of communist "justice", were taken care of by the Party according to its political considerations. The dependence of the living on the Party gradually loosened after 1963, while its history, its past, its identity, and thus the fate of its dead, continued to remain a major preoccupation of the Party. The dead, and especially victims of the Party, touched the deepest layers of the identity of the regime, thus no public discourse could be tolerated about them. The dead remained completely dependent on the actual political interest of the Party leadership. When, without due reflection, the political power gave up the right of disposal over Imre Nagy's body, the Party lost its way, and, from its own logical system, accidentally fell into another and completely alien dimension.

In the course of the continuous withdrawal there was one constant fear on the minds of the leadership of the Party: "If we decide to give our consent even to this...then there remains no hope of stopping anywhere. In that case the next stop will inevitably be 23 October. This whole debate about giving or not giving permission for the reburial resembles, in a ghostlike way, the debate around 23 October 1956, when the question was whether or not to permit the demonstration that led to the outbreak of the counter-revolution...Emotions here too might get out of control, and the consequences once more could become frightful and unimaginable...I have already heard rumors that we are, after all, not as stupid as we pretend to be: that the Party is deliberately trying to provoke this whole thing; the reburial, after all, is not quite against our wishes, for we need a pretense to be able to strike hard." This is part of Jenő Fock's monologue at the meeting of the International Legal and Public Administration Committee of the Hungarian Socialist Workers' Party on 28 April 1989.[9] Fock knew very well what he was talking about: in 1956 he was a member of the Central Committee, and in 1958 he was one of the signatories of the minutes of that closed session of the Politburo that prove that the highest leadership of the Party made a political decision about Imre Nagy's legal case, which ended with his death sentence.

It is clear from the documents of the Central Committee of the Party and from the secret police files that, following the 1956 revolution, the Party leadership was haunted by the memory of 23 October 1956, when, after bloody street fights, the demonstrators had seized the building of Hungarian Radio.[10] The communist leaders, the opposition to the regime, and the whole country learned that uprisings start with fighting in the streets, with attempts to occupy the radio station and the vital centers of information control, and with the occupation of the headquarters of power. With the nearing of the day of the reburial there remained nothing else for the leaders of the Party and the secret services to do than to try to avoid another 23 October. According to the available documents, in the end all their efforts were concentrated in preventing the reburial, the resurrection, the demonstration from turning into an uncontrollable and tragic turmoil, an armed uprising, a violent attempt to overthrow the regime. The leaders of the state security services believed—and under the given circumstances they could not have been expected to think anything else—that as long as the secret services were capable of manipulating the leaders of the opposition, of misinforming and misleading the foreign diplomats and the foreign intelligence services; as long as the events remained in the desired peaceful channel; and as long as there was no sign of the return of 1956, there was still a good chance for them and for the regime to survive.

"Our volunteer agents, under the cover names 'Bamboo' in *Magyar Világ* [Hungarian World] and 'Willow' in *Magyar Hirlap* [Hungarian Herald], are publishing articles in which the funeral is described as an important political step in the direction of social peace and concord, as proof of the sincere wish of the present leadership to leave behind the mistakes of the past and work for the development of true democracy...With the help of our agents we are initiating the publication of articles in *Magyar Nemzet* [the Hungarian Nation—the most important newspaper in 1989] that will call for national reconciliation and the preservation of public order."[11] The files of the former Secret Police archives are a rich repository of such orders and suggestions. Reading the newspapers of the spring and early summer of 1989 one cannot help but feel that the secret services really did do a successful job: the papers are full of articles and reports that call for reconciliation and caution among all parties involved. But the reader might easily become the victim of an optical illusion. At its 29 May 1989 meeting the "State Security Operative Committee in Charge of the Preparation for the Funeral of Imre Nagy and His Companions" stated: "The national press, partly on our inspiration but partly *independently of us*, calls for the avoidance of confrontation and for the paying of tribute to the dead in a dignified way".[12] The journalists and the organizers of the funeral did—and would have done so anyway, independently of the maneuvering of the secret services—what the agencies, not having any other options open to them, had planned for them to do. The secret services were able to present the situation as if they had been able to manipulate all the actors, who did not have any connection whatsoever with those secret agencies but who were acting simply out of their best convictions. The files of the Secret Police archive do not contain any known document from the period between 5 May and July 1989 (i.e., the period before and right after the 16 June reburial) that would suggest that the opposition was preparing for anything other than a peaceful and dignified act of homage to the victims of the post-revolutionary terror. Naturally, not all the documents are available as yet, but it would have been in the real interests of the former communists and the secret services to make such documents publicly available, and to blame the former opposition for conspiring towards the violent overthrow of the regime.

"Now we have the chance here to influence events; partly indirectly, but in part in the most direct way", said one Politburo secretary in charge of national security and the secret services, at the meeting of the Politburo on 14 June 1988, almost a year before the reburial.[13] According to the available documents—and fortunately a large quantity of vital documents are publicly available concerning the role of the secret services in the last year of the communist period—in the months preceding the reburial the services collected information from, infiltrated, informed, and misinformed all the organizations that had anything to do with the upcoming reburial. The services felt that they were able to manipulate not only the most important actors in the events but even those foreign governments, including the Vatican, and foreign agencies that played a decisive role in shaping international politics. It is evident from the sources cited by the services, and from the analyses of the secret services themselves, that all the actors involved in the organizational work wanted to use the funeral to pay tribute to the dead and not to incite a violent overthrow of the regime. Since the secret services—in the last months of communism—had no other option available for them but to accept the fact of the reburial and allow the peaceful event to go ahead, they could proudly present to the leadership of the Party that it was due to their successful intervention and irreplaceable role that no attempt was made at a violent and armed overthrow of the regime; everything went according to the plan of the agencies.

"Via our officer in charge in the Ministry of Foreign Affairs, Mark Palmer, the American Ambassador in Hungary, should be briefed and, under the guise of a 'friendly chat', he should be asked to make use of his connections in the alternative organizations and to dissuade these groups from turning the funeral into a political demonstration."[14] "Through legal and illegal channels, messages should be sent to the governmental agencies of the NATO member states, especially to the American and German Federal agencies, to warn them that certain extreme forces are trying to prevent the peaceful, dignified funeral and to use the occasion for political adventures, endangering the ever strengthening process of democratization", proposed the III/III Department of the

Ministry of the Interior in one of its internal documents in May 1989. The report reads as if it had been the Ministry of the Interior that had proposed the reburial in the first place in order to strengthen "the process of democratization".[15] "In the framework of our operation code-named 'Canasta', our connection under the cover name 'Hedgehog-cactus' will send the following information to CIA headquarters: certain extremist groups want to use Imre Nagy's funeral to incite anti-government disturbances. If they succeed, the government will retaliate with force. The Ministry of the Interior has mobilized its special forces...In the framework of the operation code-named 'Ulti', our agent, code-named 'Ragweed', will verbally inform the officers at BND (the West-German Federal Intelligence Agency) about the preparations for the upcoming funeral. He will mention the plans of those extreme groups conspiring to disturb the peaceful event. He will also brief the West German officers about the expected reaction of our Party's leadership. He should emphasize that any disturbance and conflict would have a negative impact on the developing democratization process."[16] "Our men have already delivered all the necessary tasks (sic!) to the Vatican, which urge the leadership of the Catholic Church to accept the views of the Hungarian church leadership as the only official view in these matters."[17]

All these documents show that the state security agencies—even though they were not able to verify it and obviously did not believe in it at all themselves—insisted on misinforming themselves and claiming that certain groups wanted to use the funeral as a signal to provoke violent acts. It was obviously in the interests of the services to insist on this: otherwise they would not have been able to cling onto the fiction of their irreplaceable status. They needed the myth of possible provocation, for what else could have legitimized their existence in the summer of 1989?

"According to *our operational plan*, we have accomplished our mission in providing security for the funeral service, aimed at contributing to national reconciliation...According to the *planned schedule*, at 7 a.m. the crowd started to assemble on Heroes' Square...No extraordinary event worth mentioning took place in the course of our daily activities. There was no need for any police action", concluded the head of the III/III Department in his report at the close of the day of the reburial, on 16 June 1989.[18]

"According to our operational plan", and "according to the planned schedule", were the phrases used by the head of the department in charge of the surveillance of the "internal enemy"—as if the reburial had been planned by the security services; as if it had been their idea in the first place; as if this is what they had always been fighting for: "national reconciliation" and the "strengthening of the process of democratization".

"No extraordinary event worth mentioning", wrote the chief security officer, as if reburying the executed prime minister of the 1956 revolution, who had been sentenced to death by Kádár's order, had been the ordinary, everyday activity of the communist regime. The conclusion of these reports is that as long as it was possible for the regime to withdraw; as long as there was a place to withdraw to, there was still space available for the regime and for its services. This is why it was possible for these services to feel that there was still a sufficiently large ground for them to play on, that they could still play an important role, that eventually it was they who planned, organized, manipulated, secured, and succeeded. Until the regime and communism fell, they operated and therefore existed. And their existence and their capacity to operate were sure proof of the existence of the regime. It was not pure fiction.

By 16 June 1989, only one real and operative goal remained for the regime and its secret services: to avoid the violent overthrow of the regime. "And in my opinion we should try to come to an agreement in advance with them: we should agree that this day of the reburial should not be the day of transition, it should not be the day of regime change. They should not do this, should not transform this day into a day of clashes, because we cannot afford another clash. We should avoid this. We could, we should, agree that the speeches should not aim at saying: 'let's go and let's start from here, let's get rid of the system'", the minister of the interior had muttered at a meeting of the Special Committee of the Central Committee of the Party, back on 28 April 1989.[19] As long as there is no shooting at the radio building the trouble is not terminal. At the close of the day, the head of the III/III Department wrote a summary in which he described the atmosphere at the reception that the organizers gave in the evening following the reburial. (The organizers of the reception and of the reburial—despite appearances to the contrary as presented in the reports of the agencies—were not the secret services but the opposition groups, led by the Committee for Historical Justice headed by Miklós Vásárhelyi, Imre Nagy's former press secretary, one of the defendants at the Imre Nagy trial and the chair of the Board of the Hungarian Soros Foundation.) "The foreigners, political émigrés among them, had a very positive view of the organization of the funeral", wrote the department head in self-congratulatory mode... "Some former political émigrés expressed their wish to move back permanently to Hungary. Some former political prisoners went as far as to say that this wave of rehabilitation [the reburial of the former enemies of the regime] would make their past role appear as if it had been a fight not against, but for, the communist regime, and in the end they may have to feel ashamed of that."[20] The services accomplished the task they had set for themselves:

they prevented another 23 October from happening—although nobody had wanted it to happen. And by having prevented something that nobody wanted to happen, they assisted in accomplishing something that nobody noticed happening: the accomplishment of the peaceful and dignified transition.

After 1956 the opposition was as much afraid of another 23 October as the regime was: the opposition had also learned that after the first shootings events become uncontrollable, nobody is in full charge anymore, acts have unforeseen consequences, the communists lose their heads, the Soviets come back in, and this can lead to unwanted and unavoidable tragedy. Another 1956 was what the opposition wanted least. The secret services—and this is due to the logic of the workings of such services—always sense conspiracy, secret organization, clandestine plans; these are the things that keep them alive. The lack of such activities, according to the logic of the services, cannot be due to anything else but to the successful working and countermeasures of the services themselves. In this logic, the peaceful nature of the reburial was proof of the splendid performance of those services. They had saved the communist regime once more. And their logic made them blind to the fact that what they had tried to prevent so hard had already happened with their assistance: the day of the reburial was in fact the day of the transition. They simply missed the moment.

When, after the funeral, the deputy minister of the interior in charge of the secret services, among them the III/III Department, evaluated the lessons of the work of the services at the funeral and started preparing the security measures for the possible 23 October demonstration (the first democratic election took place only in March 1990; in October 1989 the communists were still in power), he drew the following conclusions: "The activities of the state security forces should be organized according to the same principles that were followed before the 16 June funeral. Our guiding principles should once more be securing the growth of new nationwide reconciliation and peaceful political development. [There is a note in the margin of this document: 'development into democratic socialism!, Pallagi F.'] We should aim to find a common denominator for all those individuals who fought on different sides of the barricade [in 1956]. This common denominator could be a dynamically developing socialist Hungary. We should suggest [note in the margin: 'if necessary, then very powerfully!!, Pallagi F.'] that the society demonstrated its maturity on 16 June, but on 23 October what will be needed is a qualitatively higher stage of maturity."[21]

On 28 July 1989, just weeks after the reburial of Imre Nagy and not long after the death of his murderer, János Kádár, a confused Central

Committee of the Hungarian Socialist Workers' Party—as another preparation for the expected 23 October demonstration—discussed the proposal for a "day of national reconciliation". The suggestion was that the date set for the day of reconciliation should be 23 October. On that day, according to the proposal, a popular uprising had broken out against a regime that had alienated the people. The revolt was a reaction to great offenses against national sovereignty by the Soviets and their Hungarian henchmen. "The now renewed Hungarian Socialist Workers' Party", stated the proposal, "sees 23 October as the symbol of the movement for democratic socialism, for national sovereignty, for comprehensive and deep reforms...We bow our heads before those, too, who, led by good intentions and by their own convictions, became the victims of assaults or atrocities while fighting on both sides, even on the other side."[22]

After a close reading of the "day of reconciliation" proposal, a Central Committee member with a hermeneutical bent pointed to contradictions in the sentence "We bow our heads before those, too, who, led by good intentions and by their own convictions, became the victims of assaults or atrocities while fighting on both sides, even on the other side." He noted that "in the context of the text, 'we' are in fact 'the other side' as well".[23] He continues (I paraphrase): If everybody fought for democratic socialism, for the sovereignty of the nation, for far-reaching reforms, than we are the heirs of everybody; then we are on both this side and the other one (if "the other side" has any meaning at all). We shot at ourselves while defending ourselves from ourselves, and either we are the Soviets, too, or both of us (that is, we) were invaded and finally defeated.[24]

When the deputy minister of the interior referred in his memo to "those individuals who fought on different sides of the barricade" but who should be united under the umbrella of "a common denominator", those whom he had in mind were exactly those who, according to one of the members of the Central Committee, "while fighting on both sides" were "in the context of the text 'we'". "*We are in fact the other side as well*", as that member of the Central Committee so poignantly observed.

After the revolution, one of the most important tasks of the restored communist regime became to find suitable measures to erase 1956 from the public memory. Detailed operational plans, secret strategies, agitation and propaganda memoranda were constantly designed aiming at securing public silence on the subject of 1956. While the surface remained mute, almost without any mention of the events of the revolution, the offices behind the closed doors and curtains remained preoccupied by the frightful memory of 1956. After a while the country did not remember anymore; there was no historical context in which those memories could have been utilized. Before 1956, both the communist leaders and the citizens of Hungary felt that the situation was but temporary: the communists were waiting for World War III or for the worldwide victory of communism, while the majority of the citizens took the American "liberation theory" or the "liberation rhetoric" of the Truman and Eisenhower administration seriously. They believed that when the appropriate moment arrived the American army would come to liberate the oppressed nation. When, in 1956, the seemingly appropriate moment arrived, but not the American army, the people understood that Yalta, and the agreement that had allegedly been reached there, should be taken with deadly seriousness. After the launch of the first Sputnik in 1957 it became clear that the times were not transitory: communism was here to stay. So there was no point in remembering anymore. The promises of the "liberation theory", together with the non-fulfillment of those very same promises, contributed to the worldwide stabilization of communism after 1956.

With Imre Nagy's reemergence and his unexpected resurrection, 1956, and especially the retribution that followed the revolution, found a new historical context. It made sense to remember, to rediscover lost memories. Around the time of the funeral 1956 and 1958, the year of the execution of the revolutionary prime minister, were on everybody's mind. It is understandable that the ghost of the tragedy that everybody tried to avoid served as a warning for all the participants in the event. The Central Committee, in its effort to domesticate the memory of the revolution, unexpectedly found itself on both sides of the barricade and bowed its head before those "who, led by good intentions, fought on both sides"...and shot themselves while defending themselves from themselves.

A violent, defeated revolution and a victorious, peaceful, negotiated transition is an antinomy. However, in my view, it was in large part due to the memory of the bloody and tragic revolution that the transition in Hungary could take place without bloodshed, in a peaceful and dignified way. And in this process, as I have tried to argue, the secret police collaborated with the opposition to the regime. It was not only Imre Nagy's body that served as a tie between 1956 and 1989: in a strange way, the peaceful transition was the post mortem victory of the revolution.

Notes

1 Cf. Victor Neuman (2000). "A fost Revolutie in decembrie 1989?" In *Orizont*, No. 1416, 20 January.

2 On the tapes recorded at the meetings of the National Salvation Front soon after the changes, one of the army generals who had played an important role during the events of December 1989 told how the National Salvation Front had come into existence well before the December 1989 changes. His words fueled the suspicion that what had seemed to be a revolution had in fact been a well-orchestrated coup. Florin Iaru (1990). "*Popurul era sa fure revolutia Securitatii*". In "22", 11 May. pp. 8–9. Quoted by Mihaela Sitariu (2000). "Revolution or coup d'état in Romania?" Unpublished paper, p. 6.

3 Kenneth Jowitt (1992). "The Leninist Legacy". In Ivo Banac (ed.), *Europe in Revolution.* Cornell University Press, p. 209.

4 The novels by Pavel Corut, a former high-ranking Securitate officer combine Thracian-Dacian mythology, Orthodox symbolism, science fiction, and the exaltation of the Securitate as the stronghold of Romanian patriotic virtue. In spite of, or exactly as a consequence of, their ludicrous fabrications, hundreds of thousands of copies of his novels, such as *Floarea de Argint* and *Cintecul Nemuririi,* were sold. See Mihaela Sitario, op. cit. pp. 9–10.

5 Cf. Richard Andrew Hall. "The Uses of Absurdity: The stage War Theory and the Romanian Revolution of December 1989". In *East European Politics and Societies*, Fall 1999. Vol. 13. No. 3. pp. 501–542.

6 Quoted by Petr Roubal (2000). "November 17. Renaissance of a Forgotten Revolution". Manuscript, p. 3.

7 Ibid. p. 4.

8 Richard Cobb (1970). *The Police and the People. French Popular Protest 1789–1820.* Oxford University Press, p.8. (Emphases in the original.)

9 MOL (Hungarian National Archive). Fond 288, 1958. 5/65 ö.e.

10 See János Kenedi (1996). *Kis Állambiztonsági Olvasókönyv. Október 23.-március 15.-június 16. a Kádár korszakban* (Small Hungarian State-Security Reader. 23 October, 15 March, 16 June in the Kádár era). Budapest.

11 BM (Ministry of the Interior) III/III Department (the department in charge of the surveillance of the political opposition inside the country). Operational Plan, May 1989; and BM III/III. Press Plan, 19 May 1989. Quoted by Kenedi, op cit. Vol. II, pp. 268–269 and pp. 280–281.

12 Op. cit. p. 309. (Emphases added.)

13 Minutes of the meeting of the Politburo of the Hungarian Socialist Workers' Party on 14 June 1988. Quoted in Kenedi, op. cit. p. 202.

14 Memo after the 9 May 1989 meeting of the State Security Operative Committee in Charge of the Preparation for the Funeral of Imre Nagy and his Companions. Kenedi, op. cit. pp. 260–261.

15 Kenedi, op. cit. p. 265.

16 Ibid. p. 265.

17 Memo after the 15 May 1989 meeting of the State Security Operative Committee in Charge of the Preparation for the Funeral of Imre Nagy and his Companions. Kenedi, op. cit. p. 278.
18 Kenedi, op. cit. p. 385–387. (Emphases added.)
19 Ibid. pp. 241–242.
20 Ibid. pp. 387–388.
21 Ibid. pp. 398–399. (Ferenc Pallagi was the name of the deputy minister of the interior.)
22 A Magyar Szocialist Munkáspárt Központi Bizottságának 1989. Évi Jegyzőkönyvei (The Central Committee of the Hungarian Socialist Workers' Party. Annual Proceedings, 1989). Budapest: Magyar Országos Levéltár, 1993, Vol. 2. p. 1403.
23 Ibid., p. 1359.
24 Ibid., p. 1377.

18 *Exile and Emigration. The Strange Survival of "German Culture"**

WOLF LEPENIES

By "German Culture" I understand the traditional overrating of culture at the expense of politics. It has been a threat to the intellectual and moral life not just of Germany and of Europe, but also of the United States. It represents one of the most dangerous, unintended consequences of cultural policy in modern times.

"German Culture" Abroad: Victorious in Defeat

While the Allies fought Hitler, German thought conquered the West. "The new American lifestyle [became] a Disneyland version of the Weimar Republic for the whole family."[1] This is a quotation from what the *New York Times* called "that rarest of documents, a genuinely profound book".[2] Allan Bloom's *The Closing of the American Mind* is, in my view, not a particularly good diagnosis, but it is a striking symptom of the uneasiness that the survival of "German Culture" caused in the United States. Bloom deplores an invasion that led to a dramatic change in American philosophical thought and to the formation of a new language, one the Americans from now on felt compelled to speak in analyzing their own culture. Cab drivers all of a sudden used words like *Gestalt* and Max Weber's terminology invaded everyday life, like the *Charisma Cleaners*, which Bloom, to his horror, found in Chicago.

In the nineteenth century, when authors like John Stuart Mill and Matthew Arnold tried to soften utilitarian thought by propagating what

* Delivered as a Tanner Lecture on Human Values at Harvard University, 1999. Printed with the permission of the Tanner Lectures on Human Values, a Corporation, University of Utah, Salt Lake City, Utah.

they called the "culture of the feelings", they turned to German philosophy and poetry—as did the French whenever they tired of their Cartesianism. The same happened in the United States. Nietzsche's rejection of rationalism on rational grounds, Freud's discovery of the unconscious, Max Weber's attempt at disenchanting the world, Heidegger's Hellenism, Thomas Mann's mysteries and sufferings as described in *Death in Venice*—they all joined in a successful attack on the rational project of American culture. Americans thus became utterly dependent on German missionaries for their knowledge of Greece and Rome, Judaism and Christianity. Admiringly, Bloom tells the story of Alexandre Koyré, who was excited when, in 1940 in Chicago, one of his students, unaware that the philosopher was not his contemporary, always spoke in his paper of "Mr. Aristotle". That was Bloom's American dream: to send Professor Weber back to Heidelberg and Dr. Freud back to Vienna, while not only Mr. Aristotle, but also Mr. Plato and Mr. Locke and even Monsieur Rousseau would be granted permanent residency in the United States.

Allan Bloom's teacher in Chicago was an émigré—Leo Strauss. One could argue that *The Closing of the American Mind* is nothing but an updated sequel to *Natural Right and History*, the Walgreen Lectures that Leo Strauss gave in 1949, the year two separate German states were founded. He asked whether the American nation still believed in its original faith, that is, the self-evidence of the natural and divine foundations of the rights of man. He came to the conclusion that there was no longer any difference between the abandonment of the idea of natural right and the adherence to it. The difference between German thought on the one hand, and that of Western Europe and the United States on the other, had completely vanished. Leo Strauss concluded: "It would not be the first time that a nation, defeated on the battlefield and, as it were, annihilated as a political being, has deprived its conquerors of the most sublime fruit of victory by imposing on them the yoke of its own thought."[3] Victorious in defeat, "German Culture" had proven its fundamental assumption: it could not only compensate, it could even take its revenge on politics.

Lessons in Diminished Particularity

If there is such a thing as a German ideology, it consists in playing off romanticism against the Enlightenment, the Middle Ages against the modern world, culture against civilization, and *Gemeinschaft* against

Gesellschaft. This "exceptionalism" was always a point of pride—not least because it was based on cultural aspirations and achievements. The inward realm established by German idealism, the classic literature of Weimar, and the classical and romantic styles in music preceded the founding of the political nation by more than a hundred years. Thereafter, they legitimated any withdrawal of the individual from society into the sphere of culture and private life.

Having given a similar conclusion in a book some years ago, I was pleased when Hans Magnus Enzensberger quoted it at length in one of his essays. Pleasure turned into perplexity, though, when I realized that he had used my own words to characterize the modern history of—Spain. Thus, I was taught an ironic lesson: German history is not nearly as exceptional as the Germans are inclined to believe. In recent decades, this lesson in diminished particularity has been convincingly taught in attempts to show the persistence of the *ancien régime* in all of modern Europe; in the examination of the interconnectedness of Europe's societies and their politics in the decade after the First World War; in the reconstruction of a cycle of German national doctrines whose ideological transitions, rather than ideological persistence, are seen as characteristic; and in the assurance that cultural pessimism was not a German specialty, but rather a feature of bourgeois societies in general.[4]

These attempts to counteract "the chronic overstatement of the unfolding and ultimate triumph of modernity"[5] did much to reinsert Germany's peculiar past into a broader context of European history. They reflect a climate of opinion that enticed revisionist historians to insist on the imitative character of National Socialism, whose ideology, they alleged, was modeled on the earlier fascisms of Latin Europe, and whose atrocities mirrored the earlier crimes of Stalinism. Using chronology not only as an explanation but, equally falsely, also as an excuse, German particularity was thus seen as almost a European normality. The Holocaust was reduced to not much other than a dreadful accident on a road where careless and ideology-intoxicated driving was not the exception but the rule. The search for embeddedness led to understanding and understanding eventually led to forgiveness and to oblivion: *Tout comprendre c'est tout pardonner*.

To understand German history and its peculiarities has been a challenge not only for professional historians, but for philosophers as well. Even more: it seemed as if only philosophy could come up with an explanation for historical developments that, at first glance, eluded historical understanding. That was the argument in John Dewey's *German Philosophy and Politics,* as well as in George Santayana's *Egotism in German Philosophy*, which were published in 1915 and 1916, respectively. Dewey singled out Kant's doctrine of the two realms—"one outer, physical and necessary, the other inner, ideal and free [...] primacy always [lying] with the inner"[6]—as the most important element for understanding German national life; and George Santayana did the same when he described transcendental philosophy as its preferred "method of looking in one's own breast"—adding, somewhat caustically, that "the German breast was no longer that anatomical region which Locke had intended to probe, but a purely metaphysical point of departure [...]".[7] For Santayana, the perversity of German thought consisted in glorifying an egotism that other nations regarded as an impediment to be gotten rid of as quickly as possible. But Dewey, who was not less critical, also admired the pervasiveness of the transcendental method which had made Germany the only country in the world where even cavalry generals employed philosophy to bring home practical lessons. The most striking parallel between Dewey and Santayana, however, is that at the beginning of, and during, the Second World War, both republished books they had written in the middle of the First World War and now felt entitled to reprint without any alteration. Apparently, Germany and German culture had not changed at all.

The Typical German

Thus it was not only Germans themselves who saw inwardness as Germany's political predicament and cultural ideal. Foreign authors asserted this as well—and possibly more than the Germans did. When, in 1942 and 1943, the London Institute of Sociology organized a series of lectures on *The German Mind and Outlook*, the result was quite flattering for the nation with which England found itself at war for the second time in a generation. The debates were chaired by G.P. Gooch, who proudly identified himself not only as the president of the Institute of Sociology, but also of the English Goethe Society. The Institute's secretary summed up the debates: "Whatever may be the coming shape of German society, it is impossible to envisage a condition that shall be stable, pacific and humane, unless it embodies the master ideas of Goethe: faith in individual development, sympathy and unity with nature, vision and imagination unceasingly transforming the mundane and commonplace into symbol, drama, and poetry."[8] This meant that the failure of German politics must be repaired at home—and that, in fact, it could be repaired by drama and by poetry. The better Germany, the cultural nation, would survive the war unharmed.

Debates like those of the London Sociological Society, which ended in a kind of Goethe epiphany, still matter today in the land of poets and thinkers. In 1949, the Allensbach Institut, the German equivalent of the Gallup Institute, asked a representative sample of Germans about their knowledge of, and relationship to, Goethe. This was the year when the Federal Republic was founded, as the institute proudly recalls. Generously funded by the largest German TV station, the Goethe poll was repeated this year, when the poet's two hundred and fiftieth anniversary was celebrated with much pomp and circumstance.[9] Mentioned abroad, these polls sound rather funny—at home they were, and are still, taken seriously indeed. In 1949, for instance, Germans were asked whether, after 1945, they had had "a major spiritual experience". Only a disappointing 46 percent answered "Yes"—a result the pollsters judged so dismal that it had to be compensated by the answer of a publisher, who claimed he had a major spiritual experience each day. Somewhat mischievously he added: "This is a stupid question indeed. I would go so far as to say that any German who had not had a major spiritual experience since 1945 had better hang himself."

The Goethe polls make it possible to compare the Germans of 1949 with those of today and to compare East and West almost ten years after unification. Asked, for instance, whether they considered Goethe a typical German, 47 percent in the East, but only 31 percent in the West, answered in the affirmative. Asked "Do you know at least one Goethe poem by heart?", only 10 percent in the West, but 25 percent in the East said they did. East Germans seem to feel closer to Goethe and his legacy than West Germans do. The German press found much food for thought in the fact that, in 1949, the majority of Germans considered Faust the most important character in Goethe's drama, whereas fifty years later Mephistopheles had sneaked into first place—if only in the West. In the East, Faust still played the leading role.

The most intriguing aspect of the Goethe polls, however, does not lie in the answers they yielded, but in the importance both the interviewers and the public attributed to these surveys. The people's image of Goethe was seen as a litmus test for the state of the nation. Two results were especially reassuring. First, Goethe's popularity had not dramatically diminished since 1949. Second, Goethe was even more popular in the East than in the West. This meant that the cultural nation was alive and well. It also meant that German unification had turned out to be an asset, not a liability, in the attempt to preserve the best that Germany has to offer to itself and to the world: culture. The polls also showed some disturbing results: for instance, why do only 27 percent of those Germans who regard themselves as moderately leftist see in Goethe the typical

German, whereas 48 percent of the political Right do? This question has remained unanswered, because unasked.

A Strange Indifference to Politics

Whenever George Santayana taught German metaphysics at Harvard College, he felt "something sinister at work, something at once hollow and aggressive"[10]—a statement of inspired vagueness sharpened, twenty-five years later, by John Dewey, who spoke of the "strains of continuity connecting the creed of Hitler with the classic philosophic tradition of Germany".[11] Such claims of continuity, which often were stretched to claims of causality, have not been very convincing—regardless of whether individuals like Luther, Kant, Schelling, and Nietzsche, or intellectual movements like Idealism or Romanticism, were seen as the beginning of a road that inevitably, with Hitler, turned out to be a dead end.

The question of how Germany could become a modern economy without fostering modern social values and political institutions is generally answered by referring to the preponderance of the state, which gave from above what, in other countries, the bourgeoisie had to fight for and acquire through its own efforts. Modern Germany, it has been argued, "thought primarily in terms of the might and majesty of the state, modern England primarily in terms of the rights and liberties of the citizen".[12] This view has come under heavy attack. Still, one can hardly deny that idolization of the state has shaped the contours of German society and the course of German history to a large extent. This has involved a considerable weakening of politics and of the public sphere. At times, it could seem as if Germany was a state without politics. Yet it never aimed at being a state without culture.

Fritz Stern has convincingly argued that the strange indifference to politics that characterized German private and public life can be largely explained by the high premium placed on cultural preeminence and on the illiberal elitism that prevailed in Germany after the time of Weimar classicism. Culture was the arena of the absolute, a realm without compromise. Its exaltation led to the illusion that culture could be a substitute for power and therefore a substitute for politics.[13] Let me repeat: whenever I speak of "German Culture" I use the term in exactly this sense. Unlike "civilization", "culture" has remained a term that, in the German language, is almost naturally distant from, if not contrary to, politics. The connotations of "culture" are as positive, warm, and promising as those of "politics" are ambivalent, cold, and suspicious. Even today, the term "Weimar Republic" suffers from linguistic bruises, whereas "Weimar Culture" is nostalgically remembered as a great promise that has remained largely unfulfilled.

The Holocaust, the great divide of Western civilization, should have marked the point of no return, after which the exaltation of culture over politics was no longer possible in Germany. That is, I believe, what Theodor Adorno wanted to say when he called barbarous any attempt to write a poem after Auschwitz. The poems Paul Celan wrote after Auschwitz were anything but barbarous—because his poetry reflected the helplessness, not the power, of culture. Yet the Holocaust did not mark the end of "German Culture". One reason for this was the aesthetic appeal of fascism and later of National Socialism.

The Aesthetic Appeal of Fascism

Today we are inclined to think of National Socialism and culture as a contradiction in terms. A look at Adolf Hitler at the Munich exhibition of "degenerate art" in 1937, poking fun at some of the greatest expressionist paintings of our century, is enough to strengthen our belief that the Nazis could not but destroy the *Kulturstaat* which had, for centuries, been the idol of German self-understanding and national pride. True, many Nazi figures—Hitler the painter, Goebbels the novelist, and Albert Speer the architect—still carried the artistic ambitions of their youth around with them after they seized power, sometimes turning meetings of the inner circle of the Nazi party's leadership into a quixotic *salon des refusés*. Yet we can only laugh or shake our heads in disbelief when we read about Hitler telling Sir Nevile Henderson, the British ambassador, that he was tired of politics and longed to return to oil painting, "as soon as I have carried out my program for Germany [...]. I feel that I have it in my soul to become one of the great artists of the age and that future historians will remember me, not for what I have done for Germany, but for my art."[14]

More through ritual than through belief, National Socialism was able to cast an aesthetic spell on many intellectuals even outside Germany. Wyndham Lewis—in his book on the Hitler cult published after the outbreak of the Second World War—was not the only one who originally regarded Hitler as a politician with a muse, though he added immediately, as if shocked by his own words, that if Hitler were a poet he would be "one of the most boring poets".[15] In France, members of the political far Right envied Germany because National Socialism was seen as the legitimate heir to the fascist movements that had their origin in the Latin countries of Europe. While fascism had become sclerotic and unsure of itself in both Italy and France, it had been vigorously transformed in Germany. National Socialism had preserved the anarchistic and artistic attitudes characteristic of early Fascism: a youthful disrespect for established authority and the general will to *épater le bourgeois*, especially since the bourgeoisie was, to a large extent, identified with Jewish culture.[16]

Rilke had once seen in Mussolini above all a man of poetic qualities. Fascism was seen by many as the equivalent of *l'art pour l'art* in politics.[17] In France, admiration for what Brasillach would call "the aesthetic sensibilities" of Hitler as an individual and National Socialism as a movement had disastrous consequences.[18] Many *hommes de lettres* who were skeptics when they set out to attend the rallies of the National Socialist party returned as fanatics: "Oui, Hitler est bon", was Alphonse de Chateaubriant's resumé in 1937, whereby a strange aesthetic fascination was turned into a dangerous moral judgment.[19] These writers and intellectuals created a context of empathy and understanding that made collaboration not only possible but honorable and even necessary. Among the last troops defending Hitler's chancery in Berlin against the Red Army was the SS division "Charlemagne", which consisted of French and francophone volunteers. They believed they were fighting a culture war in which European values had to be defended against Asian bolshevism and American materialism. It is this far-reaching cultural underpinning of National Socialist politics that makes it so wrong, in my view, to make light of the films of Leni Riefenstahl or an author like Paul de Man's predilections for German "aesthetic nationalism"[20], to see them as expressions of a merely peripheral and hence morally defensible sympathy for Nazism. They point to the heart of the matter.

Art and Morality

In 1939, an extraordinary and shocking portrait of Hitler was published in *Esquire*. The portrait was shocking not least because of its title: "That Man is My Brother". The author was Thomas Mann. With him, a great artist seemed to take Hitler's artistic claims seriously. The disappointed bohemian painter who passed unopposed from one political triumph to the other was a catastrophe, a miserable phenomenon, and yet one could not help viewing him with a certain shuddering admiration: "Must I not, however much it hurts", wrote Thomas Mann, "regard the man as an artist-phenomenon? Mortifyingly enough, it is all there: the difficulty, the laziness, the pathetic formlessness in youth [...]. The [...] vegetating existence in the depths of a moral and mental Bohemia; the fundamental arrogance that thinks itself too good for any sensible and honorable activity, on the grounds of its vague intuition that it is reserved for something else [...]. A brother—a rather unpleasant and mortifying brother. He makes me nervous, the relationship is painful to a degree. But I will not disclaim it."[21]

"That Man is My Brother" is a literary masterpiece. It points to the moral limits of art and literature. Caught in irony, Thomas Mann the artist was unable to come to terms with a phenomenon like Hitler, since "the moral sphere [...] is really not altogether the artist's concern." It was the moral distance inherent in the arts and in literature which, in European history, had led many to regard the great man, the genius, as usually an aesthetic, not an ethical phenomenon. So, whether one liked it or not, Hitler—in part an aesthetic phenomenon in which madness was tempered with discretion—must also be called a genius. In portraying Hitler, Thomas Mann anticipated that, with National Socialism, "German Culture", strictly speaking, must come to an end. He also pointed to the moral limits of artistic aspiration and aesthetic judgment. He did not fall prey to the illusion that there is an elective affinity between artistic modernism and democratic beliefs. Almost the opposite seems to be true. Among the great painters whom Hitler and his comrades publicly despised, quite a few would have been only too glad to be accepted by their third-rate colleague, because they felt close to his ideas. In calling Hitler his brother, Thomas Mann helped an uncomfortable truth come to light. At its core, artistic modernism was by no means genuinely democratic; rather, it overtly displayed a propensity for authoritarian, if not totalitarian, views. As an aesthetic program, however, modernism could not be condemned on moral grounds. To avoid censorship it had to be contained, as it were, in a social context in which moral considerations permeated politics and public life.

That is why the illusory overrating of culture played such a dangerous role in German history. When culture was accepted as a compensation for politics, the absence of morality in the public sphere was accepted as well. The aesthetic appeal first of fascism, and later of National Socialism, was not a superficial phenomenon. It must be a core element in any attempt to explain the attractiveness of Nazi ideology for a large segment of the German bourgeoisie and many German artists and intellectuals. When members of the London Institute of Sociology predicted that Germany would be able to survive Nazism only if its core cultural values, represented by Goethe, were restored, it fell prey to the grand German illusion: culture came first, politics followed. The contrary was true. To survive the civilizational break it had inflicted upon Europe, Germany would have to give up the most German of all ideologies: the illusion that culture can compensate for politics. This process took a long time. "German Culture" survived the Second World War well into the second German republic. One of the reasons for this was a blurring of exile and emigration.

The Blurring of Exile and Emigration

In the summer of 1948, the German writer Gottfried Benn, a physician whose poems and prose had tested the German language to the extreme, offered a sweeping explanation for the past and future catastrophes of his times: "In my view", he wrote in a letter from Berlin, "the West is doomed not at all by the totalitarian systems or the crimes of the SS, not even by its material impoverishment or the Gottwalds and Molotovs, but by the abject surrender of its intelligentsia to political concepts. The *zoon politicon*, that Greek blunder, that Balkan notion—that is the germ of our impending doom."[22] Benn, a master of surprising prose, thus turned the classical problem of Germany's intelligentsia upside down. He did not deplore the aloofness of the German intelligentsia from the public realm that had made them easy prey for the Nazis—he pretended that the intellectual had failed to remain unpolitical and had thereby contributed to a political catastrophe. He closed his letter with bitter irony: "And so farewell, and greetings from this blockaded city without electric power, from the very part of the city which, in consequence of that Greek blunder and the resulting historical world, is on the brink of famine [...]. But it is the city whose brilliance I loved, whose misery I now endure as that of the place where I belong, the city in which I lived to see the Second, the Third, and now the Fourth Reich, and from which nothing will ever make me emigrate." Neither the open disdain for democracy nor the tacit acceptance of the Nazi regime as a legitimate period in German history is the most important passage in this disturbing document. What is so disturbing about it is the poet's belief that he had—while serving as a physician in the German army—lived in exile, artistically as well as politically. When the war ended, emigration and exile had become, in Germany, blurred genres of existence.[23]

Not 1945, the year in which the Second World War ended, but 1948, the year of the monetary reform, must be seen as the turning point in the history of postwar Germany. Not bad conscience but a new currency propelled the change that brought with it a new society. German history in the twentieth century is a disclaimer of discontinuities. Neither the year 1945 nor the year 1933 marked a break—at least not for large segments of the scientific intelligentsia and the cultural elite. When intellectual temperaments, similar in their anti-democratic *ressentiment* and yet as different from each other as the philosopher Martin Heidegger, the jurist Carl Schmitt, the poet Gottfried Benn, and the officer and anarchist Ernst Juenger, expressed their sympathy for the Nazi's seizure of power, one must not see this as a conversion but as a sign of continuity. The ominous year 1933 was not a break, it was the fulfillment of German history. In the state of the Nazis, the cultural nation would be reborn.

It was the aesthetic appeal that turned large segments of the German intelligentsia into followers of the Nazi regime—at least for a while. The sympathies of many fellow travelers dwindled only when, on June 30, 1934, dissidents within the National Socialist party and suspected enemies of the state were executed without trial. Members of the intelligentsia who had sympathized with the Nazis reacted with disgust. However, it was more the absence of taste than the lawlessness that they found intolerable in the behavior of the Nazi death squads. They were not morally appalled, but aesthetically disappointed. This had been the dream of much of the cultural elite: that Germany would become a state in which politics and culture would no longer be separated. It was the fascist dream of a theatrical state.[24] When the dream turned out to be an illusion, it was disappointment, not distance or opposition, that followed. After 1934, many German intellectuals would have gladly remained fascists—if the Nazis had only tolerated it.

Reluctance to Emigrate

When Gottfried Benn was asked why he had remained in Germany even after 1934, he replied that the idea of emigrating had never occurred to him. To go into exile was no viable intellectual option, because it had no tradition in Germany. The notion of "emigration", which would only later acquire its ethical weight, did not yet exist. When members of his generation left Germany, Benn said, they were not acting politically, they were just trying to escape personal hardship and unpleasant circumstances by traveling elsewhere. That was a cynical statement indeed. There was also an anti-Semitic tone in the rejection of emigration and exile: a German could not possibly adopt what had been the fate of the Jewish people for centuries.[25]

One may be inclined not to take Benn's argument too seriously. After all, it did not explain anything, it was just an excuse. The case of Thomas Mann, however, shows how difficult it was for a non-Jewish German intellectual to accept the idea of emigration and of exile. In February 1933 Thomas Mann had left Germany for Amsterdam, Brussels, and Paris, where, after a triumphant beginning in Munich, he was scheduled to talk about Richard Wagner, whose art, as Thomas Mann was eager to remind his audiences at home and abroad, was the epitome of "German Culture" insofar as it displayed "a complete anarchistic indifference to the state, as long as the spiritually German, the 'Deutsche Kunst' survives."[26] A vacation in Switzerland was to follow. There, his children convinced him to stay. Yet the thought of returning home remained with him. For a long time his wish was to go back to Germany and live there in a kind of inner emigration. For him as well, the point of no return was reached with the Röhm massacres. Until then, Thomas Mann had withstood pressure to react publicly to what was happening in Germany. Eventually, he yielded. The decision to act politically came with an artistic farewell. On August 9, 1934, Thomas Mann wrote in his diary: "The whole day nothing but rain and thunderstorms, so that one cannot go out. I made excerpts for my political statement...In the evening I browsed through my diaries and noted passages of political importance...Katia and the children were listening to the radio, which was broadcasting the 'Twilight of the Gods' from Bayreuth, which was constantly disturbed by the thunderstorm. I resisted listening to it, I do not want to hear anything from Germany anymore...It's nothing but cultural propaganda. My toothache is coming back."[27] In order to accept his existence in exile Thomas Mann had to reject "German Culture".

"German Culture" at Home: A Moral Failure Turned to Intellectual Advantage

Fifty years ago, Leo Strauss complained that German thought had become indistinguishable from Western thought in general. In retrospect, one must see this complaint by a German émigré as the prophecy of one of the great political success stories of the twentieth century. First the Federal Republic and then all of Germany became part of the West. The *Sonderweg*, German exceptionalism, has finally flowed into the mainstream of parliamentary democracy, the market, and the rule of law. The revolt of culture against civilization is over. It no longer makes sense to think of culture as a compensation for politics. Today we are witnessing the end of "German Culture". Fifty years ago, however, things looked different.

In the West, "German Culture" did not merely survive the war. It fared well after defeat and capitulation. Politics seemed to be discredited forever, a remilitarization of the country was unthinkable, only culture—due not least to the "inner exile" where so many intellectuals had taken refuge—was left with a legitimate past and hopes for the future. At the same time, it was shaped by emigration, exile, and re-immigration. It became difficult to identify purely German traditions of thought and scholarship; as a rule, a mixture of domestic and especially Anglo-Saxon traditions prevailed. The Federal Republic's political and military loyalty to the West was thus enhanced by its cultural "Westernization".

In 1964, when German sociologists recalled that an economist named Max Weber had written some interesting stuff around the turn of the century, the scholars they invited to talk about him were an émigré philosopher, Herbert Marcuse, then teaching in California; a French political scientist who had studied in Berlin, Raymond Aron; and an American sociologist who had graduated from Heidelberg, Talcott Parsons. It is almost beyond belief that in France an author like Emile Durkheim could have become a French classic only after a detour abroad. Ideas and ideologies of German origin, methods and men were not simply stored in exile; they survived in another cultural milieu by actively adapting to it before they returned to West Germany. It was still easy for Georg Simmel to unmask pragmatism as nothing more than Nietzsche's thought in American disguise. After the Second World War it had become much more difficult to identify the thoughts and traditions that first emigrated and then returned to Germany. Empirical social research, for instance, was widely regarded as an instrument of Anglo–Saxon re-education; not many knew that it was already flourishing in Vienna when Columbia University was just taking shape.

The situation in the East was different. Forced political loyalty to the communist regime in the Soviet Union was not conducive to restructuring scientific thought or cultural belief systems in innovative ways. Yet, while the Federal Republic was Westernized, the German Democratic Republic did not undergo a similar process of Russification. While broken English became the *lingua franca* for West German tourists, many East Germans simply refused to speak Russian. The West was internationalized, while the East remained a province where the *Internationale* had to be sung daily. Censorship took its toll. In the East, the years from 1933 to 1989 belong to a single epoch conspicuously lacking in cultural modernity.

In West Germany, a moral failure turned into intellectual advantage. Denazification foundered. The old elites were reactivated rather soon. The confrontation between émigrés and fellow travelers, between opponents of the regime and its collaborators, between Jews who had been driven out of their fatherland and anti-Semites who had been responsible for their flight led to the production of works of art and scholarly books both provocative and full of innovative energy. In philosophy, the intellectual tension created by a constellation of thinkers like Heidegger, Jaspers, Karl Löwith, and Hannah Arendt was awesome. In sociology, the confrontation of the Frankfurt School with the émigré Karl Popper on the one hand, and scholars like Arnold Gehlen and Helmut Schelsky, both members of the Nazi party, on the other, shaped the development of the discipline. To this day, German historians are caught in bitter feuds over their professional legacy, haunted by past masters who were both moral cowards and intellectual bravados during the time of the Third Reich.

In East Germany, good moral intentions turned out to be an intellectual disaster. Communists who had survived Nazi persecution and Russian exile tried to make denazification work. Culture became politically correct, but also boring and repetitive. Debates among the intelligentsia dealt with minor corrections of the established cultural canon, but they never questioned the canon itself. Once seen as stimulating within the intellectual micro-climate of the GDR, these debates have today rightly been forgotten. Bertolt Brecht was something of an exception, but even he turned more and more into a principal who was, above all, interested in the survival of his company. The communist émigrés first helped the GDR to win moral recognition, but this recognition withered away with the fall of communism. When the archives of the Communist Party in Moscow were opened, it became evident what an ignominious role heroes of German emigration to the East had played during the purges and political trials of the thirties. They had left one totalitarian regime—only to succumb to another.

The Failure of the Interpreting Class

What the cultural elite of the GDR had learned better than anything was the art of being ruled (Wyndham Lewis). Unlike Poland or Czechoslovakia, East Germany never had a sizable samizdat nor a catacomb culture; and unlike Hungary it did not—and could not—produce groups of engaged émigrés. A Czech writer who fled to Paris or to London thereby became an alienated speaker. A writer from Leipzig who went to Munich or to Berlin was still living in Germany. More important still: he remained a native speaker. Those who stayed in the GDR found, as a rule, ways and means to come to an understanding with the nomenklatura. Not all intellectuals became fellow travelers, to be sure, but a great many of them enjoyed the security and subsidies accorded to the cultural elite by a communist regime that leveled, but never equalized. When Carlyle spoke of the man of letters as a modern priest, and of the "Priesthood of the Writers of Books" that had become so influential in modern times, he was not speaking merely metaphorically. He believed that literary men who wanted to fulfill their mission ought to be poor. They had to form a monastic order. Communist regimes in Central and Eastern Europe probably committed their worst mistake in forcing members of the cultural elite to either collaborate or join the lower classes. Many of them had to work as furnace stokers and road sweepers, as cab drivers and handymen. Thus they became members of mendicant orders indeed. The communist regimes in the East were dealt a deadly blow by an intellectual proletariat they themselves had created. The situation in the GDR was different. Its cultural elite suffered from a lack of discriminative strain: it lived in a milieu with blurred moral alternatives. Put to the test with the breakdown of the regime, the failure of the cultural elite became obvious. It was the failure of the interpreting class.

The first successful German revolution was a true and spontaneous *levée en masse*—aided by the very visible hand of Michail Gorbachev. It was neither the result of a long and open struggle against communist rule, like the fight of Solidarity in Poland, nor the final triumph of twenty years of resistance in the underground of Prague, nor of shrewd piecemeal reform in Budapest. The German November revolution was neither led by a worker's union nor designed by the cultural and intellectual elite. Its heroes were hundreds and thousands of ordinary people who grasped the chance to leave a dictatorship by fleeing to the West German embassies in Prague and Budapest. Its heroes were thousands and hundreds of thousands who took to the streets of Leipzig and of Dresden. Their exit and their voice created the revolution.[28] In this revolution the intellectuals were with the crowd, but not of it. The heroes of this revolution were, with a few exceptions, not intellectuals. In contrast to the upheaval in Prague, for instance, artists and students were not spearheading the revolt.

"*Wir sind das Volk*" (We are the people) was a most appropriate slogan indeed. Intellectuals admired the slogan—and misunderstood it completely. In the framework of their own mentality, this slogan had to be read as the wish for the immediate realization of a socialist dream, while in reality it expressed the farewell to any socialist utopia. When the Berlin wall was breached on the eve of November 9, ten years ago, the slogan was only slightly changed. Then the masses no longer chanted "We are the people", but "We are one people". This minor exchange of just one single word, however, revealed their true intentions: to join the capitalist West. At that time it became obvious that the cultural elite—in the East as well as in the West—had been unable to read the public mood. Intellectuals had failed on their own ground. They had not only misjudged a political power structure and overrated the strength of the Eastern economy, they had misunderstood the meaning of words. Culture is about interpretation and making sense. In Germany, the cultural elite has had great difficulties in making sense of unification. The failure of the cultural elite was neither the misjudgment of amateur politicians nor the miscalculation of would-be economists: it was the failure of the interpreting class. This failure preserved "German Culture"—the traditional overrating of culture at the expense of politics—beyond the process of political unification.

In his attack on German philosophical egotism, George Santayana had written that "just as in pantheism God is naturalized into a cosmic force, so in German philosophy the biblical piety of the earlier Protestants is secularized into social and patriotic zeal."[29] Political opposition in the GDR was, to a considerable extent, propelled by Protestant zeal. The Lutheran Church knew how to get along with the socialist state, but at the same time it was able to resist and to contradict, often at great personal sacrifice for individual members of the church. Their moral convictions, however, never developed into a political strategy. The moralization of politics in the tradition of "German Culture" led to a mentality of "all or nothing", which, in the end, desecrated for all time the concept of politics, at least of party politics, which is nothing else than politics in a democracy. I vividly remember a meeting of a small group of former East German dissidents with Senator Edward Kennedy and Willy Brandt shortly after the fall of the Berlin wall. The dissidents, sticking to principles, and the senator, trying to promote pragmatism, had nothing to say to each other. It was especially sad that Willy Brandt, the émigré, was not able to translate between the two "camps" and remained silent virtually throughout the meeting.

So, unlike after the end of the Second World War, when the confrontation of moral alternatives, the coexistence of fellow travelers and refugees, of victims and perpetrators, of internal and external exile, had created a cultural milieu full of tension and thus creativity, nothing comparable happened after 1989. The moral alternatives confronting each other were murky. There were no real émigrés and only a few dissidents. Most important perhaps was another difference: though many of them nostalgically represented the best of Germany's cultural past, the émigrés who returned after 1945 were also carriers of new ideas, whereas the East German dissidents were molded by a milieu conspicuously lacking cultural modernity. After 1945, pragmatism and a culture of compromise entered Germany; after 1989, idealism and inwardness began to come back. Even when the dissidents had won their freedom of political expression, their fundamental contempt for politics and the procedural elements of democracy remained. "We had hoped for justice, and all we got was the rule of the law", one of them quipped. Most of the dissidents rejected the idea of forming a party, and when parties were formed it happened with great inner resistance indeed. The anti-politics of the East German protest movement thus created a political vacuum that furthered the resurgence of the Communist Party in the East and remained without any influence in the West. Cultural protest in Germany continued to be inefficient because compromise was not accepted as a political value. Once more "German Culture", with "a voice as tender and as powerful as religion itself"[30], claimed to be the better politics.

Epilogue: Weimar and St. Helena

On April 30, 1932, one hundred years after the poet's death, Paul Valéry gave an address in honor of Goethe in the *Grand Amphithéâtre* of the Sorbonne. Valéry had great difficulties in preparing his speech, as he wrote in a letter to André Gide. He did not know German and not much of Goethe, having read only few of his works, among them *Faust* in French translation and some biological stuff, *crâne et plante*, which he called, somewhat condescendingly, "not bad at all". It had taken him five whole days to type the speech on his old Remington typewriter, and when it was written he no longer wanted to read it. There was something in Goethe that disturbed him: "*Il y a quelque chose qui me gêne chez Goethe.*" And yet I do not know of a greater tribute to Goethe, "the most complex figure in the world", than this speech. Valéry used the opportunity of his talk in the Sorbonne to dwell on a theme that had been the *idée directrice* of many of his own works: How might the world, and especially Europe, have developed, if political and intellectual power "had been able to join forces, or at least if the relations between them had been less precarious."[31] Valéry never stopped dreaming of what he called a *politique de l'esprit*, but he knew that he was only dreaming: "The two forms of power may well be incommensurable quantities; and it is no doubt necessary that they should be so."

Among the handful of men in which Valéry's dream seemed to have come true were Napoleon and Goethe, "one of them no doubt […] the wisest, the other perhaps the maddest of mortals […] both of them […] the most exciting characters in the world."[32] That is why the year 1808, when Goethe and Napoleon met in Erfurt, was such a priceless moment in world history: "Coquetry was essential at such a meeting. Each wanted to appear at his ease, and carefully arranged his smile. They were two magicians attempting to charm one another. Napoleon assumed the role of emperor of the mind and even of literature. Goethe appeared as the embodiment of mind itself."[33] Valéry's description of the Erfurt meeting is extraordinary, a drama in itself, full of a tension that, even today, has lost nothing of its vibrant power. Goethe is nothing less than the incorporation of "German Culture", that is, of inwardness far from politics. He is "courtier, confidant, minister, a diligent official, a poet, collector, and naturalist" at the same time; the great, in Germany perhaps the greatest "apologist of the world of Appearances […]. In the evening of his days, in the heart of Europe, himself the center of attraction and admiration of all intelligent people", Valéry writes: Goethe probably thought of Napoleon, "perhaps his greatest memory, whose look still lingered in his eyes."[34] The French writer does not hesitate to admire a German poet who admires a French genius, but into his glowing admiration Valéry stirs a pinch of disturbing, and in the end devastating, critique—not so much of Goethe as of the German understanding of him: "Wolfgang von Goethe was to die a little more than ten years after the death of the emperor, in that little Weimar which was a sort of delicious St. Helena for him […]."[35]

Weimar, "*une sorte de Sainte-Hélène délicieuse*"—that meant that the happy coexistence of political and intellectual power had been nothing but an episode in German history, a remote island, an exile from which no Goethe would return. In Germany there was a political promise in culture then which had not been fulfilled.

Notes

1 Allan Bloom (1987). *The Closing of the American Mind.* New York: Simon and Schuster, p. 147.

2 Roger Kimball (1987). "The Groves of Ignorance". *The New York Times Book Review*, April 5, p. 7.

3 Leo Strauss (1971). *Natural Right and History.* Chicago, London: The University of Chicago Press, p. 2.

4 I am alluding to publications by Arno Mayer, Charles Maier, Harold James, Jim Sheehan, David Blackbourn, and Geoff Eley.

5 Arno J. Mayer (1981). *The Persistence of the Old Regime. Europe to the Great War.* New York: Pantheon, p. 5.

6 John Dewey (1942). *German Philosophy and Politics.* Freeport, N.Y.: Books for Libraries Press, p. 69.

7 George Santayana (1940). *Egotism in German Philosophy.* New York: Charles Scribner's Sons, p. 21.

8 Alexander Farquharson (1945). "Summary". In *The German Mind and Outlook*, ed. G.P. Gooch et al. London: Chapman & Hall, p. 218.

9 Institut fuer Demoskopie Allensbach (1999). *Demoskopie und Kulturgeschichte.* Eine Goethe-Umfrage fuer das Nachtprogramm des NWDR 1949 wird 1999 fuer das ZDF-Nachtstudio wiederholt, Allensbach/Bodensee.

10 Santayana, op.cit., p. viii.

11 Dewey, op.cit., p. 15.

12 Gooch et al., op.cit., p. viii.

13 Cf. Fritz Stern's books *The Politics of Cultural Despair: A Study in the Rise of the Germanic Ideology* [1961], Berkeley: University of California Press 1974; and *The Failure of Illiberalism*, New York: Alfred A. Knopf, 1972.

14 As reported in an article in *Time,* September 11, 1939, p. 29. The caption for the article was "Painters' War", alluding thereby to the fact that the Polish commander-in-chief, Marshall Edward Smigly-Rydz, was "an able if academic landscapist".

15 Wyndham Lewis (1972), *The Hitler Cult* [1939]. New York: Gordon Press, p. 47.

16 Here I cannot pay due attention to the difference between "collaboration with Germany" and "collaborationism with the Nazis" which has been stressed by Stanley Hoffmann. Cf. his article "Self-Ensnared: Collaboration with Nazi Germany", in *Decline or Renewal? France since the 1930s*, New York: The Viking Press (1974), pp. 26–44.

17 Cf. Erwin von Beckerath (1927). *Wesen und Werden des faschistischen Staates.* Berlin: Julius Springer.

18 William R. Tucker (1962). "Politics and Aesthetics: The Fascism of Robert Brasillach". *The Western Political Quarterly* XV, p. 608.

19 Alphonse de Chateaubriant (1937). *La Gerbe des Forces (Nouvelle Allemagne).* Paris: Bernard Grasset, p. 69. But not only the French fascists were impressed by the Nuremberg party rallies. In 1937, Nevile Henderson went there for the first time: "The effect, which was both solemn and beautiful, was like being inside a cathedral of ice [...]. I had spent six years in St. Petersburg before the war in the best days of the old Russian ballet, but in grandiose beauty I have never seen a ballet to compare with it." Nevile Henderson (1940). *Failure of a Mission.* New York: G.P. Putnam's Sons, pp. 66–67.

20 Cf. Lindsay Waters (1989). "Paul de Man: A Sketch of Two Generations". In *Responses. On Paul de Man's Wartime Journalism*, ed. Werner Hamacher et al. Lincoln: Nebraska University Press, pp. 397–403.

21 Thomas Mann (1939). "That Man is My Brother". *Esquire* 11, No.3, pp. 3, 132.

22 Gottfried Benn (1987). "Letter from Berlin, July 1948". In *Prose, Essays, Poems*, ed. Volkmar Sander. New York: Continuum, p. 80.

23 The allusion is, of course, to Clifford Geertz's "Blurred Genres: The Refiguration of Social Thought", *The American Scholar* 49 (1980), No.2, pp. 165–179.

24 I have not used the term "theatre state" because Clifford Geertz wrote that "the expressive nature of the Balinese state…was always pointed not toward tyranny" and that in Bali "power served pomp, not pomp served power." This qualification almost precludes the borrowing of even a term, not to mention a concept. Cf. Clifford Geertz (1980). *Negara. The Theatre State in Nineteenth-Century Bali.* Princeton: Princeton University Press, p. 13.

25 In July 1934, Thomas Mann speculated about the fate of the German people after the end of the Nazi regime: "Perhaps history has in fact intended for them the role of the Jews, one which even Goethe thought befitted them: to be one day scattered throughout the world and to view their existence with an intellectually proud self-irony." Thomas Mann (1933). In *Past Masters*, translated by H.T. Lowe-Porter. New York: Alfred Knopf, p. 220.

26 Thomas Mann (1933). "The Sufferings and Greatness of Richard Wagner" In *Past Masters*, op.cit., pp. 86, 90.

27 Ibid., p. 502 (My translation).

28 Cf. Albert O. Hirschman's brilliant interpretation of the collapse of the German Democratic Republic: "Exit, Voice, and the Fate of the German Democratic Republic". In *A Propensity to Self-Subversion*. Cambridge, Mass.: Harvard University Press (1995), pp. 9–44.

29 George Santayana, *Egotism in German Philosophy*, op.cit., p. 12.

30 Fritz Stern, *The Failure of Illiberalism*, op.cit., p. 5.

31 Paul Valéry (1968). "Address in Honor of Goethe". In *The Collected Works of Paul Valéry*, ed. Jackson Mathews. Princeton: Princeton University Press, Vol. 9, p. 147.

32 Ibid., p. 173.

33 Ibid., p. 171.

34 Ibid., pp. 156, 161. In this context it is interesting to note that Maurice Barrès called Goethe's drama *Iphigenie* "a civilizing work which 'defends the rights of society against the arrogance of the spirit'"—a rejection of "German Culture" if ever there was one. I am quoting Barrčs from Thomas Mann's speech "Goethe and Democracy", which he delivered in the Library of Congress on May 2, 1949. It seems to me that this speech, in which Thomas Mann mentions the Sorbonne address from 1932, is an implicit answer to Paul Valéry—and full of complicity.

35 Ibid., pp. 174, 175.

19 *Giordano Bruno Nolanus: Authoritarian Sage and Martyr for Free Speech*

RIVKA FELDHAY

Giordano Bruno was burned at the stake in Campo dei Fiori in Rome on 17 February 1600. For fifteen years he had wandered throughout Europe, inciting debate and provoking anger in its main intellectual centers. Often he was forced to leave one refuge for another, vulnerable, persecuted, and in search of new patrons.

Bruno, who was born in Nola in the south of Italy, began his vagabond life after escaping from the Neapolitan monastery where he had first taken the Dominican habit. There he was twice suspected of holding unorthodox opinions concerning Jesus, the Trinity, and the images of Christian saints. From Rome and Turin he arrived in Geneva, where he converted to Calvinism and graduated from the Academy. In Geneva Bruno printed his first little booklet in which he identified twenty philosophical errors in one lecture by a respected philosopher. This episode taught him a lesson he would never forget about the harsh intolerance of the reformers. It also crystallized his loathing for their theology.

Forced to leave the city after attacking its ministers, Bruno arrived in France where he succeeded in gaining support at the court of Henry III and obtaining a position at the Collège de Combrai. The nucleus of a Brunian discourse first appeared in a series of early works published in Paris. *De Umbris Idearum* (On the shadows of ideas) contained the seeds of his deep philosophical intuitions, especially the insight that human cognition is fundamentally occluded, and hence the need to get access to "sensible forms"—images—in which human ideas—the shadows of the divine idea—are vested. Bruno conceived of such "sensible forms" as nodal points mediating between God's lighted world and the darkish world of nature and man. The philosophical themes that would preoccupy him for the rest of his life—the connection between the infinite and the finite, between God and his universe; the nature of human cognition;

the ethical "limit" of man—surface in the *De Umbris*, together with the principles of the "art of memory" that brought him fame in France. Bruno's talent for satirical writing, verging on the obscene, also emerged during this period and found expression in the play *Il Candelaio*. So did his first experimentation with dialogue form—*Cantus Circaeus*—which testified to his lifelong experience of a deep philosophical, religious, and sociopolitical crisis to which he responded in his work. An emancipatory impulse coupled with a sense of uniqueness and vocation in Bruno's early work persisted throughout the tortured trajectory of his life that would eventually lead him to his final and tragic choice.

Bruno insisted that he left Paris for England of his own free will. However, there is no doubt that his arguments with professors at the Sorbonne became a source of embarrassment to the king. He arrived in London in April 1582 with a letter of introduction from Henri III that gained him residence at the house of the French ambassador, and the status of a gentleman of the ambassador's entourage who occasionally made his appearance at Queen Elizabeth's court. Two and a half years in England gave birth to the six Italian dialogues that constitute the heart of his physical, metaphysical, ethical, and theological thought and exemplify his peculiar literary taste. The *Cena de le Ceneri* (Ash Wednesday Supper), the first of the dialogues written in England, apparently presents a departure from a Copernican world-view towards Bruno's cosmological speculations concerning universal motion in the universe, mutability on earth, and the earth's "four" motions. However, the *Cena* contains much more than that, as we shall soon see. Bruno's perception of the social world around him, and his utopian vision of a better society with a special role for intellectuals, are presented in the form of a social comedy and an interesting piece of sociology of knowledge. In a nutshell, the *Cena* contained most of the themes that would be developed in the later cosmological and moral dialogues. The two following dialogues—*Della Causa* and *De Infinito*—depict a much more developed picture of the universe than that presented in the *Cena*, consisting mainly of arguments for its homogeneity and infinity, for the plurality of worlds, and for the relativity of all positions in it. Furthermore, these dialogues, in spite of their more philosophical tone, involve themes connected to the social, political, and religious scenes of Bruno's life that are mixed, however, with fictional elements representing Bruno's discursive interests. The *Spaccio* and the *Cabala* are more concerned with the moral reform of humanity than with cosmological matters. Here, the restitution of true religion, morality, and politics seems to be connected to the evocation of the ancient religion Bruno refined from the hermetic writings that he admired. In the last dialogue written in England—*Gli Heroici Furori*—

Bruno returns to the principles that underlie his whole discourse, develops his critique of equality on all levels of existence, and envisions his reform of the individual aspiring to divinity, based on such critique.

Bruno left London for Paris in 1585, when his patron's mission there came to its end. He was soon implicated in several disputes that forced him to leave the city again, and for good, this time for Germany. After a short stay in Mainz, Wiesbaden, and Marburg he arrived in Wittenberg where he taught for almost two years. Between 1588 and 1592 he moved to Prague, back to Marburg, and then to Frankfurt, where he published his Latin poems but was expelled by a Senate order. He then went to Zurich for a short while, before returning to Frankfurt. It was in Frankfurt that he received two letters from the Venetian patrician Giovanni Mocenigo, who invited Bruno to teach him the art of memory. In 1592 he decided to go back to Italy. He stayed a few months in Padua, where he went on printing his works, before finally leaving for Venice to reside in Mocenigo's house. After two months Mocenigo handed his complaint regarding Bruno's unorthodox opinions to the Venetian Inquisition, which immediately led to his arrest.

The Latin poems printed in Frankfurt (*De Minimo, De Monade, De Immenso*) and the fragment *De Magia* are no doubt the most outstanding among the many works written in the years of his wandering in Germany. In the first three Bruno reassumed and developed the ontological and cosmological aspects of his work, while in the *Magia* he returned to ethical—political—ones, but also unified the principles of his whole oeuvre. Bruno's infinite universe, conceived as an effect of God's infinity, emerges most clearly in these writings, as Bruno himself testified before the Inquisition. For him, infinity is twofold: an infinite number of worlds similar to the earth that he considers to be a planet like all others; and an infinite time—space continuum in which these worlds are situated. Due to universal providence all things in this universe are alive and move according to their own perfection. Bruno's cosmology entailed a radical change in the relation between God and the universe, culminating in his assumption about their mutual necessity. "The divinity is a matter which creates all and becomes all", wrote Alfonso Ingegno in his introduction to the *Causa* (p. xxviii). "The perfect human being is one who, by elevating himself to the infinite in contemplation of the divine, actualizing in the infinite his cognitive potency, is capable of assimilating everything because he knows how to transform himself into it." This, in a nutshell, is Bruno's image of God, man, and the relationship between them.

For fifteen years Giordano Bruno had wandered throughout Europe. He then spent eight years in the hands of the Venetian and Roman Inquisition, until at last the Catholic regime came to terms with one of its most severe challengers and critics. The Dominican monk who ridiculed the Holy Bible and the Eucharist, argued irreverently with Aristotle, and wrote satires about his peripatetic followers; the self-professed sage who dismissed Ptolemy together with a whole tradition of astronomy and natural philosophy, was finally silenced by the inquisitorial machine of the Catholic Church.

Giordano Bruno (1548–1600) is one of the most controversial authors in the Western tradition, variously interpreted as religious heretic, Renaissance poet, philosopher-scientist, and hermetic magus: an enigmatic figure of great literary fertility, whose work, no less than his life, is marked by obscurity. The enigma of his lonely life and his ability to identify the fundamental subjects of modern philosophical discourse—the discovery of infinite worlds on the minute and immense levels; the connection between the finite and the infinite, between the individual and the universal, between light and shadow—were certainly behind the Promethean myth that portrayed Bruno the iconoclast, striving to destroy any tradition. Moreover, his consciously chosen end in a desperate attempt to safeguard the philosophical core of his life's work has created the myth of a martyr for the sake of free thought, the figure of the modern individual who preferred death to abjuring his innermost beliefs. The historical Giordano Bruno, however, never developed the rhetoric of incommensurability between the old and the new. Rather, he naturally used, and sometimes abused, anything of tradition—from the Lullian art of memory to Aristotelian, Neo-Platonic and Hermetic concepts—that served his needs and purposes. And it is doubtful that his death, indeed an act of defiance, can be interpreted through abstracting from it a principle of the universal right to free speech. In the following pages I shall confront the myths of modernity invested in Bruno's persona—Bruno the iconoclast and the martyr for freedom of speech—with the figure of the author that emerges from a careful reconstruction of some of his works. Bruno rejected the whole institution of traditional authorship as a web of commentaries. He refused to become a commentator of texts that gained authority through tradition. He was also unwilling, or unable, to become part of the institutional structures within which tradition was replicated. The series of dislocations that constituted his life, the trajectory of the vagabond which I have delineated above, are a symptom of a radical rejection not simply of the contents of tradition but of its modes of authorization and legitimization.

Bruno's attempt to construct for himself an independent authorial position is the subject of this essay. It includes his attempt to imagine a system of interrelations with other speakers in the same discourse and to embed it in a utopian social vision. This boundless ambition, however, stood in sharp contrast to his lack of any support system in the real world. His ambition, then, had to be fulfilled through his own texts, and by the manipulation of his own life. Many of the paradoxes of modernity may be discerned in the paradoxes underlying Giordano Bruno's strategies in his heroic and tragic lifelong enterprise of creating himself an authorial position.

The trajectory of Bruno's life and work testifies to the emergence of a metaphysical and cosmological vision that departs from a critique of the Copernican point of view and develops the infinite universe and the plurality of worlds as manifestations of God's infinitude. Simultaneously, this vision asserts the ability of man—a certain type of man, though, not all men—to ascend to divinity.

How does Bruno attempt to establish himself as the author of such a radical vision, so remote from anything accepted by the culture of his time?

The answer involves an analysis of three moments in Bruno's discourse: the contents of the vision; the persona of the author; and the relationship of the discourse to the social environment. These three dimensions may be best reconstructed through a reading of one of Bruno's dialogues that exhibits all three dimensions and the relationships between them. The *Ash Wednesday Supper* was the first Italian Dialogue written by Bruno in England. While it contains the rudiments of Bruno's cosmology, this cosmology is presented to the reader as an object of debate between a discursive representative of Bruno—the Nolan—and his opponents. Furthermore, the debate is not directly introduced in the way that the Copernican system, for example, is portrayed by Galileo in the context of his Dialogue. Rather, a story about the debate is told in the course of another conversation that takes place between Bruno's mouthpiece—Theophilo—and three other interlocutors. The second moment of the discourse—the author's persona—may thus be reconstructed by deciphering the rules of debate and conversation represented in the story that contains the story of the dialogue between the Nolan and his two opponents on cosmological and metaphysical contents. Lastly, the *Ash Wednesday Supper* includes a description of the location of the debate—the house of a noble patron of the arts—and the journey to that location. It also contains many digressions on the social and political environment that surrounds the debate. These are the relevant materials for reconstructing the relationships Bruno envisages between his discourse and its context.

At the end of my short excursus into Bruno's philosophy, authorial position, and social relationships, I shall propose my reinterpretation of the myth of Bruno, the martyr for free speech. The paradox at the heart of Bruno's life and work will be exposed as a usually occluded but real paradox of modernity.

Cosmological Vision

The Copernican claims about the large dimensions of the universe and the motion of the earth were Bruno's points of departure for introducing his infinitism. Bruno dissolved the limit of the Copernican cosmos—still confined within the now immobile and very distant sphere of the stars—and populated it with an infinite number of worlds. These worlds consist of two kinds of bodies: cold earths and hot suns, which are, in fact, varying forms of the same universal infinite substance. No privileged point within that unbounded space could distinguish center from circumference, inner from outer region, in which all positions have become relative. Likewise, no essential difference separates hot and cold bodies. Earths receive light and heat from their suns, but also communicate that light and heat further to bodies on them. This need to receive and communicate heat and light is the only cause of universal motion—both of celestial bodies and of bodies on earth. The soul is the moving source of such universal motion. Each and every body has a soul that moves it. This vision is well defined in Hilary Gatty's *Giordano Bruno and Renaissance Science*: "From the recognition that the earth moves, not just around itself with diurnal motion but also around the sun with annual motion, Bruno deduces the movements of all earths in the infinite universe around central suns which supply them with the necessary heat and light for life to exist."

Underlying Bruno's original cosmology is an old ontology, according to which the world is organized as a network of similitude relationships. Things behave as they do because they share a spatial proximity, because there is sympathy or antipathy between them, because they manifest some kind of analogy, or because they tend to emulate each other. For example, a stone thrown from the top of the mast on a moving ship will fall to its feet—and not some distance behind—because it shares spatial proximity with the ship and thus expresses sympathy with it. A network of reciprocal relations stretches infinitely in time and space, and potentially links every object to every other object. At some place and at some time in the past or in the future, everything that is now invisible has surfaced or will surface, and so has entered or will enter into a relation of similitude with every other visible element. The changing patterns of objects entering a reciprocal relationship with each other constitute movement that is essential for the life-giving process of constant vicissitude and metamorphosis. Thus the Nolan, Bruno's discursive persona, explains universal celestial motion: "It happens, then, that there is no part in the center and the midst of the star which does not come to the outside and circumference of it; there is no external or outside portion of it which at some time does not of necessity come inside or become internal." The earth's four motions, which express its respiratory and reproductive needs through the sun's heat, are actually the irregular way each part of the earth interchanges with every other part.

Like Bruno's oeuvre in general, the *Ash Wednesday Supper* offers more than cosmology and ontology. Through a display of the Nolan's supreme knowledge—about which Theophilo informs his interlocutors—the reader is acquainted with the nature of true knowledge and the way it is acquired in Bruno's discursive world. If every motion, and more generally every change, is understood as the manifestation of some kind of sympathy, analogy, or spatial proximity between two objects, then the act of identifying these two objects and the type of relationship they share is the only relevant type of knowledge. The Nolan exemplifies such knowledge in his identification of the four motions of the earth. According to him the earth exposes itself to the sun daily for respiratory needs, annually for reproductive needs, and very slowly—to enable the interchange of each part of its parts with every other part, through which the entire expression and renovation of its surface is accomplished. These motions manifest relationships of affinity and mutuality which the ontology of similitude requires. Bruno in fact offers an interpretation of the Copernican theses that consciously defies Copernicus and the Copernicans, claiming that "he [the Nolan] holds the mobility of the earth on other, more solid ground of his own" (139). For although it is to be admitted that the procedures of geometers and astronomers can provide some insights that direct the search for truth, they are too superficial for proving the truth about nature. Similitude, on the other hand, provides a more comprehensive and general principle than mathematical relationships. However, nowhere in the text is there offered a key, a method, a code for making the right analogies that would lead to the right interpretation. On the contrary, usually all codes for interpretation, either of texts or of nature, or even of social behavior, are rejected. Distinctions can be significant only on the basis of prior knowledge, and only prior knowledge—which the presence of the Nolan alone can assure—can tell significant from insignificant distinctions. To the request of his interlocutor, Smith, for a guide who would help him out of the chaos of knowledge, Theophilo can only offer a "gift of the gods" for a lucky person who happens to follow the true sage. Learning from texts, or from the Book of Nature, is either a miraculous success (if a gifted person meets a "true guide"), or a march of folly (if the person is not gifted or the true guide is not found). The Nolan does not teach one how to read texts or how to observe nature, but only the meaning of that which one reads or observes. Learning is never a process of mastering rules, but of following a master who becomes the ruler of one's mind. This is the reason the Nolan is unable to conduct a dialogue with his disciples and followers. For the truths and meanings that emanate from him, he only demands "assent and love".

Authorial Position

The pre-text of the *Ash Wednesday Supper* was a journey Bruno made to Oxford in June 1583. This journey, during which he debated with some Oxford "doctors" in the presence of a Polish prince, Albert Laski, has been established as a historical fact. Apparently Bruno suffered a shameful defeat in this exchange; he was even accused of using Marsilio Ficino's ideas as his own. Some passages in the *Supper* suggest that Bruno wrote his dialogue as an attempt to make up for the painful episode in Oxford. Bruno, however, does not incorporate the humiliating experience into the text as such. Rather, he alludes to the historical event in an indirect, highly crafted manner. First, he locates a debate between the Nolan and two Aristotelians in the house of Sir Fulke Greville, an English gentleman, well known in sixteenth-century London as a patron of the arts and sciences. This is a distortion of history but not a complete fabrication, since from Bruno's testimony to the Venetian Inquisition we know that on Ash Wednesday some event took place in the French ambassador's residence, where Bruno was staying. However, even this half-fantasized event is not directly presented: rather, the event is reported by Theophilo, who tells his three interlocutors about the Nolan's conversation in London. The reader is thus faced with three distinct scenes, located in three different places: the historical affair at Oxford, which is only suggested and kept in the background; the fictional debate in London, in which the discursive persona of the Nolan is presented; and the enveloping scene, which takes place through five consecutive days in some non-place, and in which Theophilo is presented as the Nolan's mouthpiece.

The three scenes already suggest the complications involved in Bruno's attempt to gain authority. The historical figure who was defeated in a debate at Oxford is identical to the author who composes the story of a debate in London. The story itself is told by a fictional figure, Theophilo, who supposedly presents the author's views. The hero of the story is a figure always mentioned as "the Nolan", whose views are also supposedly those of its author, and whose name is often used by the author as part of his own name—Giordano Bruno Nolanus. The persona of Giordano Bruno, the historical author, is thus divided into three: Bruno the author, and the man defeated in Oxford; "the Nolan", Bruno's discursive persona and the hero of the debate in London; and Theophilo, a fictional-dramatic figure who serves as a kind of mediator between Bruno, the historical author, and his discursive persona "the Nolan". Theophilo, the mediator, enacts an elaborate technique, the purpose of which is to let the historical Bruno disappear and the discursive Bruno—the Nolan—appear. This technique consists of two separate, parallel moves. Theophilo portrays the Nolan's character as noble and refined in ways unlike the historical Bruno, while including in his portrait features typical of the historical Bruno. Correspondingly, he praises the Nolan's wisdom in terms Bruno never heard from his audience, while making allusions to Bruno's historical writings.

The goal of Bruno's technique is essential to the production of an author's position in all modern discourses. Refusing the authority of tradition meant that authority had somehow to be gained from a recognized source of support—a community of scholars, for example, or a recognized patron. After many failures to achieve support from the outside, Bruno, in an extremely original move, tried to create a position for himself, through his own text. The *Supper* encapsulated this attempt and foreshadowed its inevitable failure. For it created a paradoxical situation. The historical writer, Bruno, who occupies a minor position on the margin of several traditional discursive fields—mnemonics, poetry, philosophy, and astronomy—attempts to endow the discursive/fictional Nolan with the authority of the wisest of all men. But first, the historical Bruno must take a privileged position in a discursive field which only the fictional Nolan can create and make accessible to him (Bruno). Bruno will be acknowledged as the author he wishes only if the Nolan is acknowledged as a sage; but the sage will be acknowledged only after his author is acknowledged. In this context the Nolan is shamelessly praised; he is placed in a position occupied by no previous sage and held by no previous hero. He is placed at the top of a hierarchy that includes the legendary Phidias, the mythical Typhys, and the historical Columbus. Yet he differs from these figures; while they intervened violently, adding disorder to an already turbulent world, he endows the world with order and intelligibility. On the scale of transformations of known worlds and of the transcendent positions of their protagonists, the Nolan's conceptual revolution is perceived as the most radical, in terms of both transformation and transcendence. The supposed transformative power of his discourse shifts the very nature and status of the discourse itself, and elevates his position within it to a level unrecognized in any traditional discursive field.

Social and Political Context

The revolutionary concept of an omniscient author is pregnant with subversive implications, not only in the realm of discourse but also in the realm of politics. Herein lies the political significance of the *Supper*. Through Theophilo's description of the journey to Sir Fulke Greville's house the current political structure of English society is depicted, and at the same time the main features of a reformed political structure in an imagined better world is presented. Of the main segments of English society which Theophilo observes—the queen and her circle on the one hand, and the common people on the other hand—Bruno approves of the former and expresses sharp criticism of the latter. The fictive world depicted at the end of the real description reflects Bruno's proposal for reform.

Bruno emphasizes social stratification in his envisioned society, a society of servants in which he counts four ranks. The first is that of the impoverished gentlemen, loyal to their lords because of their need for protection. The second rank of servants consists of "bankrupt petty merchants or artisans, or those who have studied how to read (or some other art), but without any result" (123): they are distinguished by their "heraldic livery" (122). The servants of the third rank are sluggards, trying to escape hard labor. They do not wear livery, either because their masters are not grand enough, or because they are deemed unworthy. Last come the servants of the fourth rank, "the servants of servants", a miscellany of desperadoes who have fallen into disgrace with their masters. This fourfold division, and the distinguishing marks that announce it, can be reduced to a division between two approaches to authority, one of which is highly praised, the other severely criticized. Among the servants of the higher rank one finds willingness to serve, politeness, and loyalty. These gentle servants are reconciled to the social order and their position within it; they need no heraldic devices to remind them of the sharp line of demarcation that differentiates them from their masters. Against the politeness of the gentlemen, Theophilo sets the aggression of the mob, which includes all the other ranks. It is not aggression as such that provokes Bruno's criticism, but the fact that it is directed towards all foreigners, regardless of their sagacity or their discursive authority. There can be little doubt that Bruno includes in this aggressive mob his own disputants—the Nolan's pedantic, vulgar disputants—and indeed, anyone who does not agree with his teaching. Bruno does not reject the aggression of the mob in the name of abstract principles of justice. Rather, he is interested in securing a calm environment for his discourse, which would not be possible without the support of an unchallenged political authority and a stable, well-ordered social system. In order to portray the kind of reformed society about which he dreams, Bruno alludes to one of his own texts, *L'arca di Noe*, a work that contains a symbolic representation of human society after the Day of Judgment. The mob, the common people in this vision, appear not as strong and cruel beasts, but as submissive, humble sheep, and as weak children. This picture complements Bruno's vision of a hierarchical society, in which authority emanates from the queen to the council, to the gentlemen (who are, in fact, servants), and finally to the ranks of docile servants. When authority is thus centralized and hierarchized, a foreigner and non-author like Bruno need only gain the recognition of the queen. He goes on to assert that the queen needs his recognition.

A long digression on the "power of princes to exalt low things" introduces the issue of political authority. One of Theophilo's interlocutors argues that it is wiser on the part of princes to confer their benevolence upon ignoble persons than upon the great, because "otherwise, superior men would retain their superiority by saying that their position was fitting not because of the favor, kindness, and generosity of the prince, but because of Justice and Reason" (117). In other words, authority ought to be the source of justice and reason, and not vice versa. The same structure of authority holds in the discursive and political realm. Bruno suggests that authority should be independent of a method of reasoning, and should become the ground of all methods.

Precisely because the Nolan has no one to recommend him but himself (and his fictional figures)—in other words, because he is such a political absurdity—it is in the queen's interest to legitimize his discourse. In exalting Bruno, a non-entity, the sovereign exalts herself. At this point, the reading of the first book of Samuel is suggested, in order to clarify the digression on the power of princes. The literary allusion subtly inverts the relationship between sovereign and sage. For in the case of Samuel and Saul, it is the prophet—that is, the sage—who legitimizes the prince. An elaborate panegyric upon Queen Elizabeth from the mouth of Theophilo follows, where the Nolan's wisdom appears as a potentially great contribution to his queen's reputation.

What Theophilo actually suggests here are the terms of exchange between the discursive and political domains. The Nolan could offer—besides his unbounded loyalty—a conception of an unbounded universe for the queen's aspiration, and of a well-ordered, strictly hierarchized society for the queen's undisturbed rule. In return, Bruno hopes to receive political legitimization for his discourse and for his position within it. "[Political] authority", says Theophilo, "is worth [much more] than merit", and "merit is worth nothing if authority does not tolerate it" (118).

A discourse in which truth is the privilege of the sage, communicated by emanation in exchange for "assent and love", requires a society based on the idea of "service" from below and the emanation of authority from above. Between the sage and the sovereign there can be no institutionalized mediation, for the sage, the sole source of discursive authority, must be wholly independent of institutionalized discursive constraints. But in order to be thus independent, the sage must become entirely dependent on the sovereign, conceived of as the sole source of political authority. Bruno, whose aspirations knew no limit, could hardly have entered into a more vulnerable position.

***

Bruno's vulnerability, as I have tried to show, was not simply a historically contingent fact that casually brought upon him a tragic end. It was a structural feature of his position in a cultural field that rejected him, but that, in other ways, was manipulated by him in a paradoxical attempt to invent, ex nihilo, a whole discourse, including a completely new set of discursive rules and the concept of an omniscient author. The circumstances of his imprisonment by the Venetian and Roman Inquisition dramatized his loneliness and provided the occasion for turning a life story into a powerful cultural icon. The long years in prison clarified his thought and galvanized his will towards a clear-sighted vision of what was at stake. Already in Venice he crystallized a strategy of defense that had persisted throughout the two trials: he insisted on the liberty to speculate freely within the boundaries of philosophy, even while repenting in the field of theology. This manipulation of the old established doctrine of the "double truth" was rejected by the church of his own day, as it had been earlier rejected by the medieval church. Bruno, however, remained serenely faithful to his own beliefs. "You who have pronounced this sentence against me", he said after having heard the verdict, "you are more afraid than I, who submit." These unforgettable words have become his legacy to succeeding generations. What could not be gained in his real life was achieved through death: what seemed ridiculous in his own discourse was transformed by culture into a universal moral value.

Bibliography

Bruno, Giordano (1977). *The Ash Wednesday Supper.* Ed. E. A. Gosselin and L.S. Lerner. Hamden, Conn.

Gatty, H. (1999). *Giordano Bruno and Renaissance Science.* Ithaca and London: Cornell University Press.

Ingegno A. (1998). Introduction in: G. Bruno. *Cause, Principle and Unity and Essays on Magic*. Cambridge: Cambridge University Press.

VI The Philosophical Dimension

20 *Science and an Open Society: Is the Scientific Community a Genuinely Open One?*

W. H. NEWTON-SMITH

In the seventeenth century Francis Bacon expressed his hope and expectation that the new knowledge would provide us with power over nature. That became the agenda for modern science. The sciences, in particular the natural sciences, have been overwhelmingly successful in delivering the goods. For better or for worse, no institution has had more impact on the character of our existence than science. Its products—technological spin-offs—dominate our lives. Sometimes it enriches our lives: sometimes it impoverishes them or even takes them away. In light of this manifest power we have come to regard science as special. We accept the stories science tells and in so doing form radically different pictures of the universe, of ourselves, and of our place in it. Claims that are endorsed by the social institution of science are given a credibility accorded to no other social institution.

In light of this overwhelming success it is not surprising that much philosophical endeavour has been, and is, devoted to explaining what it is that enables the natural sciences to be so successful. The classical answer to this is scientific method. The scientific community has discovered some technique for weighing the relative merits of rival hypotheses and theories. The scientist has tacit knowledge of this technique. Philosophers, from Mill and Whewell through the logical positivists and Popper to contemporary Bayesians, have offered a bewildering array of rival attempts to render explicit this tacit knowledge. Just what the philosopher has been seeking is nicely encapsulated in Ernest Nagel's regret that "we do not possess at present a generally accepted, explicitly formulated, and fully comprehensive schema for weighing the evidence for any arbitrarily given hypothesis so that the logical worth of alternative conclusions relative to the evidence available for each can be compared" (Nagel 1953, p. 700). With respect to this approach, that I will call the *standard picture*, scientific method gives us a technique for evaluation not discovery. The actual discovery of hypotheses to be evaluated is left to conjecture, intuition, and hunch. However, once the hypothesis has been advanced there is an objective technique for evaluation.

To explain the success of science the standard picture adds a further ingredient: the exemplary qualities of the scientists themselves. With respect to this picture the members of the scientific community by and large bind themselves to accepting the dictates of the scientific method, setting aside all considerations of personal interest and avoiding all social pressures. The standard picture explains success by reference to the discovery of a technique of evaluation, the scientific method, and the unwavering commitment to accepting the results of the application of that technique. In the abstract, the standard picture has its attractions. Suppose someone is particularly successful in playing some complex version of tic-tac-toe. We would be inclined to explain this by positing that he has discovered some algorithm, which is being carefully applied. But as I shall argue in this paper, science is not like tic-tac-toe. There is no such thing as the scientific method. The explanation of the success of science lies more in the character of its social organization. Interestingly, the aspect of its social organization that contributes particularly to its success is its *closed* character. As will be argued, this conclusion is perhaps paradoxical and certainly ironic for a Popperian. For Popper saw at least some aspects of his conception of an open society as flowing from his analysis of science.

The bold claim that there is no scientific method needs immediate qualification. By this I mean that there are no epistemic principles for evaluating beliefs or hypotheses that are unique to science, and which could thereby be a major part of the story of its success. Given the limitations of space I will do no more than illustrate this idea with reference to three of the many attempts to characterize scientific methods: that of Popper, of contemporary realists, and of Kuhn.

Popper's account has the virtue of simplicity. Popper followed Hume in arguing that no inductive inference is ever rationally justified. Finding that a million randomly selected samples of sodium burn with a yellow flame provides no reason whatsoever for thinking that all pieces of sodium will burn with a yellow flame according to Hume and Popper. What we would normally count as evidence for such a hypothesis does not even give fallible grounds for thinking it is more probably true than false. Inductive arguments, arguments in which the premise does not entail the conclusion but purports to support it, simply have no rational force. Consequently, Popper sought to rely entirely on deductive argumentation. While we can never have the least positive reason for thinking that a hypothesis is true or probably true, we can use a deductive argument to show that it is false. Given that we have observed one black swan we can deductively infer that it is false that all swans are white. This is the crux of Popper's philosophy of science. It is only the rejection of beliefs or hypotheses that can have the sanction of reason (but see below).

Unlike Popper, Hume never sought to persuade us to abandon induction. For him, it is part of our nature to proceed inductively. Custom and habit carry us forward where reason fails. To put the point anachronistically, for Hume we are "hard-wired" to induce. It is simply a bemusing feature of the human condition for Hume that our inductive procedures do not have the sanction of reason. But for Popper, on the other hand, we do not, or should not, proceed inductively. And he claims that good scientists never do so. The Popperian scientist, equipped with a fertile imagination, simply makes a bold conjecture, the bolder the better. He then seeks to refute that conjecture by observation and experimentation. If a contrary instance is found the conjecture is falsified and hence rejected. In this case the scientist starts again with a new conjecture. If a conjecture is not falsified in a test it has been "corroborated". Corroboration, as defined by Popper, does not provide any reason for thinking that the hypothesis has any likelihood of holding in the future. It is simply a report that it has not yet failed. Critics have wondered why, in this case, we should trust even a highly corroborated hypothesis. Clearly we do so when, for example, we trust our fate to aeroplanes designed on the basis of aeronautical theories. The answer for Popper is that we have no reason at all to do so. We proceed by blind faith! Critics also object that rejecting a hypothesis in the face of a contrary instance is itself a disguised form of induction. For in so doing we are assuming that the future will be like the past: what failed on Monday will also fail on Tuesday.

In utterly rejecting anything other than deductive justification, Popper committed himself to a very strong form of fallibilism, according to which not only can we not have certain knowledge in science or in everyday life, we can have no positive reasons, however weak, for holding that particular beliefs in science or in everyday life are even more likely to be true than false. For Popper's fallibilism applies equally to the beliefs we form about what we observe. Consequently, it follows that we can have no rational grounds for claiming to have discovered that a hypothesis has been falsified. For we can have no more reason for rejecting a hypothesis than we have for our belief that we have observed a counter-example. On this Popper is quite explicit. To accept an observation report is to make a *decision* that can have no grounds. He feared that if he allowed that reports of observations were grounded his critics would claim that the only possible grounds would be inductive. Admitting induction here would lead to the charge that there was then no reason for admitting it elsewhere, in which case his system loses its uniqueness and hence its interest. But if there cannot even be grounded observation reports, Popper's fallibilism amounts to an extreme form of scepticism. We can have no reasons for thinking that any empirical proposition is true; nor can we have any reasons for thinking that it is false. So it is fifty/fifty that there are even objects to observe!

If we take Popper seriously, the success of science cannot be explained. Having rejected as illegitimate anything but deductive reasoning, the only epistemic tool available to him is consistency. That is, the only criticism that a Popperian can legitimately make of a theory, or of someone's belief system, is that it is inconsistent. No doubt scientists respect consistency. That fact is not enough to explain their special success. For we all respect consistency. This is seen in the fact that it is not even intelligible to embrace an explicit contradiction.

Casual readers of Popper sometimes fail to note that for him there are, and can be, no grounded judgements on the basis of which a theory can be criticised. On this causal reading the Popperian system does not appear to be completely implausible. And this suggests revising Popper to produce Popper*. Popper* holds that we can have good reasons for some of our beliefs concerning low-level observational reports. Popper* still rejects induction but embraces a form of direct realism, according to which we are simply given justified beliefs about low-level perceptual judgements (see McDowell 1994). On the basis of those beliefs we can criticise theories. Given that we have grounds for these beliefs those criticisms can have real force. Science is a matter of making bold conjectures and subjecting them to real criticism. Popper* sees the willingness to accept falsification of his beliefs as being the hallmark of the true scientist. "Do not hold beliefs in a way that renders them immune to falsification." Newton and Einstein acted in accordance with this; Adler, Freud, and Marx did not, and therein lies the explanation of the success of the former and the failure of the latter.

No doubt, the willingness to admit the possibility of error is a virtue. However, it is not uniquely a scientific virtue, and so Popper* cannot use this in explaining the special success of science. It is a general epistemic virtue. Someone who holds a view that another person is dishonest or that a minority is prone to theft, and refuses to consider any contrary evidence, or to give it its due weight, holds that view in a non-falsifiable way. We regard this as a deficiency in a person. So we need to consider whether there is at least a difference of degree. Perhaps among scientists it is standard practice to hold scientific views in a highly falsifiable manner and to hold them particularly lightly; that is, to be particularly sensitive to criticism. The evidence that this is so is lacking. As Lakatos once asked: "Do you know a scientist who wants to have his views falsified?" A commitment to theories is a crucial strategy in the development of science. The Newtonian system was "falsified" from its very inception. We would not have had the successful development of modern science had these falsifications not been ignored. Popper himself was forced to make the damaging concession that even in science a certain degree of dogmatism is required—in any event, as will be argued below, to the extent that if there is something in this it arises not so much from commitment to some principle of falsificationism but to the socialisation of that commitment in science.

The Popperian account of scientific method is fatally flawed and hence can offer us no explanation as to the special success of the natural sciences. A neo-Popperian account, Popper*, equally fails to account for the success of science. It draws attention to a general virtue, but fails to elucidate anything particularly special about science. Indeed, as indicated, successful science has not displayed strong adherence to this virtue.

As a second illustration of this general difficulty in using what philosophers have offered as characterisations of scientific method to explain the success of science, I turn to the opposite end of the spectrum and consider the current fashion for highlighting the importance in science of what has been called "Inference to the Best Explanation". This approach, which derives from Charles Sanders Peirce's work on abduction, has been particularly prominent in the writings of contemporary realists. The realist argues that the aim of science is to give true, or approximately true, accounts of the theoretical structures in the world that explain our observations. The realist holds that science has been impressively successful in providing good reasons for believing that our theories are at least on track for producing better approximations to the truth.

Inference to the Best Explanation (hereafter referred to as IBE) is explicitly an inductivist turn. It is argued, contrary to Hume and Popper, that we can have good non-deductive reasons to believe a hypothesis or a theory if the hypothesis or theory provides the best explanation of our observations. To illustrate, consider the period during the early years of the last century when the atomic theory was highly controversial. Oswald, in the preface to his much used 1905 physical chemistry textbook, warned the reader against taking the atomic hypothesis seriously. He advised regarding it only as a useful device. Einstein argued, on the contrary, for the truth of the atomic hypothesis, on the grounds that it provided the best possible explanation of Brownian motion. This is the apparently random motion we observe when pollen particles are immersed in water. If water were composed of atoms in motion, collisions between the atoms and the pollen particles would explain their erratic motion.

The realist sees the success of modern science as arising from our willingness to make such inductive leaps. For him, we rightly come to believe in electrons, quarks, and black holes that we cannot observe, through the explanatory power of the theories we have evolved about these items. Using IBE is no doubt an important part of what scientists do. But reference to this cannot be the explanation of the success of science. For IBE is as much a part of non-scientific practice as it is of science. I posit the existence of moles in my fields to explain the regular appearance of small piles of earth on the grass. I have never seen a mole but I can think of no better explanation. My neighbour might be placing the piles of earth as some sort of lame practical joke. But there are no signs that anyone has been in the field, and besides, he is too lazy to do this so frequently and so systematically. Consequently, I go with the postulation of moles. While I do not observe the moles, they could in principle be observed. Perhaps the difference is that in science we use IBE in postulating what cannot, even in principle, be observed. However, if we reflect on psychological states we see that IBE is something we learn to use in postulating what cannot be observed, even in principle, at our parents' knees.

In the face of certain telltale signs I postulate that a student is nervous about the forthcoming examinations, or that my daughter is in love. Being nervous, being in love are psychological states that are not observable in principle based on any reasonable criterion of what it is to be observable. Attempts by behaviourists to define such states in terms of their behaviour manifestations are pathetic failures. These states are not to be equated with the associated behaviour. These states are what explain the behaviour. Thus we see that using IBE to postulate what cannot be observed, even in principle, is not unique to science. Consequently, the use of IBE in science does not explain its particular success.

If we turn to Kuhn, who did more than anyone else to move philosophers away from the search for the kind of algorithmic representation of scientific method that Nagel sought, we find the same story. Kuhn enumerated the criteria that he saw as guiding scientists in theory choice. A good theory should be simple, fertile, broad in scope, consistent, and accurate. For Kuhn, an allegiance to these criteria was constitutive of what it was to be a scientist. These are merely guiding principles that do not define a unique choice. Different scientists will give different interpretations to the different factors. And furthermore, the factors will not all point in the same direction in all cases. Different scientists will give different weights to them. Consequently, science is bound to be a messy business with running controversies (Kuhn 1977, p. 321–22). However, important as these may be in defining the parameters of scientific debate, they are not uniquely scientific virtues. These factors represent general epistemic virtues. We do, or should, value consistency in everything. Accuracy is as much a virtue for the carpenter as it is for the scientist. Even philosophers recognise the virtue of simplicity in theories. The preference for hypotheses of broad scope is quite general. I explain the fact that my students work hard by reference to their concern with the job market and not by reference to the more flattering hypothesis that my teaching is particularly stimulating. The hypothesis of a concern with the job market is broader in scope. For it also explains why students are changing from philosophy to the vocationally more promising subjects of law and management. As with Popper and IBE, the approach of Kuhn does not identify factors unique for science and so it cannot be a crucial ingredient in explaining the success of science.

Any fully satisfactory explanation of the success of science must look to the social character of science, to science as a social institution. We can set aside the straightforward explanation offered by that arch-cynic of science, Paul Feyerabend. For him, the success of science flowed simply from the fact that, relatively speaking, science has all the resources. What wonders, he muses, might have been obtained by alchemy, magic, and witchcraft if the financial cards had not been stacked against them! Certainly resource allocation is part of the story. But we need a less superficial explanation. Science has the resources it has not just because of the lobbying of the scientists. We, or our governments and industries, allocate resources to science because of a perception that science delivers the goods. We need to explain from what that success stems.

Space precludes giving more than an indication of directions to be explored in seeking to understand the role that the social organisation of science plays in the story of its success. The features to be considered are those that contribute to the success of science as an epistemic engine. In an important sense the investigation of these features is not a purely sociological matter. It is part of what Goldman called "social epistemology", the social counterpart of the traditional philosophical epistemology that focused exclusively on the individual (Goldman 1999). Social epistemology investigates the contribution of social organisation to the production of knowledge, where that knowledge has resulted from collaborative effort. Unfortunately, philosophers of science have almost completely neglected this crucial aspect of the explanation of the success of science. To the extent that they have taken an interest in the sociology of science it has been mainly given over to a polemic against a particular tendency in the sociology of science, the so-called strong programme in the sociology of scientific knowledge (Barnes 1974, and Bloor 1976). The proponents of this programme deny that any real distinction can be drawn between rationality and rhetoric. Thus for them there is no real knowledge or justified belief in science, as those terms are understood by the philosophers. The evolution of science is to be explained purely in terms of social and psychological factors. Philosophers of science, believing that science is a successful epistemic engine, rightly reject the strong programme. But in order to explain that success they need a partnership with the sociologist of science to investigate how social organisation contributes to the generation of real knowledge. The considerable polarisation between philosophers and sociologists of science has inhibited the development of this.

From the point of social epistemics, science can best be pictured as a sort of social club with precise standards for admission and rigorously enforced rules. The features to be adduced below quite obviously contribute to the epistemic success of science. What is not obvious and needs detailed sociological investigation is the precise mechanism that induces conformity to the rules. Just how to craft an efficient epistemic engine was something we had to discover. Bacon, writing in 1624, gave his vision of how this might be done in his fable of the "Colleges of Six Days Work". He rightly saw that individuals working in isolation could not successfully pursue new knowledge. He argued that a social organisation supported by the state would be needed. But he got at least one thing importantly wrong. He argued that the workers in the Colleges should take an oath of secrecy not to reveal their results to outsiders. We have discovered the importance of putting scientific work in the public domain and have developed a complex apparatus of rewards and promotions to encourage this. We had to discover the importance of this. In the early days of the Royal Society pressure had to be put on members to present their ideas. Notoriously, Newton never made public his alchemical work. Even in the eighteenth century mathematicians were still sending colleagues theorems that they had proved but declined to provide the proofs.

It seems to us obvious that the requirement that ideas be made public serves progress. By being made public ideas can be critically discussed. The resulting debate can serve to encourage or discourage further work in a cost-effective manner. In a word, scientific ideas should have originators but not owners. That they are so regarded both explains in part the success of science and differentiates that institution from others. Consider, for instance, technology. In the case of technology, if ideas were made public instead of being owned and protected by patents, the capital investments necessary to exploit the ideas would not be made.

This aspect of the organisation of science might suggest that science is a model of an open society; a social institution where all are encouraged to put their views forward for public discussion. However, in other ways it is the very antithesis of any open society. For instance, science has evolved a complex mechanism for authenticating experts. Without this, science could not possibly succeed as it does. In any scientific investigation an individual scientist, or more likely a team of scientists, has to rely on the results of numerous other scientists. In order to ensure that what they rely on is reliable, those who provide it need to be authenticated as experts. Authenticated experts have the power to close debate. For instance, cold fusion was a nine-day wonder. Once the experts had unanimously judged it non-existent the discussion was over: no more published papers, no more conferences. This is in stark contrast to Popper's vision of an open society where open debate and criticism is never foreclosed.

Some sociologists of science regard the expert as being purely a social construct. That is, for them there is no content to being an expert other than having been authenticated as such. This is not convincing. If this was correct it would be a surprise that science could so systematically provide "power over nature". The truth of the matter is that the social system of authentication has a non-social basis. By and large it authenticates those who have the expertise. The extent to which the system makes mistakes is open to investigations that may suggest ways of improving it. But given the reliance in science on experts, its success provides evidence for the general reliability of the mechanisms of authentication.

In other ways, too, science is far from Popper's ideal of an open society. Science has very tight conditions of membership. The institution has norms of behaviour that contribute to its success, the violation of which leads to expulsion. For instance, consider the norms surrounding experimental data. You are not allowed to suppress your data from coworkers. One is just not supposed to tear out those pages of one's laboratory notebook that go against the hypothesis one has advanced in print. Clearly this norm serves the epistemic ends in science. And it highlights a contrast with other institutions such as politics or diplomacy. In the case of these institutions the suppression of data is often seen as a positive virtue. The diplomat sent to negotiate a peace settlement with a tyrant is unlikely to be successful if he insists on first outlining the history of that tyrant's violations of human rights. In the political sphere, unlike science, not only is the suppression of data not forbidden, it is sometimes even encouraged. When the secretary to the cabinet of the British government, Sir Robert Armstrong, was caught doing just that in the "Spy

Catcher" court case he replied that he had merely been economical with the truth. His career did not suffer. The career of a young scientist caught out in this way would indeed suffer.

A related social norm of epistemic value in science is the prohibition against the invention of data. Such activity is considered as particularly reprehensible. When suspicions came to light, after his death, that Cyril Burt had invented data in his studies designed to show that IQ was more influenced by hereditary factors than by environmental factors, he was posthumously expelled from the British Psychological Association. An institution that goes to the lengths of using posthumous expulsion is very closed.

Authenticated experts who can close debate and professional associations that can close off membership are but two aspects of the social organisation of science that contributes to its success. In drawing attention to them I seek to do no more than draw attention to the importance of the character of the social organisation of science in accounting for its success. Philosophers of science who seek to explain its success have erred in focusing on the chimera of scientific method rather than looking to social mechanisms.

I have intentionally overstated the case against scientific method in seeking to highlight the importance of the social organisation of science in accounting for its impressive epistemic and instrumental successes. There are general things to be said about method in science. Any full account would include Kuhn's list of scientific virtues and various general guiding maxims—for instance, "focus on falsifiable theories". The problem in accounting for the special success of science is that these turn out to be general epistemic virtues and principles that cannot bear the full explanatory weight. If we turn to the details of the specific sciences or particular areas of the specific sciences we will find methodological principles that are part of the explanation of the success of that branch or area of science. For instance, it was an important discovery that we need to use blinded techniques in clinical trials of drugs to control for the placebo effect. But by virtue of being specific to particular areas of science these do not constitute the sort of subject-neutral account of scientific method that the philosophers, including Popper, sought. Nor can I ignore the fact that scientific activity has led to the discovery of techniques used across the sciences that contribute generally to their successes, such as sophisticated statistical methods. My intention has been to draw attention to the inadequacies of the standard picture. Any convincing general explanation of the success of science is going to be a messier, more complicated business than philosophers who sought to explicate scientific method imagined. And the explanatory story will be woefully inadequate unless it focuses equally on the features of the social organisation of science that contribute to its epistemic and instrumental successes.

Popper thought he had captured the essence of scientific method in his slogan "bold conjectures and refutations". He certainly thought that adherence to that method generated the successes of science. I have argued that his account of method is fatally flawed from the theoretical point of view and fails to give due prominence to features of the social organisation of science. Interestingly, Popper insisted that some aspects of his conception of an open society flowed from his analysis of science. In his *Unended Quest* and elsewhere he stresses

> that the critical method, though it will use tests wherever possible, and preferably practical tests, can be generalized into what I described as the critical or rational attitude. I argued that one of the best senses of "reason" and "reasonableness" was openness to criticism—readiness to be criticized, and eagerness to criticize oneself; and I tried to argue that this critical attitude of reasonableness should be extended as far as possible. (Popper 1976, p. 115)

While one might well regard an openness to criticism as a generalisation of the method of falsificationism in science, the sort of openness to criticism that Popper stresses as characteristic of the open society is not a characteristic of science as it is actually practised. As actually practised, science needs dogmatism and it requires for its proper functioning a system of experts whose opinions count for more than others. An open society is supposed to be a democracy. Science is more aptly pictured as an oligarchy than a democracy. Unlike an ideal democracy, science would not flourish if each person's opinion counted equally.

The history of science shows that to flourish it needs periods which Kuhn called "normal science", dominated by a paradigm. During these periods the paradigm is not up for question. In normal science, as Kuhn has remarked, doing an experiment on the theory tests the experimenter rather than the theory. It is not a criticism of science to remark that there are periods when criticism is kept in limited bounds. The elaboration of the paradigm is essential for scientific progress and this requires commitment more than criticism. Eventually, the elaboration brings the limitations of the paradigm to the fore and a scientific revolution leads to its replacement. In noting this feature of scientific history, I am not at all subscribing to Kuhn's more outlandish views that rival paradigms are incommensurable and, consequently, that the transition from one to the other is not a rational process. Understanding the success of science requires the recognition of the importance of revolutions to scientific progress. And this provides another important difference between an open society as characterised by Popper, and the institution of science. Open societies are supposed to proceed by piecemeal social engineering, not by revolutions. Had Popper generalised not from his schematic fantasy of science but from the actual practice of science he would have arrived at a radically different vision of the ideal form of social organisation!

In science we have a social institution marvellously well adapted to achieving its aim of giving us power over nature. It is not an institution that gives us a model to follow in the social or political sphere. What makes dogmatism and authority appropriate to science are features special to science. In the natural sciences we have the possibilities of objectively testing our theories for success. Theories give us prediction and control, or they do not. This objectivity enables us to identify the dogmas that are currently contributing to success. Experts are those who are playing their part successfully in this. We have no easy analogues in the social sphere. Hence we do, or should, distrust authority. Prudence in the social and political spheres means avoiding dogmatism and proceeding by piecemeal means where possible. What constitutes human flourishing is, rightly, essentially contestable, unlike what constitutes scientific flourishing. At the end of the day, Popper's conception of an open society is so lightly sketched that a comparison with science as a social institution is bound to be fraught. However, in so far as the notion of an open society is clear, it is equally clear that science is not a model of one. The diversity and openness Popper thought of as characterising the open society is just what science does not want or need.

The special success of science that I have been considering inclines some to think of science as the very paradigm of rationality. Indeed, for the logical positivists science exhausted the sphere of the rational. On their verificationist principle of meaning, unless a sentence was true in virtue of the meaning of the terms contained within, it could only have cognitive content in virtue of being empirically verifiable. Science was the sole tool for empirical investigation, and hence it was to science that we were to turn for the answers to any meaningful questions. There could be no rationally significant non-scientific discussion of ethical or political issues. And even many non-positivists think of science as the paradigm of the rational. But that is mistaken. Science is only an impressive rational activity in relation to its own goal of giving us power over nature. And indeed there is an important sense in which science as an institution is not all that rational and is open to severe criticism from the perspective of an open society.

Rationality is not only a matter of having efficient means towards a goal, it also involves assessing that goal to see if it can be realised and to see if it is acceptable. Science is an efficient means to its goal and that goal is being realised. It is less clear that the goal is as important as the natural scientist would have us think. At least one philosopher has argued that it would have been better if all research in physics had been permanently stopped in 1900 (Dummett 1981). Less radically, we need at least to pose the question of the rationality of deploying the resources we do deploy on science, particularly "big science". Human flourishing would probably be enhanced if those resources were appropriately deployed in assisting the Third World with education, health, and economic development. And even if the resources were held constant, redeploying them away from expensive "big science" to the intellectually less exciting sciences relevant to, say, agriculture, would produce considerably enhanced benefits to the human community.

The scientific community has been deficient from the point of view of rationality in not promoting discussions of the reasonableness of devoting such large resources to science. And, equally, it has been deficient in not promoting discussion of the possible redeployment of resources within science to areas with the potential for greater general human benefit. One does not expect a boxer, for example, to take the lead in promoting a public debate on the issue of whether boxing should be outlawed. It might seem equally inappropriate to expect the scientist to challenge his own raison d'être. But there is a difference. Science is an intellectual activity and scientists see themselves as especially rational. In light of that, the dictates of rationality require them to be more proactive on the question of their future activities.

The very success of science stands in the way of responsible public policy discussion considering resource allocation. In so far as scientists promote consideration of resource allocation, it tends to take the form of appealing to past success in arguing for still more resources. A case in point is the British Science Campaign in the United Kingdom. Without denigrating the success of science we need to be moved by open-society considerations to a balanced assessment of resource allocation. You can have too much of a good thing.

I have argued that the special success of science owes as much to the character of its social organisation as it does to anything worthy of being called "the scientific method". And I have maintained, contrary to Popper, that once this is appreciated it becomes clear that science as a social institution is a bad model for an open society. One further conclusion is now warranted. While we cannot get from science to a viable concept of an open society, open-society considerations, if properly brought to bear on science, can give us a more socially responsible and socially beneficial institution.

References

Barnes, S.B. (1974). *Scientific Knowledge and Sociological Theory.* London: Routledge and Kegan Paul.

Bloor, D. (1976). *Knowledge and Social Imagery.* London: Routledge and Kegan Paul.

Dummett, M.A.E. (1981). "Ought research to be restricted?" *Grazer Philosophische Studien*, 12/13: 281–98.

Feyerabend, P. (1975). *Against Method.* London: New Left Books.

Goldman, A. (1999). *Knowledge in a Social World.* Oxford: Clarendon Press.

Kuhn, T.S. (1970). *The Structure of Scientific Revolutions.* 2nd enlarged edition. Chicago: Chicago University Press.

—— (1977). *The Essential Tension*. Chicago: Chicago University Press.

McDowell, J. (1994). *Mind and World.* Cambridge, Mass.: Harvard University Press.

Nagel, E. (1953). "The logic of historical analysis". In Feigl H. and Broadbeck M. (eds.), *Readings in the Philosophy of Science*. New York: Appleton–Century–Crafts, pp. 688–700.

Newton-Smith, W.H. (1981). *The Rationality of Science.* London: Routledge and Kegan Paul.

Popper, K. (1945) *The Open Society and Its Enemies.* London: Routledge and Kegan Paul.

—— (1959). *The Logic of Scientific Discovery.* London: Hutchison.

—— (1963). *Conjectures and Refutations.* London: Routledge and Kegan Paul.

—— (1976). *Unended Quest: An Intellectual Autobiography.* London: Collins.

Robertson, J.M. (ed.) (1905). *The Philosophical Works of Francis Bacon.* London: George Routledge and Sons.

21 *Art History at the Crossroads*

HANS BELTING

The discipline of art history entered its active phase as one of the humanities at about the same time as museums began to be founded. The field took a museum-bound direction in examining art—understandably enough, since it focused on the old works hanging in museums. Correct names and appropriate historical dates are needed in order to classify such works. Even the writing of a label to accompany a painting exhibited in a museum requires information on the master and on the work's place in his artistic oeuvre. But dates alone say very little if they are not embedded in a personal or general development that gives them their meaning. Likewise, biographies of artists make sense only if they can be arranged within a general history, for example the history of the "school" to which an artist belongs. The "French school", of course, was one that received particular emphasis in the collections of the Louvre. "Schools" were general terms of classification in art as long as it was conceived in national categories. But their scope did not correspond exactly to the borders of modern nations. Otherwise there could never have been a Venetian or Florentine school, the existence of which indicates that Italy had at that time only just set out on the path to nationhood. The early catalogues of the Louvre try to go a step beyond simply naming the artist and school, and to present the *marche* of the arts through the ages as a universal process. Naturally inherent *progrés* was seen as one of the motors of a "history of art" that had nevertheless reached perfection, once in Classical Antiquity and once in the Renaissance, whose classicism cast doubt on the idea of progress. Thus, from the beginning, two paradigms confronted each other, whose contradictions were hard to reconcile.

Quatremère de Quincy, a representative of the *ancien régime*, was hardly in agreement with this change in the understanding of art in 1815, when he published his famous critique of the museum, still a young institution at the time. According to him, those who wanted to make the museum a site of chronology were aiming to "tuer l'Art pour en fair l'Histoire". For a long time, art history's primary concern was the ordering of knowledge about works in museums or in churches, palaces, and gardens. After all, the founding of the Louvre Museum had become necessary after the Grand Revolution, in order to put the now homeless works of art that had been the property of the palaces and churches into the possession of the people as an example of general art history. For this reason, questions of the meaning of the themes in works of art receded into the background for a long time. Only in the twentieth century did such questions become popular in the field of research founded by the German emigrant Erwin Panofsky in Princeton, under the name "iconology". However, iconology has never been able to provide the kind of general method for analyzing pictures that its name seems to promise. It concerned itself solely with art, not with pictures outside of art, and it never asked what the works of art meant for the culture and history of their times; instead, it asked what current cultural conditions had entered into the works under examination. Art history thus willingly insulated itself from the rest of the humanities and claimed the autonomy of art for itself as well, by avoiding associating art with other textual or material evidence of history.

This schematic description explains the path that art history has taken in the two hundred years of its existence. Its tradition displays an intense selection of topics that has left its traces to this day. I would like briefly to characterize this selection in three ways. First, there is modern art, which did not become a favored object of research for a very long time. This did not change until after World War Two and has since led directly to a schism in the field, which resembles the division of museums and their tasks. Two different yardsticks are applied. Controversies flare up intermittently about how serious modern art is and whether it can really be integrated within a general history of art. In this respect, practitioners have remained consciously, or unconsciously, faithful to the tradition of the field since its beginnings in the early nineteenth century.

Similar reasons have necessarily led the tradition of art historiography to exclude non-Western art from the field's specialties. To this day, self-understanding in this field (and self-misunderstanding, too) suffers from the fact that it believes it is writing a universal history of art, while a closer look reveals it addresses solely the art of Europe, and more recently also of the United States. This contradiction is a familiar aspect of modernism's aggressive self-understanding, which, on the one hand, declared the rest of the world to be autonomous, but, on the other hand, arrogated the right to speak for, and depict, the whole world with its own ideas. Art history has gladly left the art of the rest of the world to anthropology, leading to the famous dispute about whether African masks, to name only one example, should be exhibited as works of art or as anthropological artifacts. This dispute has continued right up until the most recent founding of museums in Paris, although for a hundred years, and since the so-called Primitive movement, avant-garde artists have striven to declare so-called primitive art to be the true art.

However, in a third way the field's own tradition in the last two centuries has affected its profile and themes. Revealingly, art history took off at the same time as the invention of modern technical image media, such as photography and later film, and consciously excluded them from its purview. It behaved in a retrospective and curatorial manner in the conflict with the mass media's contemporaneous image production. In its view, art was, and would remain, defined solely by the old genres—painting, sculpture, and the graphic arts—which in turn were the areas on which the Louvre focused in its collections. Thus a tenacious and retarding conflict set in concerning the integration of other media. Photography received attention only after it had taken on the certified status of art and had been admitted to the museums. Artists had to make these media acceptable before art historians took notice of them. This situation is repeating itself even more intensely with today's media. Video and computer-generated art are mistrusted, as if they were betraying art and thus threatening the discipline's identity. At the same time, paradoxically, these technologies are seeking to gain more freedom in society by receiving confirmation of their aura as art.

This situation can be described in other ways than the approach I have taken here. It can be understood as an option to maintain the canon of a specifically European concept of art and to defend it against all tendencies to dissolve it. This option is justified, if it reflects upon itself and knows its own motivations. This in turn is only possible as long as it maintains dialogue with other positions, rather than merely turning its eyes away and sinking into a cultural pessimism that is demonstrated with special alacrity in regard to art, especially by those who are not primarily concerned with art. In this situation, art history, by contrast, is the prisoner of a tradition that arose in a very different era and that was motivated by other interests. A tradition must continually be filled with new life, or it degenerates into a dead ritual of repetition. Polemics about contemporary art also always involve a ritual that reveals that its glance is extraneous to art. Such polemics want to punish art as a warning to someone or something else, without even wanting to realize that some artists express themselves on the problems of the time with more originality and freedom than do the official makers of opinion. It is worth recalling that Josef Kosuth's slogan "Art after Philosophy" anticipated, in the opposite sense, Arthur C. Danto's choice of theme, "Philosophy after Art".

In France, it is important to consider a specific dichotomy in art literature that is not as pronounced in Germany. French art research has long found itself on the defensive in relation to literary and philosophical authors who have made a great name for themselves in art literature. As a result of the early founding of the museums and of the importance of the annual *Salon*, art criticism in France was a public matter; and as a consequence, writers such as Balzac, Gautier, Baudelaire, Paul Valéry, Sartre, Foucault, and Lyotard took it as their province. The hermeneutics of art were thus opened for a literature in which no disciplinary rules existed and in which language was the medium. So it is understandable that academic art research in France developed archaeological tendencies and withdrew into the factual, while the aesthetic and philosophical questions were left to the writers. The discipline thus defended the knowledge of the experts against the free interpretation of the others (the old tradition of the artists, the *amateurs*, and the laymen repeats itself). But in Germany, art history fulfilled a public function as a venue of hermeneutics.

I find myself in a somewhat delicate position in relation to the theme I am treating in this essay, since I have published two books—two different books—with the same title, *Das Ende der Kunstgeschichte* (The end of art history). The title of the first book is a question and is based on an inaugural speech I made at the University of Munich. I regret that only this first book is available in a French edition. The second book has as its subtitle "a revision after ten years". I wrote it after I moved from the university to the media college in Karlsruhe, where I have since taught art history in surroundings dominated by the new media—a college whose name, by the way, was adopted from the Bauhaus: the Hochschule für Gestaltung, or College of Design. The two books differ in that the earlier gives precedence to methodological questions and is primarily concerned with the role of modern art within general art historiography. The later book turns its glance to the changes in the world that exert an influence on art history, regardless of whether art history accepts and reflects upon them or not. Consider the new constellation of Eastern and Western Europe, the growing distance between Europe and the United States, and finally globalization, which manifests itself in the numerous new art biennials all around the world. But in both cases, my speaking of the end of art history does not refer to what one might suspect, namely, the end of the tasks of a discipline. Rather, I speak of the need to revise a canon, namely, the canon meant until now by the term "history of art".

The canon is a question of cultural identity. It creates the consensus for the history of what we in Western culture call art, to stick to my example. The canon of what art history contains as accumulated knowledge, however, has changed again and again in the last two centuries, something we have hardly noticed. This has happened not only because of the new material that has entered our field of vision with the temporal progress of art, but also because of a temporal and spatial expansion to include other epochs. Thus, at the opening of the Louvre, only the *beaux temps* of art were exhibited—which meant Classical Antiquity and the Renaissance—whereby in France, unlike its neighboring countries, the Renaissance led not to the Baroque, but to the "Classicism" of the *Grand Siècle*. Painters before Raphael were still excluded as "primitives". Gradually, the canon came to include the Middle Ages and then, step by step, modern art, although even today battles are still fought here over what should be considered canonical and what is merely an ephemeral art fashion.

Instead of the canon, I once introduced the metaphor of art history as a frame in which everything that fits is art, and everything that does not fit need not be recognized as art. But in this regard we have meanwhile become more liberal, if also more self-contradictory. We recognize much in the world as art, including much in primitive cultures, and yet we do not take it up into the "*grand récit*" by which we are accustomed to describe the history of art. So we tacitly maintain the consensus that only what can be placed in an art-history description in the time-tested manner is to be identified as art. The existence of this invisible space in which we represent historical art is indirectly confirmed by the fact that many minorities do not find themselves in this frame, and, as a result, polemically declare that the frame is a mere fiction created by the dominant culture. As an example, let me refer to art created by women and the female viewpoint, which have attracted attention in gender studies, particularly in the United States. So the frame of what belongs to art history is too narrow in two ways: inwardly, through the exclusion of minorities; and outwardly through the exclusion of the art of other cultures (especially those in which no Western-style modernism has taken place). Here, art history is experiencing nothing other than what is currently happening in all areas of study and training: a revision of the canon. But specialization in the discipline of art history precludes a perception of this change of paradigm. The atomization of the material studied leads to a situation in which each person feels he is the master of events in his own special area: thus he or she no longer represents art history, but only his or her own interests.

Europe's opening to the East has complicated art history's situation there. The countries of Eastern Europe, for example Georgia, a country I recently visited with a group of young researchers from Germany, want to be represented in what I have described as the frame of the tradition of Western art history. This is achieved by claiming a place in official art history for the country's medieval art—an old, pre-modern *Koine*—and for its national avant-garde artists. Having missed out on the Renaissance, which was spread throughout the Catholic world and its communications routes in the Baroque period, the Orthodox world in the East did not want to be excluded from the identity-producing period of modernism as well. But transporting the Western narrative of culture and art to their own situation results in far-fetched constructions of history, and few attempts have been made to inaugurate an alternative art history with other temporal and spatial priorities.

In their own way, modern artists in the West were busy for a long time carrying forward the history of art and securing a canon in which they wanted to be represented. Although the avant-garde wanted to break with tradition, at the same time it also wanted to carry the history of art along a linear path of progress to the future. So there were repeated attempts by artists to set themselves at the peak of the history of art, thus implying that they were carrying forward a long period of development towards its goal. The recapitulation of the entire history of art was part of a ritual of explanation and justification as soon as artists began writing about themselves. But there was also an opposite tendency: that of freeing oneself from the constraint of tradition and leaving the historical one-way street of art, thus "dropping out" of the history of art. This began with flight into other artistic traditions (Japan for Van Gogh and Oceania for Gauguin). Primitivism was a temptation to leave the history of art to the traditionalists and to flee into other cultures, where, in Hegel's opinion, no history had happened at all. About twenty years ago a performance was staged in the Centre Pompidou that inspired me to give my book the title *The End of Art History*. The artist Hervé Fischer used the ringing of an alarm clock to declare the end of the history of art, which he described in the book *L'Histoire de L'Art est terminée*.

If at that time Fischer was still pleading for freedom from mandatory repetition as well as from mandatory innovation, from today's vantage point we must say that such a plea would no longer be required. Rather, it has become difficult to recognize any mandatory historical pattern at all in recent art production. What was once seen as freedom from the history of art must now be seen rather as the loss of this history in contemporary art. It is a loss, in that artists no longer legitimate their activity in the time-tested genres, nor with reference to a binding tradition. I would like briefly to list some factors that have contributed to this. First, in the long conflict between High Culture and Low Culture, the latter seems to have won for good, which means that the concept of art no longer derives from an elite culture, but has adopted the forms and contents of the mass media.

Second, there has been the victory of the new technologies, as well as the more traditional modern pictorial media, in which personal authorship and its unmistakable signature no longer have any great significance. This explains why, since the 1970s, video artists have included their own images to demonstrate their authorship of their work and, as if bodily, their personal point of view. Even photography, when it transformed itself into art, was difficult to fit into the traditional work history of an artist, which is the standard model in the history of art. Finally, the opening of the boundary between Western art and the art of other cultures is leading to a new situation in the practice and theory of art-historical work. The initial effect of this is felt on the contemporary scene, where the old self-isolation of the West no longer functions. But it also affects the historical themes of art.

This also affects the concept of modernism. The West clung so tightly to the guiding image of classical modernism, especially in the visual arts, that, when the earlier ideals lost their validity, it wanted to distance itself from modernism in so-called postmodernism. In the United States, this separation from "modernism"—a phenomenon that did not last as long there—is all the more dramatic for that reason. But today, modernism is threatened by global cultural developments and the resulting interference between the former center and the periphery. For those cultures that, up to now, have not taken part in the history of modernism, are now redefining modernism. The crisis of modernism is turning into a crisis of the study of art, for the study of art (or rather its material) had allowed modernism a privileged self-portrayal: on the one hand, because of its formalism (the style and its independence from themes and content), and, on the other hand, because of its ideas of representation (art as the representation of the movement of history). But the highly praised dynamics of Western art repeatedly undercut their own premises by propagating the ideas of originality, innovation, and autonomy and then disavowing them again. Mass culture finally blurred the boundaries between High Culture, with its privileges, and popular culture, with its consumer behavior. But that undercut the claim that allowed the hegemonic West to feel loftier than the folk art and pseudo-modern art practices of other cultures. The model of history on which Western art's successful image is based (other cultures had no part in this model) now leads to new problems if one does not want simply to close one's eyes and defend it against the rest of the world. For a long time we did not consider that there were local genealogies and traditions that could not be depicted using the Western model of history—for example, China and Japan, which developed other models of time and space in which art was produced.

So where do we stand today when we think about the current practice and future profile of art history? It is sometimes difficult to carry out a debate when the majority of colleagues in the field are hardly willing to. They are dissatisfied with the loss of authority of the old method, but still unwilling to seek to determine a new standpoint. Many are afraid of losing a terrain where they felt protected by tradition. I myself am torn between my wishes to continue the traditions in which I grew up and my desire to make them capable of living and flexible for the future, which cannot happen without strict criticism. Art history has changed fundamentally several times in the last 200 years (its only 200 years), and it will do so again in the future. But now its most fundamental paradigm has been cast into doubt. This time it is not merely a question of recounting the historical material in a new way again, that is, of revising internal tasks. The question now is whether the official and long-practiced narrative that we call the history of art (like its theme, Western art) can still claim the privilege of a monopoly; the question is whether we can export the concept of art history, as we understand it, to the rest of the world, or if we must discuss it with the rest of the world.

In this regard, it is revealing to observe the difference between today's practice and its theory or methodological reflection. Practice is in the midst of a great change, exposing the previously existing scholarly premises to gradual erosion. But there is currently no methodological reflection on this change. Instead, everyone is trying to exercise an extreme tolerance, in whose shelter everyone can make his or her own comments. Hopefully, things will stabilize in a new state of reflection. It is especially interesting to read the program announcing the 30th International Congress for Art History in September 2000 in London. For this occasion, the desire is to "offer a platform for every conceivable kind of art-historical practice", and the Congress therefore offers "papers and sessions from every corner of the geographical and intellectual globe". There will be debates on "post-colonial theory, transculturality", "other modernities", and "non-European paradigms", as if there were already a consensus on this, or as if the discipline had initiated a dialogue on it. At the same time, the program offers the themes of the time-tested "tools of art-historical analysis", such as "revival" or "the classical" in the history of art. Thus we find, in one and the same section of the Congress, lectures on the Rococo in the ideas of the Goncourt brothers and "revival monuments" in the culture of the Maya. England has a rich colonial past and a correspondingly broad spectrum of cultural studies, but at the same time only a short tradition of art history as a university discipline. So the program is unusually open.

But the question is what the participants in a particular section will have to say to one another and whether they are able to listen to each other. Reading the themes in the program is probably more rewarding and offers greater stimulation for the imagination than actually taking part in the Congress. It is probably easier to imagine the polycentrism and complexity of the topics in one's own projection than to experience them in the routine of the Congress, which scarcely offers enough room for true dialogue (unless this goes on behind the scenes). Practice is at a different stage compared with the consciousness of method, which in turn is connected with cultural identity. The Congress stands under the polyvalent motto "Time". It is precisely the theme of time with which the new questions posed to art collide (or change), for here lie the old traditions of construing history. What is the time of history? And the time of *which* history? The topic for the first section of the London Congress is the "geohistory of art". Everyone can interpret the phrase differently. But it is apparently the constellation of time and space that is to be debated here. It can no longer be depicted using the old categories. In what spaces did what kind of history take place? Up to now, art history textbooks have created the impression that the history of art took place in Europe and was thus a characteristic specific to Western art. Things will hardly remain this way. But then it will not be the task of the Europeans to write the history of the art of the world. (Is there such a thing at all?) Rather, we will be expected to write the history of European art anew and in such a way that our depiction is capable of dialogue "with others", instead of presenting it as an exclusive model.

If we speak of such topics, the reproach of Eurocentrism is close at hand, a reproach we even direct against ourselves. But we then forget that, for Europe, too, there is no mandatory, unified model for narrating the history of art. This already begins in the Middle Ages. That was when Europe's culture possessed the highest degree of unity, but today we judge the art of the Middle Ages with a yardstick and with methods that developed in the art historiography of the Renaissance and subsequently. Thus we act as if the Middle Ages had a concept of art that only emerged in modern times. But these are not the only problems. After the Renaissance, the future nations took such different paths (France with its centralism, the Holy Roman Empire of the German Nation with its particularism) that we are not adequately able to describe art in these countries with one and the same model. The same is true for modernism. For a long time Paris was the center of modern art. German, Dutch, and Italian avant-garde artists oriented themselves toward an art metropolis whose practice of art had no foundation in their own countries, which did not catch up until much later. After World War Two, leadership in art passed to the United States, which in questions of culture had until then been a province of Europe (only in the mass media did the future begin there earlier). But this phase, too, can no longer be regarded as the latest situation. At the moment no one can say where the new centers of art production will establish themselves, or even whether they can still be centers in the old sense. The customary art history is thus merely one possible form of narrating history, and not a universal model.

But the problem of an art history adequate to the times reveals its true dimension when we consider something else. It is not at all the case that only the idea of history has changed, while the idea of art has remained the same. Rather, the idea of art is in turn embedded in the historical process that has come to an end in modernism, and is thus itself a product of history. I elaborated this in terms of the idea of the work of art in my book *The Invisible Masterpiece*, which will soon appear in a French edition. The term "*ars*/art" is old, but its meaning has always changed with use. Not until the nineteenth century can we speak of autonomous art, as we have so far understood it. It fulfilled its meaning in the avant-garde, but this meaning was already questioned again in the twentieth century. For decades, talk of the "end of art" has resurfaced again and again, and the title of a book by Arthur C. Danto already offers a doubled negation: *After the End of Art*. One could respond to this title with the question "What will come after the end of art?" But I do not want to claim here that art has come to an end. That would not be an original assertion, nor would it clarify my topic. In a recent essay I even compared the continued practice of producing art with the absurd activity of Sisyphus, whom Camus portrayed as happy because active, despite absurdity. But in the double concept of art and history, art history is exposed to a double uncertainty if it wants to maintain timeless conditions. This is the burden with which it must live.

It will always be necessary to classify the works of art in which art embodies and reifies itself. But that cannot be the sole task of a discipline reflecting on method, which must ask itself how it can open up art as an integral phenomenon of culture for interdisciplinary and intercultural dialogue. It is quite imaginable that art history should not only be interested in secured works of art, but should also take part in the general discussion of images that has begun in many of today's disciplines. Images are definitely other than objects of art, even if they do play a great role in art; and especially today they are increasingly entering our field of vision outside of art. They arise in the individual and appear before his or her eyes in numerous forms, techniques, and media. The internal representation of images from the imagination and memory, which the human being stages as a born "site of images", is something other than the external representation of what is collectively imagined in time. On the question of images, I would like to see art history loosen the restrictions it currently imposes on its own tasks. It can hardly be doubted that, in today's flood of images, this question already plays a larger and more general role than does the stereotypical discussion of the purpose of art and of whether art is still possible today.

22 *Pornography and the Repressive Function**

HENRY KRIPS

In his *History of Sexuality*, Michel Foucault argues that the Victorian period was characterized by sexual repression: "A single locus of sexuality was acknowledged in social space as well as at the heart of every household but it was a utilitarian and fertile one: the parents' bedroom. Sterile behavior carried the taint of abnormality; if it insisted on making itself too visible, it would be designated accordingly and would have to pay the penalty" (Foucault, 3, 4)". Producing a new generation to run the Empire, rather than sexual pleasure, was to be the economy of the bedchamber. "Think of England", was the advice that Victorian mothers passed onto daughters preparing for their wedding night.

This sexually repressive regime was imposed through a rigorous regime of scrutiny, moral instruction at home and at school, as well as an elaborate system of social and legal norms backed by disciplinary practices. All of these conspired to set in place habits of "self-scrutiny" that Foucault argues were rooted in practices of the Catholic confessional, and transposed into a sense of self-responsibility and personal guilt that were central to Reformation Protestant theology. Subjects were instructed to search themselves no less than others for the faintest stirrings of improper desires that evaded the universal logic of repression. If sexual pleasure managed to survive in this dark night—and it did—then it had to be deeply secret even from the subjects themselves.

The historical irony is that sexual pleasure did more than survive. It flourished, albeit in what Foucault calls "new and perverse forms", where the term "perverse" here is understood not in the moral or even psychoanalytic sense but rather in terms of its Latin roots, meaning "turned about", "twisted". The act of self-scrutiny, which involved knowing what to overlook as much as what to see, took on an erotic dimension, as did the related acts of display and concealment from oneself as well as others.

Foucault argues that sexual repression became so insidious and pervasive that it insinuated itself into the institutionalized practices and discourses through which subjects sought to liberate themselves. For example, sexual repression was produced and reproduced through the liberatory practices of psychoanalysis which, by taking the form of what Foucault calls "just another round of whispering on a bed", reproduced the "restrained, mute and hypocritical sexualities" of the Victorian bourgeois subjects, who concealed behind the closed doors of the parental bedroom what they could not display publicly (3, 5).

Not only does psychoanalysis reproduce the repression from which it seeks to liberate those whom it treats. It also produces the type of perverse sexual practices that it seeks to cure. It not only hystericizes the patient (an essential stage in the production of the "cure") but also produces the transference, an erotic relation between analyst and analysand, which, in turn, becomes a central target of analysis as the therapist struggles to induce the counter-transference.

In sum, not only does psychoanalysis produce a form of the repression from which it seeks to liberate its patients but also, as an unintended by-product of the act of searching them out, it manufactures the secret scandals that it requires a target for its liberatory project. As Foucault eloquently makes the point: "these attractions, these evasions, these circular incitements have traced around bodies and sexes, not boundaries not to be crossed, but *perpetual spirals of power and pleasure*" (45).

In this paper my concern will be to locate two similar structures of unintended consequences within the short history of the pornographic image: first, the 19th century moral crusade against pornography, on the surface a straightforward repression, but which, by laying the groundwork for the commercial circulation of pornography, produced in perverse form what it sought to suppress; second, the nineteen sixties sexual revolution, that, in promoting a new category of artistic erotica, appeared as a liberation, but which, in condemning any sexually explicit images that did not fit the new category, also functioned as a repression.

This repression is illustrated by the distinctions that Roland Barthes and Slavoj Zizek draw between "erotica" and the merely pornographic. Zizek characterizes porn as that which reveals/tells all, by contrast with the erotic which discreetly screens the naked flesh. Barthes, on the other hand, distinguishes erotica by the presence of what he calls "the punctum", a concrete but mysterious detail that transforms the merely sensational and shocking into an image of artistic significance. By associating an aura of value with selected sexually explicit images, Barthes and Zizek appear to take a totally liberal stand. But what they give with one hand, they take away with the other. In particular, their promotion of one category of such images—Barthes' "erotica"—comes at the expense of the rest, which are banished to the ignominious status of valueless trash. Thus Barthes and Zizek reproduce a traditional division within the field of sexually explicit images: on the one hand, "respectable" erotica that, because of their socially redeeming qualities, may be looked at with impunity, on the other, "filth" that imperils the innocent viewer, and which the sexually perverse enjoy in secret. This division between trash and erotica exemplifies the Victorian structure of sexual repression at its most perverse: a repression masquerading as a liberation that guarantees the secret return of what it represses.

The Obscene and the Pornographic

Delineating the category of pornography poses political as well as conceptual difficulties. As Simon Watney makes the point: "The notion of pornography...reflects back only what anti-pornography campaigners already 'know', either that sex is a unified system in which all men oppress all women...or that sex is a symbolic expression of the holy sacrament of marriage" (Watney, 75). In her entry under "Pornography" in *Feminism and Psychoanalysis: A Critical Dictionary*, Alison Assiter echoes these sentiments by indicating that "pornography" is an essentially contested concept. Its definitions, she writes, are "almost as many and varied as writings on the topic. They range from the liberal, for example, 'porn has a certain function of intention; to arouse its audience sexually, and also a certain content, explicit representation of sexual materials' (Williams) to the radical feminist, for example, 'porn is the graphic depiction of women as vile whores' (Dworkin)" (Wright, 335). Laura Kipnis makes a similar point when she says: "Defining porn is one big headache. One person's pornography is another person's erotica...The celebrated dictum 'I know it when I see it' made Supreme Court Justice Potter Stewart the subject of unremitting smirks and winks" (Kipnis, 64).

These difficulties suggest that "pornography", like the term "Jew" in Nazi Germany, and "democracy" in contemporary US culture, takes on the role of what Lacan calls a "master signifier". Formally it has no precise meaning. Even within a particular context of use, there exists no single "pornographic essence" to be revealed by linguistic analysis, any more than there exists a "Jewish essence", except as a figment of anti-Semitic phantasies. Nonetheless, the term "pornography" is full of the appearance of meaning, indeed, provides an anchoring point for other terms in the discourses in which it circulates, and, in particular, provides a lens through which negative evaluations may be projected in an instantly authoritative way (calling a work with sexual content "pornographic" provides a convenient way of damning it without the need for extensive critical examination). This makes the term a powerful and flexible rhetorical resource for deploying negative meaning effects, but one which it is impossible to define in a way that does justice to its meaning, or more correctly, its lack of meaning.

Because of the difficulties in delineating a concept of pornography, I start my explorations by considering the concept of obscenity, which together with the interlinked concepts of erotica and pornography constitute a key grid through which the field of sexually explicit imagery and literature has come to be mapped. According to one traditional usage, "obscenity" is a matter of transgressing the codes of propriety or decency in connection with the presentation and/or representation of material of a sexual nature. In this context, the *Le Petit Larousse* definition is a useful guide. It defines the obscene as "that which deliberately or openly hurts modesty through representations of a sexual nature" (Frapper-Mazur, 204). In other words, obscenity is a matter of violence, or what the *Le Petit Larousse* refers to as "hurt", directed against conventions of decency or modesty.[1]

Like any other transgressive practice, the obscene may become a site of its own "anti-aesthetic". So, for example, in the utterances of those for whom it is *de rigeur* to punctuate speech with "Fuck", this obscenity loses much of its transgressive character. Equally, a remark may retain its transgressive quality but lose its shock value through being embedded in a local discourse that is uniformly obscene—familiarity breeds complacency if not contempt. In both of these cases it is difficult to say whether or not the utterances retain their obscene quality, a difficulty that indicates a certain degree of free play in the concept of obscenity. In what follows I do not seek to resolve this ambiguity, but instead keep it in play as a means of understanding the rich rhetorical resources that the concept of obscenity (along with the related concepts of pornography and erotica) offer to those who would buttress the system of sexual repression under which we continue to labor as well as to those who would undermine it.

By contrast with obscenity's violence against social convention, pornography, as usually defined, is a matter of sexual arousal. It is, as Lynn Hunt puts it in her summary history (Hunt, 10–45) "the explicit depiction of sexual organs and sexual practices with the aim of arousing sexual feelings" (10). In this sense the term has a surprisingly short and recent history. It appeared as a separate entry in the *Oxford English Dictionary* for the first time in 1857, as a term for literature about prostitutes, only later taking on its modern meaning as literature or imagery the primary function of which is sexual arousal.

This is not to deny that prior to the nineteenth century sexually explicit literature and imagery existed which, when viewed from the perspective of the present, would be considered to be pornographic. On the contrary, there exists a long and robust tradition of such literature and images (Chaucer, Rabelais, and so on) which features ecclesiastical figures, nuns, monks, priests, etc, as well as secular authorities, in sexually transgressive situations. Prior to the nineteenth century, however, pornography as such did not exist because, as Walter Kendrick argues, sexually explicit literature and imagery was employed as a means of highlighting the hypocrisy of clerical and political authorities rather than for purposes of sexual arousal.

Kendrick further argues that pornography's subsequent emergence in the nineteenth century as a category of literature concerned primarily with sexual excitement rather than sedition is linked in a complex way to this pre-history (Kendrick, 31). In brief, he argues that the category of pornography as a site of sexual contamination was invented by reactionaries who, masked as defenders of public morality, sought to regulate, and more specifically to suppress, seditious attacks upon clerical and other authorities. Thus the function of the category of pornography as it emerged in the nineteenth century was ideological in a traditional sense. It enabled a body of seditious literature to be classified as sexually arousing, and as such a moral danger ripe for suppression. In this way, political censorship could be concealed as a non-partisan defense of public morality—"in the public interest" rather than a political action of suppression.[2]

The invention of the category of pornography proved a runaway success. The imaginary space that it opened up for a new form of writing/imagery, isolated from its roots in sedition, took on a constitutive dimension. A commercial pornographic literature concerned primarily with sexual arousal rushed in to occupy the place invented for it. Pornography emerged, then, as an unintended consequence of the actions of its would-be regulators who, while seeking to stamp it out, had a covert interest in its propagation as a moral danger. As Hunt indicates (following the work of Kendrick and Darnton): "Pornography developed out of the messy, two-way, push and pull between the intention of authors, artists and engravers to test the boundaries of the 'decent' and the aim of the ecclesiastical and secular police to regulate it" (Hunt, 10). Thus the early attempts at suppressing pornography had the hallmarks of what Foucault characterizes as Victorian sexual repression: an attempt to eliminate "sterile" sexual practices— in this case the reading of pornography—that had the unintended effect of producing that which it repressed.

* * *

According to the definitions that I have endorsed, the pornographic is differentiated in its effects from the obscene: specifically, whereas the pornographic concerns itself with sexual arousal, the obscene is characterized by its transgressive nature. It is clear that these two categories coincide in particular cases, but, it seems, there exists also a space for "decent", that is, non-obscene, explicit images that nevertheless give viewers a vicarious sexual thrill. As I indicate in the next section, the existence of this space within the pornographic but outside the obscene may be seen as a constitutive condition for the existence of a category of artistically respectable works of "erotica".

Not all theoretical approaches to the pornographic and the obscene allow for the existence of a category of erotica, however. For example, from a Freudian perspective we may see the sexual as always and already set within a phantasy structure that covers over a situation—the "family romance"—, which, because it is constituted as socially transgressive, is essentially obscene.[3] Thus there exists no space for a category of non-transgressive pornography (erotica).

Other approaches also intermix the pornographic and obscene, but, as I argue in the next section, they do so while leaving a space for the category of erotica. For example, as Linda Williams indicates, in recent U.S. legal practice the pornographic and the obscene have become reciprocally constitutive. The Supreme Court decision *U.S. versus Roth* (1957) takes the obscene as that constitutive element of the pornographic which, in Justice Brennan's famous phrase, is "utterly without redeeming value" (Williams, 88). More specifically, Brennan metaphorizes the obscene as the "hard core", the "indigestible pit", at the heart of the pornographic (Kendrick, 201). Through extending Brennan's metaphor, official censorship practices are transfigured into the act of pitting, and thus making palatable, the soft, fruity body of the sexually explicit text. Such metaphors have become crucial not only for legitimating censorship practices but also for investing them with an excitement, a covert sexual charge, all of their own. It is perhaps not too far fetched to see signs of such arousal in Senator Jesse Helms' ejaculation on the floor of the U.S. Senate, while waving copies of NEA funded photographs by Robert Mapplethorpe: "Look at the pictures! Look at the pictures! Don't believe the *Washington Post*! Don't believe *The New York Times*!...I'm going to ask that all the pages, all the ladies, and maybe all the staff leave the Chamber so that senators can see exactly what they're voting on" (Williams, 285).

The Supreme Court decision *Miller v California* 1973 also ran together the pornographic (sexually arousing) and the obscene (transgressive). It defined the latter in terms of the convergence of three elements: (1) appeal to prurient interest (sex for sex's sake), (2) patently offensive depictions of sexual situations, and (3) lack of "serious literary, artistic, political or scientific value", as judged by an "average person" applying "accepted community standards" (Williams, 280).

By contrast with such tendencies to imbricate the obscene with the pornographic, I have followed the convention of distinguishing between these categories in terms of their effects. In the current context, this has two advantages. First, it enables me to nominally mark an analytic distinction between sexually arousing („pornographic") and transgressive („obscene") elements within particular sexually explicit representations. Second, it has the political advantage of introducing a critical distance from repressive elements in the concept of censorship implicit in both the *Miller v California* and *U.S. v Roth* rulings, a point to which I return.

Linda Williams adopts yet another approach to delineating the pornographic.[4] Rather than resting upon legal practice or defining the pornographic in terms of its effects, she makes a historical survey of the genres of film that, since the twenties in the U.S., have fallen under the opprobrium of being classified as pornographic. The difference between Williams' approach and mine highlights an interesting question: do the changes in genre that William's notes signal a change at the level of the pornographic in my sense of the term? Specifically, do the changes from the stag film of the twenties, that were screened to small, all male audiences during "smokers", to the "classic" Hollywood-style feature-length soft-porn movie, shown in art-film houses during the sixties and seventies, to the niche-porn, characteristic of the VCR home video industry and new "cybersex" video games, signal changes at the level of sexual desire (Williams, 293–315)? Or is it rather the case that during this period, a relatively constant sexual desire shaded in and out the arena of pornographic, in Williams' sense of the term?

Erotica and the New Sexual Repression

The emergence of "erotica" as a category, opposed to both the obscene and the pornographic, complicated the earlier nineteenth century conception of pornography. The term was first noted by the *Oxford English*

Dictionary in 1854 in the book title: *Erotica. The Elegies of Propertius.* By 1913, the dictionary indicates, it was in common usage among booksellers as a description of "the romance…in its unexpurgated form". By the 1950s, it had taken on its modern sense as "sexual writing [or imagery] with literary pretensions" (*Oxford English Dictionary*) although with an ambiguity about whether "sexual" meant sexual content in general or was restricted to sexual content that was arousing. In either case, however, by contrast with the bulk of pornography or with sexually explicit representations more generally, an aura of artistic respectability surrounded erotica, thus removing them from the category of the obscene/indecent. For example, the *Oxford English Dictionary* indicates that in 1956 Kenneth Clark included a set of "presentable erotica" in the royal art collection. In short, erotica in the contemporary sense managed the trick of being sexually explicit in content, even sexually arousing, it seems, and in that sense pornographic, while, because of their artistic value, remaining "presentable", that is, "decent", and avoiding the stigma of obscenity.[5]

Ironically, one of the conditions enabling the spread of the category of erotica, or the erotic as it is sometimes called, was Justice Brennan's conservative remark in the *U.S. v Roth* decision, that "hard core" porn, which showed sex merely for sex's sake, was "utterly without socially redeemable importance". Brennan's surprisingly fertile metaphor of "hard core" conjured up the possibility of removing the valueless filth at the heart of pornography, thus leaving behind a softer, more palatable residue of sexually explicit literature and imagery. This new category of "respectable" pornography includes, indeed, may be seen as coinciding with, the category of erotica. In short, despite its conservative intent, Brennan's ruling unintentionally made an imaginary space for erotica. As Williams notes:

> The ironic effect of Brennan's [ruling]…was that all sorts of surprising works were discovered to be not without some 'nugget' of social, historical, or even aesthetic worth…The Roth decision marked 'the opening of the floodgates' [Kendrick's phrase—Kendrick, 202–204] to U.S. publication of all the long-suppressed classics—*My Secret Life* (1888) and D.H. Lawrence's *Lady Chatterly's Lover* (1929) in 1959, John Cleland's *Fanny Hill* in 1966. (Williams, 89)

In particular, the sexual liberation movement of the sixties took up Brennan's phrase "socially redeeming importance" as a clarion call for a new tolerance (some might say promiscuity) in the arena of sexually explicit images and writing, thus turning his words in a totally unexpected direction. (In less kindly vein, one might say that the sexual liberation movement exploited a loophole in the *U.S. v Roth* decision.) This clarion call demanded the recognition, even cultivation, of a category of sexually explicit literature and images—what I have called "erotica"—that, in virtue of their "socially redeeming importance", could be separated from hard core porn. As Lynda Neal makes the point, in the sixties, the promotion, one might say invention, of the category of erotica functioned as a means of legitimizing sexual representations through forestalling a "collapse into the pornographic". (Neal, 147)[6]

Various contemporary critics, such as Barthes and Zizek, have lent their authority to claims that there exists a distinction between erotica and pornography. In keeping with the liberal reading of Brennan's opinion, they reclassify works of pornography that have "artistic value" as an important new category of sexually explicit representations. Barthes, for example, contends that the key distinction between erotica and "mere" pornography resides in the fact that the former incorporate what he calls a *punctum*—a concrete and accidental detail, which, by subtly disturbing the culturally encoded expectations and conventions that comprise what he calls "the *studium*", lends artistic value to an image.[7] (Barthes' conception of the *punctum* presupposes a modernist, and specifically avant-garde, notion of art that needs revision in the light of postmodern artistic productions, but I cannot discuss that complication here.)

Barthes illustrates the *punctum* by odd juxtapositions that transcend the artifice of the conventional photographic pose—contingencies and coincidences that are formally meaningless but which, in virtue of their surprising nature, gesture towards some hidden meaning: "a backlighted nude in a doorway, the front of an old car in the grass…two benches in a field, a woman's buttocks at a farmhouse window, an egg on a naked belly" (34). Thus the *punctum* is like the coincidence between my birth date and a row of numbers that surprises me on a cinema ticket—an event or situation that, although perfectly consistent with the laws of the Universe, seems to point to a meaning beyond meaning. *Film Noir*, with its strangely meaningless signifiers—shadows through a venetian blind cast across the hero's face, mysterious strings of names and numbers—gesturing towards a sinister, hidden order of reality, illustrates this ill-logic of the *punctum*.[8]

According to Barthes, by contrast with erotica, pornographic images violate the *studium* in an unsubtle, that is, mechanical and unequivocal way, directly exposing sexual materials which, according to codes of decency, should remain discreetly out of sight. Thus, Barthes' "pornographic" is what I have called the obscene, that which directly, crudely violates/transgresses the law. As such, the obscene (Barthes' pornographic) is highly coded—determined as a simple permutation, indeed reversal, of the proper order of things. That is why, although it may shock me to see the obscene, its content never comes as a surprise in the sense of telling me something I do not know already. In short, the obscene falls under the *studium* even while contradicting its codes—the exception that proves the rule/that the rule anticipates.

The erotic *punctum*, by contrast, is "uncoded", slipping between the categories of the law rather than simply opposing them, "composed according to no creative logic" (51, 42).[9] For example, unlike obscene representations of genitals, the punctal close-ups of fabric in Mapplethorpe's erotic photographs of revealingly draped male bodies do not simply reverse usual conventions of representation. Instead, it is as if the detail of the fabric has wondered in from some other photo—something which, like the coincidence between the row of numbers on my cinema ticket and my date of birth, makes perfect sense in its own right, yet its existence surprises me:

> Another unary photograph is the pornographic photograph (I am not saying the erotic photograph: the erotic is a porno[-]graphic that has been disturbed, fissured)...Like a shop window which shows only one illuminated piece of jewelry, [the pornographic photograph] is completely constituted by the presentation of only one thing: sex: no secondary, untimely object ever manages to half conceal, delay, or distract...A proof *a contrario*: Mapplethorpe shifts his close-ups of genitalia from the pornographic to the erotic by photographing the fabric of underwear at very close range: the photograph is no longer unary, since I am interested in the texture of the material.(Barthes 41–42)[10]

The air of surprise that attends the erotic *punctum* goes beyond that of mere coincidence. As Barthes indicates, at first sight the *punctum* may appear quite ordinary, even banal. Yet on second glance or in memory it comes to disturb viewers' equilibrium, haunting their consciousness, retrospectively deepening and extending their reaction—as Barthes says, "pricking" or "wounding" them in their sovereign consciousness, rendering what they see "exceptional" beyond the appearance of mere coincidence (26–27, 53).

In Freudian terms, one may describe such a reaction as a response to an uncanniness (*Unheimlichkeit*) that results from unconscious connections of a metonymic or synecdochal kind between the *punctum* and some violent, indeed traumatic, sexualized "other scene" that has been repressed.[11] Or as Barthes makes the point, the erotic *punctum* is not itself sexual in content but instead subtly evokes the sexual through juxtaposition or causal connections with some "beyond of desire", some unattainable and imaginary "blissful eroticism" that, from a Freudian perspective, is the other side of the repressed sexual trauma: "The erotic photograph...(and this is its very condition), does not make the sexual organs into a central object; it may very well not show them at all...The *punctum*, then, is a kind of subtle *beyond*—as if the image launched desire beyond what it permits us to see...towards "the rest" of the nakedness" (59).[12]

The role of the *punctum* as a hook for unconscious meanings is clear from Barthes comments on a 1926 photograph by James Van der Zee of a family group of African–Americans dressed in their Sunday best (Barthes, 44). Initially, Barthes indicates, he was mistaken about what "moved" him in this picture, namely the strapped pumps of the black woman. But, then, in retrospect, as the memory of the image "worked" upon him, he hit upon the significant element:

> Later on I realized that the real *punctum* was the necklace she was wearing; for no doubt it was this same necklace (a slender ribbon of braided gold) which I had seen worn by someone in my own family, and which, once she died, remained shut up in a family box of old jewelry (the sister of my father never married, lived with her mother as an old maid, and I had always been saddened whenever I thought of her dreary life.) I had just realized that however immediate and incisive it was, the *punctum* could accommodate a certain latency (but never any scrutiny).
>
> Ultimately—or at the limit—in order to see a photograph well, it is best to close your eyes. "The necessary condition for an image is sight," Janouch told Kafka; and Kafka smiled and replied: "We photograph things in order to drive them out of our minds. My stories are a way of shutting my eyes." (53)

Here it is apparent that for Barthes the necklace is striking, "pricks" him, because it combines at an unconscious or barely conscious level themes and sources of anxiety from his own histories: Barthes, like "the old maid", hopeless in love, desperately alone in his old age, deserted in death by his beloved mother; Freud's well-known history of the jewel box, with all its sexual connotations; the history of Barthes' mother who, alone from an early stage in her marriage, had been uncomplaining, devoted to her son, etc. (Barthes' last book, *Incidents*, rehearses many of these themes.) In short, the photographic *punctum* is like a rigorously censored version of a dream image: a site at which several trains of unconscious associations converge but, because it is produced in strict accord with the reality principle, it is purged of fantastic, "unrealistic" elements permitted in dreams.

In Freudian terms, then, the structure of the erotic *punctum* is fetishistic. It is an obscenity at one remove, so to speak, connected to a forbidden "other" sexual scene through a logic of substitution based upon juxtaposition, causal connection, or other such relations. As Barthes puts it succinctly: "it allows me to accede to an infra-knowledge: it supplies me with a collection of partial objects [Barthes' name for the detail] and can flatter a certain fetishism of mine" (30).[13]

Zizek echoes central aspects of Barthes' account of the relation of pornography to erotica. He argues along surprisingly conventional lines that, by revealing all, the pornographic image "does *not* gaze back at us…it is 'flat', without any mysterious 'spot' needing to be looked at awry". "In porn", he goes on to say, "the spectator…gaze[s] stupidly at the image that reveals all…the spectators are reduced to a "paralyzed object-gaze". Rather than surprising us, the "effect is extremely vulgar and depressing…charm is dispelled…Instead of the sublime Thing, we are stuck with vulgar, groaning fornication" (Zizek, 180, n6).[14] It seems clear that, as for Barthes, what Zizek calls the pornographic is in our terms the obscene in the sense of that which violates standards of "good taste".

Zizek then contrasts the pornographic/obscene not with erotica (as Barthes does) but rather with other "non-vulgar" representations of the sexual, such as the "normal, nonpornographic" love story that discreetly hides the "act" itself, leaving to the reader/viewers' imagination the task of "filling in" the missing details:

> In "normal", nonpornographic film, a love scene is always built around a certain insurmountable limit: "all cannot be shown." At a certain point the image is blurred, the camera moves off, we never directly see "that" (the penetration of sexual organs, etc). In contrast…pornography goes beyond, "shows everything". The paradox is, however, that by trespassing the limit, it always *goes too far*…if we show "the thing itself," we necessarily lose what we were after. The effect is extremely vulgar and depressing (as can be confirmed by anyone who has watched any hard-core movies). (110)[15]

Thus, by contrast with pornographic/obscene images, what Zizek calls "'normal', non-pornographic love scenes" finesse and literally blur the "crotch shot". By alluding to rather than crudely exposing the genitals, in other words by discreetly drawing a veil over that which they nonetheless depict, such love scenes, according to Zizek, avoid vulgarity. These scenes act as sites for what Lacan calls "the gaze"—a point of indeterminacy in the visual field where, through making apparent to viewers that something exists, which they cannot see, an image acknowledges their existence. Through such acknowledgements, the image seems to "look back" at those who look at it, a scopic structure that Lacan associates with *trompe l'oeil* (Lacan, 112).

In sum, Barthes and Zizek adduce quite different exemplars of images which, despite their sexual content, manage to avoid falling into the cesspit of the "pornographic". Barthes takes high art erotica, such as

Mapplethorpe's images, as exemplary of the non-pornographic, whereas Zizek concentrates upon the discreetly veiled bourgeois love story. In other words, Barthes' strategy for avoiding the pornographic is to break up the *studium* of naked flesh, whereas Zizek introduces the fig leaf, with its structure of the lost object.[16] In Lacanian terms, Barthes focuses upon sexual representations that are characterized by the signifier of lack in the other (see endnote 11) whereas Zizek focuses upon images that are characterized by the gaze.

Despite their considerable theoretical differences, Barthes and Zizek are united in their opposition to and classification of what they label pornography. In particular, for both of them the target of criticism is not pornography in the sense of the sexually arousing but rather a somewhat different category, namely the obscene, specifically the vulgar and tedious images of sex in the centerfolds of magazines and hard-core pornographic movies. Thus, one might argue, their critical scorn, like that of Flaubert, is directed not against explicit, sexually arousing content—the pornographic *strictu sensu*—but rather against the vulgarity and tedium that is characteristic of the *petit bourgeois* sensibility in its transgressive mode. Nevertheless their views function rhetorically (albeit perhaps unintentionally) as an attack upon pornography writ large. This is because in making space for the category of erotica, Barthes and Zizek rework the term "pornographic" so that, by contrast to erotica, its banal and inferior instances come to stand for the category as a whole.

In reply to Zizek one might remark that vulgarity, and in particular *bourgeois* sensibility, lies as much on the side of the Hollywood "love story" and the fig leaf discreetly veiling the penis of the statue of David as it does on the side of pornography. And a similar claim may be made for the camp aesthetic recommended by Barthes. My concern is not with such aesthetic issues, however, but rather with the point that, because viewing pornography is itself a sexual activity, despite their best intentions, Barthes' and Zizek's polemics on behalf of erotica and against the pornographic, fits squarely within the Victorian regime of sexual repression that marginalizes non-procreative sexual activity.

This point returns us to the claim from which I started, namely that the short history of pornography illustrates the Victorian structure of sexual repression that Foucault describes, in which repression is accompanied by a perverse return of the repressed. In particular, by removing anything of artistic value from the category of pornography, strategies like Zizek's and Barthes', that seek to drive a wedge between art and pornography, enable viewers to disavow the sexual nature of consuming "art" (albeit with a certain ambiguity surrounding the category of erotica). Through such disavowal, Kipnis indicates, the viewing experience may take on a perverse dimension in the Freudian sense of the term: "Perhaps we're devoted to keeping art and pornography so discursively sequestered exactly because aesthetics and perversion are so contiguous (and perhaps contagious)—which is why it might seem like an important thing to firmly differentiate a Cindy Sherman photograph…from a transvestite self-portrait" (Kipnis, 83).

Barthes' and Zizek's proposals for separating erotica from pornography may be seen along exactly these lines, as making a space where viewers perversely experience the erotic pleasures of the "aesthetic", while concealing the sexual nature of their activities behind a mask of a-sexual, bourgeois refinement. Thus Barthes and Zizek partake in a Victorian form of sexual repression: maginalizing the pornographic, while creating a protected space in which viewers "get off" on looking at sexually explicit images.

In agreeing with Kipnis on this point, I am not underwriting her more general deconstructive argument, which, by adducing the sexualized nature of art appreciation, troubles the boundary between art and pornography. On the contrary, I have distinguished between, on the one hand, the obscene, which, one might argue, is what Barthes and Zizek mean by the pornographic, and, on the other, erotica as representative of the category of the artistic in the domain of images with sexual content. In particular, following Barthes, I have taken erotica as involving a *punctum,* which, while avoiding any indecently explicit sexual content, enjoys unconscious associations with a repressed and highly sexually charged primal scene. In short, artistic erotica are differentiated by a perversely disavowed and hidden sexual content in contrast with the transgressively open sexual content of the pornographic/obscene.[17]

Conclusion

By making space for, indeed celebrating, sexually explicit works of artistic value, such as Mapplethorpe's homoerotic images, Barthes seems to be on the side of sexual liberation.[18] But, I have argued, Barthes' liberatory gesture is ambivalent. By devaluing pornography, he, like Zizek, effectively suppresses, or at least marginalizes, the non-fertile sexual practice of reading pornography. Despite his liberal attitude to erotica, Barthes, like the nineteenth-century moral crusaders against pornography, reproduces the Victorian structure of sexual repression.

Barthes complicates the position of the moral crusaders, however. They engage in a self-defeating exercise of unintentionally creating a space in which the same pornographic representations that they warn against take root. Barthes also engages in a self-defeating exercise, as does Zizek, but their's is more subtle. By separating "artistic", that is, non-vulgar, representations (high art erotica for Barthes, the Hollywood love story for Zizek) from the vulgarities of pornography, they marginalize a non-fertile sexual practice, namely the viewing of porn, and thus contribute to the Victorian structure of sexual repression. In other words, Barthes and Zizek no less than the early moral crusaders engage in repression. But whereas the latter do so openly, in the name of censorship, the former do so unintentionally, under the banner of liberation. Thus, in Foucault's terms, Barthes and Zizek are reminiscent of nineteen sixties prophets of sexual liberation (like Marcuse) whom Foucault, in his *History of Sexuality*, scathingly criticizes for unintentionally advancing the cause of sexual repression under the banner of liberation.

In a moment I qualify this rather grim diagnosis of Barthes' and Zizek's contributions. Nevertheless, the historical irony remains that, for Barthes and Zizek no less that the 19th century moral crusaders, the structure of repression in which they partake is self-defeating. The early moral crusaders established the historical conditions of possibility for the diffusion of the very thing that they opposed. Barthes and Zizek, despite, or more correctly because of, their opposition to porn, contribute to, indeed license, the inherently perverse practice of appreciating sexually arousing art work while disavowing its pornographic nature.

Coda

Barthes and Zizek claim that pornography belongs to the vulgar and banal, and thus to the *studium* rather than to the *punctum*. Kipnis, by contrast, claims that, because it is an "anti-aesthetic", all pornography retains the potential to "prick" and "disturb" the sensibilities of the viewer, and thus, in Barthes' sense, to give rise to a *punctum*: "Pornography devotes itself to thwarting aesthetic conventions wherever and whenever it can, to disrupting our precious sensibilities at every turn. It's the anti-aesthetic. This is a social undertaking not without philosophical and political significance" (92).[19]

My position falls between the two extremes represented by Barthes and Kipnis. Rather than the relation between pornographic images and the *punctum* being an all or nothing affair, I allow that some such images are punctuated while others are not. For example, for the *aficionado*, "formula porn" falls on the side of the *studium* without a *punctum*. Even for conservative viewers, because of their heavily coded, predictable nature, formulaic pornographic images, although shocking, will fall on the side of the "sensational" rather than the *punctum*. But, unless one begs the question by defining the pornographic as lacking artistic merit (as Barthes and Zizek do[20]) it does *not* follow that pornography (understood in the generalized sense of sexually arousing representations) must be devoid of a *punctum*. On the contrary, several of the images which I have mentioned—for example, the Mapplethorpe photo of genitals—are not only punctuated, and in that respect perversely sexualized, but also have an explicit content that may be sexually arousing and in that sense pornographic.

Such claims carry with them grave political risk. In our society, pornography is strongly associated with the degradation and exploitation of women. Thus conceptualizing it so that pornographic images may be "striking" even artistic, rather than merely vulgar, banal, and titillating is to risk political incorrectness. It also risks the wrath of those for whom criticizing pornography has taken on the erotic lineaments of repression.

But, as Kipnis, Watney and others argue, by marginalizing an infertile sexual practice, the condemnation of porn no less than its free circulation, reproduces the patriarchal ideology of sexual repression.[21] Thus, depending upon circumstances, to avoid such condemnation takes on the dimensions of a radical political obligation, rather than, as it is sometimes portrayed, a fall into political incorrectness.

My work here is open to an objection *tu quoque*. At a basic level it seems to be no less complicit with the structures of Victorian sexual repression than Barthes' or Zizek's. Or, to put the point more bluntly, aren't my deliberations simply another case of a man perversely looking at dirty pictures of women under the banner of sexual liberation, getting cheap kicks from what he sees, together with the vicarious sexual thrill of criticizing his male betters, Barthes and Zizek?

At one level, this objection is well taken. As Foucault himself emphasizes, structures of repression are difficult, perhaps even impossible, to avoid, since acts of resistance always tend to perversely reproduce what they resist. But this does not mean that all resistance is equally pointless, since some perverse displacements may constitute an ethical improvement upon what they displace. For example, despite its ultimate complicity with the structures of Victorian sexual repression, Barthes' and Zizek's writings constitute an improvement over the pronouncements of nineteenth-century moral crusaders against porn. In particular, their promotion of the category of erotica constitutes a positive, liberal intervention against the invidious forms of censorship practiced by the early moral crusaders. In the same way, it is to be hoped, despite a degree of perverse complicity with traditional forms of sexual repression, my work here constitutes a positive political intervention against an implicit patriarchal hypocrisy that structures the works of both Barthes and Zizek.

References

Barthes, Roland (1981). *Camera Lucida*. Trans. Richard Howard. New York: Hill and Wang.

Foucault, Michel (1978). *History of Sexuality*. Trans. Robert Hurley. New York: Pantheon.

Frapper-Mazur (1993). In *The Invention of Pornography: Obscenity and the Origins of Modernity*. Ed. Lynn Hunt. New York: Zone Books.

Hunt, Lynn (1993). In *The Invention of Pornography: Obscenity and the Origins of Modernity*. Ed. Lynn Hunt. New York: Zone Books.

Kendrick, Walter (1987). *The Secret Museum: Pornography in Modern Culture*. New York: Viking.

Kipnis, Laura (1996). *Bound and Gagged: Pornography and the Politics of Fantasy in America*. New York: Grove Press.

Krips, Henry (1999). *Fetish: An Erotics of Culture*. Ithaca: Cornell University Press.

Lacan, Jacques (1981). *Four Fundamentals of Psychoanalysis: Seminar XI*. Alan Sheridan. Trans. New York: Norton.

Neal, Lynda (1992). *The Female Nude: Art, Obscenity and Sexuality*. London: Routledge.

Watney, Simon (1987). *Policing Desire: Pornography, Aids, and the Media*. Minneapolis: University of Minnesota Press.

Williams, Linda (1999). *Hard Core: Power, Pleasure, and the "Frenzy of the Visible"*. Berkeley: University of California Press.

Wright, Elizabeth (1992). *Feminism and Psychoanalysis: A Critical Dictionary*. Oxford: Blackwell.

Zizek, Slavoj (1991). *Looking Awry: an Introduction to Jacaques Lacan through Popular Culture*. Cambridge: MIT Press.

Notes

1 The transgressive nature of obscenity is a matter of an improper excess rather than a falling short, of a braggardliness rather than undue reserve. No one would be accused of obscenity on the grounds of being unduly reticent in the display of their sexual organs—a refusal to undress during a medical examination, for instance, or while taking a bath at home.

2 It follows, then, that the nineteenth century scandal over pornography can be understood as a special case of what Simon Watney (following Stuart Hall and Stanley Cohen) calls a "moral panic", in which "interest groups attempt to bypass the traditional

structures of democratic process in order to enforce the enactment of laws in the name of the 'good' of a population which is never consulted" (Watney, 42).

At first sight, the attack against pornography seems to be quite different from the usual form of moral panic, which, Watney asserts, is a defensive ideological rear-guard action which has been mounted on behalf of 'the family' for more than a century". That is, in most moral panics, the interests of the family are covertly protected in the name of public order and morality, so that what amounts to a danger merely to the historically and culturally specific institutional arrangements of the bourgeois family unit is *ipso facto* a danger to the moral fabric of society writ large. By contrast, although the attack on pornography conjures up a risk to public order and morality, the "real" ideological stakes involved are the defense of the Church or the political establishment rather than the family. But this contrast commits a mistake that, Watney claims, is characteristic of traditional moral panic theory more generally, namely to "contrast 'representation' to the arbitration of 'the real'" (41). Instead, Watney suggests, the history of moral panics reveals "the mobility of ideological confrontations across the entire field of public representations" (42).

Note too that Watney links moral panics to the development of the mass media, which, he claims, were invented specifically for the task of spreading such panics (Watney, 42). In the context of this remark, it is apposite to note the development of the mass circulation newspaper in the nineteenth century.

A similar moral panic is evident in the testimony heard by the Meese commission (the US congressional committee on pornography). As Carol Vance recounts it: "Judith Trevallian from Citizens Against Pornography, Michigan, brought a portable tape recorder to reproduce for the audience 'the chilling horror I felt in my kitchen after my first encounter with Dial-a-Porn'"; and a Miami resident testified that "By the age of sixteen after a steady diet of *Playboy*, *Penthouse*, *Scandinavian Children*, etc, I had to see a doctor for neuralgia of the prostate...If it weren't for my faith in God and the forgiveness of Jesus Christ, I would now be a pervert, an alcoholic, or dead" (cited in Watney, 69). In short, "The pornographer is seen as a vampire: he wishes to 'infect' society...Jerry Falwell inveighs against smut as it is's a sub-genre of 'sick' homosexuality; for Robin Morgan 'pornography' is the theory and rape the practice" (Watney, 63).

3 Levi-Strauss follows Freud in taking the prohibition of incest as a constitutive moment of the social.

4 I hesitate to say "defining" rather than "delineating", since, like Kendrick, albeit without fully endorsing his reasons, she distances herself from attempts to set up a precise definition of this term (Williams, 11–15).

5 In legal practice, the issue of artistic and/or educational merit seems to carry decisive weight in connection with the equally difficult question of obscenity. As Watney points out, for a work to be obscene, according to the US Supreme Court, it must "lack serious literary, artistic, political, or scientific value" (Watney, 61).

6 Contemporary censorship practices, in particular the X- and R-rating systems, also depend upon the assumption of a distinction between "good" (or at least harmless) erotica and "bad" hard core porn. In *History of Sexuality* Foucault argues that, despite their often tolerant intent, such assumptions, and he claims, the sexual liberation

movement more generally, have brought with them their own ambiguous form of repression, a point to which I return later.

7 Barthes, 26–27, 41–43. Barthes develops the concept of the *punctum* in the context of the photographic image, but it applies equally to literature and speech.

8 But in so far as such signifiers become incorporated within their own aesthetic, they lose the ephemeral, unpredictable status of the *punctum*.

9 Nevertheless, both *punctum* and obscenity share a temporal structure that is split between the pastness of the trace and the lively presentnesss of a break from the *studium*.

10 A controversial and rather romantic conception of the artistic informs Barthes' views. I make this point not in order to question his conception, but rather to raise a more basic question of whether it offers creative insight into the matters at issue here or merely begs the question.

11 The *studium*, by contrast, is *heimlich*—the imaginary, wholesome, "good body" of the Mother, unblemished/uncrossed by the Oedipus—Barthes, 40. In Lacanian terms, then, the *punctum* is a signifier of lack in the (M)Other. I owe the latter point to Jennifer Friedlander, from whose input this paper has benefited considerably.

12 The relation of the erotic *punctum* to the sexualized primal scene cannot be a matter of similarity (metaphor) since such similarity may stray all too easily into the arena of the obscene.

13 One can only wonder at the historical circumstances which led Barthes to avoid an explicit and systematic invocation of Freud as a theoretical underpinning to his phenomenology of the photograph, and in particular of the *punctum*. This avoidance that is clear in his unwillingness to refer to the unconscious—"infra-knowledge", and "subtle beyond" function as substitute terms in the previous two quotations. At work in this avoidance, one might argue, is the rejection of Freud characteristic of early French structuralist thought—the work of Claude Levi-Strauss for example, and of Barthes in *Mythologies* (on this point see the Appendix to my 1999 *Fetish*). Also contributing to these processes is the institutional and perhaps also personal importance placed by Barthes on differentiating "his" particular shift to post-structuralism from that of Lacan. The effect of such factors is apparent elsewhere in *Camera Lucida*, as Barthes distances himself from the Lacanian sense of the gaze as "the shiny point of light that makes your head swim" (Barthes, 18–19).

14 Zizek's shares with Barthes the claim that the pornographic is vulgar.

15 Because they manifest the structure of the "lost object", Zizek aligns such non-pornographic romances with the "nostalgic".

16 This suggests that Zizek's real concern is to obviate obscenity rather than pornography, and that his emphasis upon pornography is merely a result of not distinguishing it carefully enough from obscenity. One might also object to Zizek's account on the grounds that discreet veiling may excite rather than inhibit sexual effects, and thus contribute to rather than detract from an image's pornographic nature. And, one might argue, his failure to anticipate this objection is yet another instance of his confusing the obscene with the pornographic.

A similar objection can be raised against Barthes. Through begging the question of pornography's "vulgar" nature, he too seems to confuse pornography with obscenity.

(One might additionally question whether obscenity must be "vulgar" in the aesthetic sense: a "proper" work of art, one might argue, may be obscene in the interests of undermining dominant conventions.) As true as they may be, however, these criticisms simply miss the point that Barthes and Zizek are proposing reversionary concepts of the pornographic, which tie it closely to the vulgar and thus to works devoid of artistic value.

17 In endorsing such a distinction, however, I am not agreeing with Barthes' claim that it can be inflected into the aesthetic realm in terms of a difference between the properly artistic and the vulgar.

18 By contrast those who, while asserting that it lacks artistic merit, expand the category of pornography to include all works with sexually explicit content, seem to be on the side of sexual repression.

19 It seems clear that Kipnis is too quickly running together the obscene with the pornographic, although it is also clear that the disagreement between her and Barthes extends to more than this definitional issue. In particular, they divide over the issue whether the disruptive "anti-aesthetic" constituted around the obscene moments that punctuate the pornographic text comprise a *punctum* in the Barthesian sense (Kipnis) or not (Barthes).

20 Zizek and Barthes simply rule out this possibility by definitional *fiat*. That is, for them, by definition, pornography is boring, tedious, and repetitious. This *fiat* smacks of the ideological—what Marcuse describes as the ideology of sexual repression.

21 Thus the risk is not the loss of which Larry Flynt complains, namely that censoring pornography amounts to loss of the right of free expression.

23 *Unexpected Consequences: Portfolio Screening and the Ethics of Trading**

MARK JOHNSTON

> [I have] never known much good done by those who affected to trade for the public benefit. It is an affectation, indeed, not very common among merchants, and very few words need be employed in dissuading them from it.
>
> *Adam Smith*

It is no secret that throughout George Soros's extraordinary career as a trader and a philanthropist there has remained a first mistress, who never quite let him go. It is philosophy, of course, that Soros has been fascinated with, has worked on intermittently, and has tried to bring to bear on the markets and, more recently, on the world economy as a whole. For Soros, it is primarily social epistemology that is relevant to the speculative markets. As he explains, participants always have a biased perspective, which sometimes leads to self-fulfilling expectations, with a resultant boom (or bust) in the misperceived stock, commodity, or other asset. Once the trend-followers jump on the bandwagon, what was originally a misperception of reality can actually be verified, both at the level of price and at the level of fundamental value, at least to the extent that value is itself dependent on price. But the perception-based virtuous cycle can easily devolve into a vicious one, at least as overdone on the downside as it was on the upside. Soros's great ability as a trader was to recognize many such reversal or "inflection" points, and perhaps more importantly, to consistently back his judgement with enormous and often highly leveraged bets. As a philanthropist, Soros has drawn on the same combination of contrarian thinking, flexibility, and decisiveness to do many things that have a real chance of making the world better. I have had the good fortune to be able to observe at close range one of his greater philanthropic achievements—the magnificent Central European University, which rightly honors him on his seventieth birthday.

As a philosopher, who particularly admires this achievement and who is grateful for the return of real philosophy to Central Europe, I offer George Soros, on the occasion of his seventieth birthday, the following *bagatelle*—a little contrarian essay on the ethics of speculation.

One kind of bias that determines participants' perceptions of the rightness and wrongness of a proposed course of action is their sense of how good or bad they would *feel* if they pursued the course of action in question. In small-scale interpersonal settings, focussing on how one *would feel if...* is an entirely justified heuristic, since minimal empathy will ensure that one will feel badly when harming this or that particular person. But in certain institutional settings, where the real consequences of one's actions are obscured by the mass action of others, this otherwise useful heuristic can lead to mere "emotional interior decorating"; that is, to the choice of a course of action only because it makes one feel that one has done a good thing, and not because of any reflection on the real consequences of one's acts.

In what follows, I argue that this is the case with so-called ethical investing. Given the structure of the financial markets, divesting or portfolio screening is, from the consequentialist point of view, typically either ineffectual or self-defeating. The oft-broached analogy with sanctions against South Africa is thus completely misleading. In general, divestment or ethical screening does not move markets, and even if it did the effect would only be to provide indifferent or unethical money with stocks at discounted prices. (Compare a fad that directs money away from stocks whose names begin with "A" through "L". They become relatively cheap while the other stocks become relatively expensive.) By this and other considerations, the consequentialist arguments for portfolio screening and divestment are easily seen as very weak. Because they are *easily* seen to be so, there can be no significant symbolic utility in screening divesting. Rare and recherché cases aside, you cannot, by certain acts, signal to the world the importance of a certain standard if it is an easy inference that the consequences, if any, of your acts actually favor those who care nothing for that standard. Perhaps more unexpectedly I shall also argue that, consequences aside, it may actually be an unethical form of ducking responsibility to divest the stocks of morally dubious companies.

The basic issues involve the ethical constraints on speculation: Is it permissible to trade in order to profit from significantly good or significantly bad outcomes? I first defend a principle—*the reciprocity principle*—which implies that the answer has to be simply *yes* or simply *no*, not *yes* to trading in order to profit from the good outcomes and *no* to trading to profit from the bad outcomes. This leaves open two conflicting applications of the reciprocity principle. On the inclusive application it is permissible to trade stocks to profit from significantly good *or* bad outcomes. On the exclusive application it is not permissible *either way*. The inclusive application can be shown to follow from a technical observation about stocks and options: buying a stock can be modeled as an option-like bet with the creditors of the firm to the effect that, in the event of bankruptcy, the market value of the firm's assets will exceed the liabilities to creditors. This model, and the more familiar model of a "synthetic" stock stitched together out of a long at-the-money call purchased with the premium from selling the corresponding put, help to show two important things neglected by almost all writers on portfolio screening. First, stockholding is more like side-betting than like holding certificates of partial ownership. Second, to the extent that stockholding is side-betting, holding the stocks of even morally dubious companies is permissible. The results apply *a fortiori* to the futures, forex and options markets: even if it were a bad thing for the British pound to drop precipitously overnight, it is not bad to trade to profit from this outcome, unless of course you are thereby aiming to cause it to occur.

My final point will be this: even at the level of moral character it may be possible to trade for profit contingent upon bad outcomes without thereby being or becoming base or callous. This is—if you like—a sort of transcendental argument for the possibility of George Soros, as we now find him.

Let us then begin with some influential, popular literature on ethical investing.

Ethical Investing, or Rules for the Misdirection of Funds

Over the past decade or so, partly encouraged by the perceived success of the sanctions directed at the South African regime, there has been a flood of books and articles on so-called ethical or "socially responsible" investing (SRI). And deeds are accompanying the words. Now, even the large brokerage houses are likely to include, among the smorgasbord of investment vehicles offered to clients, ethically "screened" mutual funds,

funds which screen out or exclude the stocks of companies, however profitable, which pollute, have contracts with the Department of Defense, have bad product quality or unhealthy consumer relations, are lackluster in their hiring and promotion of women and minorities, or profit from alcohol, tobacco, or gambling. These "socially responsible" funds absorb the money of investors who desire to guide the invisible hand to ethical ends that it might not reach were it simply left to its own mysterious groping.

Jack Brill and Alan Reder, authors of *Investing From the Heart* (New York: Wiley, 1993) write:

> Suppose each of your investment dollars—including every dollar in your bank account—could help build the world you want for yourself and your family and earn you a healthy return besides? Well that is exactly what your money can do. With every passing day, more individuals and institutions are joining the parade of socially responsible investors, which means that their influence is making ever greater impact on the marketplace. As of last year, more than $625 billion were invested according to some social criteria, and that number...is expanding rapidly.
>
> As for returns, the range and quality of investments now screened for social issues is such that you do not have to sacrifice just because you care enough to invest according to your ethical principles. You can do just as well as or better than investors who pay no attention to ethical criteria. *In fact, based on past performance, many of the products available to you as a socially responsible investor do better than the average investments in those categories*. (p. 11)

One of the "products" that Brill and Reder have in mind is the Domini Social Index, a basket of 400 stocks, not only screened according to the "social criteria" listed above but chosen to have capitalizations and betas (the beta is a measure of the volatility or variance of returns on the stock relative to a given stock index) comparable to those of the stocks that make up the S&P 500. A few years ago, when you called the money managers at the Domini Social Index Trust Fund, they told you rather proudly that their index had outperformed the S&P over the previous two years.[1] The same emphasis on the happy coincidence of doing good and doing well is found in Elizabeth Judd's *Investing With A Social Conscience* (New York: Pharos Books, 1990). Judd writes:

> Although corporations are not like cowboy movies where good always triumphs over evil, many believe that over the long run companies with sound ethical and business practices will outperform their less responsible (and less responsive) peers... Examples abound: most socially responsible investors would have shunned Union Carbide, and so would have remained economically unhurt by

> the Bhopal tragedy. Ditto for the *Exxon Valdez* catastrophe. In many ways socially responsible investing is a very conservative approach to stock picking since investors following their consciences generally steer clear of potential problems before they strike. One ethical investor says that he sleeps better knowing it won't be his companies making the morning headlines for an environmental spill or equal employment lawsuit. (p. 13)

Nor does Judd hesitate to urge her readers to jump on the ethical bandwagon earlier rather than later:

> While one socially responsible investor is not about to cripple Royal Dutch/Shell, the boycotts against it for its South African operations do have a financial impact on the company and its stock price. Beyond all of the technical and fundamental reasons for a rise in stock price, a company's shares go up because people are spending more money to buy those shares than to sell them. If applying ethical criteria to investments becomes a widely accepted practice there will be a flow of funds toward stocks considered socially responsible and away from those perceived as objectionable. This translates into the prices of ethical issues rising and of others falling. Therefore, people who have made ethical investments early are likely to make a profit from their principled behavior.

If you're so good, why ain't you rich? Too much insistence on the idea that the investor can do very well from ethical stocks threatens to take the ethical element out of ethical investing. "Ethical criteria" may or may not correlate with conservative growth criteria and may or may not represent a new investing trend off which the foresighted investor can profit. But to the extent that advocates of ethical investing exclusively emphasizes such correlations and trends they come to sound more like the familiar financial touts talking up the portfolio they have already sold to their own clients.

Does Ethical Screening Work?

Brill writes:

> People really want to make a difference in the world, and SRI gives them that chance—*with interest.* In the lingo of the behavioral psychologist, money withdrawn from companies and government agencies that behave unethically "punishes that behavior" and makes it less likely to occur in the future. Money invested in companies and government agencies that are socially beneficial "reinforces that behavior" and makes it more likely to occur in the future. (*Investing From The Heart,* p. 4)

To this, the redoubtable Judd adds:

> When funds from the over $2 trillion chunk of pension assets—obviously a formidable force in the market—were directed toward companies with South African restrictions, this put pressure on corporations to change their policies on doing business with South Africa. It also meant that funds poured into companies without South African ties helped push up their stock prices. Because the market is so complicated there are no statistics on the effect of this flow of funds, however it was an obvious boon. Although the South African divestment movement has slowed, a similar flow of funds could benefit a different group of stocks if social pressure were applied. With activism growing about environmental issues, buying companies with strong records on this issue might be a smart move...
>
> As in all investing, being first to spot a trend could mean big profits. That this might coincide with what the investor views as the ethical thing to do makes it even more attractive.

The alleged mechanism that produces socially good effects and profitable returns for the ethical investor is supposed to operate as follows. Ethical screening directs funds away from the stocks of "unethical" and indifferent companies towards the stocks of the "ethical" companies. As a result, the ethical companies are "rewarded" and the unethical companies are "punished", that is, the ethical stocks go up in value and the unethical stocks go down in value. And as the price of the ethical stocks goes up, the quicker ethical investors make money—presumably thanks to the subsequent investments of their slower ethical brethren.

Now, if the metaphors of positive and negative reinforcement are actually to mean anything here it must be that corporate officers in the companies in question (a) notice the change in stock price and (b) associate that change in price with their firms scoring well or poorly by a set of ethical criteria that they recognize to be widely employed. But further, to produce in the unethical company the change of heart desired by the ethical investor, corporate officers must (c) regard their stock's decrease in value as a bad thing rather than an attractive opportunity to buy their own stock back at a bargain price.

This picture is mostly moonshine. As things presently stand there is no evidence that ethical screens have any real effect on stock prices. The stock market is so closely combed by bargain hunters—so called "value investors"—that any discernible deviation of a stock's price from estimates by value investors of its fair value is very short lived. Moreover, there is in the market enough noise of short-term price fluctuation having little to do with any fundamental information about companies that the signal sent by any relatively small flow of funds guided by already widely known fundamental information about the company will tend to be drowned out. Short-term trading off intraday volatility breakouts, intraday changes in bond yields, gold prices, and the dollar, government reports, and intraday chartists' observations of "double bottoms", "breakaway gaps", "island reversals", etc. create an atmosphere in which the reasons for many price changes are, for all practical purposes, unknowable. (Financial news services unwittingly cover up this fact by requiring their reporters to offer diagnostic comments after the event—every market observer has a story to tell about why things had to happen as they did—every market observer, that is, except for successful floor traders and specialists, who have a visceral knowledge of price action and so need not indulge in ex post facto rationalizations.)

With respect to (b), corporate officers quickly learn that the stock market is (in William Baumol's phrase) a quite imperfect taskmaster, whose disciplining of companies by denying them capital is a very erratic process. So although they are sensitized to the price of their company's stock, only a well-announced and well-orchestrated attack on the company's stock by ethical short sellers would make it reasonable for corporate officers to associate a downturn in their stock's price with their company's less than worthy activities as judged by some ethical standard widely shared by investment funds. Well-orchestrated speculative attacks by ethical short sellers are probably unprecedented and certainly illegal. Yet without them there will typically be no analog to the salient, unmistakable connection between financial downturn and unsavory activity found in the oft-mentioned case of South Africa.

Finally, with respect to (c), even if the reports of the ethical analysts came to move markets in salient and traceable ways, the net effect would not be the economic punishment of unethical agents and the rewarding of ethical interests. Whenever the proffered negative ethical report was not simply a way of talking about negative economic fundamentals bedeviling the firm and hence affecting its future as a reliable stream of dividends, this can be said: in so far as the report redirects funds away from unethical firms it provides unethical and indifferent money with profitable stocks at bargain prices. Conversely, in so far as ethical analysts succeed in moving money towards the ethical stocks, ethical investors are forced to pay a premium for the ethical stocks. Compare the effects of a fad that persuades lots of people to buy stocks whose names begin with the letters "A" through "L". Those stocks become expensive or overvalued while the others become correspondingly cheaper.

Ethically screened investment does not in fact move markets. But if it were to come to move markets it would economically punish ethical investors and economically reward indifferent or unethical investors.

Screening stock investments for ethical influence is therefore either ineffectual or self-defeating.

Another fantasized element in the alleged mechanism by which ethical money imposes special economic benefits and costs on corporate behavior deserves some comment. Much of the discussion of the effects of buying a stock, consequently driving up the price of the stock and thereby making it easier for the company to acquire future capital, conveniently ignores the fact that any sane market transaction has two parts. First there is the part when you buy the stock and then there is the part when you sell it to realize your profit or loss. Whereas the buying contributes, however incrementally, to upside rallies in the stock price or at least inhibits, however minutely, downturns in price, these small effects are reversed when the full transaction is completed. Buyers of ethical stocks or their heirs are also at some time or another sellers of ethical stocks. Any realistic discussion of the effects of ethical investing must focus on this obvious fact.

How Useful a Model Was South Africa?

The precise effects on the white South African government of the separable campaigns of stock divestment; worldwide rejection of black and white South African athletes; embargoes on weapons, oil, coal, and nuclear fuel technology; prohibition of krugerrand sales; and boycotts on trade in agricultural products will long remain a matter of dispute.

What does seem clear is that it was institutional investors driven by a desire for secure profit who imposed one of the most dramatic of the economic sanctions: the critical shortage of international loan capital which choked South African economic growth in the mid-eighties and precipitated the liquidity crisis which led to Pretoria's unilateral moratorium on debt repayment. The major cause of this destabilizing crisis was the refusal in mid-1985 by several U.S. banks to roll over existing loans to South Africa because of the escalating level of political unrest in the country.

Foreign divestment certainly imposed a burden. In March 1985, the American Chamber of Commerce in South Africa pressed the South African government for significant reform. It was not immediately forthcoming. In the event, hundreds of U.S. and European companies actually pulled out, many selling their plant and equipment at bargain-basement prices, all of which likely benefited rich whites. Many blacks lost their jobs as a result, and tens of thousands of skilled workers left the country rather than accept an uncertain economic future and the continuing taint of an evil, discredited regime.

It was worldwide economic and cultural warfare that brought the South African economy to its knees and helped bring the ruling National Party to its senses. Like any war, this economic and cultural war imposed massive and indiscriminate burdens on the people of South Africa, black and white alike.

Thus, in point of their scale, coordination, and very destructive long term effects, the South African sanctions are not an appropriate model for either motivating or understanding divestment programs directed against less-than-worthy public companies traded on the major stock exchanges of the world. If anything, the massive South African boycott is most analogous to a long-term and widely coordinated speculative attack on the stock of a company, that is, just the sort of operation policed and prevented by the Security and Exchange Commission and its counterparts in other countries.

Divestment As Ducking Wrong

So far, encouraged by the grosser literature on ethical investing, I have written as if ethical stock investors were driven by purely consequentialist considerations. But this of course is an oversimplification. Suppose I inherit a portfolio of stocks which includes First Beelzebub, Baal Financial, and Lucifer Light and Gas. I find out that these are evil companies, that is, in the normal course of their business operations evil acts are regularly committed. Suppose that I regard it as a grave wrong to own the stocks of an evil company. Then, even if I am a large shareholder of these companies and know that my dumping my stock on the market will deflate the prices of these three stocks and so provide bargains for indifferent or unethical money, I may still want to divest. I may want to divest, independently of the consequences, just because I see it as gravely wrong to hold the stocks of an evil company. So I call my broker to have him sell.

My broker asks me to think about what I am doing. First, he reminds me of the empirical fact that when I sell the evil stocks there will be, on the other side of the trade, at least one person who will buy the evil stocks. Then he reminds me of the ethical fact that I am not the center of the ethical universe, so that the wrongness of *my* owning the evil stocks is just the wrongness of *someone's* owning the evil stocks. This means, of course, that it is just as wrong for the person on the other side of my divesting trade to own the evil stocks as it is for me to own them. And if there is more than one counterparty to my divesting trade then a number of people will come to do something that is gravely wrong as a result of my divesting. He tells me that it follows from my own views that my divesting will most probably increase the number of gravely wrong acts.

I become very annoyed and shout at him over the phone to dump the stock. In a calm, rational voice he replies that perhaps I should consider the following analogy.

> You are waiting in a line at an ATM by a bank. In front of you in the line are two postmen. As they approach the machine a crazed bank robber runs out of the bank with a gun in one hand and a bag of cash in the other. As he passes by you the mask slips from his face. Fearing that you will get a good look at him he turns to fire a shot in your direction. You instinctively begin to duck, and as you hear the bullet whistle over your shoulder you realize that you have exposed the two postmen in front of you in the line. One of them will take the bullet in your place.
>
> You feel terrible. For a long time afterwards you wonder whether your ducking was really a reflex you couldn't help, whether you really knew before you ducked that one of the postmen would take the bullet. You think that if you really could have helped ducking then two bad things happened outside that bank on that day. An innocent person took a bullet. And that person took that bullet because another person did not have the courage to take the bullet himself.

The import of the analogy is clear to me. My broker is saying that just as it is cowardly to transfer the impending harm by ducking the bullet, it is cowardly for me to transfer the wrong of holding the evil stocks by divesting them. Momentarily flummoxed, I do what one should never do. I ask my broker for advice.

He explains that "we" have a problem: unlike the ownership of many other things, stock ownership cannot be alienated without being transferred. One cannot destroy stocks, and even if one could, this would only serve to increase the value of the holdings of the unethical or indifferent investors who do not destroy their stocks. There are, he tells me, some brokers trained in casuistry who advise their clients in similar situations to find buyers already steeped in the grave wrong of owning the stocks of the evil companies in question, owners whose equity is already so great that there is no question of their committing more wrongs by coming to own more of the stock. Because he is unsure of the moral mathematics involved, he himself does not favor this approach. He wonders why, if it is bad to own 10,000 shares of Baal Financial, it isn't 10 percent worse to own 11,000 shares.

Finally, in that calm, rational voice, my broker tells me that he thinks there are two morally consistent things that I can do. *I can become an active shareholder in Beelzebub, Baal, and Lucifer*. I can attend shareholder meetings, organize other shareholders, get proxy votes, and put pressure on the managements of these companies to change their evil ways. *As well as this, I can engage in what he calls "moral hedging"*. I can use the dividends from these shares to try to mitigate the bad consequences of the evil activities of the three companies. He reiterates that I would only be ducking these two sorts of obligations by passing them onto someone else in a divesting trade.

It seems that by inheriting the evil stocks I have inherited grave responsibilities. I quietly put down the phone and start thinking about moving my account.

Is Moral Hedging Illogical?

Michael Harrington believes that moral hedging is inconsistent in practice. On the one hand, the investor has created or contributed to the social evil in question; and on the other, he is giving away money to help deal with an evil he has helped create. In *Investing With Your Conscience: How to Achieve High Returns Using Socially Responsible Investing* (New York: Wiley, 1992), Harrington writes:

> Suppose that I am an environmentalist. Should I invest in and provide capital for a company that is expanding its production of CFCs, which destroy the stratospheric ozone layer that protects the earth from harmful ultraviolet rays, and then turn around and give the money I earn from my investments to the Natural Resources Defence Council (NDRC)? This would make no sense! I'd be donating money to clean up a problem I helped create by providing the capital to produce the harmful substance.
>
> Examples like this one abound. If I were an American steel worker, I certainly wouldn't want my pension fund investing in the Japanese steel industry whose success could ultimately cost me my job and my pension. Should the pension fund of the American Medical Association invest in Philip Morris, whose cigarettes cause a major health problem? Such an action would defy logic!

Harrington seems to have no taste for diversification. It does not "defy logic" for the American worker to reason that he can hedge against the prospect of foreign competition squeezing his own firm's profit margin by making part of his future income correlate with the success of the foreign competition. And if I am an environmentalist it may be sensible for me to invest in a company that is not ideal environmentally but provides the kind of excess returns that allow for the mopping up of more of the environment than the firm despoils. Even in the chlorofluorocarbon case, where the damage is severe, it is not senseless for me to reason that a significant environmental advantage would be secured if many of the shareholders of the company were environmentalists engaged in a moral hedge. For then substantial profits from the company's operations *that would take place anyway* will at least be channeled into environmental causes. As a stock investor my choices are not to fund this enterprise or to let it wither away. My choices are rather to direct, if I am lucky, some profit away from this company to the things I care about or leave the stock to others to use to direct funds towards their concerns.

The case of the AMA and Philip Morris is a special and quite different one. Professional medical associations have a specific duty to promote public health. This not only needs to be done, it needs to be seen to be done. The AMA needs consistently to signal its commitment to public health. So it would simply be inept, dissonant signaling for the AMA to trade to profit from the good fortunes of a cigarette company (or of a fast-food chain like MacDonald's.)

Harrington's remarks both feed, and feed off, the popular and socially destructive fantasy about "investing" in the stock market; a fantasy according to which stock investing is just a safer version of what a venture capitalist does when he literally provides capital for an entrepreneur starting a new business. According to this picture, habitually presented to the innocent by brokerage firms and pension funds, buying stocks is a way of giving Corporate America and its hardworking employees (yourself among them) a helping hand, while making a nice profit besides. This would have a chance of being close to the truth if the stock market were mostly a primary market where companies floated their stocks to raise needed capital. It would not be too far from the truth if the stock market were a primary market wedded to a secondary market whose size was not much larger than it needed to be to provide liquidity in order to reassure buyers in the primary market that they would not be stuck with their stocks should the stocks turn sour. But the picture completely misrepresents the modern stock market in which secondary transactions have metastasized far beyond what is needed to provide liquidity for the buyers of initial public offerings.

When you buy a stock you are not providing or loaning money to a company, you are gambling on the future returns from a very particular kind of financial instrument. Of course, the fate of that instrument is partly tied to the fortunes of a particular company, but it is also tied to short- and long-term interest rates, exchange rates, tax rates, government policies, investor sentiment, technical market moves, and future innovations in competitive investments. Your bet on a stock is a bet encompassing all this. And surely it is not an insignificant fact that many of the professional gamblers in this game would happily trade some knowledge of the future fundamentals of companies in return for some knowledge of future rates, policies, and sentiment.

Nor is it very clearheaded to think that owners of non-controlling blocks of shares are partial owners of the company. What they own are financial instruments which carry with them a certain limited right to bring forward and vote on resolutions at stockholders' meetings, and a highly contingent right to have some proportion of their losses covered in the event of the bankruptcy and liquidation of the firm. These are the rights legitimately extended to those who reasonably want to protect their original wager, rather than the rights of partial ownership. This at least is the view of the U.S. Securities and Exchange Commission (SEC), which accordingly oversees and restricts the topics shareholders bring forward in proxy ballots to prevent the outcomes of these ballots from impinging on the "ordinary business" of firms. So the SEC found that shareholders could not use the proxy process to challenge Cracker Barrel's ban on employing homosexuals and that Wal-mart shareholders could be refused information on Wal-mart's employment and advancement of women and minorities. These are not restrictions which could be seriously entertained for the part-owners of a firm. What you own when you buy a stock is just a stock, a certain kind of financial instrument.

It is not the best use of words to say that people and institutions invest in the stock market. Such talk suggests the wrong models—limited partnerships, private corporations, venture capital, research and development, buying or refurbishing plant and equipment. Better to say that market participants wager, punt, gamble, bet, flutter, speculate—sometimes on propositions that are not very risky and sometimes over the longish run. What motivates the change in idiom is the nice technical work of Fisher Black and Myron Scholes. As well as providing a model for the fair pricing of those side bets on the performance of stocks known as stock options, Black and Scholes showed that a stock position is equivalent to a combined position in these side bets. (More on this below.) Something equivalent to a combination of bets is a bet. The change in idiom provides two chastening reminders: even good bets can backfire, and after all, isn't there something wrong with excessive betting even if it doesn't backfire?

This in turn raises the question of why governments, universities, corporations, and church groups are so comfortable about supporting the funneling of what would otherwise be the present income of employees into the hands of the professional gamblers known as pension fund managers.

One might ask "If buying a stock is betting, with *whom* am I betting when I buy a stock?" Traders often talk of the "greater fool" theory of trading. In order to realize your profit on a stock that has gone up you have to find, or have your agents find, someone you regard as more foolish than yourself, someone who is, by your lights, prepared to buy the stock at precisely the point where it promises little in the way of future returns. The buyer regards you as the greater fool for relinquishing the stock at a point where it is likely to go up further. So you might say that in buying a stock the buyer is making a bet with the seller of the stock. The buyer is betting that the stock will go up further, and if he is right the seller suffers an opportunity cost and the buyer is paid the difference between his purchase price and the price of the stock when he, in his turn, sells it. The seller is betting that the stock will not go up significantly and if he is right he gets the present use value of the money he had in the stock while he suffers little or no opportunity cost. (But see below for a discussion of a deeper model: stocks as bets with the holders of the company's debt.)

The betting model for stock investment is particularly appropriate in the age of the "commodification of securities", a phrase referring to the way in which the major participants in the market are more and more interested in stocks not as individual assets but as elements with certain risk and return characteristics, elements which, like modular building blocks, are to be put together to form a single composite asset—the portfolio. Thus investment managers now prefer to trade their portfolios as aggregate commodities through program trades that buy and sell entire portfolios all at once. Such trades do not break apart the financial characteristics of the aggregate asset—the total portfolio—on whose performance the investment fund manager is judged. The commodification of securities is partly the product of the massive diversion of capital into investment funds, and partly a product of the discoveries of Modern Portfolio Theory—a sub-field of the theory of gambling. Modern Portfolio Theory describes how to scrutinize certain measures of risk and return of individual assets so as to construct aggregate assets that provide the optimal returns for a given level of risk. Investment funds competing for massive gambling stakes must take into account the results of Modern Portfolio Theory, which can be crudely summarized in three words—"Diversify, Diversify, Diversify". The larger and better diversified these portfolios become, the more each becomes like all the others and the more they come to resemble the very indexes, such as the S&P 500, used as a benchmark for measuring fund manager performance. So how does a fund manager then get an edge in competing for a larger gambling stake?

Modern Portfolio Theory to the rescue once more: When the fund manager has a portfolio with a beta (a measure of the volatility of returns) close to unity relative to the S&P cash index, he can attempt to acquire an edge over his competitors by trading in index futures contracts on the S&P 500. When the S&P futures contract becomes cheap relative to the cash price of the index, the fund manager can buy futures contracts and sell his portfolio in a large program trade. Then when the S&P futures become overpriced relative to the cash market, the manager buys back his original portfolio in a large program trade. Thanks to such automated brokerage arrangements as the NYSE Super Dot system, these large block trades can usually be handled with relative ease and the canny fund manager may hop back and forth between a futures and cash position several times a week, or even several times a day.

So it is now very difficult to find a pension fund "investing" in Philip Morris as opposed to making and unmaking very complex bets that are only remotely connected to the fate of that or any other particular company.

Are Derivatives the Devil's Tools?

Knowing that I am concerned about investing in dubious companies, my new broker calls and explains that he has just the thing for me. There is, he tells me, an options market in which put and call contracts on stocks are traded. Buying a put is buying a contract which gives me the right to sell the underlying stock at a predetermined price (the "strike price") before a predetermined time (the "date of expiration" of the option.) So buying a put is a bet that the underlying stock will fall significantly below the strike price before expiration, while selling a put is a bet that it will not. On the other hand, buying a call with a strike price of say $50 is a bet that the stock price will climb significantly above $50 before the date of expiration.

Thanks to the existence of puts and calls I need never buy the stock of a dubious company with high returns. For I can, for a slightly higher commission, acquire in the options market a synthetic asset whose returns match those of the stock. So instead of buying 1,000 shares of Sin Enterprises, presently trading at $50 a share, I am to sell 10 "at the money" puts and use the money I receive from the sale to buy 10 "at the money" calls. Since each pair of options "controls" 100 shares, I now have a position which exactly mimics the returns on 1,000 shares of Sin. For as Sin moves up a dollar in price the calls I bought increase in value and the puts I sold decrease in value, with a net return to me of $100 per pair of options. At the time of expiration of the puts and calls my returns will be exactly what they would have been if I had bought Sin outright. If Sin is then trading at $55, the puts I sold will expire worthless while the calls I bought will be worth $500 each, for a total profit of $5000.

Of course, as my broker explains, technically I am at expiration[2] able to exercise my calls so as to acquire 1,000 shares of Sin at $50 rather than the market price of $55. But that is just what I do not want to do. And in this respect I will be like most option traders, for whom exercise is something they do to keep physically fit. As with the stock market, the original primary function of the option market—the buying and selling of opportunities that the buyers want to act on—has been swamped by pure trading. More than 90 percent of options go unexercised.

Arbitrage aside, the options market is largely an autonomous market. Though the American Stock Exchange, the Philadelphia Stock Exchange, and the Pacific Stock Exchange all operate active options exchanges along with the Chicago Board Options Exchange, all U.S. options exchanges clear through the Options Clearing Corporation, which guarantees the contracts and guards against counterparty default. So, as my broker assures me, I never have to touch stocks—for every possible view about the pattern of future return from any given stock I can design the appropriate side bet in the option market.[3]

Being the worrying type, I begin to wonder whether it could be wrong even to buy and sell side bets on the fate of an evil or dubious enterprise. Eventually, I reassure myself with the following line of thought. It can be morally permissible to bet if the bet is not immoderate and does not risk wealth needed for important personal and social goals. Moreover, it is not wrong to profit by betting on the downturn or demise of an evil enterprise. (My father made a tidy sum by betting late in 1940 against his defeatist, though loyal, British comrades that Hitler would not soon conquer Britain.) But if I bet on a dubious enterprise doing badly then the person taking my bet is betting so as to profit from the continued success of the dubious enterprise. And yet the bet is an unforced, open, and reciprocal exchange; that is, unlike, say, blackmail it seems to be just the sort of exchange in which it is permissible for one party to engage if, and only if, it is permissible for the counterparty or parties to engage.[4] This is the *reciprocity principle.* So I conclude that it is permissible to aim to profit, and indeed actually to profit, from side bets on the success of an evil enterprise. Thus it is permissible for me to enter into a synthetic long position in Sin via the option market.

I then apply another principle which seems to me compelling: if two financial instruments are equivalent in their attendant risks, returns, rights, responsibilities, and practical effects, then buying (or selling) the one has the same ethical import as buying (or selling) the other. This is the *equivalence principle*. So I reason that there can be no ethical consideration in favor of the synthetic long position in Sin, stitched together from options, over an outright long position in Sin stocks. Since the reciprocity principle entails that the synthetic long position in Sin is permissible, it follows that I can buy Sin stocks outright with a clear conscience. [5]

Running the Argument in Reverse

Some who accept the reciprocity principle will be inclined to argue in reverse. They will say that since one morally cannot bet to profit from the upturn or success of an evil or dubious enterprise, it is also morally wrong to take the other side of such bets. But then they must also conclude that one morally cannot bet in order to profit from a significantly good outcome. For if I am betting on that then my counterparty is the one who is betting to profit from bad outcomes, that is, the non-occurrence of a significant good that had some real likelihood of occurring. In the presence of the reciprocity principle the conclusion should be that it is wrong to bet on significant outcomes, good or bad.

The friend of this exclusive application of the reciprocity principle might therefore offer it as an argument for the moral necessity of a common feature of wagering. I mean the fact that the result of the wager typically is settled by an outcome—the turn of a card, the roll of dice, the winning of a race by a dog, a horse, or a fly—either in itself trivial or, as in boxing, somewhat immunized against its usual moral import by the prior agreement of the participants.

There are then two valid applications of the reciprocity principle that lead to two very different conclusions. Why favor the application that allows one to *include* betting to profit from bad outcomes under the heading of the permissible, rather than the application that *excludes* even betting to profit from good outcomes?

Why indeed? Since the successes and failures of companies are not in themselves trivial outcomes, the exclusive application directly scotches all but a small class of transactions in the options market. For aficionados, delta-neutral and certain other pure volatility trades in which all the counterparties are also engaged in volatility trades will be in principle permissible. But since no trader can ever reasonably believe that he knows enough about the intentions of all his counterparties to suppose that they are all involved in volatility trades, then the exclusive application indirectly rules out all option trades.

Some will say, rightly, that shortish term fluctuations in the prices of stocks are trivial and that those more narrowly bounded bets represented by some option spreads, which are precisely bets on short-term fluctuations, are allowed by the exclusive application when the counterparties to the trades are likewise involved in such spreading. This again is true in theory, but in practice an option spreader can be pretty confident that among his counterparties are so-called lottery-ticket buyers, using options as highly leveraged instruments to bet on serious if unlikely downturns or rallies in the fortunes of companies. These would be significantly good or bad outcomes. So the exclusive application of the reciprocity principle presents a moral bar to pretty much all option trading. That includes trading in stock synthetics—long calls wedded to short puts. But then the equivalence principle will imply that there is likewise a bar to trading in equivalent instruments, that is, any stocks, no matter what the character of the companies they represent. So the consequence of the exclusive application of the reciprocity principle is that "ethical stock investing", far from being the pleonasm that the pension fund managers would like us to think that it is, is actually an oxymoron. Tantalizing as this conclusion might seem, it is obviously a *reductio ad absurdum* of the exclusive application of the reciprocity principle.

Isn't a Stock a European Option?

The same result is suggested by a less obvious relationship between stocks and options of a different sort, a relationship worth review because it illuminates just what a stock is.

The exclusive application of the reciprocity principle tells us that since options are bets, it is wrong to trade in options on significantly good or significantly bad outcomes. But given the structure of bankruptcy law in the U.S. and elsewhere, a stock can be modeled as a call option on the assets of the company, an option which is sold by the corporation's creditors to those who then become common shareholders of the corporation, and which is exercisable in the event of the bankruptcy of the company. If this can be made out, then the moral ban on options trading on significant outcomes will automatically extend to stock trading. Let me explain.

In U.S. law—and it is not atypical in this respect—upon the bankruptcy of a corporation the corporation's assets are sold and distributed to the legal claimants on those assets according to the "seniority" of their claims. The owners of the company's mortgaged bonds (debt instruments collaterized with the company's assets) have the prior or most senior claim on the assets of the corporation. They are the first to be paid out of the assets of the company. Next to be recompensed are the owners of the unsecured debts of the company. Then come the holders of the preferred stock, and then the holders of common stock, if there is anything left. Holders of common stock have the most "junior" claims.

So we can think of the creditors as selling stocks in the form of calls on what remains of the company's assets after the creditors have been paid. Unlike American options, which can be exercised at any time until expiration, these calls are European options, exercisable only upon the bankruptcy of the company. The calls will expire worthless if the market value of the assets of the company at bankruptcy do not exceed the claims of the creditors. The stockholders will then lose all of the "premium" they originally paid for the call. But if the assets are greater than the liabilities, then the shareholders' calls expire "in the money". They can hope to get some of their original premium back. Now these calls are obviously expensive and risky. No one would buy them unless there were some further consideration in the deal. And indeed there is. The company promises to pay, or promises to get into a position to pay, out of its future profits a dividend to the call holders that are its stockholders. What consideration do the creditors receive by way of the premium for the option they sell? They receive continued security on their loans. Money is raised for the company that owes them money, but by selling calls rather than issuing further debt instruments.

Nor is this model simply an abstract flight of fantasy divorced from the real value of the company to its stockholders. The stock-as-call-plus-enticement model provides one of the best ways of valuing the debt and equity of a leveraged company. Nevertheless, those less comfortable with the transformations of ways of looking at things provided by option models may feel that all that these considerations show is that buying a stock involves an option-like bet with the creditors that, in the event of bankruptcy, the market value of the firm's assets will exceed the liabilities to creditors.

But this concession is sufficient to yield a startling claim. Every seller of a call is, among other things, betting that the call will expire worthless. If, in the event of the bankruptcy of the company, the calls of the stockholders do not expire worthless, then the dividends paid to stockholders by the company will represent an unnecessary opportunity cost born by the creditors, *viz.* an increase in the insecurity of their own loans to the company. So the creditors are *inter alia* betting that in the event of one bad outcome—the bankruptcy of the company—another bad outcome—the expiration of the stockholders calls as worthless—will occur. Otherwise the creditors can reason that the stockholders were paid or promised too much in the way of dividend to lure them into buying the stocks or calls they hold.

It should be recalled that the exclusive application of the reciprocity principle tells us that it is ethically wrong to bet on a significantly bad or significantly good outcome. We have just seen that buying a stock is entering into a transaction with parties who are *inter alia* making such a bet. So the exclusive application tells us that it is ethically wrong to buy stocks. Any stocks.

But again, that is a *reductio ad absurdum* of the exclusive application of the reciprocity principle. For, given the more or less unrevisable basis of bankruptcy law, the exclusive application absurdly implies that nothing could be done in practice to ethically legitimate stock trading, however moderate that trading might be. Thanks to the exclusive application, even a primary market in stocks will count as ethically illegitimate. And the same applies to the corporate bond market, for to buy corporate bonds is to become a counterparty to an option trade with the stockholders of the corporation. Such a conclusion should lead us to look back at our premises rather than rest content with their upshot.

In Defense of the Inclusive Application

I therefore believe that we should accept the inclusive application of the reciprocity principle and so conclude that the reciprocity principle and the equivalence principle entail that it is not unethical to hold the stocks of morally dubious companies. The false appeal of the exclusive application seems to me to depend on running together different ways of profiting from bad activity. One way to profit from bad activity is to engage in it and profit as a result. Robbery, fraud, and the unfair securing of government favors are obvious examples. At the other extreme is the case in which the occurrence of bad or very bad things is a necessary condition of one's profiting or benefiting. Yet this is the situation of most, if not all of us. For among the de facto necessary conditions of our coming to exist, and so of our being in a position to profit from anything at all, has been the occurrence of many and great evils. (For example, my parents would never have met were it not for the horrific and disruptive work of Stalin.)

The interesting question is how to view the intermediate case of seeking to attach or correlate one's benefiting with the occurrence of bad things. That is what I do when I bet that some bad outcome will take place. What seems ethically important here is that I do not encourage evil or dubious activity as a result of my betting, either by having my betting egg on the agents in question to do evil, or by weakening my or another's revulsion by endorsing such activity. In cases where this encouragement is entirely absent, there need be no wrong in arranging things so that I profit from evil. Consider the case in which a university professor applies for and receives a grant from one of those large family foundations whose fortune has truly Stendhalian origins.[6] It seems that the professor does no wrong in getting herself into a position to profit from a fortune that was built up in criminal or evil ways. The evil or criminal activity is long done; with the passage of generations, greed has been transmuted into civility, and the family is widely engaged in, and taken to be engaged in, honorable and beneficent activity. Although in accepting the grant the professor benefits from the original evil acquisition of wealth, she does not thereby encourage or endorse evil activity, and so does not do wrong. On the other hand, a certain distinguished university was probably right to refuse the offer of a very substantial gift from Ivan Boesky while he was facing conviction for insider trading. This would have been, and would have been seen as, endorsing dubious activity. As such, it would have had some tendency to further erode the moral environment in which contempt is rightly felt for profiting by cheating and theft.

However, when I buy soybean calls in anticipation of a bad harvest in the Midwest, I am engaged in a private transaction which has no tendency to weaken public concern for the fortunes of farmers and which will not effect the likelihood of a bad harvest in the Midwest. In this respect, I am more like the professor seeking the grant than like a university that accepts a Boesky-style offer. I do nothing either to promote misfortune or to discourage resistance to evil. But in buying soybean calls, or taking a long position in gold futures in anticipation of further turmoil in Russia, am I not hoping for an outcome which is very bad for many people, and is this not a base and callous thing to do?

It certainly would be base and callous either to hope for such bad outcomes or to fear that they will not occur. But it is not likewise wrong to find oneself believing that such outcomes are likely given the evidence. (Contrast believing a person will not recover from a serious illness with hoping that he won't.) One of the moral hazards inherent in trading is precisely this: that because of the trader's anxiety for the money he has placed at risk, the trader's original expectation of a bad outcome can easily transform into a mixture of hope for the outcome and fear that it will not occur. If this happens frequently enough, then, over time, the trader's sympathy for others in potential trouble becomes blunted due to the fact that he is often in a position to profit from that trouble.

However, there are good reasons to believe that this kind of morally bad trader will also be a badly unsuccessful trader. And experienced traders are themselves among the first to elaborate the reasons for this. They regard trading with fear or hope as a reliable symptom that something has already gone wrong with the trade from the purely prudential point of view. Either the trader is under too much background stress to trade well or he has brought the present anxiety upon himself by investing a disproportionate amount of his trading capital in this particular trade, thereby violating the rules of sound money management. Moreover, experienced and successful traders regard their incipient fear and hope as signs that the original objective rationale for entering the trade either is not what it seemed when nothing was yet at risk, or has not stood the test of time. So once a disciplined trader starts feeling hope or fear concerning the outcome of some trade he will examine the rationale for the trade, and if his objective expectations do not still justify the trade he will exit the market. Similarly, there is, among serious traders, an informal ban on telling others about one's market positions, despite the marginal utility of the bandwagon effect this might sometimes produce. For telling others that you have bought or sold so and so on such and such a basis leads one to become committed to these positions in a way that is not fully sensitive to the rapidly changing evidence for and against them. Not only must you not fall in love with your positions, you must not even especially like them.

A successful trader needs to diversify across many, many trades so that he can capitalize on his edge, such as it is. That means that he must invest a small proportion of his total risk capital in any particular trade and must evaluate his performance in terms of returns and drawdowns over the longish run. In this respect he is much like a counter at blackjack who knows that he has a smallish statistical edge over the casino and so works with a predetermined long-term betting plan which leads him to be relatively indifferent to the outcome of any particular hand. Unless this is the attitude of the trader, unless his aim is to make each trade a good rational bet rather than to profit from each trade, he has little chance of surviving. Since he is practically guaranteed that many, if not most, of his trades will be losers, he is bound to eat himself up with frustration if with each trade he aims to profit. It is ironic that the vagaries of the financial markets encourage in those traders who survive precisely the aim or maxim which a Kantian moralist would most admire, namely, not to profit from this trade but to here instantiate sound trading practice.

Notes

1 These results have not held up over the last few years.
2 Or beforehand, if I am trading American options on Sin.
3 My broker is, of course, glossing over certain niceties concerning margin requirements and the present value of money, but let that pass.
4 I mean *intrinsically* permissible. You may have stolen the money you use to bet with me. That is wrong. But nothing in the act of betting itself adds to this wrong, at least not in any way that could be non-symmetric as between you and me.
5 The appeal to the equivalence principle is made simpler by abstracting away from the issues arising over dividends and voting rights. Stock options often include a dividend premium, but they never confer voting rights. Strictly, we should say that if one is not an active shareholder then the synthetic stock and the stock are equivalent instruments. So strictly there are two sensible paths; either become an active shareholder or treat the stock as if it were a synthetic side bet. Notice that neither path involves divesting.
6 Stendhal wrote that behind every great fortune there is a great crime.

Biography of George Soros

George Soros was born in Budapest, Hungary, in 1930. In 1947 he emigrated to England, where he graduated from the London School of Economics. While a student at the London School of Economics, Mr. Soros became familiar with the work of the philosopher Karl Popper, who had a profound influence on his thinking and, later, on his philanthropic activities. In 1956 he moved to the United States, where he began to accumulate a large fortune through an international investment fund that he founded and managed.

Mr. Soros currently serves as chairman of Soros Fund Management LLC, a private investment management firm which serves as principal investment advisor to the Quantum Group of Funds. The Quantum Fund N.V., the oldest and largest fund within the Quantum Group, is generally recognized as having the best performance record of any investment fund in the world in its thirty-year history.

Mr. Soros established his first foundation, the Open Society Fund, in New York in 1979, and his first Eastern European foundation in Hungary in 1984. He now funds a network of foundations that operate in thirty-one countries throughout Central and Eastern Europe, the former Soviet Union and Central Eurasia, as well as in Southern Africa, Haiti, Guatemala, and the United States. These foundations are dedicated to building and maintaining the infrastructure and institutions of an open society. Mr. Soros has also founded other major institutions, such as the Central European University and the International Science Foundation. In 1994 the foundations within the network spent a total of approximately $300 million; in 1995, $350 million; in 1996, $362 million; in 1997, $428 million; and in 1998, $574 million. Giving for 1999 and 2000 is expected to be maintained at similar levels.

In addition to many articles on the political and economic changes in Eastern Europe and the former Soviet Union, Mr. Soros is the author of *The Alchemy of Finance*, published by Simon & Schuster in 1987 and republished in 1994 by John Wiley & Sons; *Opening the Soviet System*, published by Weidenfeld &

Nicholson in 1990; *Underwriting Democracy*, published by The Free Press in 1991; and *Soros on Soros: Staying Ahead of the Curve*, published by John Wiley & Sons in 1995. Mr. Soros's most recent book, *The Crisis of Global Capitalism: Open Society Endangered*, was published by Public Affairs in November 1998.

Mr. Soros has received honorary doctoral degrees from the New School for Social Research, the University of Oxford, the Budapest University of Economics, and Yale University. In 1995 the University of Bologna awarded Mr. Soros its highest honor, the Laurea Honoris Causa, in recognition of his efforts to promote open societies throughout the world.

Works of George Soros

Books

The Crisis of Global Capitalism: Open Society Endangered, Public Affairs (1998).

Soros on Soros: Staying Ahead of the Curve, John Wiley & Sons, Inc. (1995).

The Alchemy of Finance, John Wiley & Sons, Inc. (1987, 1994).

Underwriting Democracy, The Free Press (a division of Macmillan, Inc.) (1992).

Opening the Soviet System, Weidenfeld and Nicolson, Ltd. (1990).

Op-Eds and Essays

1983–1984

July 1983, March 1984, May 1984: Morgan Stanley Papers—„The International Debt Problem".

1987

24 April: "A Plan to Ease Global Stresses", *The New York Times*.
13 August: "A Global New Deal", *The New York Review of Books*.
14 October: "Japan's Stock Market: This Time the Turning Point Has Been Reached", *Financial Times*.

1988

14 January: "Brady Commission Should've Stressed Market Stability", *The Wall Street Journal.*
Spring: "After Black Monday", *Foreign Policy* (No. 70).
15 June: "Joint Ventures: A Way to Make Perestroika Work", *Financial Times.*

1989

1 June: "Gorbachev—Dream & Reality", *The New York Review of Books.*
2 July: "Incredible Shrinking Superpowers: Can We (or the Soviets) Tolerate Arms Cuts That Would Erode Our Global Dominance?", *Newsday.*
7 July: "How to Help Poland", *The Washington Post.*
10 July: "Chores for the West: Invest in a Polish Reform Process", *International Herald Tribune.*
7 December: "Can the Soviet Economy be Saved?—Not Without U.S. Aid", *The Wall Street Journal.*

1990

19 October: "Gorbachev's Reform Plan Is a Bust", *The New York Times.*

1991

4 April: "An EC Gift for the Hungarian Economy", *The Wall Street Journal Europe.*
15 July: "The Centre Cannot Hold", *The Independent.*
13 September: "U.S.S.R.: See the Future, Make it Work", *The Wall Street Journal.*
undated: "I Welcome the Changes Now Underway in the USSR." (Pamphlet.)

1992

30 May: "Situation in Russia Has Ceased to Concern Russians Only" (translation from the Russian), *Izvestia.*
5 October: "Termites are Devouring Hungary", *The New York Times.*
11 November: "A Cold-Cash Winter Proposal for Russia", *The Wall Street Journal.*

1993

4 January: "A Social Safety Net for Russia", *The Washington Post.*
25 February: "Reconstruire le SME, Sinon...", *Le Figaro.*

26 July: "Pourquoi je ne spécule pas contre le franc", *Le Figaro*.
2 August: "Why Appeasement Must Not Have Another Chance", *The Times*. (Extracted from "Opinions" on Channel 4.)

1994

6 January: "Get Serious About Helping Russia Go Straight", *International Herald Tribune*.
March: "Help Macedonia and Pressure Greece if Necessary", *International Herald Tribune*.
17 March: "The Other Balkan Mess", *The New York Times*. (Similar piece to above.)
18 March: "Ein Land Braucht Hilfe", *Die Zeit*.

1995

Spring: "Toward Open Societies", *Foreign Policy*.
16 July: "This is the Moment of Truth" (Bosnia), *The Washington Post*.

1996

29 May: "Postpone the Bosnian Elections", *The Wall Street Journal*.
9 July: "Hoodwinked Again in Bosnia", *The Wall Street Journal*.
September/October: "Can Europe Work?" *Foreign Affairs*.
2 October: "Immigrants' Burden", *The New York Times*.
2 October: "Relighting a Lamp Outside America's Darkening Door", *Los Angeles Times*.

1997

February: "The Capitalist Threat", *The Atlantic Monthly*.
2 February: "The Drug War Cannot be Won", *The Washington Post*.
4 February: "Imagine It's 2007", *International Herald Tribune*.
22 August: "Legal Immigrants Deserve a Safety Net", *The New York Times*.
31 December: "Avoiding a Breakdown", *Financial Times*.

1998

January: "Toward a Global Open Society", *The Atlantic Monthly*.
13 August: "A G7-backed, $50bn currency board is the only way for Russian to end its crisis", *Financial Times*. (Letter to the editor.)
15 September: "The Crisis of Global Capitalism", *The Wall Street Journal*.
7 December: "The Crisis of Global Capitalism: Prosperity in Peril" *Newsweek*. (Book excerpt.)

1999

4 January: "To Avert the Next Crisis", *Financial Times*.
12 April: "Global Capital Markets: An Exchange (with Robert Solow)", *The New Republic.*
4 May: "I'm Ready to Fund Organized Programs" (After School Corporation opinion piece), *New York Daily News* et al.
6 July: "Breaking Down Borders", *Financial Times*.
29 July: "Balkan Opening", *The Washington Post.*
9 November: "Breaking The Cycle of Violence", *Financial Times*.
23 November: "It Isn't Enough to Shed Communism", *The Washington Post.*

2000

13 April: "Who Lost Russia?" *The New York Review of Books*.

George Soros' Philanthropic Initiatives

(including foundations and programs)

I. Open Society Institute – Programs

International

- Arts and Culture Programs
- Burma Project
- Central Eurasia Project
- Consortium for Academic Partnership
  - Virtual University
  - Fellowships, Scholarships, and Supplementary Grants
- East-East Program
- English-Language Program
- Forced Migration Projects
- Internet Communications
- Land Mines Project
- National Science Foundation Grant
- Network Scholarship Program
- Regional Children and Youth Programs
  - Regional Preschool Project
  - Regional High-School Debate Program
  - Regional Secondary-School Scholarship Program
  - Regional Youth Program
  - Regional Health Education Program
- Regional Media Programs
- Regional Medical and Health Care Programs
- Regional Internet and E-mail Program
- Science Journals Donation Program
- Soros Centers for the Contemporary Arts
- Southern Africa Project
- Step-by-Step
- Tajikistan Project

United States

Campaign Finance Reform
Center on Crime, Communities and Culture
Education and Youth Development
Emma Lazarus Fund
Fellowship Programs
Governance and Public Policy
The Lindesmith Center
Medicine as a Profession
Program on Law and Society
Project on Death in America
Reproductive Health and Rights
Soros Documentary Fund
Urban Initiatives
Welfare Reform
Women's Program
Youth Initiatives

Budapest

Education Program Support Unit
Higher Education Support Program (1993)
  Civic Education
  Research Support Scheme
International Higher Education Support Program (1995)
Institute for Educational Policy
Institute for Local Government and Public Service (ILGPS)
Library Program
Open Society Archives
Regional Library Program
Regional Publishing Program—Network Publishing Development
Special Projects
  Albanian Education Development Project
  Constitutional and Legal Policy Institute
  Open Society City of Şarajevo Project
  Regional Media Programs
  Roma Participation Program
  Sarajevo Film Festival
  Technical Support for Education Development in Macedonia

II. Foundations

United States

Open Society Institute
Baltimore
Los Angeles
New York
San Francisco
Washington D.C.

International

Open Society Foundation of Albania
Open Society Institute Assistance Foundation – Armenia
Open Society Institute – Azerbaijan
Soros Foundation – Belarus
Open Society Fund – Bosnia and Herzegovina
Open Society Institute – Brussels
Open Society Institute – Budapest
Open Society Fund – Sofia (Bulgaria)
Open Society Institute – Croatia
Open Society Fund – Prague (Czech Republic)
Open Estonia Foundation
Open Society Georgia Foundation
Fundacion Soros – Guatemala
Fondation Connaissance et Liberté (Haiti)
Soros Foundation – Hungary
TIFA Foundation (Indonesia) (in formation)
Soros Foundation – Kazakhstan
Kosova Foundation for Open Society
Soros Foundation – Kyrgyzstan
Soros Foundation – Latvia
Open Society Fund – Lithuania
Open Society Institute – Macedonia
Soros Foundation – Moldova
Mongolian Foundation for Open Society
Open Society Institute – Montenegro
Open Society Institute – Paris
Stefan Batory Foundation (Poland)

Soros Foundation for an Open Society (Romania)
Open Society Institute – Russia
International Cultural Initiative Foundation (Russia)
Open Society Fund – Bratislava (Slovakia)
Open Society Fund – Slovenia
Open Society Foundation for South Africa
Open Society Initiative for Southern Africa
Open Society Institute – Tajikistan
International Renaissance Foundation (Ukraine)
Open Society Institute – Uzbekistan
Open Society Initiative for West Africa (in formation)
Soros Yugoslavia Foundation

III. Other Soros-Related Entities

Albanian Education Development Project (AEDP)
Baltic-American Partnership Fund (BAPF)
Belarus Initiatives
Central European University (CEU)
Budapest Campus
  Prague Campus
  Warsaw Campus
  Centre for the Study of Nationalism
  Institute for Nationalism and Ethnic Conflict Research (Prague Campus)
  Privatization Project (International Association of Privatization)
Transition Program
CEU Press
East-West Management Institute (EWMI)
European Roma Rights Center (ERRC)
International Science Foundation (ISF)
International Soros Science Education Program (ISSEP)
Iris Foundation
Kerepesi Conference Center
Media Development Loan Fund (MDLF)
Non-Profit Foundation in Support of Culture, Education, and New Information Technologies („NEWCO") (Collier's Encyclopedia)
Open Media Research Institute (OMRI)
Open Society Fund (OSF)
Research and Policy Reform Center (RPR)

Soros Charitable Foundation
Soros Economic Development Fund (SEDF)
Soros Humanitarian Foundation
Soros Foundation – Newly Independent/Baltic States (SFNI-BS)
Soros Training for Economic Transformation Network
Soros Business and Management Foundation (SBMF)
The After-School Corporation (TASC)
The Soros Roma Foundation
Telecommunication Center "Science and Society", Autonomous non-profit organization ("Science and Society")

List of Contributors

Åslund, Anders – Senior Associate, Carnegie Endowment for International Peace, Washington, D.C.

Belting, Hans – Professor of the History of Art, Staatliche Hochschule für Gestaltung, Karlsruhe

Botstein, Leon – President, Bard College, New York

Dornbusch, Rudiger – Ford Professor of Economics and International Management, MIT Department of Economics, Cambridge, MA

Feldhay, Rivka – Director, Institute of the History and Philosophy of Science and Ideas, School of History, Tel Aviv University

Geremek, Bronisław – Minister of Foreign Affairs of the Republic of Poland

Göncz Árpád – President of the Republic of Hungary

Johnston, Mark – Chairman, Department of Philosophy, Princeton University, New Jersey, MA

Kis János – Chairman, Department of Political Science, Central European University, Budapest

Klaniczay Gábor – Rector, Collegium Budapest

Kornai János – Professor of Economics, Harvard University and Collegium Budapest

Krastev, Ivan – Program Director, Center for Liberal Strategies, Sofia

Krips, Henry – Professor of Communication, University of Pittsburgh

Lepenies, Wolf – Rector, Wissenschaftskolleg zu Berlin

Michnik, Adam – Editor-in-Chief, Gazeta Wyborcza, Poland

Mokrzycki, Edmund – Professor of Sociology, Central European University, Warsaw

Neier, Aryeh – President, Open Society Institute, New York

Newton-Smith, William – Fellow & Tutor in Philosophy, Balliol College, University of Oxford; Chairman, Higher Education Support Program, OSI, Budapest

Osiatyński, Wiktor – Professor of Law, Central European University, Budapest

Pleşu, Andrei – Rector, Collegium Nuova Europa, Bucharest

Rév István – Director, Open Society Archives, Central European University, Budapest

Rieber, Alfred – Professor of History, Central European University, Budapest

Sajó András – Professor of Law, Chair of the Comparative Constitutional Law Program, Central European University, Budapest

JESUS HAMILTON PEÑA
CALLE RIVAS Nº 41
NAIGUATA, MUNICIPIO VARGAS
C.P. 1166
VENEZUELA

TO ANY
WALL
UNITED

R 019

1998

January

Dear Sir:
My name is Jesús Hamilton Peña. I'm
I should like to sell my pictures
Please, help me.
Please, write me

Thank you.

Sincerelly your,